Scorched Earth, Black Snow

About the Author

Journalist Andrew Salmon covers the Koreas for *Forbes, The South China Morning Post, The Times* and *The Washington Times*. Educated at Elizabeth College Guernsey, the University of Kent and the School of Oriental and African Studies, University of London, he is the author of business history *American Business and the Korean Miracle* and battlefield history *To the Last Round: The Epic British Stand on the Imjin River, Korea, 1951*. The latter was the unanimous winner of the Hampshire Libraries/Osprey Publishing 'Best Military Book of 2009' award. In 2010, he was honoured at Seoul's National Assembly with a 'Korean Wave' award for his contribution to the literature of the Korean War. He lives in Seoul with wife Ji-young and daughter Hannah.

Website: http://tothelastround.wordpress.com/

Praise for Andrew Salmon's *To the Last Round*

'In a list of very strong military books, this is an excellent book, which well-deserves the winning award' Professor Richard Holmes, awarding *To the Last Round* the Hampshire Libraries inaugural 'Best Military Book of the Year' prize for 2009

'Gripping . . . exhaustively researched and expertly written' Saul David, *The Times*

'An enthralling, action-packed book [that] relives every moment of this astonishing battle' David Hardman, *Daily Mail*

'War porn at its finest, all the more delicious for being totally true' James Delingpole, *The Spectator*

'One of the most interesting books about Korea, 2010' *Wall Street Journal*

'Salmon's vivid use of recollections and dramatic quotes brings alive an unjustly forgotten conflict' Tim Newark, *Time Out*

'Over a thousand British servicemen lost their lives in the Korean War and here, at last, is a compelling account of a defining moment in the conflict' *Good Book Guide*

'Filled with detail enough to win the attention even of those for whom military histories may seem irrelevant when stacked against social and political analysis' Don Kirk, *Far Eastern Economic Review*

'A superb book which showcases British courage during a now almost forgotten last stand' *Soldier* magazine

Scorched Earth, Black Snow

Britain and Australia in the Korean War

Andrew Salmon

First published 2011 by
Aurum Press Limited
7 Greenland Street
London NW1 0ND

www.aurumpress.co.uk

Map Design: Kim Him-chan

A catalogue record for this book
is available from the British Library.

ISBN 978 1 84513 619 2

1 3 5 7 9 10 8 6 4 2

2011 2013 2015 2014 2012

Typeset in Granjon by
SX Composing DTP, Rayleigh, Essex

Printed and bound in Great Britain by
Clays, St Ives plc

I see black snow! This must be modern warfare . . .
Marshal Peng Te-huai, Korea, 1950

At the frontier
They say the soil now
Is more bones than earth . . .
Wei Chuang, Tang Dynasty, ninth century

And it's War! 'Orderly, hold the light.
You can lay him down on the table; so.
Easily – gently! Thanks – you may go.'
And it's War! But the part that is not for show . . .
Edgar Wallace

Contents

Introduction

Distant Holocaust, Forgotten Men

God of our fathers, known of old,
Lord of our far-flung battle-line,
Beneath whose awful hand we hold,
Dominion over palm and pine,
Lord God of Hosts, be with us yet,
Lest we forget – lest we forget!
Rudyard Kipling

Since the turn of the millennium, the British public has been forced to relearn a painful lesson: Soldiers die in war.

While this might seem self-evident, the events of the 1980s and '90s – bar that oddly old-fashioned conflagration, the Falklands War – seemed to prove it invalid. In peace-keeping operations in Africa and the Balkans, counterinsurgency in Northern Ireland and the one-sided adventure of Desert Storm, Britons suffered a reassuringly gentle trickle of casualties. The armed forces, it seemed, were so well trained and equipped that they could operate, either independently in low-level conflicts, or in alliance with their mighty American allies in larger ones, at minimal risk.

That shibboleth now lies shattered. In interventions in Iraq and Afghanistan, the army met a foe who, though lightly armed, fought skilfully, using guerilla tactics fired by religious zeal. Not only did he not collapse, he inflicted losses that soon exceeded a trickle, though have not (yet) reached a flood.

These conflicts are the best-covered wars the UK has ever fought, blazing across TV reports, video-sharing websites and the print of innumerable articles and books. Perhaps it is this firestorm of coverage that has led some commentators to suggest that the intensity of combat, the losses incurred and the perils faced, are unprecedented in the British Army's post-1945 experience.

Nonsense. A conflict that received scant attention at the time, and which is today almost unknown in the UK, remains far and away the biggest, bloodiest, most brutal war fought by British troops since the Second World War: Korea.

The biggest: A war of advances and retreats of hundreds of miles, fought against the army of the world's most populous nation. The bloodiest: 1,087 British servicemen fell in Korea in barely three years of fighting, a number greater than the total killed in the Falklands (255), Iraq (179) and Afghanistan (349) combined – 783.[1] And the most brutal: A sampling of incidents in this book should make that clear.

The military's ability to fight operations of scale and intensity rests upon national will, but twenty-first century Britain is casualty sensitive and cost-conscious. The slipped discs in today's national spine – epitomised in 2007's humiliating retreat from Basra – contrast with the solid backbone Britain exhibited in 1950. Then, the UK was bankrupt from the Second World War, abandoning empire and suffering military overstretch. But London had obligations: As a charter member of the UN, as an ally of the United States and as the defender of a state facing aggression. Even when China surged into the war, even when casualties soared, even though it meant lengthening National Service and raising the defence budget – Britain stayed the course. This was honourable conduct.

In 1950, an under-equipped, under-gunned British brigade was deployed into a high-risk conflict in a distant, primitive theatre against an unknown, alien enemy at ludicrously short notice. As in Afghanistan, they were fighting alongside US troops, though in the early months of the Korean War, the American Army was at a nadir. The scratch 27th Brigade – a good, but hardly elite formation – proved so effective, that despite lacking transport, armour and artillery, it was tasked with key missions. Meanwhile, the crack 41 Commando – a unit that did not even exist at the outbreak of hostilities – was embedded with America's finest troops, the 1st US Marine Division. In the most harrowing campaign of the war, the commandos won a US Presidential Unit Citation and plaudits from their comrades that still echo six decades later.

* * *

This book is not a full history of the war – Sir Max Hastings' *The Korean War* is recommended for casual readers, Dr Allen Millet's *The War in Korea* trilogy is the best for the specialist. Nor does it detail the featured units' full participation in Korea: All continued operations well into 1951.* What it is, is a narrative history of those formations during the war's most dramatic period: summer to the end of the 'Year of the Tiger', 1950.

Those months cover the defence of South Korea and the charge into North Korea; the shock Chinese intervention and the catastrophic defeat of UN forces; the hellish retreat and the tragedy of a nation put to the sword. Even the weather mirrored the drama, as the seasons transitioned from summer to autumn to winter. This period has been covered by American historians, but this book features a group of actors whose experiences have gone largely unrecorded: the Australians and Britons who made up the UN Command's first non-Korean, non-American ground troops.

Episodes include the worst 'friendly fire' disaster suffered by the British Army since the Second World War; a barely believable 'mistaken identity' action fought at handshake range; a desperate breakout to escape entrapment; and a harrowing fighting retreat amid Siberian temperatures. The units covered are large enough to encompass a broad range of experience, but small enough for individual characters to stand out. How, then, to tell their tale?

There are, essentially, three approaches to writing military history. The first is military science: the general's art, the strategic picture, the broad sweep of arrow on map. The second is technical: The weapons of the combatants, their capabilities and drawbacks.

---

*The author's *To the Last Round* picks up the story of British troops in Korea in 1951, where this book leaves off, albeit the action turns to 29th Brigade.

The third is the human story: What actually happens to men in war? What do they see, do, think, feel?

For context, I have sketched in the broad background as it unfolded in the politicians' chamber and across the generals' maps, and included information on weapons and equipment, but my preferred approach is the third. War is – like all history – a jigsaw of biographies. While I have referenced books, articles, letters, unit diaries and personal notebooks, the meat of this story is oral, allowing the reader, I hope, to 'meet' these men, to witness the war through their eyes.

*　　*　　*

While conducting the interviews that are the heart of this book, I was surprised at how old soldiers opened up and told stories that, in many cases, nobody had ever asked them about before. There was emotion. One veteran choked back tears as he recalled the inspirational leadership of his platoon commander in their first battle. A commando, describing one desperate moment, flung his arm out, sending coffee flying over his carpet. His wife made no complaint, but confided that her husband would struggle in bed that night: Discussing the war would bring nightmares back to the surface. Another man handed me an essay he had written about his wartime experiences, then told me and two fellow veterans of a war crime he had witnessed but not committed to paper; I had the sense he had never spoken about the killing previously. The traumas of Korea may be judged by the fact that some veterans, haunted by the restless dead, still sleep with their lights on sixty years later.

Yet their war is non-existent in popular culture. There are few books, fewer films. The predominant visual references, black and white photographs, do little justice to the war's sights: the sparkling emerald summer paddies, the orange blossoms of napalm, the icy blue of winter mountains. The disinterest of filmmakers and novelists, and the resultant public amnesia is odd, for the drama of this war remains unsurpassed in the post-1945 era. It changed pace and character with an intensity the wider world struggled to comprehend, and which was, for the men with the rifles, bewildering and terrifying. Korea escalated from a civil–ideological war to the first UN war. It featured the only free world invasion of a communist state and the first (and only) battlefield clash of superpowers. Those soldiers of 1950 were in the eye of the hurricane when modern China stormed, shockingly, onto the global stage.

Some veterans expressed surprise at the spotlight focused on today's troops, fighting a campaign significantly less perilous than that of half a century previously. Today, almost every death in Afghanistan merits media coverage, but in Korea, it was not simply individuals who faced extinction: This was the only war fought by the UK and US since the Second World War when entire units were consumed. In 1950, British troops were peripherally involved in the trial-by-fire of the 2nd Infantry Division at Kunu-ri, and fought with 1st US Marine Division as it broke free of the massive trap sprung at Chosin Reservoir. For the US Army, the decimation of two regiments at Kunu-ri, and the destruction of another at Chosin, were disasters unequalled even in the heaviest combat in Vietnam.

Survivors still struggle to verbalise the near-Biblical devastation of the 'scorched earth' retreat from the north. One likened it to the climax of a James Bond film, when, in the final scene, the set explodes and collapses around the hero as he fights clear in the nick of time.

In no Cold War conflict were the furies unleashed with such demonic energy, for the war raged over a peninsula brutalised by thirty-five years of Japanese rule, then polarised for five years by contrasting ideologies. Most atrocities were intra-Korean affairs – every veteran recalls civilians slaughtered by one side or the other, heaped in ditches or among ruins – but the reader will also encounter brutalities committed by Australian and British troops: the burning of villages; the shooting of wounded and captured enemy; the killing of civilians.

From the comfort of armchairs and the viewpoint of six decades, should we judge? Perhaps. But as citizens of a democracy, we must acknowledge that when our government dispatches men to do a dirty job we must bear some responsibility for deeds done in our name by those cultured, educated and raised among – and by – us.

* * *

This is not a happy tale. As Melville wrote of *Moby Dick*: 'a Polar wind blows through it, and birds of prey hover over it.' Every character in this book left friends in Korea's rocky soil. For South Koreans, the war fought to defend them spun out of control, to the point where the cure – UN intervention – became almost as bad as the disease – communist invasion. Yet if anyone questions the author's opinion on the broad issues, let me be clear, for I am as unequivocal on this as a falling guillotine: Korea was a just war.

The 1950 attack was naked aggression, abetted by Josef Stalin, one of the most murderous figures of mankind's deadliest century. It was ordered by Kim Il-sung, a leader who engineered a state that, today, grinds down the human spirit more than any other. Kim's 'achievements' – if they can be so dignified – grant post-event justification to the UN cause. In fact, UN troops had largely reunified the peninsula in November 1950: It was Mao's counteroffensive that guaranteed Kim's continued existence and almost extinguished South Korea.

Almost. The agonised efforts of the soldiers of 1950 proved sufficient. The UN Command escaped annihilation, enabling its own regeneration in 1951. In 1953, an uneasy armistice was signed. While some soldiers, experiencing first-hand the horrors of the war, questioned the justice of the cause then, none who have returned on veteran revisits – where they are greeted with remarkable warmth by South Koreans – harbour any doubts now.

South Korea did not just survive, it thrived, becoming a model of economic, and more latterly, political and social advancement. The events in this book show how fragile the existence of the greatest national success story of the twentieth century was a mere six decades ago – a time-span that lies comfortably within a human lifetime.

* * *

In their autumn years, Korea veterans have an eye on posterity. At the conclusion of several interviews, I was thanked by those whose memories I had mined. The gratitude is mine. As a writer I felt privileged – in some cases, humbled – to record such great and terrible, but largely unknown, events.

And these memories have contemporary significance, for these events could re-occur; the final act of Korea's tragedy remains unwritten. North Korea remains one of the world's most dangerous states and China continues to support her wartime ally. With the flashpoint peninsula frequently splashed across front pages, it is germane to remember – or learn of – the staggering devastation and appalling carnage of war in Korea.

Specialists on the conflict will learn nothing new herein on politics or strategy. But by zeroing in on its human stories, I hope that, six decades after the outbreak of the 'Forgotten War', this work will reopen a window onto the holocaust that laid waste the ill-starred peninsula in 1950. I hope, further, that it will breathe a spark of life back into the forgotten men of 27th Commonwealth Brigade and 41 Commando, before living memories of the tragedy they played so distinguished a role in are extinguished forever.

Andrew Salmon
Seoul, January 2011

Glossary

Unit Structure

Section: 8–10 men. Commander: Corporal

Platoon: (three sections); 30–35 men. Commander: Lieutenant

Company: (three platoons and company headquarters); 120–150 men. Commander: Major

Battalion: (three or four rifle companies; one headquarters company of administrative, supply and signals units; one support company of machine gun, mortar and anti-tank platoons); 600–700 men. Commander: Lieutenant Colonel

Brigade: (Three battalions, plus supportive units, though 27th Brigade lacked these); 2,500–5,000 men. Commander: Brigadier (In US parlance, Regimental Combat Teams)

Division: Three brigades; 15,000 men. Commander: Major General

Corps: (Two or three divisions); 40,000 + men. Commander: Lieutenant General

Note: The above are based on Korean War strengths. Note also that American units tended to have heavier manpower and firepower allotments than British units.

Acronyms and Terms

2ID – 2nd Infantry Division (US)

ACT – Air Contact Team; a team embedded with infantry who control air strikes by radio

Assault Pioneers – Engineers attached to infantry battalions

AP – Associated Press (US news agency)

APD – Assault Personnel Destroyer. US warships which carried troops on coastal raids

AWOL – Absent without leave

BAR – Browning Automatic Rifle. US light machine gun, fed with a 20-round magazine. Generally considered inferior to the Bren

Bivvy – Short for bivouac. Can refer to a small tent, or simply a basic encampment for the night. Noun or verb

BOAC – British Overseas Airways Corporation; predecessor to British Airways

Bren – Czech-designed light machine gun used by British forces. Popular for its accuracy, reliability and fast barrel-change but had a slow (500 rounds per minute) rate of fire and was fed by a 30-round magazine

'Brew up' – Noun or verb, with two distinct meanings, dependent upon context: either making a cup of tea, or blowing up/setting fire to a vehicle/armoured vehicle

'Burp gun' – Russian-built Shpagin PPSH 41 submachine gun. Rugged, dependable, and with a 71-round drum magazine, it was a formidable weapon, superior to the scrappy British equivalent, the Sten. Its fast rate of fire gave it a 'brrrppp' sound – hence its nickname

CCF – Chinese Communist Forces

CO – Commanding officer of a battalion. Usually a lieutenant colonel

Corpsman – Medic attached to US marines

CP – Command Post

CPV – Chinese People's Volunteer. In actual fact, not a volunteer, but a regular soldier of the PLA deployed to fight in Korea

CPVA – Chinese People's Volunteer Army

Dead ground – Military term for a dip in the ground, or ground behind a hill or ridge, which it is impossible to see into

DMZ – De-militarised Zone. The heavily militarised border which divides the Korean peninsula

DPRK – Democratic People's Republic of Korea, i.e. North Korea

FOO – Forward Observation Officer (pronounced 'Foo'). Artillery officer with forward troops. With a signaller, his job is to call in and to adjust the fire of artillery

'Fire for Effect' – Fire control order. Once the enemy's position and distance is known, and fall of shot or ranging fire (often with smoke shells) has been noted, infantry or artillery fire can cause actual casualties among the enemy

Garand – US service rifle of the Second World War and Korea. Generally considered better than the Lee Enfield due to its semiautomatic, rather than bolt action, function

GI – 'General Issue'; slang term for US serviceman

'Gook' – Korean War slang for Asian; noun or adjective. Fifty years before Korea, the pejorative 'goo-goo' was used to describe the guerilla enemy during the American war against the 'Moros' in the Philippines in a brutal campaign that lasted from 1898 to 1902. The word was possibly a derivative of the 'gobbledy-gook' American troops thought the natives spoke. It is unclear if 'gook' was a carryover from then, or whether it arose in Korea independently of the Philippine experience. If the latter, in origin, it was probably innocent. The Korean word for America/American is 'Miguk' and when Koreans saw US soldiers they would have used this word to describe them. Americans overhearing this could have misinterpreted this as 'Me, gook' – and so started using it describe Koreans themselves. The term took on a negative tone, becoming a racial pejorative, and was used in Vietnam

IGS – Imperial General Staff

IWM – Imperial War Museum

KIA – Killed in Action

LMG – Light Machine gun. A portable machine gun, crewed by two men, but operable by one. In the British Army, this was the much-loved Bren

LOC – Line of Communication. The road at the rear of a unit's position

LOE – Limit of Exploitation. The line at which an attacking unit will not advance beyond

LP – Listening Post

LST – Landing Ship Tank; a large landing craft

Mansei – Korean for '10,000 years', or 'long life'. Same meaning as (and often mistaken for) the Japanese banzai

MARDIV – US Marine Division

MASH – Mobile Army Surgical Hospital

MFC – Mortar Fire Controller; essentially, the same job as an artillery FOO, but for mortars

MIA – Missing in Action

MLR – Main Line of Resistance. The main – rather than the forward or fallback – line of a defensive position

MMG – Medium Machine gun. In the British Army in Korea, this was issued at the battalion level and was the trusty, belt-fed and water-cooled Vickers, a weapon which could fire non-stop for hours

MO – Medical officer; the doctor attached to a battalion

MP – Military policeman, or provost

MSR – Main Supply Route. A road or track used exclusively for military traffic; civilians were not permitted on it

'Mucker' – Best friend

NCO – Non Commissioned Officer, such as corporal or sergeant

NKPA – North Korean People's Army

OC – Officer commanding a company. Usually a major

'O' Group – Officers Group or Orders Group; a briefing for a group of officers

OP – Observation post

POW – Prisoner of War

PLA – People's Liberation Army; i.e. the regular army of communist China

PTI – Physical Training Instructor

PTSD – Post Traumatic Stress Disorder

RAMC – Royal Army Medical Corps

RAP – Regimental Aid Post. A field dressing station, usually set up at Battalion HQ, to stabilise battle casualties before they can be sent rearward

RAR – Royal Australian Regiment

Recce – British Army shorthand for reconnaissance, pronounced 'recky'. Noun or verb

ROK – Republic of Korea, i.e. South Korea. Pronounced 'Rock'. During the Korean War, the acronym also referred to the country's army and its soldiers ('ROKs')

REME – Royal Electrical and Mechanical Engineers

RV – Rendevous

Sangar – A legacy of the British Army's long service on the Indian subcontinent, 'sangar' is a Pushtu word for an embrasure of stones or rocks, raised when it is impossible to dig into ground

Sapper – Military engineer

SBA– Sick Berth Attendant; medics recruited from the Royal Navy and attached to commando units

SBS – Special Boat Squadron. Royal Marine Commando special force

'Stag' – Night sentry duty

Start line – The point from which an attack is launched. Ideally, this is reconnoitered and marked, often with tape. In reality, often just a line on the map

Sten – Mass-produced, unreliable and unpopular British SMG

SMG – Submachine gun, such as the British Sten or the Russian 'burp gun'

'Stonk' – British military slang, meaning bombard with mortars or artillery. Noun and verb

UN – United Nations. Although US and ROK troops made up its mains elements, the forces fighting in defence of South Korea were deployed following UN resolutions

UNC – United Nations Command. The American-led multinational force established in response to UN Security Council Resolutions to repel the attack on South Korea and to establish 'international peace and security in the area'

USMC – United States Marine Corps

WGC – War Graves Commission

WIA – Wounded in Action

Note to the Reader

On spellings:
In 2000, the South Korean government changed its official Romanisation system for Korean words; Pusan became Busan, Inchon became Incheon, and so on. I have stuck to the old spellings. For consistency's sake, I have also stuck with the pre-Pinyin spellings of Chinese, hence Mao Tse-tung not Mao Zedong, Peking not Beijing.

On notations:
Interesting information that would break narrative flow or remove the reader from the timescale of the events in the text, have been added as footnotes. Endnotes are exclusively used to identify sources.

On sources:
Sources in the narrative not end-noted are oral sources (for details of oral and written sources, see Acknowledgements and Sources, at end of book, for details). Some sources – e.g. Jack Gallaway, Fred Hayhurst, Ben O'Dowd, John Shipster and David Wilson – granted interviews and published accounts. In cases where they are not endnoted, their quotes are from oral sources.

Part One
Triumph

Oh, nefarious war! I see why arms
Were so seldom used by benign sovereigns
Li Po, 8th Century

Prologue

Strangers in the Night

Welcome tae yer gorie bed
Or tae victorie!

Robert Burns

15:20, 17 October. Western axis of advance.[1]

Bright, late afternoon sunlight bore down. On the hard-baked dirt track south of the town, the line of tanks, trucks and jeeps ground to a halt. Perched on the vehicles, soldiers in faded combat uniforms peered ahead. Engines idled. Clouds of mustard-coloured dust billowed into the air behind the stationary column. Officers raised field glasses and focused on the town ahead.

Sariwon. Another grid reference, another town, another target on the advance up this blighted peninsula. Dominating a key crossroads on the highway to Pyongyang, the enemy capital, it was an industrial centre and communications hub. Sariwon. It did not look like much. Scanning through binoculars, officers could see the railway suburb south of the town proper, and beyond it, streets lined with the ubiquitous wooden telegraph poles threading through a conglomeration of traditional Korean cottages, utilitarian concrete buildings and warehouses – even a spired church. But it was not what it had been just months ago. War, in the shape of B-26 bombers, had visited. Many buildings were mere shells, empty holes smashed from the sky. Sariwon.

Silhouettes broke the skyline on a ridge overlooking the town. Enemy. Machine guns on tank turrets barked. The silhouettes disappeared.[2] Signallers spoke into radio mikes. Orders were passed along to platoons, sections. Sherman tanks clattered and squeaked as they took up positions. Infantrymen, bulky with canvas bandoleers and stuffed ammunition pouches, dropped heavily from the vehicles, brought weapons into the ready position and fanned out into assault lines.

In their first major action a month earlier, these soldiers had suffered a disaster that had wiped out a company. Then, they had choked on the dust hurled up as their American allies led the advance. Now, they were the spearhead, the vanguard of the United Nations' war machine as it stabbed into enemy territory. Would the town be a fortress? It was the last major obstacle before the Pyongyang plain. Senior officers expected 'a big fight'.[3] Casting long afternoon shadows, 1st Battalion, Argyll and Sutherland Highlanders, descended upon Sariwon.

Fighting in built up areas is the most nerve-wracking form of combat. Every street is a valley, dominated by rooftops; every building a potential strong point. Every window can hold a snipe, every doorway, a booby trap. C Company advanced up the main road. Private Ronald Yetman – an Englishman, who at 6-foot, was, like many of the bigger Argylls, a Bren gunner – moved warily. Occasional rounds – sniper fire – cracked overhead, but the advance continued; trained soldiers only halt when fire becomes effective or when they hit resistance. Nothing. The town, like so many others, was eerily empty.

Tension evaporated. Yetman and his mates relaxed into covering positions while B Company's commander, Major Alastair Gordon-Ingram, and his second-in-command, Captain Colin Mitchell, carried out a short vehicle recce. Meanwhile, trucks and tanks crowded with grinning infantry in broad-brimmed hats rumbled by: 3rd Battalion, Royal Australian Regiment was passing through to set up a block to the north. Soon it was quiet again.

A Company, which had fought a sharp action on Sariwon's outskirts, arrived. Their OC, Major David Wilson, slumped into the chair of a deserted barbershop, its walls lined with tall, American-style mirrors. It was an unexpected find in this half-ruined town – particularly for an officer who had been living in the field for weeks. Outside, the B Company officers had just returned from their recce when their battalion commander, Lieutenant Colonel Leslie Neilson, drove up and called them over. The three were conferring over maps in the middle of the street when a truck drew up alongside and halted, apparently to ask directions. The conversation was stillborn; the realisation hit all participants at the same moment.[4] The vehicle was bristling with armed enemy.

Around Wilson, the barbershop mirrors disintegrated into crystal fragments. A crescendo of North Korean fire – the ripping 'brrrrrppp' of PPsh 41 submachine guns – was amplified by the close walls. Outside, with bullets whipping overhead, Neilson abandoned his vehicle and dived behind a low wall. As he attempted to return fire, he was struck by one of those embarrassments that is not meant to affect colonels: His Sten gun jammed. Gordon-Ingram was having more success: Standing upright next to the land rover, 'looking exactly like the sheriff in an old-time Western', he picked off enemy with carefully aimed shots of his revolver.[5] By now, Yetman and his mates had reacted. Bullets hammered through the bodywork of the vehicle, coverless in the centre of the road. North Koreans vaulted off the truck and into a monsoon ditch running alongside the road. Mistake. Argylls were above the drain, in defilade. Rapid firing along the length of the ditch, the Highlanders tumbled the North Koreans down, dead.

The driver attempted to accelerate out of the fusillade. As his perforated vehicle juddered forward, a member of Yetman's platoon scurried alongside in the monsoon ditch and hurled a grenade. It detonated on the truck bed. Brewing up, the vehicle careened to the side of the street, its occupants dead. Sudden silence. The contact had been, Yetman thought, 'a bit dodgy'. Remarkably, given the extreme close range – no more than the width of a street – no Argyll had been hit. Thirty North Koreans – including a group of prisoners taken earlier and mown down in the crossfire – sprawled on the road.[6] There were no wounded to be tended, no captured to be interrogated. 'When you are firing at a range of 20 feet and you get an angry Jock – well, he shoots to kill,' said the battalion adjutant, Captain John Slim. Flames flickering up from the burning truck lit the ruined street. Daylight was fading.

Orders arrived from Brigade HQ: Neilson was to consolidate his battalion and establish blocking positions west of Sariwon. By radio, Neilson summoned C Company, clearing the north of the town, back to the south. Then with his battalion second-in-command, Major John Sloane, he drove out of the town down the southwest road in a land rover and a tracked carrier to recce the blocking position. A CO and second-in-command should not be together; it was a rare mistake by Neilson.

The clock ticked. The party did not return. The radio was silent. 'This was quite fun!' thought Intelligence Officer Sandy Boswell grimly: The battalion was leaderless in an unsecured town with night falling. Gordon-Ingram took command in Neilson's absence.

It was now some time after 18:00. As evening gloom cloaked Sariwon's arena of broken streets, perhaps the most extraordinary encounter of the Korean War was about to take place; an encounter that, were it fiction, would defy credibility.

C Company, along with the mortar platoon and a troop of American tanks, was returning south along the main road. With sporadic sniping echoing through the streets, the column was tactically deployed. Behind the turret of the leading Sherman, stood a green National Service officer: Second Lieutenant Alan Lauder, a Dunfermline native. Beside him, well-spaced Jocks of his platoon were pacing on either side of the crawling tank. The column entered the illumination of a stationary truck's headlights. Abandoned. A Jock broke ranks and smashed the lights with his rifle butt. Then, from his vantage point at the head of the column, Lauder made out 'a horde of people' advancing up the street towards him. He could see that they were armed and accompanied by stacked ox carts. As the two columns converged, the newcomers – now recognisable as Asian troops – politely dragged their carts to the side of the road to let the Argylls pass. 'They were giving us a friendly reception, waving and rubbing shoulders with our guys,' Lauder recalled. Obviously, the men were South Korean allies. But as the Sherman trundled by, the American tank commander's head popped out of his turret and scrutinised the strangers. 'They're goddamned Gooks!' he hissed.

For the first time in his life, the Scotsman experienced something

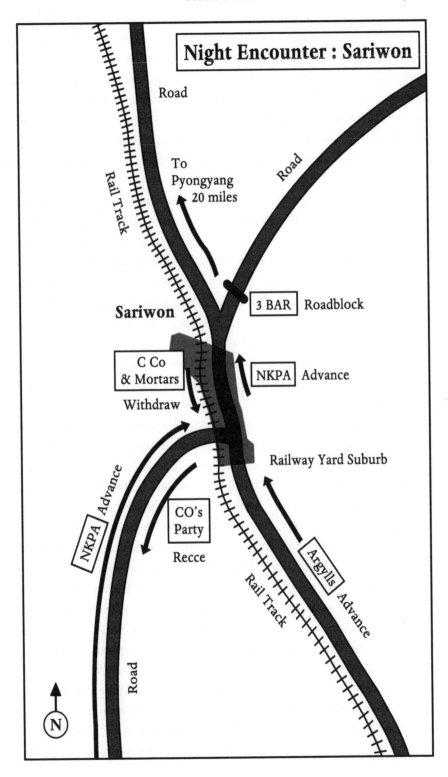

Night Encounter : Sariwon

Road

To Pyongyang 20 miles

Road

Rail Track

3 BAR Roadblock

Sariwon

C Co & Mortars

NKPA Advance

Withdraw

NKPA Advance

Railway Yard Suburb

CO's Party

Recce

Argylls Advance

Rail Track

Road

N

he had only read about: A crawling sensation on the back of his neck as hairs bristled up in a primeval response to fear: 'Gook' was the slang GIs used for enemy. 'What am I gonna do?' asked the tank commander. 'For God's sake keep motoring,' Lauder retorted. 'I'm not going to start a fight here!' The American disappeared inside his armoured shell, clanging his top hatch closed. Ahead was a junction. The enemy column seemed endless. Seeing the opportunity to escape, Lauder led his column off the main road, down a side street. The nerve-wracking drive, Lauder estimated, had taken 10 minutes; somehow, the Argylls had got away with it. Then, from behind, a shot rang out.

The rear of Lauder's column consisted of a couple of US tanks and the Argyll Mortar Platoon, mounted in seven Bren gun carriers: low, open boxes of armour on caterpillar tracks. Some mortar men were in the carriers; others pacing alongside, shepherding half a dozen POWs captured north of the town. At the rear of the platoon was a Glasgow-born private, Henry 'Chick' Cochrane. The column halted. Cochrane saw why: A crowd of Korean troops was approaching. The soldiers and the idling armoured vehicles in the town square reminded Cochrane fleetingly of Colchester. 'I said, "South Koreans – how the hell did they get here?"' He called one over. The man walked across, smiling. As he approached, Cochrane felt a lurching shock: There was a red star in the man's cap. 'I said, "Enemy troops! We are not gonna see daylight tomorrow!"' Circumspectly, Cochrane approached his platoon commander, Captain Robin Fairrie. Echoing the American tanker's enquiry to Lauder, he whispered urgently, 'What are ye gonna do?' Fairrie, a heavyweight boxer popular with the Jocks for his boyish sense of mischief, was nonplussed: 'You tell me!' he replied. This delicate scenario was not covered at Sandhurst.

The mingling North Koreans seemed delighted, pointing excitedly at the white stars stencilled on the hulls of the fighting vehicles (UN air recognition signals). Grins flashed, mutually incomprehensible greetings were exchanged, cigarettes and souvenirs passed back and forth. Passing enemy clapped Jocks on the back, murmuring, 'Russki!' The penny dropped: As the Argylls were returning from the north of Sariwon to the south, the enemy, entering the town from a separate road, had mistaken them for Russian allies joining the war. The Argylls' kit reinforced the North Koreans' belief, for the Jocks were wearing knitted cap comforters – similar to Red Army headgear of the Second World War – and carrying British, not American, small arms.*

Another mortar man, Adam MacKenzie, was walking beside a carrier; Fairrie had somehow passed word to his men that they were not to speak, only nod, and to keep the prisoners moving. The POWs seem not to have realised what was going on – or were too frightened to take advantage. 'Let's get out of here!' MacKenzie fretted. But fraternisation continued: A North Korean officer approached Fairrie. 'Russki?' he enquired. Fairrie replied with the only Russian he knew: 'Tovarisch!'[7] This was enough to secure a special favour: A uniformed North Korean female joined him on his jeep, motioning playfully for the speechless officer to pass her his balmoral.[8]

Tension wound tighter; this impossible, ludicrous situation could not last. Inside carriers, Jocks quietly pulled the cocking levers of Bren guns and loosened hand grenade pins. 'There was going to be a big skirmish in a minute,' said Cochrane. 'Ye could hear it: The calm before the storm!' As the head of the column, led by Lauder, was trundling down the junction, one of the American tank commanders at the rear got into an altercation with a North Korean. The sergeant reached down from his turret, grabbed a Korean's rifle by the barrel, and tried to yank it away. The Korean squeezed the trigger. The GI slumped, gut-shot. 'We'd been rumbled!' MacKenzie realised. Almost immediately, the second US tank opened up with

---

* Why should so many NKPA soldiers have been expecting Soviet assistance at this stage of the war? Kim Il-sung, the North Korean dictator, had served in the Red Army in the Second World War; the Red Army that had liberated North Korean in 1945 and equipped, trained and advised the NKPA in the earlier fighting. Kim had written to Stalin on 29 September begging for assistance. For the first two weeks of October, debate and correspondence flowed between Pyongyang, Moscow and Peking on possible intervention in Korea. (For details, see Mansourov). NKPA combat troops were not party to these discussions, but Dr Andrei Lankov, a Russian-born professor at Seoul's Kookmin University and an expert on North Korea, told the author of his belief that news of Kim's pleas to Stalin would have leaked out – even to field soldiers.

machine guns. The convivial scene disintegrated into pandemonium.

MacKenzie hit the deck – North Koreans were frantically setting up machine guns – then vaulted into a carrier. Cochrane did the same. Jocks were emptying Brens and Stens and hurling hand grenades over the sides of the armour, while staying as low as possible. In the confusion, the prisoners disappeared, while astounded enemy – those not scythed down – scattered. One appeared around a corner from Cochrane, raised his rifle and squeezed the trigger; it clicked on an empty chamber. 'There was no fear,' he said. 'The fear had left ye, all your emphasis was to get them off ye and get under cover somewhere!' A big North Korean dived through the rice paper window of a house. In mid-air, a phosphorous grenade hit him. Soldier and house flared up[9] Suddenly, the street was clear; the mortar men and North Koreans had broken away from each other.

But the town was crawling with desperate enemy seeking exits. The CO was still absent. Most of the battalion regrouped to the south of the town proper – but not all. Small groups of Jocks took position in buildings, waiting nervously for dawn. Sudden bursts of firing and crumps of grenades echoed through the streets as frantic North Koreans blundered into Argylls and each other. Even the battalion medical officer found himself shooting. 'There happened to be people milling about in the darkness, I had a carbine, I fired at a shadow, and have regretted it ever since,' said Dr Douglas Haldane. 'I was caught up in the atmosphere, it was a melee, bedlam.' Parts of Sariwon were burning; the orange glow was reflected in the clouds above.

Dawn finally lit the scene. The streets were littered with the stiffening bodies of some 150 North Koreans. Remarkably, only one Argyll had been killed.[10]

The mystery of the missing colonel was solved, when Neilson and his party motored in with a remarkable tale. They had barely left Sariwon the previous evening when they came upon a double column of troops plodding up the road towards them: North Koreans. There was a short burst from the leading enemy, but the officers could not turn their vehicles on the narrow track. Neilson ordered, 'Step on the gas!'[11] The British vehicles drove straight between the marching lines.

There were hundreds of enemy – but they were defeated, exhausted, and did not identify the unfamiliar vehicles. Mitchell – one of the Argylls' most aggressive officers – stood in the leading carrier, Second World War Luger clutched in his fist. Feeling 'a sense of detachment . . . excited, alert and amused at the same time', he could not help bursting into laughter; his 'ashen faced' driver was less amused at their knife-edge predicament.[12] In nightmare slow-motion, the drive through some 2,000 enemy soldiers continued for over 4 miles. Finally, the column was behind them. The party pulled off the track, camouflaged their vehicles, and formed a tight defensive perimeter in a roadside ditch – the colonel himself taking a turn on sentry duty – hoping that neither enemy, nor advancing Americans, would fire on them. Meanwhile, the North Korean column had entered the town – where they met Lauder.

The fate of the enemy mass soon became known. Word came that their big column, having fled the hammer of the Argylls, had stumbled into the anvil of the Australians. Surprised but fast-thinking Diggers had taken 1,982 prisoners. Enemy numbers justified Lauder's circumspection the previous night. 'I've often wondered what I should have done,' he said. 'I think I did the right thing.' Indeed: his company and the mortar platoon had walked into an enemy regiment.

Some men felt remorseful over the amiable enemy. 'Later, you seen what you'd done,' said Cochrane, ruminating on the North Koreans killed. 'It was laughable after – but no joke at the time.' One Jock retained a North Korean epaulette from the exchanges; another a lapel badge.[13] Fairrie recovered his balmoral; his North Korean admirer had bolted in the firefight.[14]

Still, Sariwon had fallen.* Concentrated, the battalion pressed onward. At the town entrance the Scots planted a laconic sign for the benefit of troops coming through: 'Have no fear[15] – the Argylls were here.'

---

* The extraordinary story of Sariwon was under-reported at the time – not due to censorship, but because correspondents' copy bogged down in the 8th Army PR process. See Thompson, 1951, p 202.

Chapter One
Thunder in the East

On the idle hill of summer,
Sleepy with the flow of streams,
Far I hear the steady drummer
Drumming like a noise in dreams.
A.E. Housman

Evening, 19 August. Kowloon, Hong Kong.

Near the waterfront, a swimming gala was underway. It was a typical Saturday event at the colony's premier sporting venue, the Portuguese Club, in the summer of 1950. The competitors were 1st Battalion, the Middlesex Regiment – a young, sport-focused infantry battalion – versus local defence force volunteers. The ambience was cheerful; colourful, too. Defying the humidity, officers were tooled up in, 'No 1 dress, or mess kit or that kind of ridiculous stuff,' said Major Dennis Rendell. His CO, Lieutenant Colonel Andrew Man, was about to stand up and speak to the assemblage, when someone appeared and whispered in his ear. Without ado, the colonel departed. Officers were always being called away for one thing or another, so his absence was barely remarked upon. 'We went back to having a jolly good time,' Rendell said. In due course, Man returned. The gala continued.[1]

Swimming galas were just one of a number of pleasant diversions for servicemen in the Crown Colony, for 1950s Hong Kong was perhaps the most enviable posting in the British Army. Elsewhere, Britain was pulling back from an empire on which the sun was setting. Military commitments in India had wound down with independence; a messy counter-insurgency campaign had just been completed in Palestine; jungle operations against communist guerillas were underway in the Malay jungle. In Europe, the army was manning a range of garrisons across a tense, devastated continent, while home duty in grim barracks in the UK, a nation threadbare after the Second World War, was a dreary prospect.

Hong Kong was different. The colony was a trading port and the atmosphere in the stores, markets, cinemas, pubs, clubs and restaurants of 'the shopping window of the Far East' was sizzling.[2] Streets were bustling, shop fronts were enlivened with colourful Chinese signage, rickshaws ran hither and yon. In the days before international tourism, this exoticism was exciting. 'I had never been on a train till I joined the army, never seen a ship,' said Jake Mutch, a private soldier in the Argyll and Sutherland Highlanders. 'It was all marvellous, all new to me; really exciting.' For young Britons raised in the rationed UK, the goods offered were near miraculous – and available at prices even lowly soldiers could afford. 'Coming up in the war years, I'd never had steak,' said Middlesex Private Edgar Green, a 19-year-old National Serviceman from Herne Hill, London. 'But in Hong Kong, if you went to a service club – "The Cheerio Club" or "The Soldiers and Sailors Club" – you would get steak, egg and chips for not even two shillings!' Shopping opportunities were 'out of this world'; Green sent his mother nylon stockings so fine he could post them in a letter.

The weather, sporting facilities and scenery made Hong Kong a healthy as well as a popular posting. 'Ah, Hong Kong – a playboy existence!' said Lieutenant Peter Baldwin, a former boy soldier and Signals Officer attached to the headquarters of 27th Infantry Brigade, part of the defence force posted in the New Territories. On weekends, soldiers could swim off fine beaches, though there were constant reminders of the fact that this was not Europe. 'There was a float out in the bay, and junks and sampans used to come in, and they'd defecate over the side,' said Argyll Roy Vincent. 'Lads used to get a bit annoyed; strong swimmers would swim out and rock them.'

Still, relations with the Chinese were good; it tended to be British expatriates who looked down upon soldiers. 'The Chinese businessmen organised beach parties and barbeques,' Vincent said.

'If you wanted a lift, you went to the end of road and you flagged down cars. British cars would bowl past you like you weren't there, but Chinamen would stop, I once got a ride with a Chinaman in a Rolls Royce. I thought, "If he can do that, why can't British?"'

The gentle sex was abundant and of pleasing variety. Captain Andrew Brown, the Argylls' ever-cheerful quartermaster, noted, as he took the Star Ferry plying between Kowloon and Hong Kong island, that British soldiers would gawp at the sudden flash of thigh revealed by the slit in a Chinese *cheongsam* dress, but ignore the generous cleavage displayed by European girls; Chinese males, on the other hand, goggled at buxom foreign bosoms, while paying little attention to slender local legs.[3]

Then as now, the Wild, Wild East was famed for its night life. Beer – San Miguel and Tiger – was cheap, chilled and good. More dubious indulgences were close at hand. The Middlesex's padre advised his flock to avoid the notorious red-light district, Wanchai, with some robust advice: 'He said, "Do what the good Lord said: Take it in your own hand and satisfy yourself!"' recalled Corporal Bob Yerby, a Middlesex regular. 'He was a great padre for the lads!' Spiritual warnings, however, did not dissuade amorous squaddies. 'There was one place you could go in and get a tattoo, a meal, a tooth out, a drink and it was a brothel – all under one roof!' said Mutch. 'The police would raid and they'd say, "Where you been?" and you'd say, "Dentist!" They'd say to the next man, "Where you been?" and it was, "Tattoo!"'

Those who caught a dose of Cupid's Arrows ended up with twenty-eight days in the guardhouse – and a rocket from officers.[4] 'There was bloke called "Major Snowball", he was second-in-command, and a bloke from our company was up for trial because he had gonorrhea,' recalled Mutch. 'This guy from our company, his greens were black with ink because Snowball had thrown an inkpot at him and yelled, "You filthy brute!" He had to change his clothes, then go to jail.'

And of course, there was the tomfoolery that British military units customarily indulge in. When the NAAFI closed, Argyll Corporal Joseph Fairhurst and his mates filled a kit bag with beer, then retired to a monsoon ditch to drink under the stars. The battalion had a small shop set up in a tent, selling odds and ends; accounts were noted via a ledger: 'You handed over a few cents or put your name down in the account book,' Mutch said. One night, a tropical storm wreaked havoc on the tented camp. While men were dashing around dealing with the after effects of the deluge, others found time to visit the shop. 'The first thing some lads did in this storm was go to the tent, get hold of the book and tear it up,' said Mutch. 'A clean sheet!'

An NCO in one battalion was dressed down by his CO after he paraded a full Royal Guard to welcome the San Miguel truck when it arrived to refill the sergeants' mess. Men from the same unit took imaginative revenge on an unpopular company sergeant major with a drinking habit. The CSM staggered into his room one night after an heroic night at the mess bar and collapsed into bed. Early the next morning, soldiers nearby heard horrified screams, before the NCO appeared in dramatic fashion – leaping through his window and clipping a chip off his scalp on the window frame. Long-suffering soldiers had disinterred a corpse from a Chinese grave on the hill behind their base, and planted it carefully in the CSM's bed while he was indulging in his wassails. Hungover, he woke beside a mouldering corpse.[5]

The pleasant off-duty existence soldiers enjoyed over weekends and the Quixotic episodes that enlivened barrack life did not, however, detract from the geo-political realities that necessitated a Hong Kong garrison. The colony had been seized in a particularly savage battle by the Japanese in 1942; in 1949, there were fears of a replay, for after years of fighting, Chiang Kai-shek's ragtag nationalists had been driven from China by Mao Tse-tung's communists. It was unclear how the new Peking would view an outpost of rampant capitalism on its southern flank. Whitehall had dispatched its quick reaction force, 27th Infantry Brigade – the 1st battalions of the Argyll and Sutherland Highlanders, the Middlesex Regiment and the Royal Leicestershire Regiment – to bolster 40th Division, the 20,000-strong force defending the colony. The brigade landed in July, 1949.[6]

Duties were tough. Days started with a mug of water and a

paladrine tablet to keep malaria at bay, then a run through the assault course or PT. Then came the primary activity: Digging defences into the hills of the New Territories overlooking the China border. 'Those hills, they were all solid bloody rock so to dig a hole you would put a charge down, blow it and then shore it up,' Green said. Wearing only shorts, boots and berets, men laboured up the slopes with shovels, stakes, bags of cement and dixies of water. Over sun-drenched hillsides, sweat-soaked soldiers unrolled miles and miles of barbed wire, and carved trenches into the contours. Men grew lean and fit. Bunkers and observation points sprouted. From these positions, binoculars were aimed into the newly communised land.

'It was very interesting, you were looking into China proper,' said Ralph Horsfield, a Doncaster lad serving with the Argylls. 'You'd pick up different things: How many vehicles crossed a bridge? Who got on them?' Movements were noted in logs and passed to higher command. The Chinese were doing the same. 'The communists had big blockhouses on the other side,' said Wigan native Corporal Joseph Fairhurst, another Englishman in the Argylls. 'We could see them; they could see us.'

Soldiers, patrolling the border fences, were wary of local wildlife in the thigh-deep mud and water of the rice fields. 'All the paddies were filled with snakes,' said Middlesex Lance Corporal Don Barrett. 'Every sergeant carried a razor blade to cut the bites and suck out the blood.' The mud, water and humidity caused a number of afflictions. 'Everybody had diseases,' Barrett recalled. 'Blotches – all your scrotum goes gungy and smelly – and diarrhoea.' Men attended duty painted with blue medical liniments.

By summer 1950, geopolitical tensions were easing. Mao, it appeared, was not going to storm the border. Despite the high hills, high temperatures and rough barracks – the Argylls lived in tents, the Middlesex in stables – Hong Kong was, for the British soldier, a very agreeable existence.

The same could not be said elsewhere in the Far East. In Europe, the Cold War had stabilised, largely in favour of the capitalist democracies. Tito and Stalin had split in 1948; the following year, the Berlin Blockade was lifted, the Greek Civil War ended and NATO was founded. The centre of gravity of the great ideological conflict was shifting eastwards. China, the 'Middle Kingdom' at the continent's heart, was now red, and in February 1950, the Sino-Soviet pact had been signed. European colonial powers, their prestige shattered by early Japanese success in the Second World War were in the descendent. Communism had climbed into bed with nationalism, and leftist guerillas were fighting in the jungles of Indochina, Malaya, and the Philippines.

The message that had summoned Lieutenant Colonel Man from his battalion's swimming gala on 19 August was a harbinger of ill tidings. 27th Infantry Brigade was about to be pitch-forked from the best posting available to British troops in 1950 to the worst. Potential communist menace had brought the Argylls and Middlesex to Hong Kong; actual communist menace would propel them into the vortex of the struggle for tomorrow's Asia.

This would be no low-intensity guerilla conflict in tropical jungle, but a savage, all-out war fought over a primitive, cruel and rugged land. On 25 June 1950, an armoured invasion force, fully outfitted and advised by the USSR, had rolled over an unheralded frontier. The communist blitzkrieg was cleaving across a mountainous peninsula 525 miles long and 200 miles wide, that few Argylls or Middlesex had even heard of. Korea.

*　*　*

It was a warm, early summer day, and Kim Song-hwan, a slight, cheerful-looking high-school student was sitting with friends on a hilltop on the northern outskirts of Seoul, the capital of South Korea. At their feet were the curved tiled roofs and thatch of a typical Korean village; beyond stretched paddy fields and a dust road heading northward. All eyes were focused on the blue hills on the northern horizon, where great puffs of grey smoke were blossoming, then dispersing. Kim got to work. As always, he had pencils, watercolours and sketchbook with him, for the 17-year-old student was also an artist, earning money working for Seoul newspapers, which could not afford cameramen. The watchers knew the smoke was from artillery impacts, but were unconcerned. 'We had heard over the radio that North Korea had invaded, but were told over the radio that the South Korean Army had pushed them back,' Kim recalled. In fact, the barrage on the hills heralded not a successful defence, but the imminent arrival of armoured spearheads of the North Korean People's Army, or NKPA; its formidable T34 tanks had crushed flimsy frontier barriers and were now rattling down the road toward the capital. 'I am bitter about those broadcasts,' Kim said. 'Because of them, many people did not flee.'

The land over which was this war was raging was an ill-fated one, for though it had been independent in language, custom and governance since the Dark Ages, the Korean peninsula is the strategic heart of Northeast Asia, the crossroads between the more powerful, more populous lands of China, Japan and the Russian Far East. It was a cockpit of war. The Mongolians launched their ill-fated thirteenth-century invasions of Japan from the peninsula; the Japanese launched their equally doomed sixteenth-century invasion of China over the same terrain. After the Japanese devastation of the sixteenth century and a Manchurian onslaught in the seventeenth, the traumatised Korean people closed their gates against the outside world and hoped for the best.

It was a doomed strategy. With colonial powers thrusting ever further east, the 'Hermit Kingdom' was swimming against the historical tide. In the second half of the nineteenth century, in a dynamic response to the rising West, Japan modernised swiftly and radically. Sleepy Korea became the prize in a trilateral power game. In 1895, Tokyo defeated Peking in the Sino-Japanese War, and in 1905, smashed Moscow in the Russo-Japanese War. These victories staked her claim on the mountainous peninsula. With the acquiescence of London and Washington, Tokyo annexed a bewildered Korea in 1910. The sun sank on the house of Yi, the royal dynasty which had claimed Korea's dragon throne exactly one hundred years before Columbus had discovered America. Korea had never been much known beyond East Asia. As a colony of Japan, she was erased from global consciousness.

Tokyo would prove no benevolent overlord. In the early stages of its thirty-five-year rule, Japan governed with an iron fist. Resistance generated more lenient policies; twentieth-century infrastructure and a modern economy were installed. But come the 1930s, Japan was turning militaristic, ultra-nationalistic. Korea became the springboard for Tokyo's conquest of Manchuria in 1931, then her invasion into China proper in 1937. In 1941, war flames spread across the Pacific, to be extinguished four years later by atomic flashes over Hiroshima and Nagasaki and a last-minute Soviet thrust into Manchuria and northern Korea. Japan lay shattered.

What of her colony? In an afterthought at the end of the Second World War, the peninsula was divided by the Americans along a line on a map, the 38th parallel. In the North, Soviet forces installed Kim Il-sung, a former anti-Japanese guerilla and major in the Red Army who had fled to the Russian Far East when Manchuria got too hot for him, to rule the country's nine million people from Pyongyang. The Americans installed Rhee Syngman, an anti-Japanese nationalist who had spent the colonial years in exile in the US, over the South's twenty-one million in Seoul. The arrangement was meant to be temporary, but the Second World War had morphed into the Cold War; neither Rhee nor Kim would compromise with the other. In 1948, competing governments were established on both sides of the 38th parallel. Guerillas took up arms against the South, sparking brutality and massacre. Clashes flickered along the inter-Korean frontier. The Seoul government boasted that if war came, it would 'eat lunch in Pyongyang, dinner in Sinuiju'.[7] But with neither insurgency nor border fighting promising an end to division, it would be Kim – fully outfitted by Stalin with offensive weapons, advised by Soviet planners – who made the decisive bid for unification. In the early hours of Sunday, 25 June 1950, he launched the NKPA southward in a full-scale invasion. This was not an insurgency, nor support for said; this was naked aggression. A heretofore-unknown peninsula was about to explode onto the world's consciousness.

Among those in Seoul, as communist divisions rolled south, was a student of literature, Lee Jong-yun. A native of the border city of Kaesong, he had once read *Chong Kamnok,* a 300-year book of divination which had prophesied a terrible war in 1950, the Year of the Tiger, but living in Kaesong, had grown used to gunfire. Like many, he believed early reports of the fighting referred to frontier clashes. Then he saw refugees arriving from Uijongbu, the town 15 miles north, where Kim had watched artillery impacts. Though apolitical, Lee was convinced that the North Koreans would recruit him into their army – something he wanted to avoid. He decided to flee.

Kim, the young newspaper artist, had returned to Seoul and found a vantage point: He stood on the medieval city walls, where they climbed up the mountain side near the fortress-like East Gate, watching brown smoke rise over the adjacent market and the grey tiled roofs of the suburbs. Curious civilians crowded the walls, trying to see what was going on. Republic of Korea, or ROK soldiers were posted nervously in doorways; the war was not proceeding according to plan. An infectious panic was spreading. Desperate people were running through alleyways, bundles of possessions on their backs or their heads. Soldiers started to lose their nerve. Kim watched ROK troops changing into civilian clothes, hiding uniforms and weapons.

Rhee's army has proven unable to check the invaders. While Moscow had liberally supplied Kim with armour, artillery and warplanes, Washington – fearful that Rhee might invade the North – had withheld heavy weapons. Lacking tanks, warplanes, heavy artillery and effective anti-tank weapons, the ROK Army was disintegrating.

Lee, meanwhile, was heading south, caught up in what was becoming, for some, a mad rush: 'I ran like I was running from a volcano,' he said. Soon he was out of the city proper, moving across paddy dykes, through the rice fields and thatched hamlets of the countryside. 'It was pretty peaceful there,' Lee said. 'People were just watching what was going on.' He reached the kilometres-wide Han River. The bridges had been blown by ROK engineers – Kim was not to know it, but hundreds of civilian refugees had been obliterated in the detonations – and the brown river was swollen and fast flowing with summer rains. No ferries were available; they had been commandeered by the military. However, Lee was a strong swimmer. Stripping off, he held his clothes on his head, and entered the swirl. He was carried downstream, but reached the south bank safely.

On 28 June, Seoul fell to the NKPA. Kim watched victorious columns trundle up the tree-lined boulevards. First came the Soviet-built T34 tanks, scout cars and motorcycle side-cars and trucks pulling artillery, all heavily camouflaged with scrub. Then, lines of marching men, rifles and submachine guns slung. Finally, the logistic tail: lumbering ox carts, also well camouflaged. In tan uniforms, the troops were dusty from the road, and some eyes, under peaked caps, were wide with battle shock, but most looked stern, tough and competent; many were combat veterans of Mao's communist forces and the Chinese Civil War. Splashing colour across the scene were the red banners and flags the men from the north were carrying. Modest crowds lined the route. 'Some workers welcomed them, they thought it would be a different world!' said Kim. 'There were NKPA going by in jeeps saying, "Give them a big hand!" but it was only some workers and children who did.'

Meanwhile Lee, temporarily safe south of the Han, had halted. 'I thought I'd return to Seoul in a few days and the North Koreans would be defeated,' he said. But looking back, he could see smoke rising over the city: ROK troops were burning supplies. He stayed in a Buddhist temple for three days, buying food from nearby farming villages. Then the NKPA forded the Han. Lee set off again, heading for the south-central city of Taegu. In the town square in front of the railway station, was a sign asking for English interpreters. A student of English literature – his favourite poem was T.S. Eliot's 'The Waste Land', a work appropriate to the times – Lee spoke the language reasonably. Men like Lee were suddenly in high demand. 'The Yankees' had landed.

Kim's invasion had not gone unchallenged. Amid frantic US-led diplomacy – aided by the absence of the Soviet delegation, boycotting the organisation in protest at the UN's refusal to grant a seat to Mao's China – the UN Security Council passed resolutions on 25 and 27 June recommending UN members act to 'restore international peace and security in the area'. On 30 June, US President Harry Truman ordered the US Supreme Commander in the Far East, Tokyo-based General Douglas MacArthur, to deploy US ground forces to assist the South. On 7 July, the UN Security Council recommended that

UN forces be placed under US command. On 8 July, MacArthur was put in charge of the 'United Nations Command', or UNC.[8] For the first time in its history, the New York-based multinational body was going to war.

For MacArthur – the victor in the Pacific; a general who combined a brilliant strategic mind with the instincts of an actor and the ego of a duke – Korea was the last chance for glory. His troops had been engaged almost from the start of hostilities: On 27 June, with the US Air Force evacuating US personnel – mainly members of the 500-man military advisory group working with the ROK Army – a North Korean Yak fighter had been shot down by a US Air Force F-82. On 1 July, US ground forces landed.[9]

The first American soldiers to arrive in Korea were garrison troops from the four-division US occupation force in Japan, the 8th Army. On 5 July, the North Koreans and Americans clashed for the first time. A Regimental Combat Team, or RCT, 'Taskforce Smith' proved no match for the hard driving NKPA: The RCT's blocking position was rolled over by armour outside the town of Osan. The taskforce broke. Reinforcements landing in the southeastern port of Pusan were hastened to the front.

Among those recording events was an Associated Press photographer, Max Desfor. His editor expected the war to be over in two weeks – 'that was the prevalent opinion' – but Desfor, then in AP's Miami bureau, had leapt at the chance to shoot a real story: 'It was a hell of a lot different from catching a bunch of senators shaking hands, smiling and looking at the camera!' No stranger to combat, the Bronx native had covered the Indonesian fight for independence against the Dutch and prior to that, the battle for Okinawa in the Second World War. Not a man to cover war from HQ, Desfor headed for the front. He was unimpressed by the troops. 'There was a lot of criticism of them and I felt it too: the 24th and 25th Divisions were occupation troops, "good time Charlies",' he said. 'They were not prepared to fight and I don't know if they had any idea why they were fighting.'

With a nuclear deterrent and a strategic air force in hand, Washington had massively downsized and downgraded US ground forces after the Second World War. The 8th Army, after the easy living, booze and broads of occupied Japan, was unprepared for the primitive conditions of Korea and unfit for combat. Their leadership was third-tier: Only the lowest performing US military cadets were assigned to the Far East.[10] Many units were under strength, particularly in artillery. Less than ten per cent had combat experience. Moreover, in a budget-cutting move, the key brains and nerve centres of any army – the corps headquarters – of US forces in Japan had been eliminated.[11]

The result was that neither US nor ROK troops were capable of holding the NKPA. Retreat, defeat, retreat. A new term entered the military lexicon: 'Bug out'. Lines of refugees and soldiers slogged south down baking dust tracks winding through Korea's paddy fields, thatched hamlets and rocky hills. The summer sun burned down.

In occupied Seoul, Kim Song-hwan adjusted to new realities. Many people got on with life, but leftists had emerged and were denouncing rightists. Many scenes he saw and sketched, were snapshot tragedies he never learned the beginning to, or the end of. Camouflaged North Korean troops roughly questioning a terrified man – his face as pale as a ghost's – in a village alley. A wounded ROK soldier, abandoned by doctors and stripped of his trousers by villagers trying to find his wounds was dying on a blood-soaked stretcher. A desolate couple sobbed next to a body in a paddy. Ubiquitous corpses lying under the ubiquitous rice sacking, the ubiquitous flies buzzing around their wounds. 'There were flies everywhere,' Kim recalled. 'Some bodies attracted more than others; maybe the flies liked fresh blood?'

But as the weeks passed, indications appeared that all was not well with the communist leadership. Food was becoming difficult to obtain; Kim decided to head north to join his aunt in Kaesong. On the way, he noted how difficult it was to take transport: The skies were dominated by US aircraft. He watched North Korean soldiers in camouflaged foxholes firing in angry futility at distant bombers. In Kaesong, the ancient Korean capital on the 38th parallel, he took refuge in an inn. Like many males, he was now virtually in hiding, for the NKPA was press-ganging men into the army. When he did go out, he carried a walking stick and faked a limp to demonstrate unfitness. Hiding under the beams of the inn, sketching, the young artist thought of a pen name for himself: *Gobau* or 'Strong Rock'.

The USAF was not restricted to southern or central Korea; strike squadrons, skimming over paddies and hills, were ranging far and wide, paying visits to the towns as far from the battlefield as the industrial city of Hamhung, 150 miles northeast of Seoul. There lived Lim Geum-sook, a 19-year-old girl, no supporter of Kim's regime: 'Under communism, we were not allowed to eat white rice – we had to cook it secretly!' She detested the term 'comrade' and dreaded the thought of working in the provincial mines, where young people were encouraged to volunteer. The first indication that war had broken out was the destruction of a city centre bridge by air attack. Raids became frequent. 'There were no underground shelters, people just hid under bridges and so on,' she said. 'When planes came over, we could not see them, we just heard the sounds – how can you look up? We could not stand and watch!'

Danger came closer. The house next door was flattened; lumps of shrapnel skittered into the Lims' courtyard. The family evacuated the children to a farm in the countryside, where the men dug a bunker in the cemetery. When aircraft appeared, the children crawled underground, but it was not just the UNC air offensive Lim was hiding from. While men were dragged into the NKPA, women were press-ganged as nurses. Though the ground war was distant, the Lim family decided to escape North Korea should the opportunity arise.

On the southern front, the NKPA was forging southeast on its final offensive. A wavy line was starting to appear on UNC maps: 'The Pusan Perimeter', a rough 50–100 mile defensive rectangle, largely defined by the Naktong River, that enclosed the port city of Pusan, the funnel through which UNC reinforcements were being fed. Among those coming ashore were America's elite. After answering 'a few questions' related to his English proficiency, Lee was assigned to these troops.

'There was an older man with us, a teacher, and when he heard about joining them he disappeared – he'd read about them!' Lee said.

The new arrivals, US marines, made an immediate impression. 'They were really tough, professional fighters, they talked and talked about fighting,' he said. 'I had attended missionary school, but when I joined up, I found marines don't speak missionary English!' Lee was assigned to the Marine Provisional Brigade as an interpreter; his given name, Jong-yun, was anglicised to 'John'. He was accepted. 'In 1950, there was still the white superiority complex, it was discriminatory, but for marines, you were a marine,' he said. 'I wore marine utilities, a lieutenant's badge and became part of them culturally and psychologically.' The crack brigade was committed almost immediately to combat.

*　　*　　*

In between digging trenches, patrolling hills and heading downtown for weekend entertainment, few men of 27th Brigade had been following the war: Korea was separated from Hong Kong by the vast breadth of China, and unlike locations west and south – Singapore, Malaya, Ceylon, India – the UK had no significant historical, political or commercial interest in Korea. Moreover, nobody had heard of such a thing as a UN multinational force, and media was limited.

'There were no radios in Hong Kong in the camp, occasional newspapers, so we did not know a great deal that was going on,' said Barrett. Officers were hardly better informed. 'Once the war started, my company commander called the platoon commanders and said, "This has blown up, there is a faint possibility that some battalions will go to Korea, but not us,"' said Owen Light, a National Service second-lieutenant in the Argylls. 'I told my platoon this.' The uncertainty as to whether British troops were being sent or not extended to official visits. 'We had a visit from John Strachey, the Secretary of State for War, in early August, and the brigadier asked if we were likely to be sent to Korea,' recalled Captain Reggie Jeffes, 27th Brigade's REME officer. 'He said, "No, we are forming a brigade in the UK to go to Korea in October, you will remain here."'

In fact, members of Coad's brigade had already been in action in – or rather, off – Korea.

At the end of June, Corporal Peter Jones and two fellow Argylls had their names drawn from a hat to join the Royal Navy in Kure, Japan, for the annual Naval Regatta. The three Jocks, along with representatives of other Hong Kong-based units who boarded the heavy cruiser HMS *Jamaica* and the sloop HMS *Black Swan* were delighted at this seaborne holiday. It did not turn out as expected: The ships diverted to Korea. The Royal Naval force, with the US cruiser USS *Juneau,* was tasked with bombarding North Korean coastal supply routes and military installations, and, if possible, convoys of trucks, tanks and guns heading south.

In their first action, the soldiers were locked below decks as guns thundered above; Jones considered it like being 'enclosed in a steel tomb'. Immediately action stations ended and the hatches were flung open, the soldiers sought the Gunnery Officer and 'begged to be on deck next time, to help in any way possible'. The soldiers were appointed to pass ammunition to the four-inch guns, the cruiser's secondary armament, and the antiaircraft batteries. On 2 July, the British men-of-war made a tempting target for a group of seaborne guerillas. From the rocky coastline, six black dots appeared, speeding toward the ships, throwing up impressive wakes: A squadron of North Korean motor torpedo boats, MTBs, sallying out of their coastal lair. If the attack craft could close to torpedo range, the big ships were vulnerable: It was a race to stop them before they could launch.

Klaxons blared, orders were shouted down the tannoy: 'Alarm! Surface! Port!' The great turrets swivelled. The guns depressed. Eardrums of soldiers on deck were almost blown in as the *Jamaica* opened up with all her six-inch batteries. The ship shuddered to her keel. Simultaneously, great columns of water spurted up ahead of the racing MTBs as the broadside smashed into the waves. More salvoes followed as turret crews reloaded and fired at will. Inside the hull, unable to see outside, sailors hung on every word coming over the tannoy: 'Target stopped... possible hit... fire and smoke visible... target sinking'. Within minutes, the attackers had been wiped out. The only survivor turned tail and ran, beaching herself on the distant coast. The soldiers could just make out her crew abandoning ship and running for their lives as the naval guns found the target, blowing the beached MTB into splinters.* Then sudden silence as the Gunnery Officer commanded fire to cease. For the Argylls, the battle had been 'great to watch'. The next action would not be so one-sided.

The three ships had worked out a routine for shore bombardments: Hit high ground, bringing it crashing down on roads and rails. When NKPA convoys, which routinely travelled at night for fear of the USAF, halted and cleared the roads, they would use lights. These lights would then become targets for the blacked-out warships lurking offshore in the darkness – so close that sailors aboard could sometimes hear North Korean voices carrying over the water. On 8 July, the enemy hit back with artillery. A shell hit the base of the *Jamaica's* mast, doing little material damage, but showering those below with shrapnel. Six men were killed or mortally wounded. Under the tattered battle ensign of the cruiser, the fallen – the first British casualties of the Korean War – were buried at sea.

The brutality of events ashore soon became apparent. As the patrol continued, the crew of the *Jamaica* spotted scores of unidentifiable black lumps bobbing in the swell ahead. The ship closed. Curious crew on deck realised what they were: Between 100 and 200 bloated corpses, their hands tied behind their back and shot in the head. For one of the *Jamaica's* marines, Corporal Raymond Todd, it was 'a foretaste of atrocities to come'.[12] The soldiers aboard subsequently disembarked at Nagasaki, from whence they returned to Hong Kong.[13]

* * *

While the UK had minimal historical connection to Korea, Whitehall had been in discussions with Washington over the crisis from the

---

* In 2005, the author, on a visit to Pyongyang, asked a staffer at the capital's impressive war museum what the most heroic North Korean action of the war had been. She replied, 'The sinking of the cruiser USS *Baltimore* by our MTBs!' This sounded impressive, but I had not heard of it. Upon return to Seoul, I checked the literature. No mention. Intrigued, I contacted the Pentagon's PR department. They came back, stating that not only was the *Baltimore* not sunk, it was not assigned to Korea. And no, no other US cruisers had been sunk off Korea. I have wondered since if the 'heroic action' referred to was the raid on *Jamaica* and *Juneau* – which might, perhaps, have been reported up the chain of command as a success.

outset. As the United States' closest ally, a founder member of the UN and a member of the UN Security Council, Britain was under pressure to act. Moreover, Prime Minister Clement Attlee, though a socialist, had a deep distrust of Moscow, and recognised that Britain had to stand alongside the US in facing down what he saw as ruthless communist expansionism. He recognised further that to strengthen the hand of those Americans who favoured a strong defence for Europe, London had to support Washington in Asia. The Royal Navy had already been deployed in a blockading role. What force could the Army provide?

Britain's Imperial Strategic Reserve tasked with deployment outside the UK or Germany, had been 27th Brigade, until dispatched to Hong Kong in 1949. The duty had passed on to 29th Independent Infantry Brigade. On 28 July, Whitehall signalled 29th Brigade, ordering it to prepare for deployment to Korea – this was the brigade Jeffes had been told would do the job. But 29th Brigade was far from ready for immediate departure. Reflecting the strained status of the British Army of 1950, its units were under strength or completely detached. It would not be ready even to embark until 1 November. Though this timetable was subsequently accelerated to 1 October, the tactical situation in Korea continued to degrade.[14]

On 10 August, Air Vice-Marshall Cecil Bourchier, British liaison at MacArthur's Tokyo HQ, reported that the supreme commander, having been informed that no British brigade would arrive until December, was stressing the urgency of getting troops into action, fast. The NKPA were grinding up ROK and US troops; 500 GIs per day were being flown in on chartered aircraft, and committed, piecemeal, to the line; no other UN ally had yet landed ground troops. The Imperial General Staff, unsure whether MacArthur – a general with a taste for melodrama – was to be trusted regarding the situation's urgency, consulted with the US Joint Chiefs of Staff. The crisis was confirmed. On 17 August, the IGS decided to send to Korea, as a stop-gap, British forces from a location closer to Korea than the UK: 27th Brigade. Once 29th Brigade arrived in theatre, 27th Brigade would be withdrawn to Hong Kong.[15]

On Saturday, 19 August – the same evening Lieutenant Colonel

Man was interrupted at the swimming gala – Jeffes was in Kowloon waiting to be picked up by Brigadier Basil Coad, 27th Brigade's commander, for their customary weekend round of golf. 'He did not arrive, so I rang [Coad's] wife, and she said he had been called across to Land Forces, but he will be with you shortly,' Jeffes recalled. 'When he arrived, he said, "Reggie, no golf today: We go to Korea next Friday!"'

Orders for the deployment of 27th Brigade had arrived from Singapore the previous day.[16] The timetable was ridiculous: The departure date from Hong Kong was less than one week away.

* * *

Brigadier Basil Coad – he went by his middle name, Aubrey –was a highly experienced veteran of the Wiltshire Regiment. Tall, austere-looking, grey-haired with a lived-in visage, he was tough on senior officers, but was popular with junior officers and other ranks, for whom he flashed a frequent grin. He had led a battalion in Normandy and a brigade in Northwest Europe, winning a DSO, then briefly commanded a division, before returning to brigadier rank. He had the carefully cultivated commanders' knack of remembering names. 'He always knew you, he knew everybody,' said Argyll adjutant, Captain John Slim. 'He was very clear at commanding troops – English, Scottish or Australian.' A realist, Coad was unwilling to risk men on forlorn hopes. Anglican Reverend William Jones, a self-described 'brainless curate' who had just been posted to the Middlesex, got a sense of Coad's steady sense when he first met him. 'He looked at me and welcomed me to 27th Brigade, then he said, "I don't want any heroes in my brigade – heroes get killed!"' 27th Brigade nicknamed their brigadier, 'Daddy Coad'.[17]

A brigade customarily consists of three battalions, but so stretched were the British forces in 1950, that 27th Brigade was to enter combat with only two: 1st Argylls and 1st Middlesex. On 21 August, Canberra announced that an Australian battalion, 3rd Battalion, the Royal Australian Regiment, would join the brigade in Korea.[18]

The two Hong Kong-based battalions boasted strong cadres of combat-hardened officers and senior NCOs, but their junior ranks were heavily composed of National Servicemen. Many regulars considered them nuisances and amateurs, but some saw their quality. 'At that time about sixty per cent of the battalion were National Service, which, at that time, was eighteen months,' said Argyll Private Jake Mutch, a regular himself. 'Without them, the army would have been lost – there were lots of good tradesmen and sportsmen.'

Soldiers in any army look alike: They wear the same uniforms; are the same age; do the same job. How, then, is unit identity fostered? Infantry regiments were recruited from specific areas of the country, and 'branding'– a strategy to differentiate and raise public perceptions of a product, service or entity above near-identical competition – had been in use by British regiments long before the concept was 'invented' and commercialised by marketers. The tools used to brand units were their unique traditions, histories, insignia and nicknames. Regimental identities were instilled in recruits, forming a key component of *esprit de corps*.

The Argyll and Sutherland Highlanders were one of the British Army's most famed regiments. After the battle of Culloden in 1746 ended the Jacobite dream of returning the Stuart kings to the throne, London decided to incorporate the Jacobites' key fighting men – the Gaelic-speaking hill clansmen – into its own forces. Thus was born the legend of the Highland regiments. Hardy hill men, raised to revere courage in battle and proud of their distinct dress – jaunty headgear and kilts in clan tartan – weapons – the basket-hilted *claymore* ('great broadsword') and the *skin dubh* ('red knife') dirk – and music – the bagpipe – Highlanders became the shock troops of empire. The 91st Argyllshire Highlanders were raised in 1794 and the 93rd Sutherland Highlanders in 1799. In 1881, the two regiments were amalgamated into the Argyll and Sutherland Highlanders, usually shortened simply to 'The Argylls' or, more colloquially, 'The Jocks'. The regiments had served in the Peninsula, at Waterloo, in the Crimea, the Indian Mutiny, South Africa and both World Wars. Headquartered in Stirling, the medieval fortress at the base of the highlands associated with Scottish warrior-patriot William Wallace, they boasted one of the most famed nicknames in military history. 'The Thin Red Line' referred to an incident when their slender, scarlet-coated ranks, deployed across the valley of Balaclava, halted a mass Russian cavalry charge.

In 1950, many men in 1st Battalion were Gaelic-speaking Highlanders, though all spoke fluent (albeit, accented) English. 'They're tough, the Argylls, they stand no nonsense,' said Mutch, who reckoned the only unit which could face them down were the Cameronians, who recruited from the roughest districts of Glasgow and Hamilton. 'The Middlesex were English so we would fight them,' Mutch added. 'And it was not only the soldiers, the sergeant majors got involved too – they were proud of us!' The battalion adjutant agreed. 'Scottish regiments are always aggressive – up and at 'em!– and it's hard to stop them,' said Slim. 'Jocks are humane, but tough as they come.'

Due to its deployment to Hong Kong, the battalion had a solid core. 'The battalion had come back from Palestine, all those who had been of any value moved to other appointments and a lot of people who really were pretty second-rate were back,' said intelligence officer, Lieutenant Alexander 'Sandy' Boswell, speaking of the battalion as it had been in the UK. 'The moment we got warned that we were going to defend Hong Kong against the Chinese, those kinds of chaps disappeared.'

The commander of the Argylls in Hong Kong was Lieutenant Colonel Leslie Neilson. 'Fit but aging, determined, single minded, not a bundle of laughs, no great imagination but a thoroughly professional soldier', was the verdict of one officer.[19] 'He was a good, steady CO, personally brave,' added Slim. 'He always got around the companies.' A Highlander to the core, Neilson was usually accompanied by his pipe major and at least a couple of pipers, but there was a silent, contemplative side to him: Few knew him well.*

The battalion's second-in-command was a different kettle of fish: A quiet and pleasant, but determined and often sprightly individual, Major Kenny Muir, whose father had commanded the battalion from

*Half a century after the Korean War, Neilson's son – an Argyll officer himself – joined a group of regiment veterans on a visit to the Crimean War battlefields. During the trip, he asked some of the Korea veterans if they could tell him a little about his father, who he felt he had never really got to know. None could.

1923–27.[20] Muir Junior had served on the Northwest Frontier and throughout the Second World War in North Africa, Sicily and Northwest Europe, winning a mention in dispatches. Slight but very fit, Muir had a whimsical side: He would make the junior officers follow him in doing back flips on mess nights.[21] 'He was a peppery little bugger!' reckoned the adjutant.

The adjutant – responsible for administration and discipline in the battalion – was high-profile: John Slim was the son of the chief of the Imperial General Staff, General Bill Slim, arguably the UK's finest Second World War general. A tall, tough-looking character, 'Big John' had commanded Gurkhas in Burma during the war, and still wore a kukri. After Indian independence, he joined the Argylls: 'I exchanged one bunch of wild hillmen for another,' he said. 'The Jock is a bit like the Gurkha: He won't tell you you're any good until you prove it.' No wilting flower, Slim told his CO, 'If you won't give me a company, I'll stay with you – not in the rear area!' Neilson consented. Though a formidable fighting man, there was a playful side to Slim. 'He was a wonderful chap, a bit of a chancer, a bit wild in the night clubs,' said Quartermaster Brown. 'In Hong Kong, I played piano, and he played the drums. He was very energetic.'

Among the company commanders was Burma veteran Major Alastair Gordon-Ingram of B Company. 'He was a gentleman,' said Mutch. 'I remember once when we had not been paid and it was a Friday and Ingram had a company of 120 men and he gave us all about ten shillings each out of his own pocket – the average weekly pay of a soldier. That was the kind of thing he did.' Another high-profile officer was the aggressive, heavy-set Captain Colin Mitchell, a soldier who positively enjoyed combat: 'You'd find him where the bullets were flying,' said Slim. Mitchell had fought in Italy and after the war, been wounded in Palestine. 'He was the best tactician in the battalion,' said one of his soldiers, Adam MacKenzie. 'Quite a character.' Mitchell would later gain a more famous nickname, but in Korea, was known due to his stubby nose, as 'Piggy'.

One of the biggest Argylls was Robin Fairrie, a giant mortar officer, who, his soldiers said, could carry two heavy mortar tubes up the Hong Kong hills. Fairrie's rank yo-yoed – sometimes captain, sometimes lieutenant – due to the mischief he was constantly involved with. His latest demotion had come after a field exercise in the UK, when he had been questioned by police after the disappearance of a local pig. Fairrie had ordered his men to capture the beast, and they were planning to feed it on hardtack biscuits and slaughter it. Fairrie was denying any knowledge of the hoofed ration to the local constable and a gamekeeper when a terrified squealing erupted from a nearby trench.[22] The men adored him. 'He was a big, rough man, something of the same stamp as John Slim – no fear,' said Mutch. 'He treated men as men.'

Another character who always had a twinkle in his eye was the quartermaster, Andrew 'Dodger' Brown. An Aberdeen lad who had originally signed up in 1933 with the regimental band, he had served everywhere: Eritrea, the Sudan, the Western Desert, Sicily, Italy, Palestine. Returning to the battalion in Hong Kong from seven months combat in the jungle with the Royal Malay Regiment, he was impressed with the Jocks in Hong Kong: 'They looked tremendous, very fit and tough from running up and down the mountains,' he said. However, he was concerned when he took over the stores; there were a large number of missing items.

The regimental doctor was Lieutenant Douglas Haldane, a Paisley native and National Service officer. 'Initially, I was probably a wee bit bolshie because it was a regular unit with regular features including 06:30 sick parades,' he said. 'I tended to take the side of younger National Service officers.' His assistants were poorly trained, knowing only basic first aid; most pressingly, he did not have anyone trained to treat burns. Their inexperience placed a heavy burden on Haldane, who was inevitably nicknamed 'Jock the Doc'.

The junior officers were a mixed bunch. Some, such as intelligence officer Sandy Boswell, were regular graduates of Sandhurst; others were National Service officers who had completed a four-month platoon commanders' crash course at Eton Hall. James Stirling came from an illustrious family – his cousin, Scots Guardsman David Stirling had founded the SAS – but he was a less deadly soldier himself. 'I was the one who always fell asleep after lunch,' he recalled. Owen Light, a 19-year-old 'half-Scots, half-English half-breed' had joined the Argylls after Eton Hall and arrived in Hong Kong with two newly commissioned regular officers. The latter were greeted by the CO, 'like long-lost friends', but when Light was introduced, Neilson simply asked, 'Who are you?' Thus ended Light's interview.

The senior man in the non-commissioned ranks was the giant Regimental Sergeant Major: Paddy Boyd. He was a mystery to the other ranks: 'He would never tell us how he won the Distinguished Conduct Medal, even when we got him drunk in the mess,' said MacKenzie. 'I think he'd probably seen too much in the Second World War, and I don't think he was that popular,' said one officer.

Private Jake Mutch, a 22-year-old from Morayshire, had left school at thirteen to enter agriculture, which he had not taken to. Impressed by soldiers returning from the war, he had joined the Seaforth Highlanders, but bored with garrison duty at Fort George – 'I had joined the army to see the world, but I was just 6 miles away from the farm I had worked at' – volunteered for the Argylls and Hong Kong. 'They were a real family clique,' he said. 'Everybody for the others.'

A particularly formidable soldier was Corporal Harry Young, a Black Watch man who had been called up in 1945 then, finding that 'the services do something for you', signed on for twenty-two years and volunteered for the Argylls in Hong Kong. 'We had boys from the North and from London,' he said. 'We got together – it was a terrific team. Never knew of any problems – usually the punch-ups were Jocks and Paddies! A sense of humour helps.'

Roy Vincent was a 19-year-old Edinburgh lad who had served in the fire brigade during the war, but been unable to join the army at first try due to pneumonia scars on his lungs: 'In the fire service, you were always soaking wet.' He tried again and was accepted. He had wanted to join the Argylls after reading about the 'Thin Red Line' in a boy's comic.

This most Scottish regiment had a strong foreign contingent: 'A lot of Englishmen became good Scotsmen!' said Brown. Robert Searle from New Malden had wanted to join a Highland regiment after his father had taken him to watch the Scottish Division beating retreat. Another Englishman was Lance Corporal Joseph Fairhurst. 'They didn't hold it against us, once you were in the regiment you were in it,' he said. 'You lose your accent, you talk just like a Scotsman.'

Coad's second battalion was a London-recruited unit: 1st Middlesex.

The Middlesex, or Duke of Cambridge's Own, was born in 1881, an amalgamation of two foot regiments, the 57th and 77th. The regiment's nickname, 'The Diehards' dates to the battle of Albuerra on 16 May 1811. On that day, the dying CO of the 57th, Colonel Inglis, watching his battalion being shredded – twenty-two out of twenty-five officers were killed, along with 425 of 570 other ranks – shouted his last order: 'Die hard, my men – die hard!' The enemy commander, Marshal Soult, was astounded: 'There is no beating these troops,' he wrote. 'The day was mine, yet they would not run.' Prior to that action, the London-recruited regiment had a less illustrious brand, 'The Steelbacks', alluding to its soldiers' unusual propensity for being flogged.[23] 1st Middlesex in 1950 was a youthful, London-recruited battalion with a strong emphasis on sport. Having arrived in Hong Kong after guard duties at Buckingham Palace, they 'needed a bit more shaping', in their CO's words.

Unlike some officers, their CO, Lieutenant Colonel Andrew Man, was not blessed with wealth. Though he hoped to follow his father, an Aldershot clergyman, to Cambridge, his family was cash-strapped – 'there was no money!' – forcing the young Man, 'to look to see what I could do without costing my father.' He failed to win a university scholarship, so joined the army as a private, hoping to be commissioned – which he was. In the Middlesex, he found an organisation which treated him fairly; he repaid it with life-long loyalty. In 1944, he demanded to be relieved of a staff appointment to return to regimental frontline duties, a move a superior officer called 'professional suicide'.[24] Landing on D-Day +2, he commanded the Middlesex's 7th Battalion through France, Belgium and Holland, winning a French *Croix de Guerre* in the process. In 1949, he took command of 1st Middlesex for its Hong Kong deployment, where he shook up the battalion, gaining a reputation as a martinet: 'We used to say, "Never has so much trouble been caused by so little a Man!"' recalled Yerby, for Man stood just north of five feet. Yet he was a popular CO. 'You did not see him, he moved too fast!' said Private Ken Mankelow. 'He took an interest right down to section level, he was right in with everybody.' Mustachioed; fast-talking; waspish; no-nonsense; always smartly turned out in field cap; if Neilson was the stereotypical silent Scot, Man was the classic English officer.

As with the Argyll's mid-level officers, the Middlesex company commanders had had active wars between 1939 and 1945. D Company's leader was Major John Willoughby, who had fought in France, and been evacuated through Dunkirk before serving in the Far East – where, as a liaison officer, he met a number of the personalities running MacArthur's war machine – before finishing the war commanding a battalion in Northwest Europe. A big, fair-haired major, Willoughby did not always get along with his CO and was a man of considerable bonhomie with a well-crafted – though often irreverent – turn of phrase. On operations, he was popular with pressmen, a species Man had little time for. Willoughby was also respected by the junior ranks. Edgar Green, the 19-year-old private, became a mess barman, where he got to see the officers up close: 'Some were very nice people, some were like a load of schoolboys,' he said. Willoughby was one officer who stood the barmen a drink.

Then there was Major John Shipster, who had commanded Punjabis in some of the very worst combat in Burma, before joining the Middlesex after Indian independence. As a professional soldier, he found life in Hong Kong 'pretty dull' but his wife and their young child had just arrived in the colony, so he was preparing to settle in for the long haul – a process that meant finding better accommo-dation than the Chinese hotel room they were put up in.

Major Dennis Rendell, who led A Company, was a dashing-looking, mustachioed blade with a matching upper-class accent. He had served in the Parachute Regiment during the war, been captured and escaped in North Africa. In 1946 he had shipped out to the Far East, with 5 Parachute Brigade, sent to restore order in Indonesia pending the return of Dutch forces. Among his exploits there was the capture of an independence activist in a dawn raid: he was 'in bed with the most beautiful woman,' Rendell recalled. 'He behaved perfectly well, he was perfectly amenable; there were about 20 of us in the room!' The target Rendell had bagged was – he believed – Sukarno, soon-to-be president of Indonesia.* Rendell moved on to Palestine and Malaya before returning to his parent unit, the Middlesex in Hong Kong.

Among the platoon officers was a tall young man, Chris Lawrence, who greatly impressed a number of the men under his command, 4 Platoon, B Company 'You could not get past him,' said one of his soldiers, Private Ken 'Ted' Mankelow. 'He was very good at looking after the men, he was always calm and collected, I never saw him looking flustered, it was if he were born to it.'

Mankelow was a Croydon boy whose elder brother had served in the Middlesex; with the regiment comprised of a lot of South London faces he 'couldn't wait to join'. Corporal Harry Spicer from Tottenham was another volunteer, who had enjoyed the Army Cadets, so signed up for 'five and seven' (five years in the regulars, seven on the reserves.)

Private Edgar Green, the Herne Hill boy who so enjoyed the Hong Kong shopping, had been a railway fireman, when, called up for National Service, had asked to join the Middlesex as his uncle had served in the regiment: 'I didn't know what I was letting myself in for,' he said. 'I could have gone into the Royal Engineers, there was no need to go into the infantry.'

Private James Beverly, a Bermondsey man with the Cockney's typical disrespect for authority, was unimpressed upon arriving for basic training, but to his surprise, after going through the ten-week basic course, found himself buying into the Diehard *esprit.* 'I was not one who had a lot of respect for a regiment,' he said. 'But I did for that regiment.'

Lance-Corporal Bob Yerby was from Kingsbury. He had originally wanted to join the cavalry for five and seven, but was told he would have to sign up for twenty-two years. Instead, he joined the Middlesex. In Hong Kong, he realised that the Cockneys were different to the Scottish: 'The Jocks would fight anyone, they would

---

*The author has been unable to find any mention of this incident in the literature, indicating that Rendell was mistaken in his identification – unless he was posted to the Dutch paratroops who captured Sukarno, briefly, in 1948.

fight among themselves, but we were a sporting battalion,' he said. 'We played a lot of cricket, rugby and hockey.'

Indeed, one of the battalion's sporting achievements had been beating Hong Kong's seven-a-side rugby team, but when Man went to collect the trophy, was told he would not be allowed to take it. It was the wrong approach to take with the feisty little colonel. 'You can be assured it returned with me!' he said.

Not all the Middlesex were Londoners. Sergeant Paddy Redmond was a Dubliner who came from a family with a strong British military tradition. He volunteered in 1944, joined the elite commandos, and was *en route* to the invasion of Malaya when the war ended. 'In a way, it was a sigh of relief, in a way it was disappointing,' he said. 'We were geared up for action.' Post-war, Redmond was posted to the Middlesex. 'They were great blokes, you know what Cockneys are like, there was none of this, "He's a Paddy bastard" – everyone was the same.'

* * *

Every military unit is hardwired with an acutely sensitive, if unofficial, intelligence antenna. 27th Brigade was no exception: Its rumour service anticipated deployment orders by seven days. 'A week earlier, a corporal came and said, "A ship is in harbour waiting to transport us to Korea!"' recalled Middlesex Lance Corporal Don Barrett, originally a National Serviceman who subsequently volunteered. 'Forty eight hours later, nothing had happened, the corporal had gone into hiding and we were all saying, "lying sod!"'

27th Brigade's movement orders were shrouded in secrecy. Over the weekend of 19–20 August only commanding officers and seconds-in-command were informed. Among them was Jeffes, the REME officer who had to check transport; his arrival at battalions over the weekend was greeted with great suspicion as to why an officer was examining equipment on a Saturday afternoon. 'Everyone was highly excited about this, and of course, no one could tell them why.'

On Monday morning, Barrett's rumour was confirmed: 27th Brigade was to deploy. 'Officers were dashing around, parties were being taken off to do various jobs,' said Barrett, who found himself excited at the prospect of action. 'We'd just had six years of war, we all expected to go to war.'

In the first flurry of orders, it was unclear which two of the brigade's three battalions would go. On 19 August, it was the Leicesters; on 20 August, they were replaced by the Middlesex.[25] Quite why the Argylls and Middlesex were chosen remains unclear; it seems likely that the Leicesters had too heavy a National Service component, though theories abound. 'My theory is that the Argylls and Middlesex were troublesome,' said Barrett. 'It was going to be the Argylls and the Leicesters, and I think it was because we had this little 'to do' on Albuerra Day on 16 May. It was a jolly good do, then it got a bit nasty: I went to sleep and when I woke up, the camp had been wrecked: windows broken, the RSM had a suspected skull fracture, the CO went into the corporals' mess and supposedly someone threw a mug at him. So probably somebody said, 'Look, if these Middlesex want to fight, change 'em for the Leicesters.' And of course, the Jocks always want to fight!'

Combat is a military unit's *raison d'etre*. The word was passed down from company commanders to platoon commanders, from platoon commanders to the men. 'When I told them, "We are going", I think they all looked forward to it,' said Light, the Argyll subaltern. 'An infantry soldier is trained to want to get to grips with the enemy, you join the infantry for this – you join the Royal Army Service Corps if you want to drive lorries!' One of the brigade's least bloodthirsty men was the Argyll MO, but even 'Jock the Doc' Haldane shared the general enthusiasm. 'My reaction was, "I quite fancy this,"' Haldane said. 'It was an adventure, an opportunity to do something useful.'

More reluctant was Second Lieutenant James Stirling. 'I was horrified – this was not what I had intended – but it was what you had to do,' he said. 'Most of my men were like me, National Servicemen who had only done eight weeks training. But some wanted to get into it.'

Many men were out of camp when orders came down. 'I was in the China Fleet Club having a few drinks when the MPs came and told all Argylls and Middlesex to get back to their units, the bus was waiting, the "balloon" had gone up,' said Mankelow. 'We didn't know which "balloon" it was – all we were worried about was if someone else would drink your beer!'

Ignorant of what awaited in Korea, some veterans were unworried at the prospect. Among them was Yerby, the Middlesex lance corporal, who had served in counter-insurgency operations. 'What wars had we seen?' he said. 'Palestine gave me a whiff.'

Soldiers under nineteen were not to be sent and the Middlesex was fifty-five per cent composed of youthful National Servicemen, but such was the CO's rhetoric – 'he had a wonderful knack of talking to people,' said Yerby – that Man was 'besieged' by under-aged soldiers begging to go to Korea. 'We all wanted to go, we had trained together, we were young, fit and confident,' said Mankelow. 'You are trained to be a soldier and when a war is on, you have to go with your mates and the regiment does its job.'[26]

While professionals and fire-eaters had their own reasons for fighting, in assessing why ordinary soldiers were keen to deploy, Mankelow had put his finger on the lure of war. Some very effective armies are ideological; not the British. Politicians speak of patriotism and duty to country, and that is certainly an element, but in the British Army, soldiers are inculcated in the cult of the unit. War means battle honours, the chance for the regiment to add to its history and so elevate itself among its peers. This is a motivation; some officers consider it the key motivation: 'Everything for the regiment'.

But moving down through the unit – from 650-man battalion, to 120-man company to 30-man platoon or 8-man section – the human factor is more critical. Military subunits are groups of young men, and powerful bonds are forged between men who train, work, talk, eat, sleep, share and fight together, for months or years. It is little wonder that so many soldiers borrow Shakespeare's 'band of brothers' quote from *Henry V*, to describe intra-unit relationship ties that are, in many cases, closer than those of family. The critical motivational factor, then, is peer pressure: The determination to prove oneself to, and not to let down, one's friends in the most extreme human experience, mortal combat. This makes effective infantry units deadly fraternities, forged of bonds of friendship, led by men whose loyalties are as much to regiment as they are to their cause.

Still, if war was an exciting prospect, the battlefield and the enemy were completely unknown to most of 27th Brigade.

The limit of Man's knowledge of the country was a couple of Korean stamps he had collected as a child. That was more than many of his men, who knew absolutely nothing. 'Chris Lawrence called the platoon together and said, "We are going to Korea!" and we said, "Where is Korea?" and he said, "How the hell do I know?"' Mankelow recalled. 'We were trying to find info, it was pretty sketchy. All we knew was we were going.'

Unlike most officers, Shipster had been following Korea closely as American naval reinforcements came through Hong Kong on their way to the war. Yet his ignorance was apparent when it came to equipment, an issue he sought his CO's advice on. 'I remember asking Colonel Man if I should take my golf club and tennis raquets,' Shipster recalled. 'And he said, "By all means, John, take them."'

The war was not going well. The NKPA had exposed serious shortcomings in the training and motivation of US troops. North Koreans were fighting to drive the Americans and ROKs into the sea before reinforcements – 27th Brigade among them – transformed the strategic balance.

The ironic potential of the situation – British troops coming to the aid of pressured Americans – was not lost on the Diehard CO. 'We knew the Americans had been caught with their trousers down and there was a certain amount of banter which we thoroughly enjoyed,' Man said. 'Hitherto the Americans had come in late and said, "We won" and this time we came in late and were able to have some pretty good backchat at them – my troops particularly!'

Americans arrived to demonstrate new weapons – notably the 3.5-inch 'bazooka' anti-tank rocket launcher, essential against the NKPA T34s. Their briefings were not encouraging. 'This American intelligence officer came out and said, "It's a grave situation out there and we are thankful that you are going out there to help us, but we doubt if you will come home again,"' Green recalled. 'I thought, "Cor!"'

* * *

The deployment order blew a tornado of activity through the brigade.

'The orders were a hell of a shock,' said Brown. 'I worked all week and got something from the doctor to keep me awake so I could work all night.' Orders were delivered, then countermanded. 'It was pack this, you won't need this, you would get told one thing, then ten minutes later, told the opposite,' said Mutch. 'It was hell for leather for a few days.'

Fortunately, a brigade movement exercise had recently been completed. 'The adjutant and the quartermaster are the keys,' said Slim. 'We had rehearsed the whole business of being ready to move suddenly and had worked out what we needed if there was a battle with the Chinese in Hong Kong. It was frantic, but not a panic.' The deployment solved the problem worrying the Argyll Quartermaster: the many non-existent stores he had 'inherited' from his predecessor. 'I took all my deficiencies with me to Korea and "lost" them,' said Brown. 'That was that!'

Medical officers faced specific challenges. 'When we got orders to go to Korea I had to inoculate the battalion, so I went with a sergeant to get needles,' said Dr Stanley Boydell, the Middlesex MO. 'We had 3,000–4,000 inoculations to do and we only got about twenty needles!' Boydell sterilised and re-sterilised the needles, but it was painful for men being punctured by increasingly blunt instruments.

The most critical task was to beef up the infantry. Each battalion's fourth rifle company was disbanded to provide three up-to-strength companies. Still, the battalions would not be up to their full, on-paper war-strength of 38 officers and 948 other ranks; a minimum strength of 28 officers and 618 other ranks was set.[27] The Argylls and Middlesex absorbed volunteers from other battalions in Hong Kong.

The brigade was heading to Korea seriously under strength. It would depend totally upon the Americans for rations, heavy vehicular transport, engineering and hospitals. In 'teeth' terms it was equally lightweight. An infantry brigade should contain three battalions, an artillery regiment, a mobile/armoured force and a transport pool. 27th Brigade would have only two infantry battalions until it was joined by the Royal Australians; when that would be was unclear. It totally lacked armour – the spearhead in attack and the rearguard in retreat – and artillery – the arm that causes the most battlefield casualties – meaning that 27th Brigade lacked critical punch. In action, Coad would be heavily reliant upon his bayonets.

The scratch nature of the deployment worried thoughtful officers. 'Dwelling momentarily on our almost total un-preparedness, my blood runs cold,' wrote Middlesex Major John Willoughby. Brigade HQ, he thought, had the air of 'fairyland'.[28] Due to the *ad hoc* nature of their deployment, 27th Brigade's soldiers began to refer to themselves as 'The Woolworth's Brigade' or 'The Cinderella Brigade'. Others, reflecting the urgency with which they were being sent east, coined a new nickname: 'The For-God's-Sake-Send-Something Brigade'.

Yet the frenzied preparations paid off. Orders had been passed down on 18 August. Exactly one week later, the UK's Korean War expeditionary force, its first ever contribution to a multinational UN force was – somehow – good to go. For those responsible for getting the units ready, relief was tremendous. 'John Slim and I went out that last night and got rather pissed!' Brown said.

Pre-battle anticipation was, however, a false high. 'There was an undercurrent of excitement – we were going to kick arses! – when you are twenty, you feel invincible,' said Private Ray Rogers, a volunteer to the Middlesex from the South Staffords. 'That feeling lasted until the first action.'

Some were subconsciously roiled. On the night before the soldiers boarded their transport for the war zone, one of the Diehard barracks was awoken by a sudden uproar. 'At night-time, all hell broke lose – one of our people, Sharpe, was crying his eyes out, he didn't want to go,' said Frank Whitehouse, another South Stafford volunteer. 'He was going berserk – I had to slap his face.' Eventually, Sharpe was calmed. The barrack returned to uneasy sleep.

The day before departure, the brigade paraded for a special

address by General Sir John Harding, Commander-in-Chief, British Forces Far East, who had arrived from Singapore. The Diehards' aggressive little CO was satisfied with the message. '"Shoot straight and shoot to kill", that was the essence of it,' Man said. 'He was very inspiring.' The brigade would travel by sea from the Kowloon dockside, and it was there that a second pep talk was delivered to the bare-chested young men, formed up in ranks, by Malcolm MacDonald, British High Commissioner for the Far East. 'The enemy you are fighting are North Koreans, but the weapons they are using are Russian, their training is Russian,' he told the soldiers. 'You will be fighting as if on the soil of France or on the beaches of Britain.'[29] Then it was time to board.

At approximately 18:30, the Argylls trooped up the gangplanks of the heavy cruiser HMS *Ceylon*; the Middlesex and Brigade HQ boarded the fleet support carrier HMS *Unicorn*. The pipes of the King's Own Scottish Borderers wailed from the dock, answered by the band of the Royal Marines and the pipes of the Argylls from the quarterdeck of the *Ceylon*. Families and friends waved furiously from the quays as pipers played, 'Will ye nae came back again?'[30] With the sun setting behind the Hong Kong hills, the two men-of-war slipped their moorings and set their bows toward the darkening east. It was 25 August, 1950.

*   *   *

The brigade steamed east. Argylls found the *Ceylon* cramped. 'We were living on decks, turrets, gangways, on the floors of mess decks,' said Argyll Ralph Horsfield. 'But it was a happy ship.' Army-Navy relations soared when the *Ceylon*'s commander flew the Argyll regimental flag alongside his battle ensign. The Middlesex had more space in the cavernous hangers of the carrier HMS *Unicorn*.

Tactical adjustments were made to peace-time kit. In Hong Kong the troops' webbing had been scrubbed parade-ground clean, almost white; with combat approaching, this had to be dirtied down. All brasses were removed or blackened.[31] Sterns crackled with firing as musketry training was prioritised. Anything in the ship's wake was used as a target: boxes heaved over the side, seagulls – even surf. With no peace-time ammunition restrictions, soldiers joyfully blazed away. 'Everyone fired more than they have ever been able to before,' noted Willoughby.[32]

The big major had had a thoughtful moment as the ships left Hong Kong: An RAF overflight had dipped wings, reminding him of the last time he had seen a Royal Naval vessel with Spitfires overhead: Dunkirk.[33] A different airborne incident had some men hoping for mischief. 'The tannoy went and it was the captain, saying, "The plane going over is your commanding officer and intelligence officer,"' recalled Second Lieutenant James Stirling. 'All the guns on the ships tracked it and we all hoped someone would let off a shot, but they did not, sadly!'

A brisk lecture circuit was underway. 'We were being called together and given updates on what was going on in Korea,' Mutch said. 'The part we listened to was the casualties: We thought if this week it is the Americans, next week it could be Argylls. It was no party.' The two best-informed men aboard however, were not military. A pair of embarked reporters told Willoughby that if the war dragged on, winter would be harsh.[34] With the brigade attired in lightweight jungle greens, staff officers seemed not to have realised that Korea, in distant Northeast Asia, suffered more extreme climates than sub-tropical Hong Kong and steamy Southeast Asia.

A necessary formality of active service focused minds. 'It was bought home to you when they gave you the "next-of-kin" form; that was scary, some of the fellas, the tough guys, were in tears,' said Mutch. Green found himself a quiet nook. 'I have been told we are going into a bad situation and if I don't get home, I want to thank you for the life I have had,' he wrote to his parents.

The *Ceylon* and *Unicorn* were joined by a jaunty escort: two Australian destroyers, HMAS *Warramunga* and HMAS *Bataan*. 'One came in that fast, I thought "Bloody hell it's going to hit us!"' said Argyll Roy Vincent. 'But it came alongside it in a curve – neat work.' Due to fears of Chinese submarines off Formosa the ships blacked out and closed bulkhead doors.[35] As they approached Korea, gun crews closed up against air attack. The high-angle 4.7-inch gun turrets swivelled in search of targets, but no threat appeared in the summer skies.

* * *

The advance parties – including Coad, Man and Neilson, adjutants and quartermasters – had already landed. On boarding the aircraft in Hong Kong, Man was immediately critical of the US flight crews. 'The Americans were very casual, they flew off when they wanted to,' he said. 'We heard later that [the crews on the ships] manned the guns, the American [pilots] had no idea of the countersign. I wasn't impressed.'

First port of call was Japan, where the advance party was installed at a US Air Force base. In an era when British officers sported an understated style, Major John Shipster was take aback by an inscription in the mess hall: 'The greatest, fightingest pilots in the world go down this chow line!' He was more impressed with the pilots. 'It is one of the strange things about war: You don't find people tense in the front line, you find them tense a wee bit further back,' he said. 'Fighting elements, like pilots who will be flying missions the next day, are quite relaxed; it's part of the business to adapt this sort of pose.' Base females were shocked to be told that when the Argylls paraded in kilts they 'went regimental' – i.e. without underpants – and were soon fraternising. 'We were dancing with our birds,' said Brown. 'But the CO was keeping an eye on us like a hen, so we never got anywhere!'

Unbeknownst to Brown, senior officers enjoyed certain privileges. 'A very attractive little Jap girl with long black hair came to my room and wanted to know if she could get me a bath,' Man recalled. 'It was very civilised after the unpleasant conditions we lived in among the snakes, smells and night soil of Hong Kong.'

The following morning, the party landed at Taegu in Korea. 'I got out of the plane and much to my amazement found the airfield under shellfire,' said Shipster, armed to the teeth with sporting equipment. 'I was carrying my golf clubs and tennis racquet, so I threw them in a ditch and never saw them again.'

This was the 'Pusan Perimeter'.

Chapter Two
Under Korean Skies

Wild, dark times are rumbling toward us
Heinrich Heine

29 August, Pusan Docks.

A strange, flatulent drone, followed by an agonised wail, echoed across Pusan docks. Waiting Koreans – VIPs, military officers, a schoolgirl choir – forming a welcoming committee gazed seaward in astonishment. Men in skirts, formed up on the aft gun turret of a great, grey man-of-war and plying piped sacks, seemed to be the source of the din. Could these be the first non-American ground troops joining the UN Crusade?

27th Brigade was closing on the port. Under a bright, colourless sky, soldiers lining the decks of HMS *Ceylon* and HMS *Unicorn* could see, in the foreground, scores of ships, for Pusan was the funnel through which reinforcements were being shovelled to feed the UN war machine. Then the city itself – a dirty smudge on the landscape – and behind it, the great mountains that climbed up the peninsula, coated in the vivid green of summer scrub. The port city was the hub of UNC operations in a rectangle 50 miles deep and 100 miles wide: The 'Pusan Perimeter', the last remaining territory on the peninsula not controlled by the North Korean Peoples Army.

The Argylls and Middlesex had disembarked together in a war zone before: – they had been the first two regiments ashore in France in 1914 – but 27th Brigade's arrival in Korea was not auspicious. In Pusan HMS *Unicorn,* carrying the Diehards, ran aground. Assistance was dispatched. 'There was a very fussy Korean tug alongside with

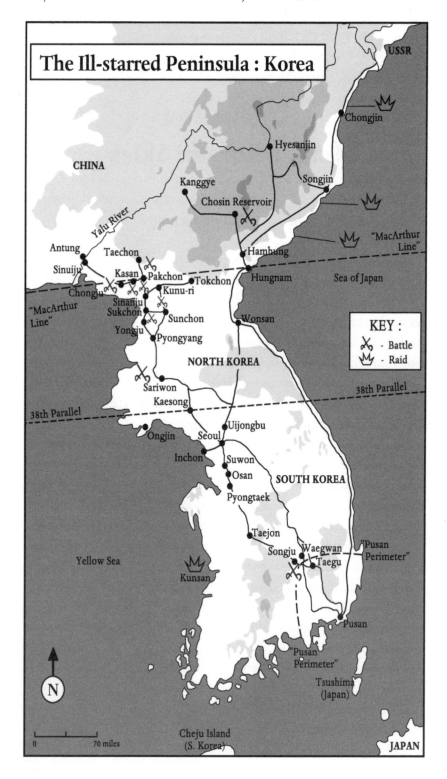

The Ill-starred Peninsula : Korea

a large funnel and the captain had more gold braid than an admiral,' said REME Captain Reggie Jeffes. 'It had a funny type of bridge – rather like a greenhouse, lots of glass and wooden bits and pieces – and the cross trees on his mast got caught up with this huge life raft on the side of the carrier; it broke loose, dropped down on his bridge and shattered it! Of course, all the troops were peering over and cheered like anything, and this was an enormous loss of face for the poor Korean captain who promptly took his tug and left in high dudgeon.'

Still, the tug had done its job. Freed, the *Unicorn* moved to dock behind the *Ceylon*.

Approaching the quay, Diehards were sent below by the *Unicorn*'s captain. 'We were told it was going to be like Dunkirk so we were all geared up, we were down below prepping guns and grenades and getting pep talks on field action,' said Corporal Bob Yerby. It was a pleasant shock when the men spotted, not NKPA machine gunners, but the Korean reception committee and inter-national media waiting to record their arrival. Aural ambience was provided by an African-American marching band blaring out ragtime, 'Colonel Bogey' and 'God Save the King'. 'Where the hell is the war?' wondered Yerby.

The Argylls on HMS *Ceylon* had not suffered the ignominy of being posted below. As the cruiser glided in, the Highlanders presented a formidably warlike array: Jocks in tam-o'-shanters thronged the decks while martial music piped the battalion ashore. 'There was great excitement among the Americans at our pipes and drums, they had never seen anything like this!' said Robert Searle. Trooping ashore, the Highlanders –'the ladies from hell' to US troops – were handed bouquets of flowers by shy schoolgirls.[1] Among the reception committee were a number of ludicrously armed US service troops, prompting the adoption among some Argylls of an ageless infantry prejudice – disdain for men in the rear. 'They all wanted to be John Wayne and Gary Cooper, with .45s, knives and carbines,' said Ralph Horsfield. 'I don't know if they were trying to impress us or what: They were base wallahs – forklift truck drives and dockside workers!' At least one Argyll, however, was not showing a heroic face to the world: Second Lieutenant Owen Light had been berthed in the gunroom with midshipmen, and on the previous night 'we allowed ourselves to be lulled with gin'. Aboard the moving warships, soldiers had been cooled by the breeze; in Pusan's sweltering humidity, Light, loaded down with gear, sweated off his hangover.

Lieutenant Colonel Andrew Man was not having a good day. Firstly, his advance party had been met on the docks by a British attaché. 'He had a face like a boot and seemed imbued with the American idea that all was lost, and pretty well told us to go back again,' Man said. 'He annoyed us intensely!' The Middlesex CO was equally irritated by the attention lavished on the Highlanders, who had disembarked before his battalion (as they had in 1914). 'The bouquets all went to the Argylls, these lovely exciting Scotsmen got all the attention,' Man sighed. 'But one always expects Scottish regiments to catch the eye.' Major John Willoughby suffered his CO's wrath as a result: 'This infuriated Andrew Man waiting on the jetty, who began shouting abuse for not having us all on deck.'[2] Willoughby's D Company remained behind to unload brigade stores into warehouses, while the rest of the troops, issued with their first American C-ration packs and 50 rounds of ammunition, marched off to the rail station for the trip up-country.[3]

'The atmosphere of their arrival was far removed from that of a military operation, it was a pageant of international goodwill,' noted the *Daily Telegraph*.[4] Men were handed gifts. James Beverly, accepting a South Korean flag made of sacking, folded it and put it in a pocket for good luck. But the seriousness of the business at hand became evident when sergeants ordered men to load and lock their weapons – orders that were never issued on trains.[5] In the station, as the locomotive gathered steam, the last carnival ambience evaporated as another train clunked to a halt alongside. Curious soldiers glanced over. Its passengers were hundreds of mangled American soldiers: fresh meat from the battlefront. 'We could see them lying there in bandages,' said Middlesex MO Stanley Boydell. 'This was rather disconcerting, to say the least.'

The grim sight was left behind as the brigade train drew out of the station.

* * *

The 'hard-class' wooden carriages the brigade was occupying had previously carried refugees. Littered with garbage and infested with lice, they had been disinfected by naval decontamination squads, but even so, 'Jock the Doc' Haldane spoke for many when he characterised the train ride as 'prehistoric'. Passing through the provisional capital of Rhee Syngman's besieged republic, few soldiers were reassured by their first sights of the land they had come to defend. 'Pusan was a filthy hole, diseased, crammed with refuges, it was quite horrible,' said Man. 'If somebody had said bubonic plague was rife, I would not have been a bit surprised.'

The utilitarian port city was swollen with countless thousands of refugees who had fled to this last refuge from the communist onslaught. Spreading from Pusan's outskirts were shanty towns of huts patched together from rough planking, the ever-present rice straw mats, and bits of military castoff material – cardboard ration boxes; cans hammered flat; military ponchos. Here, an olive green steel helmet was suspended over an open fire, in use as a cooking pot, bubbling with a watery rice porridge miserably flavoured with a few dried cabbage leaves. There, another one was lashed to the end of a pole to empty the heaving, fly-infested 'honey pot' receptacles of the rickety wooden latrines, from whence the stinking contents –'night soil' – were conveyed in carts to fertilise the paddy fields outside the city.

Even in the early months of the war, the sprawl of the 'International Market' was spreading. But this was no Asian market jammed with exotic bargains like the racy street stalls of Hong Kong; this was a bazaar of desperation, of survival. The alleyways were swarming. Grunting men hefted improbable piles of goods on wooden A-frame backpack carriers; maimed and disabled soldiers begged on corners; raucous women at makeshift stalls sold or bartered everything from fish to agricultural produce, from rubber shoes to Hershey chocolate bars. The clamour was a thousand voices shouting and arguing in staccato Korean, with, here and there, jaunty, Japanese-style music blaring from gramophones. The smell was a blend of garlic, *kimchi* – the pungent Korean pickle –wood smoke and the filth of the gutter.

Flitting through the chaos at waist height, tugging at the uniforms of wandering American soldiers were Dickensian apparitions: The ubiquitous scruffy children, holding their palms out imploringly for gum or candy and intoning '*Miguk, miguk*' – Korean for 'American'. Many UNC troops were moved to see these rag-clad, dirty-faced urchins, topped with scarecrow-like shocks of un-brushed hair. Few looked older than twelve, but many had even tinier children bound to their backs. Countless families had been broken up in the chaotic retreat, yet the duties implicit in the elder sibling relationship still compelled these pathetic orphans to somehow care for their younger, more defenceless brothers and sisters. 'I remember faces,' said Ray Rogers. 'Just these bewildered faces.' And the orphans haunting the shanties of Pusan were just one minute fragment of the vast human tragedy Kim Il-sung's invasion had precipitated.* [6]

* * *

On their stop-start train, sampling the interesting new American C-rations, 27th Brigade chugged out of Pusan into the countryside. After transferring to US trucks, they disembarked some 20 miles southeast of Taegu. The concentration area was a boulder-studded, sandy stream bed, trickling with clean running water and shaded by willows. It was an idyllic spot; here they would work up before being inserted into the line.

Nearby was the HQ of 24th Infantry Division, the first American occupation unit that had landed in Korea from Japan, and been defeated in a succession of battles, losing its commanding general, William Dean, captured in the defence of Taejon after taking on a T34. 'In welcoming Brigadier Coad, the US commander said he was particularly glad to receive a British contingent because they were

---

* The manic activity of the wartime markets planted a commercial, entrepreneurial seed that was one of the foundations of South Korea's extraordinary post-war economic ascent.

experts in retreating,' Willoughby heard. 'Well, we shall see.'[7] Their first sight of American combat troops gave some men pause for thought. Argyll adjutant John Slim looked on critically. 'They just retreated,' he said. 'Everyone runs at times, but the 24th Infantry Division was not ready for war.' Yerby got talking to one of the coloured truck drivers; the US Army of 1950 was still segregated along racial lines. 'This guy got out a sleeping bag and his feet stuck out the bottom. He said, "When the Gooks come, you pull the bag up and bug out!"' These were new terms: 'Gooks' were enemy, 'bug out' was a retreat.

Still the allies were well supplied – and generous. Haldane was woefully under-equipped: His Regimental Aid Post, or RAP, had 'a couple of crates of blankets' six stretchers, sedatives for battle fatigue casualties, and three bottles of anti-diarrhoea solution. Americans gave him a full medical pannier. 'I could have done an appendicitis operation with the instruments there!' he said.

Soldiers discovered what poor cousins they were beside the Americans. US units had stainless steel kitchen units, water-filled drums to clean their mess tins – British troops were expected to use a handful of sand – and, hanging from trees, water skins filled with ice. 'It was the first time we had seen the American way of living in the field, it was fantastic to see ice water in the field, it struck us as very funny,' said Horsfield. 'The Americans had fantastic organisation.'

The 3.5-inch 'bazooka' anti-tank rocket launchers were issued. 'One per platoon, with six rockets!' Willoughby, whose D Company had rejoined the battalion, noted. 'None of us had fired it and I had no alternative but to make two members of the crew fire one rocket each and hope I would not regret it.'[8]

Willoughby fretted at the speed with which the brigade was heading for the front. Many young soldiers were unused even to keeping their rifles – which in the depot were locked in the armoury – handy at all times, leading to urgent reproaches from NCOs. 'Wonderfully willing as our National Servicemen are, they are at best half trained and I expect they are all as frightened of being pitch-forked into battle as I am,' he wrote. 'May we have time to learn without too many casualties.'[9]

That possibility looked unlikely after company commanders were summoned for a briefing in Taegu, the market town that was, bar Pusan, the only Korean settlement of any size still in UNC hands, just behind the front. In the town, the officers noted two stalls servicing the US Army: 'Very Gentle Laundry' and 'Kindly and Clean Laundry' – both situated over open sewers. Refugees thronged side streets, and ROK recruits were drilling and singing: 'It is said they are put into the line after two weeks, where they either get their throats cut by the "Gooks" or are shot for desertion,' Willoughby noted gloomily.[10] Some ROK officers were dangerous-looking men, veterans of the Japanese Army, but many recruits were virtual children, lost in helmets and uniforms far too big for them.

One minute before midnight on 2 September, 27th Brigade was placed under command of US 1st Cavalry Division.[11] Chaos reigned. Willoughby and fellow officers had been waiting for their briefing in front of a headquarters building when an American brigadier drove up in a jeep, skidded – showering all those waiting with dirt – and raced off. 'The building came alive with figures carrying boxes of files to parked vehicles and it was evident that all was everything but well in high places.' A briefing officer arrived, stating that during the night, the NKPA had forced the Naktong in seventeen places. Willoughby noticed nearby rear echelon officers, 'frantically pumping bullets into targets almost in desperation', as they honed rusty musketry skills.[12] 'There were very dramatic descriptions about what was going on,' recalled Major John Shipster. 'I remember an American marine colonel going up to Colonel Man, and the question was, "What's cooking?" and the reply was, "We're hitting it out, punch for punch up there!" All this lingo was slightly alien.'

The headquarters seemed overrun with reporters – horrifying many British officers, whose units, unlike their American counterparts, lacked PR staff. General Hobart Gay of the US 1st Cavalry Division had just returned from a reconnaissance, and was surrounded, Willoughby stated, by 'US press, a considerable crowd of whom followed his every move, stopping him for close ups and crowding in when he issues his orders.' Brigadier Coad appeared 'rightly appalled'; Man told journalists that if they appeared in his area, they would, 'incur his greatest displeasure'.[13]

As the brigade turned in, the night was disturbed by the rumble of artillery and the glow of flares to the north.[14] Coad had hoped for an acclimatisation period. It was not feasible. 'The Americans were under such pressure they asked the brigade commander if he was prepared to go into the line,' said Jeffes, the REME officer who was still waiting for the brigade's transport to arrive from Hong Kong. 'He said, "Yes" – he had to.'

After dark, in pouring rain, a long line of trucks arrived at the brigade forming up-point. One ran over a tangle of signal cables and wrapped them round its axle. 'With great singleness of mind, one American procured a machete and hacked through every cable,' Willoughby noted. 'I could not help wondering what sort of impact this might have in the early hours, in the middle of an enemy offensive, on the HQ.' In darkness lit by distant, flickering gunfire, drenched platoons mounted up, then the convoys headed for the Naktong River, the key defensive feature of the 'Pusan Perimeter'.[15]

* * *

Throughout the night of 4 September, 27th Brigade's men deployed onto frontline positions on the east bank of the Naktong. Heavily loaded down with weapons and ammunition, the men slogged up the muddy hillside tracks under the pelting rain. The outlook was not promising.

Their hills, set back some 1,000–2,000 metres from the riverbank, were overlooked by higher, enemy-held hills on the west bank and also to the south, where the river looped around. The brigade's frontage was 16,500 metres (18,000 yards) – twice that of a division, i.e. a unit three times its size. There was a gap of 8,200 metres (9,000 yards) between the brigade and its left flank unit, the US 2nd Infantry Division.[16] Across the river, was deployed a North Korean division.[17]

Willoughby arrived at his allocated sector – 4 miles, a ludicrous frontage for a company, with an open right flank – to find GIs sitting on their trenches, firing off coloured signal lights and tracers in celebration of their imminent departure. 'That they were able to make a carnival without attracting enemy response was reassuring, but it ruled out any possibility of reoccupying their positions,' Willoughby sniffed. The American commander had a force of 200 infantry, eight AA guns, six tanks and 200 Korean police. 'The whereabouts of his troops were only too evident and we were naturally only too anxious to get his men out as quickly as possible... he was singularly unspecific concerning enemy positions and activities, beyond a warning that they operated almost always after dark with patrols regularly crossing the river and snipers left behind.'[18]

Departing GIs proved full of advice. 'They were asking about our rifles and stuff; they said, "You need to have this kind of automatic, they'll be on top of you before you know it,"' recalled Frank Whitehouse, the Stafford man who had volunteered for the Middlesex. 'Typical Americans – they talk a lot.' The Americans were surprised at the British numbers. 'They said, "Where are the rest of you?"' recalled Diehard Lance Corporal Don Barrett. 'We said, "We are the rest!"'

The key defensive priority in war is to fortify and hold high ground, dominating terrain. The soldiers furiously dug staggered, two-man slit trenches ringing the hilltops in all-round defence. 'Before you think of food or anything, you dig,' said Argyll Private Jake Mutch. 'It was bloody hard, stony, but we hacked through. You felt better when you were under cover.' Rocks were piled along trench parapets, tins filled with stones strung on foliage to give aural warning of attacks. Once positions were dug, crates of ammunition and rations were humped up. The conditioning of the New Territories paid dividends. 'We were proud fit, not bullshit fit,' said Captain John Slim. 'After Hong Kong we could run up the biggest bloody hill with a pack.'

Inexperience was glaring. When Barrett had dug in under his platoon commander's orders, the dispositions were found to be suicidal: 'He dug in three sections shooting into each others backs!' The platoon sergeant rearranged the positions. Argyll subaltern, Owen Light, was discovering who was in charge. 'The Jocks were tough, they were not people who'd be pushed around by any miserable second lieutenant,' he said. When another young lieutenant offered one soldier advice on digging, the man spat back, 'I've been a fucking miner all my life; you are going to tell me how to use a spade?'

As daylight illuminated the brigade's first day in the Naktong Valley, gruesome evidence of combat took shape. Diehard Ken Mankelow and his mates found their entrenching tools hitting the former defenders of the hill: A ROK unit who had been buried in their trenches. 'We had to dig them out, there were maggots crawling out of their skulls,' he said. Barrett, on the same position – 'Boot Hill' – found it covered in 'bits of bodies' from an attack two weeks previously; it was a 'bit pongy'. To reach a forward OP, it was necessary to crawl through human detritus, while in front of the hill, a minefield was 'chock full' of decaying North Koreans.

The brigade's neighbours on the line, it was discovered, were not soldiers. So desperate was South Korea's manpower shortage that the police force was taking on a combat role; 230 men were holding a line adjacent to the Middlesex's D Company. The first meeting between Willoughby and the constabulary proved memorable. Their leader, Captain Hong, 'an absolute caricature of a Japanese general' who smelt of stale brandy and was later to be exposed 'as an entrepreneur of anything saleable in Taegu, and in particular, army rations' appeared at Willoughby's CP. He was accompanied by a boy named Hur ('who could be fourteen or could be eighteen'), who had learned English at a missionary-run school, who acted as an interpreter. In welcome, Willoughby praised the police and told them what an honour it was having them attached to the Middlesex. In response, Hong spoke for several minutes. Willoughby waited for a translation of this lengthy speech: 'Captain Hong, he say, "Yes,"' was Hur's summary. Willoughby then asked about the police positions. This query prompted a pantomime from Hong: 'First he turned himself into a windmill, then a machine gun mowing us all down, and finally he shot himself in the temple with his forefinger.' He finished by demanding that one hundred British soldiers be placed under his command. Instead, Willoughby lent him his CSM and a Bren gun, which the NCO instructed the police in. Willoughby wondered how much faith to place in his new allies: They were 'a pretty scratch lot armed with rusty Jap rifles . . . I hope I can keep them on my side.' A Middlesex sanitary corporal, Jimmy Fields, who had learned basic Japanese as a prisoner-of-war, was made liaison officer.[19] The police, split into two companies, were dubbed 'Army Group A' and 'Army Group B' and incorporated into the brigade defences.[20]

With yawning gaps between units, Battalion HQs were sited for all-round defence; even Coad's Brigade HQ had a section of line to hold.[21] The brigadier was disgusted with the muddled state of affairs thus far. He had been ordered to insert his men into the front by first light on 5 September, then, two hours later, told they had to be in position by last light on the fourth. 'With very few exceptions, American staff officers never leave their HQs, even to visit lower formation HQs, and never in our experience did a staff officer come to look at any ground,' he seethed in a secret report to Whitehall. 'Information about the positions of flanking units has always been impossible to obtain from formation HQ.'[22]

Amid the steamy late summer humidity, 27th Brigade settled into their positions, gazed out over the landscape, and waited to see what the Korean War would bring.

*   *   *

In common with most modern conflicts, where soldiers lie in carefully camouflaged positions, the front appeared lifeless, deserted. But it was, in its way, beautiful. Korea is known as 'the land of embroidered rivers and mountains', and from their hilltops, gazing into No Man's Land, this landscape spread before the British soldiers' eyes. Above, impossibly high, spread a luminous blue sky. Beyond the foresights of rifles and Bren guns resting on the parapets of slit trenches, untended rice fields sparkled green. From higher positions, the water-filled paddies reflected the summer sky and its dazzle of sunshine like a patchwork of mirrors. Among them, here and there, were dotted hamlets of mud-walled, thatch-roofed huts and cottages, set amid little copses. All were abandoned; some were burned down; others smouldered. As the eye wandered further north, it came to the broad blue loop of the Naktong, its flow almost imperceptible.

Beyond it, largely treeless – most of the peninsula was deforested – but carpeted in lush green scrub, loomed the enemy-held hills, the shadows of clouds scudding across their slopes. And behind them, wave after wave of mountains cascading northward into a hazy blue infinity. It was a landscape that had endured for eons: the lone signs of the twentieth century, bar the soldiers' weapons, were the telegraph poles lining the empty tracks that wound through the paddies. Silence, broken only by the incessant background drone of cicadas and the occasional squawk of a radio, hung over all.

The skies were not always blue. When the post-monsoon down-pours came, they came with a vengeance. Grey clouds descended, blanketing the hills and merging onto the ridges like fog. Then, the deluge. Heavy pellets of rain speared down, churning the ground into thick ooze. On the edges of their trenches, huddling under largely useless ponchos, soldiers sat with the litter of camp life – matchboxes, cigarette packets, empty cans, ration-box cardboard – swirling around their knees. Chilled men swore at their circumstances and the rain, and waited impotently for it to cease. When it did and the sun returned, the hills gradually took shape through the grey, until all that was left of the rain clouds were tendrils drifting up from the slopes like smoke, giving the terrain the appearance of a Chinese watercolour painting. Soldiers upended boots, emptying brown water onto the mud, and strung soaked jungle greens from branches and makeshift washing lines, where they steamed in the haze. The cicadas took up their buzz once again.

'It was all peace and quiet,' said Man. 'But it was an ominous peace.' The motionless Asian landscape was primed with invisible menace, a menace Light encountered on his first morning on the Naktong, as his company commander pointed out – there were no maps – to indicate the positions his platoon was to occupy. 'We were walking in the countryside, suddenly there was this terrible bang, and we hit the deck,' Light said. Dirt geysered out of a paddy, then rained down. After a few seconds, the officers stood warily. 'We just had to get on, there was no real terror, it was surprise,' said Light. 'Someone was watching us; it brought home that this was no game, this was real.'

Across the river, brilliantly concealed, lay the angular bulk of self propelled guns, or SPGs. These Russian-made armoured vehicles – essentially, tanks without turrets, granting them low silhouettes – mounted 76mm guns. They were potent weapons, and on the Naktong, were used by the NKPA to inform 27th Brigade that there was, indeed, a war on. A sudden crack – the simultaneous shriek of a shell – the near-instantaneous crump of detonation – redundant yells to 'Take cover!' – men tumbling into water-filled trenches – dirt showering down – sudden silence. Then the pick-pick-pick as men scratched trenches a little deeper.

'Stonkings' from SPGs and mortars dug in across the river granted most men their first experience of hostile fire. 'It always seemed to be when we were going to have something to eat they would start mortaring or shelling,' said Argyll Lance Corporal Joseph Fairhurst. 'If it made a particular noise it was coming over you – shhhh – it if made another noise – sssss – it was coming on top of you.' The SPGs were most dangerous. While mortars would 'thunk' when fired, giving men a few seconds to take cover before the bomb, describing a high parabola, landed, many SPG shells were high-velocity, direct-fire weapons; they hit at the same moment the gunshot was heard. Corporal Harry Spicer's baptism of fire occurred when his position was subjected to a ten-minute mortar barrage. He knew he was largely safe against anything but a direct hit if he stayed below ground – bombs explode outward and upward – but found the noise of mortars detonating close-by 'absolutely terrifying' their volume beyond anything in his experience. The ground in Spicer's trench vibrated with each impact.

Various retaliations were plotted. 'We'd all say, "I think that's it over there, there's smoke!"' said Fairhurst. 'So they'd call in an air strike. You'd see planes come in, swoop down the valley, they'd start at the bottom of the hill firing rockets straight up to the top, they'd say, "That should've shifted them." Half an hour later, the blinking gun or mortar would start up again!' Willoughby was at Battalion HQ where he witnessed one attempt to eliminate an SPG. A sniper sergeant returned from a reconnaissance on the riverbank, saying an SPG had pointed at him. Man called his mortar officer, who contacted an American artillery battery. Coordinates were sent. Minutes later, a twenty-minute artillery barrage whooshed over the CP, its shells impacting across the river. Willoughby, uninvolved, quietly checked his target map. The 'SPG' was almost certainly a wrecked truck he had previously marked.[23]

* * *

27th Brigade had been dispatched to Korea then rushed to the line post haste but once installed on the Naktong, the war seemed to slow down. Bar maggot-eaten corpses and long-range fire, signs of fighting were surprisingly few. 'The extraordinary vulnerability of my position, and the merciful inactivity of the enemy induces a strange unreality,' wrote Willoughby.[24] 'Everything seems so peaceful... the river meanders across my front, a mirror of the cloudless sky, it is too gentle for war.'[25]

The clear air and hilltop vistas granted soldiers grandstand views of distant actions. Vincent and the Argyll mortar platoon watched one drama across the river: A flight of Mustang fighter bombers were buzzing the hills when a North Korean momentarily let his fire discipline slip. 'Somebody opened up with a machine gun,' Vincent said. 'One Mustang did a perfect loop and blew the top of the hill off. I bet he wished he'd not opened up.' Willoughby watched American jets strafing a ruined village. 'I wondered if it was worth it for them to fly from Japan for that,' he wrote.[26]

With such distances between the hilltops the soldiers inhabited, patrols were constantly roaming between them. They proved good exercise, good tactical training, and good practice in reading the maps that were now starting to be issued. The patrols – sections of eight men in jungle green, eyes shaded from the sun under jungle hats, weapons at the ready and canvas bandoleers slung across chests – passed frequently through the villages in the rear. With North Korean and local communist guerillas operating in the region, it was critical to show a presence, to dominate not just the physical, but also the 'human terrain', assuring the villagers that the UNC was present and active. On these patrols, Jocks and Diehards began to encounter South Koreans.

The Naktong Valley hamlets were huddles of cottages, many fronted with dangling bundles of bright red and green chilli peppers drying in the sun, while pungent *kimchi* fermented in half-buried earthen jars. The villagers lived under thatch, dressed in the white peasant attire they had worn for centuries and tended their paddies with oxen. 'It is a gentle countryside of rice and cotton fields and apple orchards,' wrote Willoughby. 'The village elders sit about in their white robes and tall hats smoking their long-stemmed silver pipes and none of us has the slightest idea what they are thinking of.'[27]

Being miles – and centuries – removed from the ideologies and politics of Pyongyang and Seoul, Moscow and Washington, many villagers had little idea of what was happening to their country. The destructiveness of warplanes and artillery was beyond their ken, leading some to believe that their president had hired a devastatingly powerful shaman to obliterate his enemies from the North.[28]

Private James Beverly, the Bermondsey Cockney, was amazed by both landscape – 'I was from London, I'd never seen a hill before!' – and lifestyle – 'all the manure from the water buffalo and the sewage from the Koreans went into the paddy fields. The whole country stunk.' For British troops familiar with Singapore and Hong Kong – both of which suffered pockets of poverty, but which were cosmopolitan trading hubs – Korea seemed lost in time. 'It was not similar to Hong Kong: The New Territories had modern cars and buildings, Korea was like going back in history, seeing bullocks pulling carts, no roads, and small, poorly built houses,' said Yerby. 'Lord! The world had forgotten them. I was a bit shocked that any country could be that poor and have nothing.'

*　　*　　*

On active service, many men found themselves less busy than they had been in peace-time Hong Kong. There was stand to at last light and at first light. In the evening, two-hour sentry 'stags' were arranged. But during the day, when not on patrol, there was little to do but cook, clean weapons, write letters, improve trenches and bullshit with mates.

Food was largely the US C-rations, one cardboard box per man per day. Though best eaten hot, it could be consumed cold, and contained a range of tins and brown-paper wrapped packages. The entrée, heated over a tin of solid spirit ('canned heat') varied: meat stew, spaghetti and meatballs, meat and noodles, frankfurters and beans, ham and lima beans. 'C rats' also contained hardtack crackers, an oatmeal block, instant coffee, sugar tablets, chocolate, gum, a 'jelly bar', candy, nine cigarettes and an ingenious little can opener. 'The chewing gum, the cigarettes and the toilet paper were nice – but I am no fan of frankfurters and ham and lima beans,' said Yerby. 'But there were times when the cooks managed to make a good old stew – that was good stuff.'

Field hygiene was essential as, given the intimate living conditions, were one soldier to come down with a bug, the rest of his section would suffer the same. Behind the fighting positions were latrine trenches and 'tin holes' where empty ration cans, which attracted swarms of flies, were buried. But sanitary drills did not guard against every possible infestation. Peter Jones, the Argyll who had seen naval action, found himself hosting unwanted visitors: 'It was very alarming passing an 18–24 inch tapeworm.'[29]

Real leaders were standing out. 'In Hong Kong it was more regimental: "Yes sir, no sir, stand to attention," ' said Whitehouse. 'In Korea, there was none of that, they were easygoing officers, they were very good and led from the front.' 'You tend to get more "lead swinging" when troops are not in action,' added Stanley Boydell, the Middlesex MO. 'If troops are involved in something life-threatening, a lot of attitudes change, particularly if officers are recognised as being highly competent; they may have been regarded as disciplinarians, but then troops realise they are efficient and lifesaving.'

While many subalterns lacked experience, company-level officers had learned their business in the Second World War. 'He was a very good officer, very strict,' said Argyll Ralph Horsfield of his company commander Miles Marsten. 'He had us all digging in and keep heads down and no movement whatsoever.' Willoughby was teaching his young Diehards the tricks of the trade. In the silent landscape, the loud bells of field telephones were disconnected; calls were made instead with discreet whistles down the line. To make the enemy think there were more Middlesex than they were, he sent pairs of soldiers out to different locations before daybreak to light cooking fires. He also took a 2-inch mortar crew with him whenever he went out to visit platoon positions, and sent half a dozen bombs from the positions to give an impression of greater firepower. And he disguised a Bren gun carrier as an SPG, using a pole and shell cases for the barrel and a jam tin for the muzzle brake; the decoy actually fooled a visiting ROK officer.[30]

Conversely, unfamiliarity with the countryside, and nerves, showed. Second Lieutenant James Stirling's platoon – his 'tiny little army' – found themselves cut off on their isolated position. 'We were surrounded and had an airdrop of American rations and ice in bags – this was quite dangerous, about a hundredweight of ice – as we had not been able to get water,' Stirling said. 'Then the CO walked into my perimeter; we were not surrounded at all, it was just rumour.'

Not all officers welcomed CO visits. Man and Coad visited Willoughby's company position by jeeping along the road in clear view of enemy. Three days later, Willoughby's positions came under sustained shellfire, 'No doubt a consequence of the brigade commander's circus last Sunday.'[31]

Under Korea's fierce sun, the men's lightweight jungle-green uniforms, salted with sweat, faded. Argyll quartermaster Andrew Brown found himself running out of trousers, as in Hong Kong, many of the men had their laundry done by Chinese washerwomen, who slapped the clothes on rocks, a method that cleaned them but wore the cloth. 'Eventually, you could just about recognise the battalion by their split arses,' Brown said.

Henry 'Chick' Cochrane of the Argyll mortar platoon and a mate, soaked after a downpour, approached an American supply dump in the rear to beg some clothes. 'They gave us American jackets, really good jackets, really good boots – lovely!' he said. Returning to their lines, the two bumped into Slim stalking through the paddies. 'We saluted him,' Cochrane recalled. 'He recognised us and said, "Get 'em off!" We had a laugh about it.' As the war proceeded, the rugged terrain and extreme climate would wear out British kit, and 27th Brigade would come to look increasingly American.

There were some pluses to British gear. Cochrane was talking with some GIs behind the line when discussion turned to weaponry. An argument ensued as to what was better: the bolt-operated British Lee Enfield or the semiautomatic American M1 Garand. A competition was quickly arranged: the winner would be the first man to put ten rounds through a can 50 yards distant. Bets were laid, cigarettes piled up as the winner's trophy. Cochrane used the quick-firing method taught to British troops – 'I used the bolt with my forefinger and thumb, and fired with the middle finger' – but even so, the American had only to squeeze his trigger, and was shooting faster. But after firing his eighth round, the clip pinged out of the American's M1. 'My rifle only holds eight!' the GI ejaculated. 'I know!' crowed the Argyll as he finished first: the Lee-Enfield had a ten-round magazine, obviating a reload. 'You sure caught me that time,' the American conceded. 'I'll write home about you!'

Some members of the brigade grew very fond of the GIs. 'We needed a lot of warm heartedness from the Americans to supply us – we had no guns, no tanks, and we were supplied with food and rations,' said Shipster. 'I can't speak too highly about them [Americans].'

Others were more critical. The Middlesex CO was at his most irritable when two excited US colonels arrived at his CP. They had been driving when they came under fire from a sniper on a hill, they told Man, so took cover in the monsoon ditch alongside the track. 'Along came my ration truck with a couple of fellows inside,' Man recalled. 'They stopped their truck, saw these American colonels in a ditch and went up with their rifles and sorted out this chap.' The two American officers recommended that Man award the two Diehards medals. Man was having none of it. 'They were doing a normal day's work,' he sniffed.[*]

---

[*] Man's parsimony with medals would later anger some of his soldiers. 'We had the lowest record for awards, because Colonel Man expected people just to do their job,' said Don Barrett, who, in later years, would become an unofficial regimental historian, chronicling many of the brigade's activities in Korea. 'But at the time nobody cared.'

Enemy snipers, like the mortars and SPGs, gave the brigade respect for NKPA fieldcraft. At the back of Beverly's trench was a sapling. One day a pair of bullets thudded into it, just inches from the Diehard's head. 'They could see you, but you could not see them,' Beverly said.

But despite everything – rain, mortars, SPGs and snipers – there were pleasant moments. When the sun descended, the soldiers on their hilltops were treated to a remarkable spectacle: 'There were beautiful sunsets, like nothing I had set eyes on before or since,' Julian Tunstall, a Middlesex private, wrote.[32] But once darkness settled, nerves were stretched.

'In the front line, nights are always hateful, they last for ever and the trees whisper to each other in perpetual disquiet, bushes seem to move and starving dogs from some deserted village roam among us and send old tins clattering down the hillside,' wrote Willoughby. 'All about our little perimeter . . . young soldiers in pairs leaned forward against the wet parapets of their narrow trenches grasping a rifle and staring into the darkness.'[33]

It was dangerous for men to move beyond their own slits. On Mankelow's position, the latrine trenches were at the back but one man went out in front behind a bush. 'There was a white flash, someone opened up, we all fired,' Mankelow recalled. 'Officers came and stopped it, then they were saying, "And you couldn't even hit the bloke!"' Some young officers were so spooked by the dark that they simply did not sleep. 'We thought the North Koreans were superhuman and could come at night without making any noise, so we sat up all night with fingers on triggers and every rabbit that hopped, people fired,' recalled Stirling. 'By the end of three nights, we were absolutely bushed, and an order came down from the CO: All officers were to sleep at night.'

Though the anticipated enemy assault had not materialised, British soldiers on the Naktong were being wounded and killed. The Argylls suffered their first casualty on their first day in the line: A subaltern was accidentally shot by his own sentries and evacuated on 5 September.[34]

While the dug-in men would learn that they were largely safe from sudden fire, jeeps speeding along the dust tracks between the positions were at risk. 'If you sent a jeep down the road they would shoot at you if you went along,' said Jeffes. 'And if you went too far you ran into a North Korean machine gun nest – we lost one or two vehicles where they missed the turning for the Argylls and came across this wretched machine gun.'

It was a jeep accident that would precipitate one of the war's countless little tragedies. Reg Streeter, the batman to the Middlesex Intelligence Officer, Captain Jeff Bucknell was killed when his jeep overturned near one of the forward company positions. The two men, both boxers, were 'really good mates', whose friendship, unusually, crossed rank boundaries. Bucknell subsequently armed himself and headed down to the river, toward the North Koreans, alone. He was never seen again. Dark rumours circulated. 'He was tied up with barbed wire and burned,' said Yerby. 'At least, that is what we heard.'[35]

*   *   *

Roving patrols were becoming routine. With 27th Brigade familiarised with the terrain, more dangerous operations – fighting patrols – were instituted. In the brigade's first offensive operation, the Argylls' C Company was tasked to take out a North Korean position. A force of North Koreans of unknown size had moved across the Naktong and were digging in on a hill on the Argyll's left flank, where there was a 6,000-yard gap before an American unit.[36] They had been spotted by the keen young Lance Corporal Harry Young. 'I was one of those guys who was well alert, well trained and I had been brought up in the hills: My father used to be a gamekeeper and I had done gamekeeper duty,' he said. 'I told the platoon commander I could see maybe two platoons about a mile away on this hill feature.' On 6 September, a daylight patrol under Captain Neil Buchanan was tasked to bump the enemy outpost by advancing to contact. In his briefing, Buchanan warned his men that they were facing a savage enemy; wounded had to be retrieved.[37]

27th Brigade's first offensive action got underway. In tactical formation, the patrol moved warily toward the suspected enemy-held feature. The patrol was strong – 15 men – but carried only one significant automatic, a Bren. At the hill, the patrol split into two sections, one on either side of a stream, and advanced through the cover of the pine trees dotting the hillside. The only sound was the grunt and pant of men labouring up the hillside – then the air was rent with multiple ripping crackles. Muzzle flashes flickered among the trees. 'The North Koreans had realised we were going to walk right into them, and opened fire,' said Young.

The PPSH 41 Shpagin submachine gun was the key Soviet automatic of the Second World War. Despite lacking range, accuracy, and (in common with all submachine guns), stopping power – tactically speaking, it is a better result for a man to be wounded than killed outright, for a wounded man will occupy the attention of up to four more comrades who will have to drag him away, and his screams and the sight of his wound will demoralise the rest of his unit – it boasted a fearsome rate of fire. Its nickname, 'the burp gun' derived from the distinctive, 900 rounds-per-minute 'brrrrppp' of its burst – far faster than the 500 rpm of the British Sten submachine gun and Bren light machine gun. Moreover, like most Soviet weapons, it was crude but robust, and was fed with a 71-round drum, giving it a longer burst capacity than the Bren or Sten, each fed with 30-round magazines. These were the weapons that, from cover, lit up the Argylls.

Leading men spun down, bullets ripping into them. Six of the 15-man patrol were hit in the first fusillade. Young, further back, oddly felt no fear. Programming took over. 'There's nothing going through your mind,' he said. 'It was a very serious situation – you had to go for it!' He returned fire. His targets – small men, dug into spider holes with bushes pulled overhead as top cover – were visible but he could not tell if his shooting was effective: 'It is very difficult to tell if you have a hit.'

At the head of the patrol, Buchanan had been riddled. Crippled; unable to move; realizing that any recovery attempt would bring more of his Jocks into the enemy kill zone; the captain yelled at his men to escape, ordering them to make no attempt to rescue himself or his wounded batman, lying nearby. The order – which contravened his earlier command to leave no man – sealed his own fate.

The leading men – including Walker, the patrol sergeant, bleeding from nine wounds – tumbled back under fire, extricating the way they had come. Jocks grabbed the wounded, helping them walk or dragging them backward. Young and another soldier covered the retreating survivors, rapid-firing over their heads, then withdrew themselves.

The bloodied patrol sloshed down into the rice fields. 'There were a few odd shots as we came back across the paddy,' Young said. 'But we were not pursued.' Behind them, gun smoke drifted through the pines. Supporting their wounded, the Argylls trudged back to the C Company position. As he settled down, Young found he was suffering no nervous reaction to the short but sharp firefight.[38]

Five miles from C Company, in the peasant cottage that was the Argylls' Battalion HQ, the progress of the Buchanan patrol had been grimly followed over the radio. 'We all felt it was rather an audacious patrol,' said Slim. 'He was very isolated and there was no way to support him – we had no bloody artillery when he walked into that ambush.' Lieutenant Colonel Neilson ordered his MO to jeep immediately to C Company to deal with the four casualties.

Douglas Haldane leapt into a waiting vehicle, which hurtled along the dust track toward the company. The doctor registered a distant and mysterious 'plunk, plunk'. Seconds later, fountains of mud sprayed out of the paddies, bracketing the jeep. 'They were mortars, they came out of nowhere,' said Haldane. 'It was the first time I had experienced anything like that; it was not pleasant.' 'Jock the Doc' made it to C Company unscathed, where he was confronted with his first bullet wounds. 'The ammunition the North Koreans were using was small bore, so you got entry, but not exit wounds,' he said. 'It amuses me to see cowboys and indians being shot on films with a .45 and the bullet being removed, and then they get up and go on their way: If you are hit even on the finger, you go down; even a small bore is shocking to the system.' He got to work on the four bloodied men, but there was little he could do: 'I was virtually rendering first aid with field dressings.' Haldane's treatment stabilised them for helicopter evacuation the following day. A spotter plane was requested to search for Buchanan and Taylor.[39]

As is so often the case in war, losses prompted a second, equally risky operation. 'The OC got on the wireless and said, "I want you to take a patrol to the valley where Neil was, and see if you can get a prisoner to find out what happened,"' recalled Light. The inexperienced subaltern was appalled: Not only does a snatch patrol have to advance into close – literally, hand-to-hand – range of the enemy, but Light was certain the NKPA would be waiting for just such a move. 'I thought, the man is off his head!' he recalled. 'It must have been a hornet's nest!' But orders were orders.

Light and five men smeared their faces with dirt, removed all heavy equipment, taking only weapons, and walked out of their perimeter toward the target. In visual range of the objective, they dropped and began crawling – an exhausting form of movement. 'We heard noises,' Light said. 'We crawled forward, and saw them all quite clearly digging like mad, about twenty of them, with pickaxes and spades about 30 metres away and chaps standing with rifles and burp guns. I thought, "There is no way in the world to get a prisoner!"' Light ordered a withdrawal. The Jocks exfiltrated.

As he returned, Light worried about his company commander's likely reaction. He was pleasantly surprised. 'I said, "It was impossible!" and he said, "OK, well, there you are. You've had your first active service patrol."' It is a general principle of military operations that the commander on the ground should not be overruled by those not at the situation. Marston followed that rule. Light was learning.

The clash provided the Jocks with disconcerting intelligence. 'I remember saying to the colonel, "When it comes to automatic weapons, we are outgunned!"' said Slim. 'So we got all the colour sergeants and quartermasters together with as many three ton trucks as we could, and sent them back to where the American stores were kept. We had – being a good Highland regiment – whiskey in crates marked 'Office Equipment' and we tried to buy each platoon a .30 calibre machine gun and a 'grease gun' or a Thompson submachine gun with it. Americans are good at war – they give you what you want.'

The aerial recce failed to spot the bodies of Buchanan or his batman; they remained un-recovered. The Argylls' first encounter with the NKPA had been a defeat. 'The good thing about the Highlander is that he speaks his mind, but is not rude,' Slim said. 'We drank with the Jocks, mostly beer or rum, and they'd say, "Didn't we make a bit of a mistake there?"' The Argylls settled into the hills to await the enemy's next move.

* * *

While the forward companies patrolled the paddy fields and held their hills against the NKPA, a different kind of enemy was operating behind the lines. Roy Vincent, the Argyll mortar man, became aware of this when his second fire mission – his first had been on targets at the river – was to his rear. Light learned of enemy in the rear when, on a night patrol behind his position, his patrol halted in a village and they drank from the village well. The next morning, the patrol discovered that the well was stuffed with dead bodies. The Jocks had boiled their water – 'it did not do us any harm' – but polluting wells with corpses is a classic guerilla tactic.

Roaming behind the front were bands of South Korean communists and North Korean infiltrators. In the mornings, in the mountains to their rear and on their open left flank, the brigade could see 'lots of little fires where they were brewing up their morning tea,' recalled Jeffes. On 12 September, a special unit was tasked to deal with them.

A battalion of Korean police was placed under the Diehard's second-in-command, Major Roly Gwynne: 'Rolyforce'. Gwynne was perfectly spoken and always immaculately presented with a silk cravat and gold wristwatch complimenting his combat uniform, but in defiance of his debonair appearance, he was one of those unflappable leaders of the 'officer and gentleman' school, who in Coad's words 'seemed to revel in this kind of warfare'.[40] Gwynne chose some of the Middlesex's most experienced NCOs, as well as American signallers, to buttress the police for the mission. Among the scratch force was Sergeant Paddy Redmond, the Irish ex-commando. 'Major Gwynne said, "This should suit you: We're going up into the mountains!"' The force – British soldiers, Korean police and porters – were trucked to the base of the mountains, where they dismounted, and began a six-hour climb into the granite ridges.

Reaching the summit of the range, Redmond's unit set up a covert hide, scanning for the enemy brigade believed to have infiltrated across the river. 'It was windswept, rainswept and we had no tents, no cover, just dig, sleep in shallow trenches and scan the horizon,' said Redmond. 'This is what I'd joined the commandos for.' Given the terrain, the unit's call sign was appropriate: 'Billygoat One Six'. The police, thought Redmond's unit, were a 'rag tag lot, like a paramilitary'. One company had no firearms, only hand grenades; the unit mortar had no sights and the wrong calibre bombs.[41] Redmond had little faith in them should the North Koreans mount an attack.

The hills, Gwynne's men had been briefed, were empty of civilians. Anyone moving around was hostile. Redmond and the other NCOs alternated duties, manning hides and leading reconnaissance patrols down the slopes, but it was when the Dublin native was scanning from a peak that he spotted movement 1,000 metres below. 'We located them in the valley,' he said. Through binoculars, he learned how the enemy concealed themselves: 'They had burrowed into the sides of the hills.' Now they were in the open, visible to the naked eye. Working excitedly with an attached American signaller, he called in the grid reference for an air strike. The flight arrived on time, shrieking down the valley toward North Koreans, caught out in the open. Earth erupted as bombs landed, then a great sheet of orange flame tore along the valley floor as napalm went in. 'They were very good at delivering what you asked for, it was awesome!' Redmond said. The Dubliner was so exhilarated that he forgot radio procedure, yelling, 'Fuck it, that's it!' into the handset. This was economy of force: 'We were killing them without having to fight them on the ground,' said Redmond. His party remained in their hide to scan further. 'The next day, if there was no movement, you knew it had been a good strike.'

Prowling through the mountains; operating with local troops; living on their wits; calling in destruction from above; it was an extraordinary operation for the men of 'Billygoat One Six'. 'Major Gwynne said he would not have missed it for the world,' Redmond recalled. 'It was like an adventure to us, it was away from ordinary soldiering, you had a bit of freedom.'

But there was a darker side to this war behind the lines. Because guerillas do not wear uniforms, blurring the distinction between civilian and combatant, atrocity is the handmaiden to irregular warfare. While the ROK Army battled the NKPA, ROK police and paramilitaries were waging a campaign against insurgents. Fuelling the flames was the fact that in traditional Korean society, women had rigidly defined roles and were kept firmly under the thumb of men, but invading communists had promised wider roles for females and had established women's committees in captured areas. The promise of emancipation was a strong lure for many South Korean women. One day, Redmond's Korean police squad returned from a patrol with two female prisoners. 'The cops were a law unto themselves, and they reckoned these were North Korean soldiers or South Korean sympathisers,' Redmond said. 'They were always patrolling down the mountains, and you'd hear a few screams; they took them away and just shot them. War is war.'

Other men, on the front, were coming across similarly disturbing incidents. 'Suffering thirty years of Japanese domination had taught the Koreans some really bad habits,' said Slim. Watching a group of South Korean policemen conducting an 'interrogation' – a mass beating of a suspect with batons and clubs – Tunstall wondered if his allies were worth fighting for.[42] The Middlesex MO witnessed something he did not, at the time, comprehend. 'We noticed these trucks going up into the hills crowded with people and coming back empty,' Boydell said. 'We thought they were just being transported.' Only later, when he read about atrocities, did he realise the likely fate of the trucks' occupants: execution.

* * *

On 11 September, A Company's commander, Marston, returned to the UK to Staff College. Second Lieutenant James Stirling was one of the first to meet his replacement. He went up to ask a question of

A Company's sergeant major who was talking to 'a very scruffy soldier' wearing a tam-o'-shanter and no badges of rank. 'I said, "I hear you have a new company commander, he's a bit of a fire-eater."' Stirling recalled, 'And this scruffy soldier said, "Boy! Who are you?"' It was the new company commander, Major David Wilson.

Wilson could have rested on his considerable laurels. He had fought and survived the Malayan disaster – he had escaped by sea, fought at Kohima in Burma and commanded the battalion in Palestine, but was keen to get into the new war: 'I was chuffed, this is what one joined up for,' he said. Just before departing the UK, he watched the classic Western *She Wore a Yellow Ribbon* about the 7th Cavalry – a unit he would soon get to know well. Then he was flying out. 'Within 24 hours of leaving civilisation, one was in the front line – very similar to the parachutists who jumped in Normandy,' he said. He was impressed by the Jocks on the Naktong – 'very fit, very tough' – and found the terrain and nature of the war familiar from his formative soldiering experiences on the Northwest Frontier. Many older Argylls knew Wilson. Light first saw his OC when he spotted the major stalking around in full view of the enemy. 'Look at the way he walks!' a Jock said to Light. 'He's as fit as anything!' Fearless, cheerful, scruffy, energetic and idiosyncratic – 'the Jocks would have followed him anywhere, if only out of curiosity' said Intelligence Officer Sandy Boswell – Wilson would prove one of the brigade's most effective battle leaders. It would be Wilson who, just four days after his arrival, orchestrated revenge for the Buchanan patrol.

A Company occupied the most exposed Argyll position. While enemy strength was unknown, a regiment was believed to be just over the river, and the company was in range of – and had been fired on – by enemy mortars and at least two SPGs. At 19:00 on the night of 16 September, in pouring rain, the company exfiltrated in darkness in preparation for a forthcoming river-crossing operation. At 04:00, the company was ordered to return: The operation had been aborted. Jocks cursed. They were ordered to rest up and dry out in a nearby village, and reoccupy their position on 17 September. Wilson had his company back in place at 17:30, but their various movements had not escaped the eyes of the enemy. At dawn on the 18 September, an enemy fighting patrol crept up and showered a forward Vickers section with hand grenades.[43] Light's platoon heard, but could not see the fight, when one of his men hissed, 'Somebody in front of us, sir!' A man was crawling toward them. It was a survivor from the Vickers section, which had suffered a man killed. The wounded man was taken in by Light's platoon.

The North Korean probe prompted a deadly game in the scrubby hills. That evening, the Vickers section was withdrawn and an Argyll patrol under Sergeant Morrison sent out to intercept further enemy patrols. 'I'd told him to go about 50 metres below our platoon position and do nothing and sit and watch and see what was happening and if it was a small patrol, to open fire,' said Light. At 20:30, Morrison's men spotted enemy heading toward 1 Platoon. 'He came back and reported, "At least twenty came past us!"' said Light. 'This was good information.' By whispered telephone conversation, this was passed along to all platoons. Twenty men was a strong force, a fighting patrol. With action imminent, the company's scale of sentries was quietly increased to fifty per cent.

At 04:00, gunfire and explosions shredded the night as the NKPA patrol attacked the empty Vickers position. It then opened up – 'reconnaissance by fire' – in the direction of 1 Platoon. This would usually prompt flares and a storm of reactionary shooting, giving away positions to the attackers. But in an extraordinary piece of fire discipline, the platoon, commanded by Sergeant Robertson, held its fire. 'It is difficult to describe in ordinary language the control this NCO was able to exercise over his platoon,' noted Wilson. The enemy fighting patrol was now within the company lines but would have to withdraw before daybreak – when they would be in the sights of Robertson's Jocks. The patrol had cut the company telephone lines; Wilson requested a situation report by radio. Robinson whispered that enemy were all around him, but as soon as dawn cast light, he would 'let them have it'. At 05:00, daylight broke over the position. Argylls further up the position heard an outbreak of intense firing mingled with screams and panicked North Korean shouts. At 05:15, shooting ceased.

Light was ordered to lead a fighting patrol down to sweep in front of 1 Platoon's position: battlefield clearance. Wilson's A Company After-action Report records what the patrol discovered: '10 dead with 3 wounded, which we did not recover.' No Argylls had been hit. All in all, the action had been 'A most satisfactory day's work' the report concluded.[44] The Brigade War Diary for the day reported, 'several wounded were lying on the slopes below, who probably died later from wounds'.

The war diarist may well have been ignorant of what actually happened, as the After-action Report's phrase 'did not recover' is disingenuous. It provides cover for an event which reveals how military occurrences jarring to civilian sensibilities can be buried in everyday language, while the grisly incident it camouflages demonstrates how brutalised British troops on the Naktong had become even at this early stage of the war.

Reports of North Korean atrocities had widely circulated. Tales of Japanese fanaticism in the Second World War – such as suicidal wounded soldiers grenading Allied medics who came to their aid – were common currency, and the brigade was aware that Korea had, until recently, been a Japanese colony which had, moreover, supplied some of the Emperor's most notorious POW camp guards. Light himself had seen an abandoned American tank surrounded by dead enemy: the crew had, rather than surrender, fought till they ran out of ammunition, then been killed. The NKPA's reputation for fanaticism and atrocity would not engender mercy in their enemies.

'We knew there were quite a few of them,' Light said, so took two sections – 16 men – on the clearance. The patrol moved warily down through the trees. Reaching the area of the firefight, they encountered, as expected, the victims of 1 Platoon's close-range fire. Enemy soldiers – dead, dying and wounded – lay in the dirt. The Highlanders halted and looked on. 'There were several there, we could see grenades primed under them,' Light recalled. 'Not all were dead. You couldn't touch them.' He ordered his men to stand off, then from a safe range, the Argylls opened fire, coldly finishing off the wounded. 'Those with grenades were ready to blow us to pieces,' said Light simply. 'So they were shot.'

A war crime? Not according to the officer responsible for discipline within Light's battalion. 'Quite right – those were sound tactics,' said Adjutant Slim. 'Light was an outstanding officer. We were learning about the North Koreans on the Naktong, and it is a very Oriental thing to leave your wounded crying and blubbing; if you go and talk to them, there may be another ambush. They made the right tactical decision.'

There may have been another, more personal reason behind the clinical killing, one that would not stand up in any court of law, but, as a precedent, pre-dates any judicial system. Light's men knew one Argyll had been killed, and had seen the mangled Jock from the Vickers section hit in the initial attack. 'It's always the thing,' said Slim, 'that if you share a slit trench with a man, and he gets killed, you say, "I'll get one back for him." It's legitimate.'

The killing on the lower slope of A Company's position on 19 September was not just tactical common sense; it was soldiers' justice.

* * *

On 15 September, Gwynne and his men had been ordered to leave their counter-guerilla unit and return to brigade. Command of the force was handed over to the local police chief, who left for Taegu; the operation subsequently collapsed.[45] The situation on his flank was less important to Coad than the concentration of his brigade, for orders were now coming down from higher command for an operation to force the Naktong.

The need for intelligence of enemy dispositions over the river was suddenly critical. While the brigade held its line knowledge, of the NKPA across the river was severely lacking. Willoughby has been introduced to a 'miserable looking youth' who had been offered US$2 by the Americans to reconnoiter, cross-river. The 'spy' returned to report: 'Many, many enemy on other side of river.' As intelligence, this was 'quite meaningless' Willoughby thought.[46] With nothing worthwhile or actionable coming from the local 'line crossers', on 18 September, Man sent a cautious patrol over on shallow reconnaissance. It found nothing to report. On 20 September, a deep penetration would be made.[47]

D Company was tasked. Willoughby plotted the 'tricky little operation' carefully. One platoon and a section of Vickers machine guns were sited on the riverbank as patrol base; a full platoon would cross. Telephone cables were laid from the riverbank to Company HQ, a battery of US artillery was on call, and the Vickers were sighted in; the patrol would remain within their 2,000-yard range.[48]

Among those going over was Corporal Harry Spicer. 'We were sort of excited,' he recalled. 'It was, "Ah, at last we are going to do something!"' The platoon moved down to the Naktong after dusk. In their lying-up point in a local hut on the riverbank, they were introduced to one joy of rural life. 'We all got lice,' Spicer said. 'They bite or suck and you are scratching all the time. We'd pick 'em off like little worms.'

Dawn, 20 September. The platoon silently entered canvas boats and pushed onto the misty river. The Naktong was broad, its flow sluggish. The platoon crossed without incident. A section remained to guard the boats on the sandy beach while the other two sections readied their weapons, spread out into tactical formation and began moving through the sunlit countryside parallel to the river. There was no sign of enemy, even though they were now, literally, patrolling under the noses of the North Koreans on the hills.

'We got about a mile and we were looking up the hill and saw someone moving, and then a lot of movement: It looked like a guy waving troops up from the rear of the hill,' said Spicer. Seconds later, some 130 enemy cascaded over the crest and occupied trenches on the forward slope. Still, not a shot had been fired, but parties of enemy in company strength were now visible flanking the patrol along the ridge: the patrol was being pincered.[49] Then came a multiple whiplash as bullets cracked overhead: A camouflaged machine gun on high ground was ranging in. Most of the platoon was in the cover of the riverbank, but Spicer's section was in the open, right in the gun's beaten zone. 'It was the worst moment of my life,' Spicer said. 'You can't do nothing, bullets were that close to me, I made a dent trying to get in the flaming ground!' Desperately pressing himself flat, he could not see the enemy weapon that was trying to kill him. A helpless thought flashed through his mind: 'If you are going to hit me – hit me!'

Abruptly the firing ceased – perhaps as the gunner reloaded; perhaps because all his targets had gone to ground. 'Dash to the bank!' Spicer yelled. His section got up and took off. Firing resumed. As if in a slow motion, Spicer saw bullets pelting into the ground and kicking up dust all around his platoon sergeant. A signaller ditched his radio; one man panicked as his webbing, cut by a round, fell, entangling his legs. As Platoon Sergeant Paddy Bermingham cut him free, it crossed his mind that such destruction of equipment would constitute 'a hanging offence' in the CO's book.[50] A man was hit in the back. 'It was in and out, just a flesh wound, he didn't realise,' Spicer said. 'You are so engrossed in what you were doing, you don't realise what was happening.' Focus was on immediate priorities: Get up! Move! Get down!

The Middlesex Vickers returned fire, temporarily suppressing the enemy weapon. 'We got up and moved; they fired again, we got down,' Spicer said. Two members of a three-man US artillery FOO section with the platoon disappeared, but their officer remained. 'One went down, we carried him out, but that officer was good,' said Spicer. 'He was ashamed his guys took off, he said he'd court martial 'em.'

Under intermittent fire, the patrol ran and crawled back along the riverbank for the boats. Under cover of the bank, out of the line of fire, Spicer told his platoon commander he was worried an enemy patrol might cut them off before they reached the boats. 'Oh yeah?' his platoon commander panted back. Another burst. Men took cover. Fire ceased. Quizzical looks. 'Was that you, sir?' Spicer queried. 'Er – yes,' replied the officer; he had tripped and his Sten had gone off. The dash resumed. The Vickers hammered again: Spicer later learned that an enemy patrol was, indeed, trying to cut them off, but the Diehard guns drove them back. The boats were waiting. The patrol tumbled in, pushed off, and headed for safety across the river. 'That patrol was just a couple of hours,' said Spicer. 'The only thing we found was they were on top of the hill!'

Willoughby extracted more information from the exercise. The enemy's failure to press home an attack on the patrol – which suffered two wounded – suggested the riverbank was lightly held. The major was irritated, however, that his commanding officer arrived to monitor the operation from the Vickers firing point. 'I could have done without AM's presence,' he confided. Still, at least someone was happy from the adventure: A Reuters correspondent interviewed the men who had returned from the adventure.[51]

It had been a close call. Something close to rapture swept those who had been caught in the enemy machine gun sights. One patrol member had a hole through his headgear; Spicer was amazed to discover a bullet had gone through the sleeve of his shirt. In the excitement of contact, he had not noticed. 'The reaction was, "Gee whiz!" ' Spicer recalled. 'We got away with it!'

*   *   *

For those men of 27th Brigade not involved in patrol skirmishes – i.e. the vast majority – the defence of the Naktong remained an adventure which, despite its monotony, discomfort, after-dark tensions and occasional mortal risks, still held the flavour of a rather exotic camping trip. After the urgency of deployment, the war was anticlimactic. 'We thought they had raced us out here – and nothing has happened!' said Mankelow. 'I never saw a Gook over the Naktong,' added Barrett. 'It was totally quiet.'

The unexpectedly gentle introduction to war had, however, bonded units. 'The days along the river line were heaven sent,' Willoughby wrote. 'We have barely seen any action – just enough to learn to acclimatise, to know each other.'[52] This state of affairs was about to change, drastically.

The days of defensive operations, of the restricted fronts of the 'Pusan Perimeter' were numbered. Unknown to 27th Brigade the NKPA had been ground down. The last major communist offensive against the UNC perimeter had been launched on 27 August. 27th Brigade, had, remarkably, not come under attack; the assault had fallen, instead, upon ROK and US units. By now, 8th Army Commander General Walton Walker had the benefit of interior lines of communications, greatly increased troop strength, and air and naval firepower. By 12 September – seven days after 27th Brigade entered the line – the enemy offensive had burned out. In the closing days of the month, the UNC had 156,500 troops defending Pusan against the NKPA's 70,000.[53]

The balance had changed. The UNC was shifting gear, from defensive to offensive. 8th Army Headquarters was all abuzz. Generals and colonels plotted on maps. Field telephones rang; radios squawked. Olive green typewriters clattered as clerks drafted orders. Officers packed sealed papers into valises, climbed into jeeps and motored off for CPs. In the second week of September, along the Naktong, a new rumour was making the rounds, a new word being heard: 'breakout'.

For this operation, the primary force would be the powerful I Corps, consisting of the US 1st Cavalry Division (actually a motorised infantry division), the US 24th Infantry Division, the ROK 1st Division – the best South Korean unit – and the US 24th Infantry Division. In preparation, I Corps was beefed up with extra armour, extra artillery and 27th Brigade.[54]

Coad had received preliminary orders to prepare for an offensive on 13 September: an assault river crossing. What would follow would be an example of the slack US staff work the brigadier would come to loathe. The next day, the plan was changed; instead the brigade would seize a bridgehead further north. D-Day would be the 16th. US units jumped off, but were immediately held up. 27th Brigade was ordered to proceed to its forming-up areas at 16:25 on the same day. Given the lack of progress of the US assault, Coad queried these orders – why give up ground? – but they were confirmed. The brigade's forward companies started the move from their positions but were recalled when High Command rescinded the orders at 20:50 – hence the confusion with Wilson's A Company and the subsequent firefight, as the NKPA moved to occupy the abandoned position. The confused orders also led to the disintegration of Gwynne's police operation.[55]

Only on 20 September did the brigade finally receive firm movement orders. That day – the same day that he had extricated his patrol from enemy fire across the Naktong – Willoughby and his men were summoned rearward. Relief took place after last light. Diehards trucked off to the line. Behind the front, all was intense activity. 'It seemed as if whole of 8th Army must be on the move,' the surprised major wrote.[56] The Argylls were moving too, Wilson's A Company on the flank being the last to embark. The trucks carrying his men, Wilson suspected, had been used for recent battlefield clearance: they 'smelt horribly of dead bodies'.[57]

One phase of the Korean War was drawing to a close, a new one was opening. For 27th Brigade, battle was imminent.

Chapter Three
Into the Inferno

It's hard to know if you're alive or dead
When steel and fire go roaring through your head
Robert Graves

Dawn, 21 September. Staging Area, East Bank, Naktong River.

Looking around, the recently arrived Middlesex were pleased to see their new surroundings. Having been trucked off their positions in the hours of darkness, they had been dumped here, some 600 yards east of the Naktong, beside a maize field with a clear stream flowing through it. Ahead to the west, a track wound toward a village nestling in a copse on the riverbank. Beyond, lay the river; beyond the river, a ridge of dark hills obscured further view. Disregarding the considerable activity of senior officers nearby, it was, after eighteen days on the line, idyllic. Boots were gratefully removed and feet dipped in the cool stream; coffee began to brew.[1]

Stan Boydell, the Middlesex MO was with Tac HQ party when the ground around him erupted. Shellfire. For Boydell, it was the first experience of bombardment; the first casualty in the new phase of operations was Medical Sergeant Bill Bailey, who dived into a foxhole and broke his wrist. 'No matter what was wrong with you, he'd say, "Have an aspirin,"' said Sergeant Paddy Redmond. 'When he shouted, "I've broken my wrist," someone called out, "Have an aspro!"' Amid the chaos, Father Tony Quinlain stood. 'He was very experienced, he got up in the middle of shelling,' Boydell recalled. 'He was saying, "Don't worry, these are not high-explosive, these are anti-tank shells."' Boydell and his party moved back to a US Field Hospital where they were treated to rations the British found remarkable: fresh steaks. A US tank commenced shooting across the river. 'Nothing like a few shells to increase the congregation!' Quinlain confided to Boydell

Explosions continued. The SPG was dubbed 'The bastard'.[2] Many Diehards had been anticipating a day or two's rest before going into action. An uncomfortable realisation spread: What they had assumed was their rest area was, in fact, the staging area for an attack.[3]

Soldiers had long anticipated the moment when the UNC would go over to the offensive. As that moment drew near, foreboding grew. Patrolling the Naktong was one thing; entering the crucible of battle was another. Major John Shipster, who had fought in the worst combat in the Second World War, wondered whether young National Servicemen were equal to the challenge. 'I'd been in Burma and been wounded three times with Indian troops,' he said. 'I found them extremely fine soldiers, and wondered what it would be like with British soldiers.' Others were equally nervous. 'We really knew nothing about our enemy,' Major John Willoughby confided to his notebook, 'Looking across at those fearful hills, it was no good pretending that we could scarcely wait to get among them.'[4]

The hills – approximately 3 miles across the river – constituted an NKPA defensive network, for the road leading to the crossroads town of Songju, itself some three and a half miles behind the hills, ran between them. A US armoured reconnaissance company had already forded the river, hoping to open up a secondary axis on the left flank of 24th US Infantry Division, but were halted by the entrenched hills. 27th Brigade was to seize the hills, thus opening the road, for Songju was a key link on the northwest route that led up to Kumchon, Taejon, Suwon and Seoul. The brigade would fight under 24th Division command.

Coad sited his Brigade HQ on the river's east bank. The Middlesex would carry the hills on the right side of the road; the Argylls, those on the left. But first they had to force the Naktong. The men would cross over a single-file footbridge, vehicles and heavy equipment by pontoon ferry.

At 16:00, Lieutenant Colonel Andrew Man led his company commanders across the river on the rickety bridge built by US engineers, mounted armour of the reconnaissance company and rolled up the poplar- and telegraph pole-lined track to a hamlet, a kilometre south of the hills, where the company was leaguered. En route, Willoughby saw 'a beastly sight': flattened enemy dead, run over repeatedly by trucks.[5] 'We found this collection of Americans in a complete huddle, everyone touching everyone else, obviously very unhappy,' said Man. 'We joined this rather terrified lot.' Their apprehension was understandable: armour without infantry protection is vulnerable, and they had already been mortared and attacked by a patrol. Still, Man could not help being critical of their dispositions: 'They could hardly have been sited more closely together, or have presented a more worthwhile mortar target.'[6]

Behind him, his battalion was in motion. By company, the Diehards stood, shouldered small packs, hefted weapons and, one by one, set foot on the bridge. It had been blown earlier in the war, then jury-rigged by first North Korean, later US engineers. Some 300 yards long, it was a makeshift affair: Concrete slabs from the original bridge; bits of assault boats; rubber floats; wooden planking; and sandbags.[7] The river, blue from afar, proved muddy brown, close up. Its current was swift.

In dispersed file, the Middlesex advanced. Though they could not see their camouflaged enemy, they were under observation from the hills; behind the hills, lay North Korean artillery. On both sides of the bridge, great columns of water jetted up as shells slammed into the river, soaking crossing men. The advance continued. 'People were marching as per normal, we thought the chances of being hit were remote,' said Ken Mankelow of B Company. 'And your mates were there – you had to put on a bit of a face.' For most, this was their first experience of sustained shellfire. Soldiers yelled snatches of bravado at each other to reinforce courage. 'We'd shout out to the one in front or the one behind, "Next one will get you!"' Mankelow recalled. 'This was just to get yourself psyched up.'

Over the bridge, the companies spread out to advance. Then, approximately 300 yards short of the village, shells began landing among the lines of men, blasting up clods of earth and clouds of black smoke.[8]

This was the moment of truth: Would the young Diehards crack and go to ground – a nightmare for officers, for getting stalled and frightened men moving is a dangerous, difficult business – or would they continue?

'We went to ground on a sandy beach and the officers said, "Don't stop for anything! Don't stop!"' recalled Lance Corporal Don Barrett. 'So we didn't stop, and when shells came in we kept ploughing on, suddenly the company commander shouted, "Down, Down!" and they burst across the road.'

The test was passed. 'The moment we came under fire it was just like being back in Burma again,' said Shipster who – like countless soldiers throughout the ages – found his fears evaporated as the tension of anticipation was released and the business of command commenced. 'My doubts left me completely.' Willoughby was equally heartened. 'Sometimes a whole section would disappear in the black smoke of shell bursts, only to reappear seconds later, unchecked,' he wrote. 'It was a brave sight to see these little crocodiles of eight or so men walking steadily across the open fields, without hesitating. In my heart, I felt we should be all right tomorrow.'[9]

B Company dispersed around the village; A and D Companies veered right, with A securing a preliminary ridge for the attack; the ridge proved unoccupied. All men began digging in. The advance over the river to their start lines had cost the Middlesex one killed and four wounded.[10]

It was 19:30.[11] Man had wanted to capture the first feature before dark, but time was against him. Instead, he would launch his Diehards on a consecutive, two-phase dawn attack on the 22nd. B Company would seize the preliminary feature, 'Plum Pudding Hill' (so-named for its shape), then D Company would storm the second, larger feature, 'Middlesex Hill', beyond. A Company was reserve. Once objectives were taken, the companies would go firm while the Argylls – crossing behind the Diehards – carried the hills left of the road.

In the first British assault of the Korean War, Man demanded maximum aggression. Cheerfully waving his walking stick – the only weapon he carried bar his belted service pistol – he told Corporal Bob

Yerby, 'If you don't hit the bastards, I'll reduce you from five stars to three!' – stars being the pay ranking for NCOs. In darkness, Second Lieutenant Chris Lawrence, whose 4 Platoon, B Company, would spearhead the attack, delivered a quieter briefing. 'Chris was very reassuring on this type of thing,' said Mankelow. '"We are here; do as the NCOs tell you; keep calm"; it was a good briefing.' The platoon was ordered to rest, though for most, sleep proved elusive. To their rear, the ferry bringing the brigade's vehicles and heavy weapons over the Naktong, had been knocked out.[12] And the North Koreans, anticipating a British attack, were preparing: All night long, Diehards could hear enemy above, digging in deeper.[13]

What happens in a battle? Strategists talk of different formats: The encounter battle; the battle of annihilation; etc. What would happen on the Naktong River would be the most basic battle: a violent land grab. The attackers would 'advance to contact' until they came under 'effective fire', i.e. fire that causes casualties – then fire and manoeuvre through the enemy. The challenge for attackers is dislodging the defenders, thereby enabling the land to be grabbed. The defenders can be made casualties, but if they are entrenched – as the North Koreans were – the best that can realistically be hoped for is for fire to keep their heads down while the attackers manoeuvre onto, into and through their position. If they get into close range, attackers can kill defenders with small arms, or can close to within such proximity that the enemy, seeing doom approaching, surrenders or runs. If he runs, he can be slaughtered. Given that a relatively small number of combatants actually become casualties, a battle is, essentially, a test of wills. Will the attackers give out as his ranks are cut down on the way to the objective? If so, the attack grinds to a halt, requiring a second wave to pass through: 'maintaining the momentum'. Momentum is critical, for a moving unit is harder to register and hit than a stationary one. In the worst possible case, attackers break and flee. For the defender, that outcome is best achieved by counterattack. The attacker must hope that the defenders' collective determination – for military endeavours are collectives ones – erodes as he watches the assault wave approach despite everything the defender can throw at it. If determination does, indeed, erode, individual defenders will either cower in terror, hoping desperately that the situation will pass him by; crack, drop weapons and raise hands in the (often vain) hope of being taken prisoner; or simply flee – something which may well precipitate his comrades to do the same. If neither side breaks before the actual clash, fighting enters close quarters. In that case, eviction takes place at the point of the bayonet.

* * *

B Company were roused pre-dawn. At 07:00, they rose, spread out and set off toward their objective. Covering fire from the battalion's 3-inch mortars and Vickers machine guns – which had been manhandled over the footbridge during the night by B Echelon and attached Korean porters – opened fire reassuringly, hitting the feature, but the tanks the Middlesex had expected to join the assault wave did not move.

Man was incredulous. 'The Americans were supposed to support me with tanks, my platoon commander went off and the tanks would not go with him!' he said. 'An incredible business!' In fact, the commander believed the road ahead was mined; after some discussion with B Company's OC, two American tanks began firing cover from just in front of the village.[14]

Regardless of the armour, the infantry was going in. In the vanguard, two sections up, one back, was 4 Platoon. Hefting a heavy Bren gun, Mankelow was just behind Lawrence as the lieutenant led his men up the slope. 'It was, "Here we go", and it was up the hill, keeping your eyes ahead and to the sides, make sure your mates are OK, NCOs reassuring you,' Mankelow said. The angle steepened. The platoon scrambled. They took the first ridge without opposition – it proved to be a false crest. They were, by Mankelow's reckoning, about halfway to the true summit when it started.

Willoughby was watching from below at the precise moment battle was joined. 'At once, the whole of the hill came alive with machine gun, rifle and what I guessed to be anti-tank rifles, for they gave a sharper crack and a bright white muzzle flash,' Willoughby noted. 'It was an impressive sight.'[15]

Mankelow registered shouting and a crackle of firing – then spotted a volley of grenades spinning towards him. 'I was wondering when these grenades were going to explode,' he said. 'But NCOs were shouting, "Keep going! Get under them!"' Diehards dashed upward, grenades detonated with thumps, bullets whip-lashed overhead. Mankelow was inspired by the silhouette of Lawrence leading through the smoke. 'You think, "He is a big tall bloke; they have not hit him; so why me?"' He pressed upward.

The reassurance proved momentary. Firing broke out behind Mankelow's section. North Koreans in spider holes, bypassed by the advance, were shooting. 'You think, "I hope someone will take care of him!"' he said, but maintained eyes forward. His Bren hammered against his shoulder and his No. 2 clicked on fresh magazines as he laid down fire. Some was suppressive: 'The thing was to fire back, to keep their heads down.' Some was direct: 'It was fairly heavily wooded, you just saw a bit of movement,' he said. 'If it shot back, you shot again.'

Gunfire. Shouted commands. Flying dust. Flickering gun-sight silhouettes of enemy among the dwarf pines. Suddenly, Mankelow and his section were on top of the North Koreans, 10–15 feet from their trenches: 'It got up-close and personal, not hand-to-hand but really close – we were at point-blank range – we fired, they fired – some got up and ran, they just melted away, disappeared – everything was going pretty fast.'

It took Mankelow some moments to realise his platoon, in the open, had carried the summit of 'Plum Pudding'. Lawrence's men had advanced so far, so fast, that successive platoons had not passed through: The platoon had taken B Company's entire objective.* They had been aided by the NKPA defensive layout: Their trenches were covering the road, so most were on the left of the feature, but Lawrence had attacked from the right.[16]

A single tree crowned the summit. NCOs dashed around,

---

* Lawrence won the Military Cross for the attack. 'It was his calmness that I remember,' said Mankelow. 'He would stand up and walk among you, you are lying down and there is this tall chap – very reassuring. He was brilliant.' Recounting the action sixty years later, Mankelow was moved to tears at the memory of his platoon commander's leadership.

positioning men, for the ideal moment for a counterattack is when attackers are uncoordinated. 'They spread us around and said, "Fire if you see anything!"' Mankelow recalled. No counterattack came. As their adrenalin dissipated and their tunnel vision broadened, Mankelow and his mates had leisure to look around. A sudden rip of firing below. A stretcher party heading for the hill had been ambushed by enemy in a monsoon ditch; two Diehards were killed. The North Koreans were below 4 Platoon's sights: They fired down.[17] The ambush party was wiped out. More stretcher-bearers arrived. Casualties were evacuated. An odd normalcy settled. Platoon survivors broke out rations and began eating. It was 09:00.

Twelve enemy lay stiffening on the position. Lawrence's platoon had lost three killed, three wounded. Among the former, Mankelow was struck to see the body of Teddy West: He had turned nineteen the day the battalion landed in Pusan. Among the latter was Corporal Joe Pentony, hit by a burst through the torso. 'He'd tried to take out a machine gun nest and he'd paid the price,' said Corporal Bob Yerby of A Company, who saw him at the casualty evacuation point. 'He'd had morphine and was quite relaxed; he asked me for a cigarette, then they took him away.' Sergeant Paddy Redmond, recently returned from anti-guerilla operations, was appalled to see the severity of his wounds; he had been Pentony's best man at his wedding in England one year before, just prior to the battalion's departure for Hong Kong. Pentony would die in hospital in Japan. A sight that stayed with Yerby was that of some Americans, killed by mortars. 'They were lying there and their feet were bare and each had a tag on their big toe,' he recalled. 'For some reason, that shocked me.'

A burial party was assigned to dispose of the enemy dead in a ditch, but one corpse proved unusually large. 'We could not get one chap in, so one man tried to smash his head into it with a shovel,' said Barrett. Unknown to the Middlesex, a camouflaged enemy was watching these grisly proceedings. 'This anti-tank rifle fired at us,' Barrett recalled. 'He didn't like to see this chap knocking his head in with a shovel!'

From 'Plum Pudding', B Company had a grandstand view as D

Company went in against 'Middlesex Hill'. 'We were sitting and eating and could see figures moving up the hill, and because you had gone through it yourself, you knew exactly what they were going through,' said Mankelow. He felt oddly distant. 'It was like remote control, it was like watching a movie with our own people.'

B Company's business was finished. D Company's had just begun.

* * *

Willoughby's men had moved up to their start line, a ridge held by A Company, pre-dawn. With the ferry inoperable, they had received neither rations nor reserve ammunition. The looming objective, 'Middlesex Hill' looked like, the major thought, 'a long dumbbell with a knot at each end'. It was 325 metres high: 'The whole hill stared down at me – it seemed from a fearful height – and looked awful.' Like Lawrence, Willoughby decided on an indirect approach, a flanking attack. If he could reach the foot of the steepest part of the hill on the right, his men would be in 'dead ground' – i.e. ground invisible, due to the angle of the slopes, from the top. They would scale the shoulder and site Brens on the right-hand knob to cover an assault along the ridge that would roll up the position and clear the left-hand knob. Everything depended upon making the dead ground. Mortar smoke would screen D Company as it dashed across some 800 metres of open ground in full view of the enemy.

The time was now around 8:00. Lawrence's men were winning 'Plum Pudding'. Willoughby's radio crackled: It was Man giving the command to attack. 'We're off now!' Willoughby yelled. 'Fix bayonets!' roared the lead platoon commander. 'Look the business!' As his company broke cover, Willoughby pressed the radio mike to his ear, ready to call in mortar smoke as soon as the enemy fired. Then Man came over the net, urgently, ordering an immediate halt. Willoughby was 'in two minds' to disregard this – he wanted to make the cover of the dead ground – when a barrage of 155 millimetre artillery blasted up geysers of earth directly on his line of advance.[18]

Man, attempting to direct the battle from his CP, seethed. 'The only people who had shells were the Americans, and I had the greatest difficulty in discovering who was doing it,' he said. The reconnaissance company eventually made contact with the artillery unit; its fire was directed by a spotter plane that was unaware of the British operation. 24th Division's staff work, it seemed, was sloppy. A long radio argument ensued while D Company lay exposed in front of their objective. Man overheard the discussion: The barrage could, 'on no account be stopped as a United States Reconnaissance Company was held up!' This was too much. Man grabbed the microphone, identified himself and explained 'with considerable restraint' that the hill in question was being attacked by his troops, who were assisting the reconnaissance company in question; moreover the fire was endangering British soldiers' lives. Man's message was assented to with 'a rather subdued "Roger"'.[19]

D Company's attack had been stalled, but with the artillery sorted out, there was now gun support on call – though arrangements were *ad hoc*. Willoughby directed the fire of the US medium regiment by radioing Man at his CP; Man then passed the orders by telephone to the US reconnaissance company commander; he ran across to one of his tanks, who signalled back to the observation plane; the aircraft conveyed the message to the actual guns. 'It worked quite well after a time,' Willoughby said.[20]

The barrage rolled up the hillside, erupting in clouds of earth and smoke ahead of the company. The assault recommenced. Willoughby's men made the dead ground, and began scrambling up the right shoulder. 'Hill? More like a blooming mountain,' said Frank Whitehouse. 'The tin hats went – they just got in the way – where we were it was like the side of a house, we climbed with rifles slung.' So far, so good. The lead platoon crested the rise, but as it set foot on the ridge, it was swept with automatic fire. Second Lieutenant Geoffrey White was killed instantly; his sergeant, a corporal and another man were all hit; the platoon radio ceased transmission.[21] Willoughby ordered Sergeant Paddy Bermingham to grab all spare ammunition available, go forward and sort out the platoon. Bermingham and a corporal, heavily loaded, staggered upwards and made contact. After checking that White was, indeed dead, they repositioned the platoon's Brens and radio, which had been screened by rocks.[22]

With D Company now holding just a toehold on the right of the hill, the situation was precarious. The ridge, D Company could now see, was a 200-yard long 'dog leg' under complete enfilade from enemy dug in, slightly lower down, on the hill's reverse slope. 'The smallest movement from us drew machine gun fire in long bursts, and every time I peered over the top, I was nearly blinded by stone splinters,' noted Willoughby, whose command problems were compounded: His signaller had collapsed with exhaustion. The prospect of a charge along the ridge was 'most uninviting' the big major thought. Man dispatched reinforcements; A Company began climbing the hill. But additional numbers did not solve the problem. Pondering this, Willoughby was unexpectedly joined on the ridge by an American FOO. 'He took in the situation at once and said, "Leave it to me,"' Willoughby recalled. The newcomer delivered terse coordinates over his radio.[23]

The US gunner was concerned that his battery, already firing on 'Upper Registry' would not clear the ridge but the mission was called in anyway.[24] Distant thunder – a tremendous force rushing overhead – then the whole length of the enemy position on the rear slope disappeared under thick black smoke. Dead on. Willoughby watched 'in awe and some caution, because even at 200 yards, a lot of stuff comes back'. The barrage lifted. 'I think that should do,' the American told Willoughby.[25]

A platoon each of A and D Company charged ahead, their objective the enemy-held outcrop at the far end. 'Away they went with fixed bayonets,' wrote Willoughby. 'They swept over the outcrop, kept straight on and in no time I could see them thrashing around in the enemy position, but no return fire.'[26] The ridge was taken. Three Maxim heavy machine guns, shielded and wheeled, were captured; approximately forty enemy dead lay scattered around.[27] Some were in a gruesome state. 'They had had a fire, and a North Korean who had been hit was lying in the fire,' said Corporal Harry Spicer. 'His rifle ammunition was going off and bits of him were blowing up, blood was flying up.'

Yet there were still more enemy. Willoughby moved forward to the left outcrop, where he found himself, 'looking down about 150 yards on another ridge below, manned for almost its whole length by North Korean soldiers staring up at us from their now hopelessly exposed position. One, presumably an officer, appeared to be looking me straight in the eye. Both sides seemed equally surprised.' This was the North Korean entrenchment covering the Songju road. A number of Diehards were standing around looking astonished, except for one corporal who engaged in a rifle duel with an enemy below.[28] Other men joined in; the enemy replied. 'We were looking slightly down on them, I was No 2 on a Bren, we were firing and all of a sudden, the Bren jumped out of my mate's hand – the flash eliminator had been ripped off!' said Whitehouse. 'We changed the barrel and continued firing.' Whitehouse could see the effect of his fire: Dust was churning up among the enemy trenches. Facing well-equipped, motivated troops, a recent briefing flashed through Willoughby's mind: 'We had been assured that the enemy were a motley mix of weary units from various formations . . . from our position they were anything but a rabble, from the glint of their steel helmets to dark uniforms and equipment.'[29]

The American FOO arrived again. 'Again, there was the sound of the almighty overhead, a storm of black smoke, and when it cleared there was no sign of anyone,' Willoughby wrote. 'It was a remarkable feat of gunnery for the target area was at right angles to the earlier shoot and it was not a simple question of lifting a few hundred yards and shifting right by a small angle, yet the first time, the whole length of the target was engaged. He was an exceptional character whose competence impressed me deeply.'[30]

With the last North Korean position obliterated, a platoon went down for the grisly task of checking bodies. The Diehards were as suspicious of enemy casualties as the Argylls had been. 'Someone shouted, "One here alive!" and then there was a shot,' said Whitehouse. 'Major Willoughby did not agree with that at all, but we had heard stories from Americans – they painted a terrible picture of the enemy.'

By a mixture of fire – the US bombardment had been critical – and manoeuvre – the Diehard's approach up the steepest part of the hill had taken them into the rump rather than the teeth of the enemy position – 'Middlesex Hill' had been captured. The North Korean reaction was not long in coming.

At approximately 15:00 hours, enemy riposted against A Company deployed along the ridge. 'We saw chaps coming down behind us,' said the Major Dennis Rendell. 'We got quite a lot of those.' Rendell radioed battalion mortars and as the North Koreans advanced up gullies toward him, the ex-paratrooper directed bombs in, right on top of them. 'They had a marvellous shoot,' he said. 'You saw bodies coming up when the bombs hit – very satisfying!' The counterattack was driven off.

Evening fell. D Company was almost out of ammo, and had had neither water nor food for thirty-six hours. Willoughby radioed Man twice. 'I appreciate your difficulties – out, goddamn it!' the testy CO replied. But men arrived with jerry cans of water. After his parched men had been re-hydrated, Willoughby urged them to dig: 'Dig for your lives depend on it!'[31]

Embedded in the rocky dust, A and D Companies settled in for a tense night. At around 02:00, thunderous crashes and white flashes impacted along the position. Heavy mortars: 120mm. Spicer was jolted. 'We'd thought, "Thank goodness that's over," then it was all on again,' he said. 'I stayed in the bottom of trench – you feel the ground shaking.' The fire lifted. It had been a short but violent barrage, 'a fiendish experience,' Willoughby thought as he looked out. All equipment above ground had been shattered.[32]

There was one casualty: Private Sharpe, one of the tallest men in the company. Bermingham went to check him. It was so dark that the sergeant could not see the extent of his wounds, but knowing how shallow the man's trench had been, guessed where he had been hit, and began feeling his head. Bermingham's probing hand made contact with 'a large area of jagged bones'; Sharpe's head had been over the parapet when the mortars landed, and shrapnel had carried away a chunk of skull. He was buried on the position.[33]

In a final attempt to dislodge the Middlesex, the enemy launched a pre-dawn attack on the 23 September.[34] In the gloom, the force advanced up toward the section of ridge held by A Company. Their movement was spotted almost immediately.

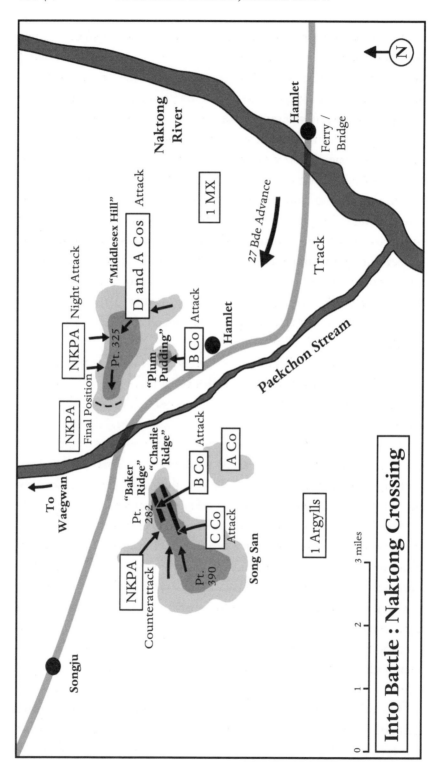

Into Battle : Naktong Crossing

'Don't ask me who fired first; it might have been us,' said James Beverley, the Cockney who had earlier thought Korea's hills looked like mountains. 'There is fear to start with, then the adrenaline kicks in and you are more interested in firing than anything else.' For Yerby, the Palestine veteran, fire orders are redundant: 'There is none of this, "Enemy in front", it was, "Pick your targets! Fire!" I don't think anyone needed any encouragement,' he said. 'You were firing at silhouettes coming up the hillside; you shot at one, and if he went down, you shot at another. Everybody had been on the ranges in Hong Kong – the firepower was hectic.' As a release of tension, rapid fire proved infectious: Along the ridge, soldiers worked bolts, squeezed triggers, braced for recoil, fired again. 'The .303 frightens you, it's got a kick like a mule, they say it can break your collarbone,' said Beverly. 'But you get used to it, you hold it in tight to the shoulder.' Some soldiers, in action, cower in cover, declining to fire, but the Middlesex had been a machine gun battalion in the Second World War, and that heritage was rubbing off; the furious shooting rate obviated the old British Army adage of 'one bullet, one body'. 'I put 150 rounds through that rifle,' Beverly said. 'Just don't ask me what I was shooting at!'

The enemy, decimated, had barely got off their start line. 'We realised then, we were in a war,' said Yerby, who had experienced nothing so intense in the Middle East. 'Up to then it had not dawned; this was our first involvement.'

The battle for 'Middlesex Hill' was over: it had cost five killed, seven wounded (one mortally).[35] The Diehards had successfully assaulted into the teeth of an entrenched position held by superior numbers, then held against counterattacks. Bermingham was ordered to check enemy cadavers on the lower slopes: The sergeant counted 253.[36] All were found to be carrying white civilian clothing – enabling them to blend in with the civilian population. The battalion's booty included the Maxim machine guns, as well as LMGs and a sniper rifle.[37]

The aftermath had a shock in store for Whitehouse. The private gasped when he heard the identity of the last man killed on 'Middlesex Hill'. Sharpe had been the soldier who had woken the barracks with his screaming the night before the brigade's departure from Hong Kong; his nightmare, Whitehouse realised, had been a premonition.

Secure on their objectives, the Diehards were perfectly positioned to watch the Argylls repeat their feat as they assaulted the hills on the western side of the Songju road. The Highlanders were advancing into what remains perhaps the most hellish combat space entered by British infantry since the Second World War.

* * *

Like the Middlesex, the Argyll's day on 21 September had begun pleasantly enough. After trucking off their defensive positions on the Naktong, the mortar platoon assembled in an orchard. 'The platoon was more curious in the orchard girls than in the battle, they were all topless and all young, picking these apples!' said Jake Mutch, the Stirling lad who had joined the Army after barely taking a train back home; in rural Korea, breasts exposed by the traditional short blouse were common. 'Soldiers were all whistling and yelling in Glasgow accents, but the girls just smiled and threw these apples – lovely apples which we stuck in our ammo pouches.'

Other units were exposed to grimmer sights, as the battle elsewhere along the front had hit serious resistance. Second Lieutenant James Stirling was shocked to see heaped trucks driving by. 'These hordes of American wounded were coming back down the road – it was not at all reassuring for a 19-year-old,' he said. Previously, the fair-skinned subaltern had only had sunburn to fear; now, with battle looming, things were getting serious: 'I was terrified I would be frightened and show it,' he said.

'The Bastard' was in full flow: Shelling was getting heavier and more accurate. Reggie Jeffes, the Brigade REME officer, was moving along the riverbank to check the ferry when, there was 'a hell of a bump right behind me, I was knocked on my face and there was a great burning sensation in the middle of my back. I thought, "My God, I have been hit!" I lay there quietly and the pain went. I had heard that if you are very seriously hurt, you won't feel anything, so I thought, "Ahhh, this is terrible."' Jeffes twitched each leg; both seemed to be working. Reaching cautiously back, he discovered a tiny shell fragment, 'about an eighth of an inch' in the pleat at the back of his uniform. It had not penetrated his skin, but, being red hot, had given him a minor scorch.

Relieved, he returned to Brigade HQ, and was drinking a mug of tea when another shell came in. The HQ was under camouflage nets, but the SPG had spotted the sun catching the windscreen of a vehicle. Jeffes and others dived into a foxhole as the shell detonated. A signaller had not moved fast enough: Shrapnel ripped through his abdomen and out through his back, taking his stomach with it, killing him outright. 'I was sick because I suddenly realised that could have been me,' said Jeffes.

With the Middlesex across, the Argylls advanced on the river. The scene was a battle portrait. 'We're ready to go, we're gonna cross the river, in big formation, well spread out, all heading for this river,' said Henry 'Chick' Cochrane. Appropriate accompaniment was on hand. 'Being Highlanders, we played the pipes as we were attacking.'

But crossing after the Middlesex, the Argylls' journey would prove dicier; the SPGs dug in outside Songju, had zeroed in.[38] Shells bracketed the bridge. Major David Wilson found the crossing 'a most unpleasant way to run the gauntlet'.[39] Stirling was showered with water and lost his tin hat, but crossed unscathed. 'It was both exciting and frightening,' said Lieutenant Sandy Boswell, the intelligence officer.

Not all men were lucky. Mutch was carrying a 36-pound mortar base plate on a Korean A-frame, a well designed, wood-and-rope peasant carrying rack, similar to an external-frame rucksack. He was mid-stream when a tremendous light flashed at his feet – Mutch felt a force like a kick in the stomach – he went down – a man behind moved to help – 'Leave him!' roared Captain Robin Fairrie, 'Get off the bridge!' – Mutch felt someone grab him by his belt – he was dragged, bumping, across. His mate, Adam MacKenzie, had ignored Fairrie's order and hauled Mutch to the far shore. There, MacKenzie dropped him in the cover of the riverbank. Momentum could not be interrupted for a single casualty.

A shell had detonated just feet in front of Mutch. Remarkably it had not severed the rickety bridge, but a slice of hot shrapnel had plunged, like a bullet, deep into Mutch's abdomen. 'At first it hurt,' he said. 'Then there was no pain at all.' Numbness signals a serious wound: Pain receptors shut down as the nervous system floods with endorphins. Mutch could see blood leaking down his uniform, feel it soaking him. Alone, he lay on the Naktong bank. A memory of his uncle – with whom he shared the same name – flickered through his mind. The uncle had been killed at Dunkirk. 'I thought, "This could be it: There's nobody here,"' he recalled.

Then, voices: 'Alright Jake, we'll look after you!' He looked up. Two orderlies had arrived, to stretcher him back over the bridge. Shelling continued. 'I thought, "Another bloody bomb!"' Mutch said, but the party passed unscathed. On the west bank, he lost consciousness. He came to briefly in the Middlesex RAP where his documents were stamped, 'Jake Mutch, Argyll and Middlesex Highlanders'. When he awoke, he was in hospital in Japan.

The rest of the platoon had got across, to a small unit of American engineers on the far bank. Incoming – mortars and SPGs – continued. 'I remember jumping over these two or three slit trenches with Americans in, they were looking at us and calling us a mad lot because they were mortaring,' said Cochrane. However, Cochrane, and his mates, mortar men themselves, were counting intervals. 'You could more or less count the seconds when one is going to drop here, one there.' A brief incident fortified morale, when an American sapper officer told his men, 'Stand up and watch the best little army in the world come through,' recalled Roy Vincent, another mortar man. 'It made us feel good,' Vincent said.

With his Jocks over the Naktong, Neilson made his pre-battle appreciation. His objectives were similar to Man's: A saddle-shaped hill, the two high points on it linked by a ridge: Points 390 and Point 282. In front of the big feature squatted a smaller hill, Hill 148. Wilson's A Company was tasked to seize this preliminary objective, securing start lines for the attack on the main feature.

Pre-attack, Wilson fell into conversation with an American master sergeant of the Reconnaissance Company, commanding five

Sherman tanks. The major's customary charm worked: The NCO agreed to support the Jocks' attack. Wilson lent him a company radio for communication and at 16:00, led his platoons as they spread out and began striding toward Point 148. They crossed Paekchon Stream, a tributary of the Naktong running adjacent to the Songju road – it was only waist deep – then the road itself.

Under fire from the tanks, and watching the Highlanders' inexorable approach, the small party of North Koreans on the hill decamped. A Company took Hill 148 without opposition and dug in. It was now 17:30.[40] With Willoughby's company facing such significant resistance on 'Middlesex Hill' Brigadier Coad – showing the prudence that, later in the campaign, his men would be so grateful for – did not want the Argylls embroiled in a fight that could drag on into darkness. He ordered Neilson to stand down his assault until dawn. [41]

The battalion prepared for battle. Beside the stream, Dr Douglas Haldane established his RAP: a makeshift shelter with ponchos and some hessian covering usually used to screen field toilets, with the medical pannier laid out. Briefings were delivered to the assault troops. B and C Companies, who would attack at dawn, took a good look at their objectives before night fell.

After it did, there was a minor drama. Stirling and fellow subaltern Jock Edington, were ordered to recce the start line, a dry riverbed forward of the lying-up area. The two officers did do –'one dry ditch looked very much like another,' Stirling reckoned – then headed back. Approaching they heard a sharp click-clack: A rifle bolt being locked. 'Password!' a Scottish voice barked. Neither officer could recall it. Edington, in front, froze; Stirling thought it sensible to take cover behind. 'What's the bloody password?' Edington hissed over his shoulder, then spotting Stirling's prudent position, added, 'What the bloody hell are you doing down there?' The sentry heard it all. 'Come in Mr Edington,' he said. 'I know who it is!' The two officers proceeded into the perimeter.

Jocks rolled up in ponchos and blankets. Orders were to make no noise; no cigarettes were to be lit. 'We were highly trained and whatever the situation was going to be up there, we were prepared to accept it,' said Harry Young, the corporal who had taken part in the Buchanan patrol. 'But I'm not sure if I slept that night.' Artillery thundered in the distance, but otherwise it was a quiet night.[42] For many Argylls, their last.

* * *

At 04:45, Neilson established his Command Post, or CP, on Point 148 with A Company. From here, he would direct the battle. Men who had managed to sleep were quietly woken. At 05:15, the Highlanders jumped off. In the grey darkness, long skirmish lines of men advanced in silence, in the classic infantry assault: Dawn attack.

Major Alastair Gordon-Ingram's B Company reached the foot of the hill without incident and began the ascent. Jocks, slung over with canvas bandoleers and pouches stuffed with Bren magazines, found it hard going through shale, boulders, dwarf pines. Lance Corporal Joseph Fairhurst was on point. 'We got going, climbing up through all these bushes, I don't know how the heck anybody didn't hear us,' he said.

The leading platoon broke skyline. This proved a false crest, a ridge that ran parallel to the main ridge, 30–40 yards further up. More interestingly, just a few yards distant sat some fifty North Koreans, cross-legged, calmly eating rice out of baskets. Corporal Richard Peet, in Fairhurst's platoon, was staggered. Each side, equally shocked, stared at the other. A moment's pause. Peet's platoon sergeant, Paddy O'Sullivan, yelled, 'Up and at 'em!' Jocks charged. 'We ran over the top and all hell broke loose,' recalled Fairhurst. O'Sullivan fell almost immediately, shot in the groin. 'He went down and then there is me running up with the chaps and all of sudden I hear a brrrrppp – it felt like someone had kicked me straight in the stomach,' said Fairhurst. 'A fellow behind a bush had fired a burp gun on me. I fell down, tried to get up, my legs would not move so I just lay there.' Peet ran over. 'Good God lad, how are you?' he spluttered. Peet and another corporal, 'Big Bob' Sweeney, dragged Fairhurst to a tree, stuck a cigarette between his lips and asked him the location of the burp gunner. Fairhurst indicated, 'and Sweeney led 'em all forward, charging with bayonets'.

Some enemy had returned fire, but most, breakfasting and without arms close at hand, were gunned down. The charge continued across the saddle and up to the far ridge, where a few enemy survivors had managed to scramble, and were throwing grenades, Peet recalled. Then the Argylls were at the top. The CSM arrived and ordered men to dig in and prepare for counterattack. B Company had lost ten men killed or wounded in the skirmish, including two lieutenants and one sergeant. Fifteen North Koreans lay dead.[43] But one position had been bypassed. In a short, sharp engagement, this was taken out by Second Lieutenant David Buchanan's platoon. All of B Company was established on the top ridge by 06:18.[44]

Meanwhile, Major Jim Gillies' C Company had been advancing with two platoons up, one back. Corporal Harry Young's platoon was on the left flank of the battalion. Closing on the hill, tank fire started to prep the position ahead of the advance. Gravel and stone showered on Young's men. They continued climbing. 'We came over the top, we took the feature, we did not see anybody,' he said. C Company had taken their objective without even encountering the enemy. They were in position at 06:30.[45] The company started to dig in. Stirling had been positioned by his company commander to cover the rear, slightly down-slope from the two roughly parallel ridges. The ground was too hard to penetrate, so Stirling's men began constructing sangars, or stone parapets.

So far, so good. The Jocks had gone firm on and around Point 282 with minimal losses. B Company was on the right, holding the higher ridge, 'Baker Ridge'. C Company was on the left, holding the lower ridge, 'Charlie Ridge'. But the knots of soldiers strung out along the granite now realised they were overlooked by a higher position, Point 390,* some 1,500 yards east of Point 282, connected by a saddle and still occupied by enemy. Neilson had hoped that C Company would exploit forward fast and take that, but they were disorganised.[46] Both companies had become entangled in the advance; redeployment would take time to sort out.

The NKPA, seeing enemy below them, beat the Argylls to the

*In some accounts, Point 388.

punch. Putting their height advantage to effect, they began firing down with machine guns and mortars. While mortar detonations kept the Highlanders' heads down, enemy began infiltrating from the high ground, using the cover of the scrub which coated the hillside to close with the Argylls' and open fire with burp guns. A series of vicious, close-range firefights broke out. The most exposed platoon, on the left and so closest to Point 390, was Second Lieutenant Jock Edington's. Edington and his platoon sergeant were both hit by gunfire, just metres away from Young. Unwounded men dragged the injured back.

Stirling and his platoon, holding the reverse slope, were not yet in the action but were seeing the results. A shirtless sergeant stumbled past the subaltern, blood leaking from seven holes stitched across his upper body. Stirling was appalled, thinking he had taken a full burst. In fact, a single high-velocity bullet had entered one arm, continued through, torn diagonally through one pectoral muscle, out, in through the next, out again, and finally lodged in his far arm. Stirling's friend Edingon arrived; he had been shot in the leg. 'He was hit in the femoral artery so I put a tourniquet on him,' Stirling said. Then he remembered a lecture by the MO who had said that it had to be constantly loosened or he would lose the leg. Stirling tried that – blood gushed. Realising that his friend needed medical evacuation, it struck him, for the first time, how difficult it would be to get wounded down 900 feet of steep-sided hill, much of which was shale: Four men would be required for each stretcher, or ground-sheet. Edington, bleeding out, lost consciousness.

Young, in Edington's platoon, had remained in position, lying low and returning fire against infiltrators. Under sensory overload – 'It's very confusing, so much is happening' – he did not realise his platoon's plunging numbers. In a lull, he looked back to find, to his amazement, that his thirty-strong unit had been reduced by casualties and those evacuating them, to just two men. It was now around 10:45.[47] Young and the other survivor, Pete Martin, fell back on the other two C Company platoons, further up the ridge. The Argyll perimeter was being compressed. Ammunition was dwindling.

Down below, the Argylls' 3-inch mortar platoon was duelling.

'We were mortared by a bigger weapon than a 3-inch and started looking for him,' said Roy Vincent. 'When you are looking for a mortar, you shift your aim and try and find him in different places.' Robert Searle was sent off to get some signalling equipment. He returned, running at a crouch in the cover of a 5-foot high paddy dyke when he heard a shrieking. 'We knew it was mortars, they exploded all around us,' he said. 'The noise was tremendous.' Soil and dirt showered down. The duel continued. 'The enemy lobbed over bombs that knocked the heck out of the hill at the back of us,' said Vincent. 'The order would come to fire five rounds rapid, then jump into the slit trench and wait for him to have his turn!' Eventually, the invisible enemy ceased fire. The Argyll mortars had no idea if they had hit him.

The position of the Argylls on and around Point 282 was now more perilous than that faced by the Diehards' A and D Companies the previous day. They had been on the highest ground, so had line of sight into the enemy positions. For the Argylls, the situation was reversed: They were overlooked. Moreover, the Middlesex had enjoyed the support of US artillery. At 11:00, with the Argylls heavily engaged and their casualties mounting, 24th Infantry Division recalled the American FOO team from the battalion.[48]

It was an extraordinary decision. With North Koreans out-gunning Jocks with automatics, abandonment by artillery meant the loss of their key equaliser, as the tanks down below could not elevate their guns high enough to support the Argylls, nor did the battalion mortars have the elevation to hit Point 390. Gillies and Gordon-Ingram both radioed Neilson; Neilson contacted Coad.[49] 'A protest was made to 24th Divisional HQ and alternative support was promised,' Coad recalled. 'But nothing arrived.'[50] Jeffes, at HQ watched things deteriorate. 'The brigade commander was absolutely furious,' he said. Lacking firepower or reinforcements, Coad and Neilson were losing control of the battle. The Jocks on Point 282 were on their own.

* * *

North Korean counterattacks were gaining steam. B Company was now under pressure as heavy as that facing C Company, as enemy assaulted up the cover of a re-entrant. '4 Platoon and 5 Platoon were holding this gully and were holding these North Koreans, I am led to believe in battalion strength, attacking these two Argyll platoons,' said Peet. Peet himself was raked with machine gun fire from Point 390; he slid down onto the reverse slope for cover. 'You'd better get back up, or we'll be overwhelmed,' a wounded sergeant lying there told him. He crawled back up; another sergeant told him to get back down again: The whole area was in the gun's beaten zone.

By 11:45, the forward companies had sustained around 50 casualties, and had lost numbers of men evacuating the casualties down the hillside – a one-hour trip each way.[51] Neilson's CP, some 400 yards from the action, was under intense pressure to assist the fighting companies. 'There were screams for help going back down the line to us and to Brigade from the forward companies,' said Intelligence Officer Sandy Boswell, listening in on the net. 'Eventually, the only support we could get was an air strike.' Neilson ordered it in on Point 390.[52]

With the brigade lacking any radio link to the ground attack pilots, Peet, up on the hill, was ordered to help spread air recognition panels – brightly coloured silk sheets, three feet long by a foot wide – on the ground in the colours of the day, so ID-ing the Argyll position for the pilots. They were laid out in the form of St Andrew's Cross; one was orange, one was crimson. Then Peet crawled into cover and began sniping at movement. For some reason, the machine gun above had ceased fire.

Perhaps the enemy gunner had taken cover, for air arrived promptly on station at 12:15.[53] Those Argylls not shooting glanced up. Three Mustang fighter bombers droned overhead, banking and circling, getting eyes on the target. 'We thought at that minute that they were going to attack this gully where the North Korean Army were,' said Peet. 'I sat there watching this airplane drop this thing. I didn't know what it was.'

* * *

The first two Mustangs swooped low along the ridge, for the

optimum drop altitude of their weapons was approximately 25 feet above ground. Plastic canisters tumbled from their bellies. Each 100-gallon egg contained a brownish, sticky solution of naphthalene and palmitate, a saturated fatty acid. This solution had been developed at Harvard in 1942, but saw only limited use late in the Second World War. It was far more widely used in Korea: So effective was it that UNC aircraft would unload approximately 250,000 pounds per day. The viscous solution itself was an incendiary, designed to burn at higher temperatures – yet more slowly – than raw gasoline. It was also designed to stick to its target. It takes its name from the first syllables of its two key ingredients: napalm.[54]

Unlike conventional explosives that burst up and out, it is not possible to escape napalm by ducking underground. Being liquid, it runs down into trenches, cracks and crevasses. Whatever it touches, it adheres to, burning into vegetation, buildings, vehicles and people at a temperature of 800° C – eight times hotter than boiling water. Humans caught in such intense conflagrations become virtual fossils: In the Second World War, the heat generated by incendiaries baked and dehydrated the dead, turning humans into mummies, known in German as *bombenbrandschrumpfeichen*, or 'firebomb shrunken flesh'.[55] Those not completely drenched but splashed with liquid fire suffer agonising wounds: So hotly does napalm ignite that it generates fifth-degree burns, scorching through skin, fat, muscle and bone; survivors suffer keloids, un-erasable scars. Finally, the intense heat of its ignition deoxygenates air, generating massive amounts of carbon monoxide: Those victims at the centre of the blast who are not cooked end up killed by carbon monoxide poisoning.

Fire terrifies all animals and most humans with a deep, perhaps atavistic fear, for it is nature's primary agent of destruction; many representations of hell across unrelated cultures and religions feature a burning pit. The demonic aspect of napalm was recognised by reporters in Korea who saw its effect and who dubbed napalm 'hell bombs'.* This was the munition dropped on Song-san at just after 12:15 on 23 September.

---

* The US Armed Forces reportedly ceased use of napalm in 2001.

The Mustangs, however, did not drop their loads on the enemy weapons on Point 390, the infiltrators advancing through the scrub on the ridge against C Company, or on the gully up which the North Korean attackers were swarming. They delivered their ordnance squarely on top of the Argylls of B Company.

For onlookers, it was a nightmare. In echelon, Quartermaster Andrew Brown, watching the battle from afar, watched the air strike with satisfaction. 'We thought, "Ah, tremendous," it was just a sheet of flame,' he said. 'Little did we know it was our fellows. Later when we found out – oh, God . . .' 'We were cock-a-hoop when the Mustangs arrived,' said Adjutant John Slim. 'Then we heard the screams.'

The napalm burst with its characteristic roaring 'whooompf'. A jet black mushroom cloud, tinted with amber, writhed into the sky. Blast-furnace heat and a petroleum stink swept Point 282 as a wave of orange flame tore along the hilltop like lava and rivulets spewed over the sides of the ridge: This was 'friendly fire' at its worst. Highlanders caught in the inferno were plunged into hell on earth. Everything in the path of the chemical – trees, rocks, soldiers – flared up. Burning, figures writhed, staggered and fell into charred heaps.

For good measure, the Mustangs dived on Point 148 in a strafing run. Jocks tumbled into slit trenches as running lines of dust fountained up across the position. 'They killed one of my corporals,' said Second Lieutenant Owen Light. 'One or two Jocks were all for opening fire with Bren guns but it would have been pointless, so I put a stop to that.' Finally, the spotter aircraft droned over the Middlesex position waggling wings: 'Mission Accomplished'.[56] The air strike had taken mere minutes.

With the napalm strike coming after the withdrawal of artillery support, there was 'almost disbelief' at the CP. An American tank commander told mortar man Roy Vincent, 'This is the first time I am ashamed to be American.'

In the wake of the attack, shocked survivors – perhaps forty men – saw sights that would be indelibly seared into their memories. 'That is one day I will never forget, it did affect me, it has never gone out of my mind,' said Peet. 'It was terrible, to see Argylls running around on fire covered in petroleum jelly, terrible, there were lads lying everywhere burnt.' 'One officer, skinned alive, took 20 minutes to die.[57] Those men who had napalm sticking to them, burning into them, screamed terribly.'

'I remember standing with my mouth open with amazement when I realised what had happened,' said Stirling, who wondered, momentarily, if the Mustangs had been enemy aircraft. His position, on the rear slope, had saved him: 'The napalm was within 100 yards of me,' he said. 'But I was behind a huge rock.' Not all his men were so well covered. One soldier, a redhead, was burned across his backside by a stream of napalm that rolled down the hillside and over him while he lay prone. Agonised, the soldier ripped off his burning uniform. Stirling ordered the man away: his pale skin stood out – a perfect target on the drab hillside.

While the redhead was lightly burned; others were horribly disfigured, skin hanging off in strips. 'There was a young fellow and the skin on his face had come off like a surgical glove,' said Peet. 'He said to me, "Dickie is my face alright?"' Peet assented, though in truth, the injury was so bad he could not recognise who it was. He urged the boy to get out. 'I said, "Don't stay there lad, we can't hold these Koreans, they are overwhelming us, you'd better come with me." He said, "Alright."' Peet started downhill, but when he looked back the soldier had not moved: He had frozen into shock. Another smouldering Argyll was given a cigarette by a mate; when he removed the cigarette, the flesh of his lips came away with it.[58]

Were such a disaster to occur in a normal situation, it would force the halt of all everyday activity in the surrounding area, as all resources are focused exclusively on assisting the victims. This was no normal situation. The battle still hung in the balance. With the napalm burning out, enemy movement up to and along the ridgeline could re-commence at any moment. It was essential to regain Point 282, where two platoons of B Company at the top of the gully had been incinerated. But the position – and the nerve – of the Argylls on the summit now balanced on a knife edge. In truly desperate situations, even the best military units can collapse; if one man flees, it can trigger a stampede. What prevents this? Discipline, example, leadership. On the ridge below Point 282, the surviving Argylls were galvanised by a man whose name would become legendary in the regiment.

* * *

Major Kenny Muir, the Argylls' second-in-command, had, in the early hours of the battle been a spare cog, for unless his commanding officer becomes a casualty, a 2I/C has little to do. On his own initiative, Muir had rounded up a party of stretcher-bearers, given them extra ammunition to carry, and with Neilson's permission led them up the hill at around 09:00. There, he had taken *de facto* command of the two companies on the ridge – arranging ammunition distribution, deployments and casualty evacuation. Amid the air attack, while everyone else was trying to make himself as small as possible, Muir had stood, waving air recognition panels around his head.[59] Was Muir simply keen to get stuck in, or was there a more personal reason behind his action?

An Argyll officer who had seen Muir the night previously, recalled the major complaining bitterly to him about the CO and the RSM, and it was well known that Muir and Neilson did not get along.[60] By getting up onto the hill, he had placed himself in a key position – where he could lead more decisively than the CO or the brigade commander, both largely ineffective witnesses to the drama. But it was in the wake of the firestorm that he showed true mettle.

'Major Muir arrived and rounded us up,' said Peet. Stirling left the wounded, as he, too, was called up to where Muir, Gillies and Gordon-Ingram were regrouping about 30 yards down-ridge from Point 282. 'Gordon-Ingram and Muir said, "We have to get this high ground,"' Stirling said. 'There were about 30 left of two companies, they told us to grab any weapons we could find, we were going to do a charge down and up to the ridge B Company had been on.' 'Baker Ridge' overlooked the valley from which enemy assaults had surged up; the NKPA were expected to launch a final attack any minute. It was essential to beat him to it, to seize Point 282, the dominant height, before the North Koreans. Remarkably, given the furnace that had been upended over the hill, Point 282 was still held by a single Argyll, the wounded Private William Watt, who was shooting onto targets below.

The entire ridge was blackened and smoking, but fires were fizzling out. Abandoned weapons lay everywhere. Stirling grabbed a Bren in each hand. Others scooped up loose ammunition. Gillies and a small group on 'Charlie Ridge' opened covering fire as Muir, armed with a Sten, led fourteen Highlanders into the charge. From Hill 148, Wilson saw, through the smoke haze, the line of running men. He understood immediately what was underway: 'This was the age-old drill that had applied on the Northwest Frontier . . . you never left wounded behind.'[61]

Yelling, Muir's motley crew surged down from 'Charlie Ridge', across the saddle and up the slope to the parallel 'Baker Ridge', thumping down next to Private Watt on his lonely outpost. There was no enemy in the immediate vicinity. Presumably terrified by the Mustangs, the North Koreans had pulled back. Highlanders took prone positions and aimed weapons down the crags. They had beaten the NKPA to the summit – just.

'You could see where they were massing down below, a lot of figures moving around, forming up to attack,' said Stirling. Jocks opened fire on the troops approaching through the trees. Green tracers from North Korean assault weapons streaked up. Red tracers from the Argylls streaked down. The wave receded. 'They all went back when enough had got wounded,' said Stirling. 'Then they'd attack again.'

The subaltern could see every detail of his enemy: 'They all had burp guns and were in dirty white military-type shirts.' His Bren kicked, targets tumbled – 'they were 150 yards away, you could see the ones you fired at going down' – but he felt no remorse at the mass homicide he was committing: 'It was them or me.' In the thick of the fight, the greatest pre-battle concern of the young subaltern whose family boasted such formidable warriors was lifted: He felt no fear. 'I was pleased about that,' Stirling said. 'That was what I had been more frightened of than anything.'

Several North Korean thrusts were stalled; the enemy seemed around 400 strong.[62] Behind the screen of fourteen Jocks – as thin a red line as any in the regiment's history – wounded and dead were dragged away by stretcher parties of Argylls, aided by Middlesex volunteers who had spontaneously dashed across to assist. Ammunition was getting critical: even a five-round 'service burst' from a Bren was 'a luxury that could be ill-afforded,' noted Gordon-Ingram.[63]

By now it was approximately 14:00. The candle was burning low on Muir's little band.[64] Their constricted perimeter around Point 282 was a maelstrom, for North Koreans had advanced through cover; the Jock screen was under fire from three sides.[65] 'The North Koreans were overwhelming, we were running out of ammunition, it was getting drastic,' said Peet. Muir was a dynamo. Having emptied a Sten, he was firing a 2-inch mortar at minimum elevation. Oblivious to incoming crossfire, he was frequently kneeling or standing to encourage his men.[66]

Impotent spectators on Hill 148 radioed for a retreat. 'I think I was the last person to talk to Kenny Muir on the wireless,' said Wilson, snatching glimpses of the fighting through field glasses while fending off a probe that was now developing against A Company. 'I said, "There is nothing I can do to help you, for goodness sake get off!"'

Muir ignored the advice. It is impossible to say what the motivation behind his behaviour – behaviour that everyone who witnessed it agreed was extraordinary – was. Perhaps there was an urge to outperform the CO. Certainly, there was determination to hold off the North Koreans and save the wounded for Muir, like Wilson, had served on the Northwest Frontier. There may have been another, more distant factor. Scientists have long been baffled by the issue of battle altruism, but some believe that heroism – essentially, selflessness, the willingness to sacrifice oneself for the group – is hardwired into human genes. According to this theory, heroism was both by-product and reinforcement of the group's cohesiveness that made certain primitive tribes successful in war, thus ensuring 'survival of the fittest'.[67]

This, then, may have been the impulse behind Muir's last actions that day. Did the 38-year-old major, who had been an Argyll officer all his adult life, and whose father had commanded a battalion of the regiment before him, see his duty as being not just to those men around him – after all, he was not a member of B or C Companies – but to a wider tribe, the Argyll and Sutherland Highlanders? This seems feasible, for though the task of evacuating the wounded had been carried out, Muir was not finished. In defiance of all odds; deaf to all advice; animated by battle spirit; the major seemed determined to retain indefinitely the ground the Jocks had won at such cost. 'Neither the Gooks or the US Air Force will get the Argylls off this ridge!' he urged his Highlanders.

They were Kenny Muir's last words. A burst of machine-gun fire raked his thighs and torso – a terrible wound. Gordon-Ingram assumed command. By now, there were only ten men – some wounded – left on the ridge, and only one magazine each for their three Bren guns.[68] Further resistance was impossible. Gordon-Ingram ordered the retreat. His party joined Gillies' cover group – also ten strong – and tumbled down the hillside in bounds, covering each other. They were all that remained of the more than 200 soldiers who had assaulted the hill nine long hours earlier.

Muir, dragged off in a groundsheet, was dead before he reached the foot of the hill. Wounded remaining on the slope were scooped up in the withdrawal. 'I saw a young man with his knee cap blown off, so I got hold of the lads with me, we put him in a groundsheet and carried him down,' said Peet. 'Flies were landing on the raw flesh so I covered his knee up, and he kept saying, "Look, I can move my foot!" He did not know his whole kneecap had gone; it was the movement of the groundsheet he was being carried in.'

Stirling was among the last men coming down the hill when his left hand registered something like an electric shock: a burp gun bullet had passed right through. 'It was a very low velocity, small bullet,' he said. 'But there was quite a bit of blood and I had no bandages.' After the stinging zap, the pain subsided. Stirling continued to level ground, where Light, at the A Company position, greeted his friend. 'The dreaded Stirling came down the hill and I said, "How did you get on?" He said, "I've been shot through the hand!" I said, "Does it hurt?" He said, "Not really, but I'm starving," so I said, "My rations are over there." ' Stirling helped himself, then departed for the RAP.

With the last Argylls retreating from Point 282, the enemy, in plain view of the mortar platoon, was advancing around the foot of the hill, threatening A Company and attempting to cut off the escapees. The Vickers and mortars opened up, the latter firing at minimum range with minimum propellant. The wound radius of a 3-inch mortar bomb is around 100 yards; the Argylls were shooting inside 500 yards. 'You just got on with it, the Number Two was plonking bombs down the barrel,' said Adam MacKenzie, who had, the previous day, dragged the wounded Mutch off the bridge. 'Afterward, we thought, "How close was that!" The bombs exploded in puffs of smoke. Hundreds of little bursts of dust in a 100-yard radius marked the impact of their shrapnel into the ground.

Unusually – for mortars fire in a parabola over hills or other obstacles – the mortar men could see the effect of their fire on the enemy. Likewise, their bombs were being ejected at such short range, and on such low charges, that the enemy could plainly see the bombs plummeting towards them. 'We saw one North Korean trying to catch a bomb,' said MacKenzie. 'It was pure instinct that made him put his hands up.' The soldier was obliterated. The enemy probe was driven off; the remnants of B and C Companies regrouped at the foot of the hill as the wounded were taken to the RAP.

*　　*　　*

Haldane had been on alert to expect casualties when Neilson warned him that 'things were not going the way they should'. A number of gunshot victims from the earlier fighting had already arrived. When the burn victims started to come in, the RAP was inundated.

'I treated them with anything I could lay my hands on,' he said. In his hessian-lined shelter, he applied yellow antiseptic cream, gauze strips coated with petroleum jelly, pain killers and American-donated plasma – though getting a drip in was difficult. 'A first-degree burn gave you redness, second- and third- went through the skin – you blister first, and the skin peels – and further degrees burned through the tissue underneath and even bone,' he said. 'There was redness, blistering and peeling. Most of those burned black were left up the hill; most of those coming down were in a lot of pain.' As more wounded arrived, those who could walk were sent back, across the stream toward where they could get transport to take them across the river. 'My job was triaging and shipping them out,' Haldane said.

With the worst cases unable to walk, American casualty evacuation helicopters were landing nearby. Stirling and other walking wounded held down the RAP's hessian strips, to prevent dust from the rotors blowing into burn wounds. The helicopter – 'egg beater' in GI parlance – was a new and unfamiliar form of ambulance; stretcher pods tied to the skids. As they lifted off, some wounded, shocked and half conscious, thought they were ascending to heaven's gate.[69]

Haldane would treat around seventy men that day. 'I don't think I'd say it was traumatic, it was a busy medical day,' he said. 'But at the end, I felt deflated.' For his efforts, a number of Argyll officers felt 'Jock the Doc' deserved a decoration. 'He was a wonderful man,' said Slim. 'He was a GP, but ended up being a bloody good surgeon – he had to hack bits off.'

The first sign the Middlesex had of the casualties was when they saw a line of blackened men stumbling from the Argyll positions toward Paekchon Stream. 'I have never smelt burning flesh before, this horrible smell,' said Yerby. 'The guys were black like they had been down a coal mine.' Men of B Company, including Don Barrett, ran to assist the Jocks. Observing the charred men, an appalling realisation struck Barrett. 'We are like pork,' he said. 'We crack like pork.'

The ordeal of those wounded not helicopter-evacuated continued. The casualty evacuation chain led across Paekchon Stream, then down to and across the Naktong. It was a fraught journey. The stream was under observation by snipers firing anti-tank rifles; two jeeps were immobilised, bullets through their engine blocks.[70] With enemy artillery observers still overlooking the Naktong, the river crossing remained dangerous: Four Middlesex stretcher-bearers suffered a direct shell hit as they crossed the Naktong bridge, killing three.[71] The bridge was cut three times that night.[72]

Fairhurst, the gut-shot lance corporal, had a particularly

harrowing trip. After being injected with morphine and evacuated off the hill unconscious, he came round at the bottom. 'There were two Yanks and a jeep with a stretcher on it and we hightailed it down the road,' he said. When they reached the stream, shelling started. 'The Yanks got me off the stretcher, and dropped me straight in the water!' It was only waist deep. Fairhurst was taken to a dressing station, then lifted into an ambulance, where a drip was put in his arm. With another casualty in the rack above him, the ambulance jerked off. 'It was getting dark and we were going along this road, two black Americans driving, bumping up and down,' he recalled. 'All of a sudden there was one hell of a bang, the ambulance tipped over and everything went hazy.'

It was pitch black when he came to. The Argyll found himself lying outside; the other casualty was hanging upside down inside the wrecked ambulance, and the cab, with its drivers, was blown apart – whether from mine or shell burst, Fairhurst could not tell. He crawled into a monsoon ditch where he lay until headlights approached. He staggered up and waved. His next memory was of waking up in hospital in Osaka covered in tubes. 'You were very lucky,' an American nurse told him. He agreed.

Stirling, shot through the hand, had a less fraught trip to and through the long line of UNC hospitals. He walked down to the river, then was taken by truck to a railhead, and placed on a hospital train. In Pusan, he boarded a hospital ship, landed in Tokyo, and was transferred to Tokyo General Hospital. From there, British military authorities dispatched him to a hospital in Hong Kong, and finally, a hospital in Glasgow with a group of other men who had been wounded on Point 282. 'That was the end of my distinguished military career!' he said.*

---

*In Scotland, Stirling had one more duty to discharge: Visiting the parents of Neil Buchanan, MIA on the Naktong, and his cousin David Buchanan, KIA on Point 282. 'That was not an easy job,' he said. Neil's mother held out some hope that he was still alive; Neil's father took Stirling outside and asked him to speak frankly. Stirling told him that he did not believe there was a chance. Neil's body was later recovered by Sandy Boswell, a school friend of Neil's, who later returned to the ambush site with Harry Young. The two visited the spot of the patrol action and coaxed village elders to show them the burial site. Buchanan's body was identified by his sidearm lanyard and shoulder pips.

On the battlefield, silent Argylls dug in around A Company – the only cohesive company left. Light had a hungry night; preparing to cook that evening, he was furious to discover that Stirling had taken all his rations. B and C Companies' remnants were amalgamated under Gordon-Ingram. Night fell. US tanks fired on the hill. 'The noise was tremendous, when a tank shell goes over, there is a tremendous crack,' said Searle, with the Mortar Platoon. 'It was unnerving everyone . . . after what had gone on earlier in the day, we were not very confident in their shooting.' Officers counted heads. The butcher's bill for Point 282 totalled seventeen killed or missing, seventy-nine wounded.[73] Of the total casualties, sixty-one had been caused by the bombing.[74]

While the day's grim events were digested at the Battalion CP, one officer was going through personal hell. 'When the air strike went onto the companies, I thought, "Oh God, I have issued the wrong panels!"' said intelligence officer Boswell. 'It was not till much later the next day that I was able to check the records and see I was right. It was a huge anxiety.'

What nobody in 27th Brigade yet knew was that the UNC's offensive, which had started on 16 September, had broken enemy resistance on the Naktong front. The British attack had been the final blow. On 23 September – the same day the Argylls went into action – NKPA besieging the Pusan Perimeter had commenced a general retreat. If the attack had been delayed by one day, the hills, abandoned, could have been taken without a fight. 'I think the battalion was a bit shocked because of what had happened and because they were unable to hold the ground,' said Haldane. 'As it turned out, the Gooks disappeared during the night. It was an awful lot of effort for no return.'

* * *

On the evening of 23 September, Brigadier Coad drove to meet US 24th Infantry Division commander General John Church, to press for artillery support – the loss of guns had led to the air strike.

'Church was not very helpful, and merely said he had NO artillery to spare,' Coad recorded.[75] He had a more satisfactory chance meeting with General Walton Walker, the 8th Army commander. The following day, the US 68th Anti-Aircraft Artillery Battalion arrived. 'That I am sure was the work of General Walker,' Coad wrote.[76]

27th Brigade was subdued after its first battle. 'We sat in little groups, with our mates, we spoke about the ones who had been killed, sort of discussed it among ourselves, then we buried it,' said Private Ken Mankelow. 'We did this while having our mugs of tea, nothing morbid – just matter-of-fact.'

The assistance the Middlesex had extended in voluntarily evacuating Argyll casualties was gratefully acknowledged. 'From that moment the Argylls and the Middlesex became allied regiments,' said Lieutenant Colonel Andrew Man. 'We are honorary members of each others messes; English and Scottish regiments don't often have that sort of link.' 'They helped us Jocks,' said Corporal Harry Young. 'We were blood brothers.'

The quality of the enemy could now be realistically assessed. 'We were quite pleased for having got bloodied and not suffered very much,' said Shipster. 'Our wariness of the enemy from that point on, I think, became less pronounced.' Other men tempered their view of the enemy's professionalism with his brutality. 'War is interesting: You can both hate and admire the enemy,' said Slim. 'The North Koreans were very good infantry soldiers,' said Barrett, whose CSM told him that a couple of men had been found tied to trees, bayoneted. 'But it seemed unwise to put your hands up – very unwise.'

In the Argylls, three topics of conversation dominated: Lost friends, Kenny Muir and the USAF. 'I felt terrible, a lot of them lads were friends of mine who had joined the army with me, we had been together for quite a while,' said Corporal Richard Peet. 'Corporal Whittington, a great pal of mine, was burned to death. I saw his platoon get covered in napalm, and I could do nothing about it.'

Nobody had expected Muir to do what he did. 'It was an amazing performance by an individual who had been slightly reserved to that day,' said Boswell. 'Muir was always cheerful, a hell of a nice little fellow,' said Vincent. 'He was a cocky little Jock.' Some wondered if he had been too fiery. 'A major up the hill with Kenny said if Kenny had not been killed, they would all have been killed,' said Quartermaster Captain Andrew Brown. 'He would not have let them go.'

Opinion was divided over the air strike. 'It made [the battalion] hopping mad,' said Wilson. 'But we realised war is war and mistakes happen.' Certainly, the USAF provided tremendous tactical advantage when on target, but some members of Brigade HQ were less equivocal. When the US anti-aircraft unit provided by Walker arrived to support the brigade, it started to move into a position that had been shelled. 'We watched the Americans move into this location and we were so angry, we did not tell them,' said Jeffes. 'And of course they had headlights on and everything, and in due course these SP guns popped at them and of course the Americans sped off very quickly.'

The first major operation under American command had not been a happy one. Poor staff work had resulted in companies leaving positions on the Naktong, then being ordered back. The Middlesex had been unsupported by US armour in their initial advance; their second-phase attack was halted by US artillery fire. US artillery support had proven critical at 'Middlesex Hill', but the Argylls had their US guns withdrawn in mid-battle, then been bombed. The Middlesex's CO passed harsh judgment. 'The Americans were utterly awful!' Man said.

Still, Jeffes, the officer who had declined to warn the American unit about shelling, would soon see the USAF in a better light – and the mystery of the invisible SPGs would be solved. 'A day or so later, an Air Contact Team went up this hill by jeep to get better communications, the SP guns started firing at this jeep and the ACT chappie spotted the smoke and put in a napalm strike and took them out,' Jeffes recalled. 'They were in the side of this hill, they had dug a tunnel there and were hiding – they would drive out, fire and then go back in. They were very difficult to spot.'*

* * *

In the aftermath, Walker signalled Tokyo for an explanation about the air strike. Air Chief Marshal Cecil Bourchier, senior British liaison officer at MacArthur's HQ, communicated with Major General Earle Partridge, the CO of the US 5th Air Force, and flew in to speak to 27th Brigade on 25 September. He dispatched a report to Whitehall on the following day.

His findings uncovered three key errors. Firstly, the US ACT were not up front, so did not have eyes on the target. Secondly, the spotter aircraft's map had a different scale to that held by the ACT. Thirdly, the plane had radioed back that the correct air recognition panels were, indeed, being displayed, but the ACT officer – who had no eyes on the target – ordered the strike in, on the basis that the NKPA often copied UNC air recognition panels.[77]

Americans were contrite. Partridge subsequently relieved all USAF officers concerned, guilty and innocent.[78] On 25 September, the US Minister in London, Julius Holmes, sent a letter of apology to Prime Minister Clement Attlee, calling it 'a tragic mistake of identity by their United States air support'.[79] On 3 October, Colonel Charles Bicking, commanding the USAF's 93rd Bombardment Wing in California, sent a cheque for US$882.85, 'a voluntary and spontaneous contribution from the personnel of the Wing . . . it will indicate in small measure our regret, as it will show our deep feeling for our comrades-in-arms'.[80]

Bourchier attempted to suppress a press release about Point 282, but it was too late: The media had got hold of the tragedy.[81] Citing Reuters and AP, the *News of the World* on 24 September led with the incident, noting that artillery support had been withdrawn and air recognition panels set out; it also reported the fury of some

---

* The lessons learned in the Korean War are still applied by the NKPA today. One of its most feared threats is its massed, long-range artillery, dug into tunnels and ranged on Seoul.

Argylls. On 25 September, *The Bulletin* editorialised with some insight: 'The real lesson of the Korean tragedy is that when British forces are sent into battle they should be far better balanced in the matter of arms and equipment . . . it seems that in this case, the US planes were called in only because the Argylls could not obtain artillery support'.*

Though Bourchier's attempt to keep the story quiet failed and the friendly fire incident was reported, there was one issue on which Whitehall did, indeed, pull off a cover up – of a sort.

The first Victoria Cross of the Korean War was awarded, posthumously, to Major Kenneth Muir. His citation, published in the *London Gazette* on 5 January 1951, records his final words as: 'The Gooks will never drive the Argylls off this hill'. The 'Gooks' were the North Koreans; at this stage of the war, 'Gook' was an American-coined term applied to the enemy, rather than the racial pejorative for Asians it was soon to become. But his full quote – 'Neither the Gooks nor the US Air Force . . .' – was reproduced in Major Gordon-Ingram's detailed B Company after-action report, a copy of which was inserted into battalion and brigade war diaries. Given that Gordon-Ingram was alongside Muir in his final action, there is no reason to doubt his veracity. Why, then, were Muir's defiant – if bitter – last words truncated? 'That part about the Yanks was conveniently left out,' said Man. The conclusion is inescapable. Whitehall wished to minimise embarrassment to Washington.

The whitewashed quote of Kenny Muir, VC, has been reproduced in every published work since.

* * *

* Although Bourchier's findings were covered in Farrar-Hockley's official history of the Korean War, rumours of a cover-up still circulate. A two-page story by Angus Macleod in Scotland's *Sunday Mail,* on 21 January 1993, 'Death on Hill 282', stated: 'Troops were told to keep quiet, newspaper reports were censored and Britain's files have been stamped Top Secret until 2025'. In fact, troops were quoted in newspaper reports on the 24 and 25 September; the coverage looks uncensored; and this author failed to find any file regarding the incident in the National Archive stamped 'Top Secret until 2025'. The US side, however, appears reluctant to discuss the issue. The official US Army history, Appleman's *From the Naktong to the Yalu* fails to mention 27th Brigade's part in the Naktong Crossing offensive at all.

Reinforcements arrived with the brigade, not simply to replace casualties, but to bring the battalions – which had deployed under strength – to appropriate manning levels. A trickle had been arriving previously, but on 28 September, a draft of volunteers from Highland regiments joined the Argylls; on 1 October, a company from the Queen's Regiment, another London and Southeastern-recruited unit, reinforced the Middlesex.

Among incoming Jocks were two National Service subalterns, Alan Lauder from Dunfermline and Edward Cunningham from Edinburgh. The pair had flown PanAm from Hong Kong in Tokyo, landing pre-dawn. At the airport, unprepared movement officers told them to find their own way to the British Embassy and enquire there how to proceed to Korea. They did so, knocked on the door, and were politely invited in for a 07:00 breakfast. Three days later, the two flew out to 27th Brigade in a C-47 alongside Bourchier, where the two learned of the Point 282 tragedy, which Bourchier was off to investigate. Upon landing, they were picked up by Quartermaster Andrew Brown in a truck and headed for the Naktong crossing. They immediately came under shellfire. 'We took cover in a Korean house where there were some dead Americans, then had to get over the bridge before they could reload,' said Lauder. 'Exciting is the only word you could use for it at that age.' These events took place within thirty minutes of landing in Korea.

The two were welcomed by Neilson at Battalion HQ, then dispatched to their respective companies; Cunningham to Wilson's A, Lauder to Gillies' C. Cunningham – 'Ted' to the British, 'Red' to the Americans, on account of his ginger hair – was greeted by Wilson, whose charisma was immediately apparent. 'There was a degree of theatre about Wilson, he was a character!' he said. The company's talk was all of Muir. 'That's where the action was,' Wilson told Cunningham, pointing at Point 282. 'That's where Kenny Muir lost his life.' Arriving at his platoon position, Lauder was greeted in a manner appropriate. A man called Kerr shouted, 'Christ boys – another officer! Ye are the third one we have had in six weeks sir, ye'll nae last long!' Lauder was the only platoon commander in the decimated C Company.

Another A Company arrival was a short, slight private from Edinburgh, Eric Gurr. His was the kind of hard luck story common in the 1930s and '40s. English by birth, he had been brought up in Scottish orphanages and been drafted in 1944; the atom bombs bought the war to an end before he saw action. He entered the hotel business but found it was, 'long hours, low pay' so rejoined the army, 'for more low pay!' He had served with the Black Watch in Palestine, then, as a re-enlistee was sent East to reinforce the Argylls. After seven days of flying from the UK, he found himself in front of Wilson: 'A smashing guy, a good company commander.'

Ronald Yetman, a professional soldier from Richmond, Surrey had joined the Argylls because one of his mates had wanted to join a Scottish regiment. He volunteered for the Hong Kong draft. 'I was a soldier, I had been trained but had not experienced war, like all young men I was eager,' he said. A six-footer and a marksman with an LMG, he was made a Bren gunner in B Company.

Joining the Middlesex was Davenport native Corporal John Pluck, a volunteer who had been through the Army's junior leaders course – the top training ground for promising NCOs. Arriving at the battalion, he found the situation confused, but morale 'first rate', with much being made of Chris Lawrence. The first few days of active service he found 'just like training'.

* * *

Operations were ongoing. Reports came in of good progress by American units advancing north. On 25 September, the 27th Brigade War Diary reads: 'The Brigade is now to move up to Songju and take up positions to deny enemy movement to the North and East and protect the left flank of I Corps'.

Led by the trundling American Shermans, the Middlesex headed into the pass through the hills they had fought for. Signs of NKPA retreat were everywhere. 'Both sides of the road through the pass are littered with every variety of military equipment: mortars, medium machine guns, anti-tank guns and vehicles,' Willoughby noted. But enemy had maintained discipline. 'I was struck by the methodical way in which in every case a vital part had been removed and in many cases a booby trap had been set up. This was a disciplined retreat.'[82]

In their wake, the NKPA had sprinkled deadly gifts for the road-centric UNC. Brigade HQ was driving in convoy on the 26 September, when, 'all of a sudden, the 15 hundredweight truck with the Defence Platoon went up with an enormous bang,' said Jeffes. One – possibly two – linked mines had gone off under the truck. One man was killed; the rest, though blown into the air, survived. A pioneer sergeant, a mine expert, arrived. 'He said, "They lay them in threes," so people prodded around and found another mine.' The column continued, until another heavy vehicle, a Bedford truck, arrived. 'That went up – the front offside of the vehicle disappeared into the air,' Jeffes said. He radioed for his Scammel recovery vehicle, but first probed the ground with his own bayonet: he could not afford to lose the Scammel. There were no more mines.

Men laid sandbags on the floors of vehicles as bottom protection, but given that mines could blow a vehicle right off the road and scatter its metalwork over one hundred yards, such measures were, at best, damage limitation. And not all traps were on the road. A Diehard foot patrol entered one empty village to discover wires everywhere; the entire settlement was rigged as a giant booby trap.[83]

Songju was occupied without resistance. In the town square stood a battery of North Korean artillery. Each muzzle was peeled back like a banana – disabled with explosives. The crossroads town, it was discovered, had been a critical supply dump for the Naktong fighting, making its capture – it had been a secondary axis – more critical than originally thought. 'They had dumps in Songju, ammunition and so forth,' said Man. 'So we made quite a name for ourselves, we British.'

The town was also the first location in which the brigade would see, close up, the devastation of the war. 'Songju had paid a dreadful price for liberation by the UN. In black heaps of smouldering ruins, only the main road offers a recognisable feature,' wrote Willoughby. 'Sadly, a tattered banner is displayed to read, "Welcome UN Army". A smell of death pervades everything.'[84] A pathetic column of civilians cautiously re-entered the town, carrying maimed neighbours and relatives, hoping for treatment. Diehards treated twenty-five civilians who had been wounded after gathering a deadly harvest:

butterfly anti-personnel bombs dropped by the USAF. Many wounds had gone septic, and fingers were lost to gangrene.[85] The Middlesex used up all their medical supplies.

Julian Tunstall, the sensitive soldier who had so enjoyed the Naktong sunsets, saw one boy with a completely shattered leg: He didn't utter a murmer. 'Then, as so often later, I was to admire the courage and endurance of these people who were suffering such insane cruelty through no fault of their own,' Tunstall wrote.[86] Even Man, no wilting flower, was moved. 'Casualties among the civilians were quite awful,' he said. 'I've seen terrible wounds, all the skin burned off – living skeletons.'

Such scenes spurred reflection. 'It made you think quite deeply whether it was morally right to go in and decimate the country of a simple people who probably did not give a damn if they were communist or what, their main concern was just to get enough food,' said Boydell, who began to question the frequent use of the word 'liberated'. 'It crossed my mind that this is a funny sort of "liberation" because these people would perhaps have been better off without us.'

With Songju secure, the Middlesex fanned out through the countryside. 'There were numerous T34s burnt out along the roadside and SU74 self-propelled guns that had been dealt with likewise,' said Shipster. 'Stark symbols of the efficiency of American air attacks.' The Middlesex War Diary noted, however, that there were few small arms found, and the roads were also littered with epaulettes – presumably torn off to prevent identification.[87] Abandoned enemy positions were masterfully constructed, Willoughby discovered. Their slit trenches, 6 feet long, 2 feet wide and 4 feet deep were similar to the British, but were 'almost an art form' with all fresh soil carefully spread and perfectly concealed. 'No wonder we could see nothing on the river line,' he thought.[88]

Though the enemy main force had departed, unlucky stragglers abandoned by their comrades lingered. In one village, Willoughby encountered a POW under guard in a house. Wounded, with his knee festering with gangrene and covered in maggots, he was clearly in great pain. The major explained that he was English, part of the UN Forces, and promised medical treatment. This was translated by

Hur, the young interpreter. The translation over, the prisoner struggled up onto one elbow. Willoughby leaned in. The POW spat squarely in the major's face. 'This was my first face-to-face experience of communist indoctrination,' Willoughby wrote. 'It left me with considerable misgivings.' The prisoner had looked to be about thirteen.[89]

Reports of enemy were vague. In a hamlet Willoughby was using for a patrol base, civilians were questioned. 'The answer is invariably, "Yesterday many enemies came and they took away one ox" and arms are stretched up toward the hills. We have no way of telling whether this refers to the remnants of a defeated army, or local brigands, or folk tales to satisfy our curiosity,' the major wrote.[90]

They were strange days. Not only enemy, but many civilians had also fled and hidden. In one empty cottage, Corporal Frank Screeche-Powell, an Irishman in the Diehards, came across an ornate brass gramophone. He wound it up and put a record on; to his astonishment, it was Bing Crosby's 'Red Sails in the Sunset'. He left it: 'It wasn't mine to steal.' Despite the autumn sunshine, abandoned villages were eerie places. Patrolling through one, Mankelow entered a cottage. 'There was an old lady there, I spoke to her, then I noticed she had wire round her neck,' he said. 'She had killed herself – I got out, quick. Those things stick in your mind.'

Everywhere were little tragedies. Columns roaring up the rural tracks left minimal room for traditional transport. When a patrol of Middlesex halted at a small bridge, Shipster looked down. Below, in the dry river-bed, a bullock cart was overturned with a family sitting astride the shaft, weeping. 'I remember getting seven or eight soldiers to go down, give them what rations we had and help them mount the side of this culvert and get on this road,' he said. 'The sad thing was we could not help them any more – their bullock was dying.' Soldiers did what they could. Screeche-Powell took a sandbag full of rations to the traumatised occupants of a half-demolished house beside the road, showing them pictures of his own wife and child. 'Sadness took my heart, going through houses, empty except for a few childrens' playthings.'

Yet the war had receded northward. 'Another lovely day . . . the past few days belong to a dreamland as if we had always been at peace,' Willoughby recorded. 'This is a strange, fey country.'[91] Struck by the beauty of the landscape – villages nestling among paddies, streams winding between hills – he was losing interest in operations. 'The sun, the blueness of the skies and the golden glory of these fields among the mountains is suddenly so unbelievably beautiful,' he wrote. 'This is unexpectedly a Shangri-La where past days are forgotten.'[92]

Information trickled in. On 29 September, the brigade received notice that it was receiving a South Korean Presidential Unit Citation for 'outstanding and heroic performance of duty'.[93] There was also more weighty news – news both exciting and disturbing.

D Company had acquired a decent radio and the announcer was talking of heavy fighting in the capital. 'The commentary is given with such intensity, as to leave one breathless and chained to the set – can anything be left of Seoul?' Willoughby wondered. But Seoul was 140 miles to the northwest. What enemy could be there? 27th Brigade had understood that the entire NKPA had been besieging the Pusan Perimeter, while the UNC force 'must have been assembled while we were told we were about to be driven into the sea', Willoughby wrote. 'Not for the first time, I am left wondering.'[94]

In wartime, intelligence is disseminated on a need-to-know basis; most men learned of the wider strategic picture through news reports. While Walker's 8th Army, with 27th Brigade attached, had been in action on the Naktong, another UNC force, the eager D Company listeners crowding around their set learned, had launched an amphibious operation aimed at Seoul. They had landed at a place called Inchon.

Chapter Four
Turned Tide and New Allies

Whenever I prepare for a journey I prepare as though for death.
Should I never return, all is in order.
Katherine Mansfield

Morning, 13 September, the Yellow Sea.

Having just returned from his first active service operation, Corporal Raymond Todd, Royal Marines, was disgusted. A fleet marine who had been serving aboard HMS *Jamaica*, the County Durham native, like a lot of servicemen who had not seen combat in the Second World War felt himself 'almost a second-class citizen against those who had chestfuls of medals'. Given this, he had jumped at the chance when he heard a call for volunteers: A special raiding force was being raised from among fleet marines and Royal Navy personnel in the Far East. The force – fourteen strong – had been training in Japan under US Marine Corps auspices since mid-August. Commanded by Royal Marine Lieutenant Derek Pounds, its remit was coastal raids. 'Pounds Force's' first mission had been a beach reconnaissance near the town of Kunsan, 90 miles south of Inchon, the port on the Han River serving Seoul, on the night of 12 September.

It had been a farce.

The unit had embarked on the frigate HMS *Whitesand Bay* together with a company of US Army Raiders. Pounds Force would recce the south of the target beach, the Raider Company would take the north. The targets were separated by a promontory. Todd was suspicious of the US units: The heavily armed Americans, in company strength, were 'too many for a reconnaissance,' he thought.

Things went wrong from the start. As the blacked-out *Whitesand Bay* glided through the offshore islets – black silhouettes in the Yellow Sea night – men on deck could see lights flashing from island to island. Signals? Regardless, the operation was launched. Pounds Forces' inflatables hit a sandbar 150 metres offshore. After extricating themselves, they paddled silently ashore. Almost immediately, there came gunfire to their left: they could see flashes on the promontory. The Americans, it seemed, were already under fire. The British advanced inland when their radio hissed. With the operation compromised, Pounds Force was ordered to extract. They returned despondently to the frigate by 01:30.[1] Aboard, they found that nine of the Raiders were missing. The frigate's captain fretted: If his ship was caught inshore at daybreak, she would be a sitting duck, but he could not abandon the Americans. At 04:45, a light flashed from the pre-arranged emergency extraction point. Seven Raiders were picked up. Two were left, dead, on the beach. The *Whitesand Bay* headed for blue water.[2]

The mission was over. 'We felt it had been an absolute failure,' said Todd.* He and other members of the force settled down and slept on the thrumming upper deck of the frigate. They were woken by a great thunder. In amazement, they looked around at a suddenly crowded seascape. 'As the dawn broke we could see this massive fleet carrying out the bombardment of what we later found to be Inchon,' he said. It was 14 September; D-Day –1 for Operation Chromite, the biggest amphibious assault since the Second World War.

*   *   *

It was an audacious plan. The invasion force – X Corps, comprising the crack US 1st Marine Division, upgraded from brigade size, plus the US Army's 7th Infantry Division; and some 2,600 ROK Marines – was a powerful one, but amphibious operations are a dodgy business, and Chromite would be amongst the dodgiest. The force has to make its way up a narrow channel, past coastal defences, while

---

* Nearly four decades later, Todd would read that the operation had, in fact, been a success. The raid was designed not as a reconnaissance, but to divert enemy attention from Inchon.

dealing with the world's highest tidal range, which granted only a two-hour landing window. Virtually everyone in the US Navy and Marines Corps had urged against it: too risky. MacArthur himself had silenced the naysayers and pushed the plan through.

The thunder that had startled Todd boomed from some 230 ships – carriers, battleships, cruisers, destroyers, rocket bombardment craft and landing ships, with, among them, a Royal Naval Taskforce – that were softening up the target beaches. On 15 September, under massive pillars of black smoke billowing from the port's blazing oil refinery, Operation Chromite jumped off. US marines disembarked from landing craft and surged up scaling ladders set against the seawalls.

Lieutenant Lee Jong-yun – now 'John Lee' – the literature student who had fled Seoul, was among them. 'They needed someone who spoke English,' he said. He could feel vibrations in the air from the bombardment – 'it was just continuous!' – and could see the sea walls, and the mountains beyond, over the ramp of the landing craft as it closed on the target beach. Then they were ashore. The objective was 'just ashes,' Lee said. Marines surged forward. Shell-shocked NKPA survivors emerged from bunkers, hands raised.

On the open bridge of his command ship USS *Mount McKinley,* MacArthur was overseeing the spectacle. In an age when battle is conducted by small, dispersed groups of men, trying to blend into terrain, the Inchon landing was a theatrical panorama that might have fired the blood of Napoleon. Overhead, squadrons of fighter bombers swooped through columns of smoke. On the sea, waves of landing craft circled, then peeled off and headed for their beaches. All around, to the horizon, were rippling flashes as men-of-war unleashed salvoes. The general – in leather jacket and peaked cap, field glasses in hand – was photographed beaming. For good reason: The operation was proceeding like clockwork. Green Beach, Red Beach, Blue Beach; all objectives were falling like dominoes. Against all advice, MacArthur had rolled the dice. They had come up sixes.

Day one had been a success. Lee, moving into Inchon itself, came across stockpiled heavy Russian weapons in caves bored into cliffs overlooking the harbour.* 'These caves were full of shells and big guns,' he said. 'But before the battle, their Russian advisers had been withdrawn, so nobody was able to operate them.' There was also a lot of propaganda: the thoughts of Josef Stalin and Kim Il-sung. 'I suppose they spent a lot of time reading this,' Lee said. ROK marines mopped up in the town, while US marines advanced on Seoul. On 18 September the US 7th Infantry Division began disembarking.

Pounds had 'negotiated' a part for his little unit in the landing. His force, together with the American Raiders, was tasked to take Kimpo, the airfield between Inchon and Seoul. It proved a sideshow. 'The marines were too fast, we were coming up behind them,' said Todd. 'They had taken Kimpo before we arrived.' There had been quite a slaughter: The airfield with strewn with wrecked aircraft and enemy bodies. Pounds Force linked up with a ROK marine battalion clearing X Corps' rear of guerillas. 'We were looking for trouble,' said 20-year-old Marine Geoff King, who had volunteered for Pounds Force after a night of drinking in Hong Kong, when he had missed the last 'liberty boat' out to their ship, and so 'borrowed' another boat – only to be caught by the duty officer.

Patrolling through the countryside, Pounds Force came upon a village. King and a mate were sent in to scout it. They advanced warily. 'There were these Gooks, I was a bit confused who they were, then I saw their rifles,' King said. He hurled a phosphorous grenade. Thatch flared up and a confused contact started as enemy broke away. Firing halted when Pounds ordered his men to assist the civilians. 'He was a real generous bloke, Pounds,' King said. That night, he dug into a convenient mound outside the village. The next morning, he gave off a sickly stench: 'It was kind of sweet and sour,' he said. 'Nobody would go near me!' The mound King had dug into had been a grave; his bed companion had been a corpse.

The patrol continued. Passing through a copse, the barbarity of this war became shockingly clear. Scattered among the trees lay some twenty young Korean males, all dead. All had been stripped and many mutilated, penises severed. One victim had been disemboweled

* Today, the high ground is Freedom Park – complete with a statue of MacArthur.

but was still, somehow, alive; he was injected with morphine to ease his passing. 'There was nothing we could do,' said King. 'We were just a recce force.' One naked corpse had been placed in a crouching position, and something dangled from its rectum. King tried not to look, but his eyes were drawn. A hand grenade had been forced up, placed so that if the corpse were moved, it would detonate – a particularly foul booby trap. 'We moved on, we never found out what'd happened,' said King. He made his mind up never to be captured. Other men were also affected. 'Life seemed cheap,' Todd mused.

Seoul, 19 miles from Inchon, proved a tougher nut to crack than its port. Inchon had been defended by 2,500 men; there were some 20,000 holding the capital, including communist cadres.[3] Seoul, home to over a million inhabitants, covered 56 square miles and the NKPA were dug in, notably in the hills of the university district in the west.[4] Streets were barricaded with sandbag walls, buildings fortified. Under the gazes of Stalin and Kim, emblazoned across huge placards throughout the city, marine squads fought up the streets. Tanks and artillery blasted strong points at point-blank range; air strikes were called in on the dime. A great pall of dust rose over the embattled capital.

Kim Song-hwan, the young artist, had already realised the war was turning against the NKPA. He had seen young soldiers in blacked-out rail stations heading for the battlefront on night marches, some without weapons. On a road, he watched a panicky North Korean officer threatening a farmer with his pistol after the man's bullock cart had knocked his motorcycle off the road. 'The North Korean was out of his mind – everybody knows how long it takes a bullock cart to stop or turn,' Kim said. 'The war was going badly for them.' Kim sketched US air strikes, silhouetted against lurid purple sunsets, diving and firing red rockets into the curved roofs of traditional houses. At his first sight of Americans, he thought the marines were in their 40s or 50s. He was astonished to learn that they were only in their late teens or early 20s. Combat stress and beards had added decades.

In the midst of it was Max Desfor, the AP photojournalist. On a

Seoul street he snapped his first great Korean War shot, a battle photograph that remains one of the most remarkable ever taken. In war – unlike in movies – it is extraordinarily rare for a camera to capture, in one frame, both friendly and enemy troops in combat. Desfor was with a marine squad held up on a wrecked street. Men were being picked off, but the sniper could not be located. There came a burst of firing. Desfor spun. An NKPA sniper, concealed under a block of cement in the gutter, had been shooting into marines from ankle level from mere yards away. 'By some luck or intuition, when he popped up, they fired and got him,' Desfor said. His shutter clicked the moment a trio of marines – barely 5 yards away – shot the prone sniper dead. Desfor had embedded with marines on Okinawa, but Korea was different. 'In the Second World War we were fighting more from a distance,' he said. 'It was not as close up as Korea.'

There could be only one end. Strong point by strong point, the NKPA were crushed. On 29 September, the day MacArthur arrived to hand the capital over to a tearful President Rhee Syngman, the city was, but for a few isolated holdouts, retaken. Some districts, bypassed by combat, were untouched; elsewhere, entire swathes lay ruined. Kim's watercolours captured the aftermath. Piles of white-clad bodies stacked in building forecourts; a pair of ragged orphans living in a stationary, tyreless car; pieces of burnt enemy soldiers, blown apart and rolled flat by vehicles.

The hour of revenge was at hand. ROK authorities had slaughtered thousands of leftists during their retreat down the peninsula; the NKPA had carried out their own massacres during their occupation, and while fleeing the UNC advance. Many soldiers arriving in Seoul – particularly the 17th ROK Regiment, formed of Christians who had fled North Korea, and many of whose families were culled during the NKPA occupation – had scores to settle.* Desfor photographed the beating of one suspected collaborator, but most 'justice' was sterner.

---

* Family ties remain punishable in North Korea today: Political criminals' families are incarcerated in labour and re-education camps alongside the transgressors themselves.

Lee mourned one particular execution: His English literature professor, Lee In-soo had been forced, during the occupation, to broadcast propaganda in English. 'When Seoul was retaken, he was handed over to the ROK 17th Regiment and was either tried and found guilty or – I am guessing here – just shot out of hand,' Lee said. 'That was a real loss.'

The tide of the war had turned. In the south, while 27th Brigade hunted guerillas, motorised units of Walker's 8th Army had been driving north. 8th Army spearheads linked up with X Corps on 27 September. This closing of the pincers did not spell annihilation, for Korea's mountains provided exfiltration routes for determined units. But Kim Il-sung's sword – the army that had astonished the world with its shock invasion and won a fearsome reputation for both martial competence and ruthless brutality – was broken. At the outset of the war, the NKPA had numbered some 137,000 men.[5] It is unlikely that more than 30,000 escaped to the North.[6]

* * *

On 28 September, the soldiers of the third nation to join the UNC trooped onto Pusan dock. Though hefting British-style weapons and clad in British-style battle dress they were distinguished by their headgear: broad-brimmed slouch hats. Big, bronzed, tough looking men, these arrivals from Japan were 3rd Battalion, Royal Australian Regiment.

Australia, like the UK, had minimal historical relations with Korea, but had sent two field observers to the 38th parallel in response to a UN request in May 1950. After the 25 June invasion, Canberra chose to follow Westminster's lead. On 29 June, when the Royal Navy was tasked with Korea operations, Australia followed with its own naval commitment; on the same day, the RAAF's Japan-based 77th Mustang Fighter Squadron, went into action.[7] On 25 July, MacArthur officially requested the commitment of Australia's only infantry unit deployed overseas: 3 RAR.

The Australian Army had forged a legendary reputation in the First World War, emerging as arguably the best infantry fielded by the then-British Empire, and had also fought with distinction in the

Second World War, in both the Middle East and the Far East. The First World War nickname, 'Digger' – believed to date from Gallipoli, where Australians had proved exceptional trench diggers – was still in use in 1950, but the post-war Australian Army was a shadow of its former self.

Canberra had decided, in 1947, that its army should henceforth consist of a single brigade, augmented by a civilian defence force. By 1950, its only overseas unit was deployed in Japan. While Australian units under command of Lieutenant General Horace 'Red Robbie' Robertson made up the key component of the British Commonwealth Occupation Force in the island nation, notably the Commonwealth base at Kure, this ground force was seriously under strength. In June, 3 RAR consisted of twenty officers and 530 men, not its establishment of thirty-three officers and 682 men. Moreover, it lacked a support company, a signals component and – like 27th Brigade's battalions – a fourth rifle company.[8]

Like US occupation units, 3 RAR enjoyed Japanese life. Houseboys and maids maintained barracks, beer was cheap, good and plentiful; and there were droves of friendly local girls. 'No Australian Digger ever had it so good,' reckoned Signals Sergeant, Jack Gallaway.[9] Being the only official Commonwealth army unit in Japan, the battalion was much in demand for ceremonials. Ian 'Robbie' Robertson, of 3 RAR's sniper section, was surprised at how friendly the ex-enemy proved. 'When we marched through Tokyo with the Union Jack and the Australian flag, Japanese were cheering and waving and I was thinking, "Only a few years ago, we were fighting to the death!"' Robertson became particularly friendly with one local, Maiko 'Miki' Higashida – to the point where he married her. Her elder brother had served in the Imperial Japanese Army, and when she asked him – the senior male in the family – for advice, he asked what unit her beau was in. 'Infantry,' she told him. Hearing this, her brother, an ex-combat soldier himself, assented to the match.

Unlike many American units, however, 3 RAR cycled its convivial ceremonial chores with combat training at Haramura Battle Camp, and being all-volunteers, all-regulars, morale was high. On 25 July, the unit's commander was informed that MacArthur had requested

3 RAR be deployed to Korea. Given that the battalion had been preparing to depart Japan for Australia – hardly welcome news – the announcements that Diggers would be committed to Korea was positively received.

'I was overjoyed,' said Captain Ben O'Dowd, HQ Company commander. 'As soon as they made the announcement, we knew it had to be us.' On 30 July, Robertson visited the battalion, and invited its members to volunteer for Korea service. All but twenty-six men did so. In early August, the battalion saw an equipment upgrade and began an intense pre-combat work-out, but remained under strength. To boost numbers, volunteers were invited from the RAR's 1st and 2nd Battalions. This was still not enough, yet there was no time to train recruits. On 21 August, a call went out nationwide for experienced servicemen to rejoin the army for three years, to include a year in Korea: 'K Force'. Recruiting stations across Australia were flooded.[10]

War is a terrible business, but there are those who enjoy the tight male bonding and comradeship that is part and parcel of close living and shared risk; the sense of self-worth that comes from being a member of a group engaged in a challenging task; and the adrenalin surge of combat. It seems fair to say that most of those who signed up for K Force fell into this unusual category of men. Most were outdoorsmen and nearly all were Second World War veterans: Tough characters who had fought in history's greatest war and found civilian life disappointing.

'The K Force guys were nearly all ex NCOs and they came in as privates,' said Gallaway, an Australia-based regular sergeant who had volunteered for 3 RAR. He was responsible for orienting and moving a group of K Force, when, prior to their departure for Japan, they were 'let loose in the town of Seymour,' Gallaway recalled. 'We got word from the publican so went in with a three-ton truck and loaded them up and as fast as we could get them out of one pub, they would be in another, so we unloaded them in the bush and marched them back to camp. I was a bit worried – I am fairly robust but was not going to tackle 40–50 blokes! But we got them in.' Another volunteer, on hearing of the war in Korea, dug a slit trench in the lawn of the Russian Embassy in Canberra to 'clean out the commos'.[11]

Soldiers such as these are potentially war-winning instruments, but they require a firm grip, a strong leader.

On a late August evening, 3 RAR officers crowded around the mess radio to listen to the Radio Australia news. They were stunned to hear the broadcaster announce that a new CO was heading out to Japan to take command. This was news, indeed: Their current CO, Lieutenant Colonel Floyd Walsh, one of those listening to the radio, was as surprised as his subordinates.[12] It was a serious breach of etiquette by senior officers, and a huge embarrassment for Walsh. To lead Australia's men in Korea, High Command had picked an officer, who, unlike Walsh, had an extensive battle record.

Lieutenant Colonel Charlie Hercules Green, 30, then a student at the Queenscliffe Army Staff College, was that man. Tall; slim; youthful but serious looking; Green had a quiet confidence backed by a remarkable Second World War CV. After joining as a private, he was almost immediately promoted to lieutenant and fought in the Western Desert. Trapped by the Germans during the Greek campaign, he led his group of men out of the trap through Greece, in to Turkey and on to Syria. Promoted to major, he then fought in one of the most horrific campaigns of the Second World War – New Guinea – where he became the youngest battalion commander in the Australian Army and won a DSO.[13] With peace, he left the army, hoping to realise his dream of becoming a farmer. It was not to be. Lacking capital, he was forced to take, instead, a poorly paid salaried position. It was a comedown for the warrior leader. 'Soon our dreams were shrinking and losing direction,' wrote his wife, Olwyn. 'Charlie's confident desire for success could not be realised in his inconsequential job.' In 1948, he joined the militia; in 1949, he rejoined the regular army.[14]

Green's return to uniform seems pre-destined, for he was a natural leader. Any concerns raised by his appointment were swiftly allayed. Arriving on 10 September, he addressed all 3 RAR officers. 'He was a quiet man, he talked in simple terms about what was expected of us and we had no doubts he meant it: He had us from that first day,' said one of the subalterns, David Butler from Perth. 'The next day he spoke to the battalion on the parade ground, and it was a tremendous *tour de force*.' Such was Green's natural comportment, that Gallaway thought his new CO came from an aristocratic background; he was surprised to learn that he had been raised on a farm, and wore dentures after having had his teeth kicked out by a stallion.

Yet, like Coad and Neilson, Green was a distant figure to his officers, who, when briefing, he never addressed by their Christian names. 'He was hard to get close to,' said O'Dowd who knew Green as well as anyone – Green had granted him a battlefield commission in New Guinea. 'He kept to himself.' By an odd coincidence, Green shared the same nickname as Argyll Major David Wilson – 'Chuckles' – though for the opposite reason: While Wilson was perennially cheerful, Green had been so dubbed, in New Guinea, for his apparent inability to smile.[15] His men dubbed him simply, 'The Boss'.

3 RAR's second-in-command was a louder and fiercer figure, Major Bruce 'Ferg' Ferguson. He had known Green in the Second World War, and like Green, had not graduated from the Royal Military Academy at Duntroon. 'He was very experienced, he had gone away in the first convoy and seen a lot of war,' said Butler. 'He had a very brusque manner and used to terrorise subalterns.' Some – not all – soldiers liked him. 'Ferguson was steely, but knew all Diggers by their nicknames,' said Robertson. Ferguson also had a whimsical side that was, perhaps, typical of the 1950s Australian Army. The battalion had adopted a little black terrier – named, in laconic style, 'Dog' – which took its place on parade every Monday morning. 'Ferg would go along the parade and this little dog was in rank, and he would always walk around this little dog and inspect it,' said Robertson. 'Nobody ever commented.'

Headquarters Company Commander O'Dowd, was another ex-ranker cut from similar cloth. A Fremantle native, he has under-educated, having 'gone out to earn a living at fourteen' and been gold mining when the Second World War broke out. He had fought in the Western desert – where he was wounded in the lung – then New Guinea, and been promoted to warrant officer before his commission. 'He was a man's man, a very capable soldier,' said

Gallaway. 'No bullshit about him, he talked to you straight; if you stepped out of line he'd hit you; he'd have you for breakfast!'

While 3 RAR's company-level officers such as O'Dowd were the Second World War veterans, the subalterns were inexperienced Duntroon graduates. For men like Butler and the Mortar Platoon's Lieutenant Phillip Bennett, serving under such thrusting commanders – and commanding highly experienced K Force volunteers – was a challenging prospect.

Many, many 3 RAR men were country boys, outdoorsmen from the Australian bush who had led hard-scrabble childhoods. Sergeant Reg Bandy of C Company was one such: Born and bred on a farm north of Perth, he and a mate tried to enlist in the Navy at the age of seventeen for sartorial reasons: 'I was attracted to the Navy, everyone wore bell bottoms!' Told he would have to wait for two months, he joined the Army instead. He almost made it to the Navy during the war, serving in an amphibious group in New Guinea for three years.

Younger men without war experience wanted it. Sniper Robertson was a volunteer whose father had fought at Gallipoli and whose elder brother had fought in the Middle East in the Second World War; Robbie himself joined up in 1945, underage, but was found out, so rejoined officially in 1946. A crack shot – he used to shoot rabbits in the bush – he had come second in the Queen's Medal Marksmanship competition, so joined the battalion sniper section, where much of his time was spent as the CO's bodyguard.

Twenty-four-year-old Brisbane native Mick Servos was typical of the K Force men shipping out to Japan in that he had served in the Second World War, but was untypical in that he had seen no action; he had been too young to go overseas. Two brothers had been killed in the war and he 'wanted to do some fighting on their behalf' so volunteered, though he knew nothing of Korea. Raised in an orphanage – 'it was good training for the army; I could survive half starved and I was independent'– Servos considered himself tough, but found his new section mates tougher: 'They were mainly ex-NCOs and warrant officers, all ex-Middle East and New Guinea,' he said. 'I had to learn in a bit of a hurry!'

Servos was not the only man impressed by the fighting quality of the new intake. 'They were gung ho sorts of people, they relished the thought of getting back into the army,' said Stan Connelly, a young regular from Melbourne. 'I can only say that we young guys who formed most of the battalion respected their experience and looked up to them.'

One such – who has been described as 'a stone-cold killer' though he had a gentler interest in model railways – was the Second World War veteran Private Len Opie. In Australia, a depot NCO had jeered, 'When you go up there, you'll be on the Imperial Palace Guard,' referring to 3 RAR's Japanese ceremonial role. 'We're not going up there,' Opie replied. 'We're going to Korea to fight.' Opie's enthusiasm and talent for combat would soon astonish even fellow Diggers.

The flood of K Force men bought 3 RAR (unlike the Argylls and Middlesex) fully up to strength and the raw material was excellent. 'There was no conscription or National Service, so it was a pretty reliable and well-trained battalion,' said Bennett. 'You don't see too many of those.' Still, there was little time to prepare for war, and the sudden reinforcement meant that many men did not know each other or their officers. Green had a major task to gel his unit into a cohesive force.

Ceremonial duties were ditched, tactical exercises conducted. On 21 September, the battalion got a taste of Green's single-mindedness. At the end of the exercise, a vehicle convoy arrived to return the men to barracks. The CO ordered it to depart; cursing Diggers marched 20 miles to base, arriving at midnight.[16] On 23 September – the day 27th Brigade was attacking over the Naktong – General Robertson ordered Green to prepare to deploy to Korea.[17] What was not clear, however, was whether 3 RAR's would-be warriors would have a war to fight. Their troopship, the *Aiken Victory*, departed Japan on 27 September. At 21:00, an announcement was piped over the tannoy: A broadcast from MacArthur, finishing with, 'All organised resistance has ceased.'[18]

On 28 September, in Pusan, the Diggers landed to the now-customary welcome of marching band and schoolgirl choir. 'The CO was given a wreath of flowers by a Korean girl; he passed it to the second-in-command on his left, who then passed it just as quickly to the adjutant, who passed it to the RSM,' recalled the Intelligence Officer, Melbourne native and Duntroon graduate Lieutenant Alf Argent. 'As there was nobody else in the line, he was left holding it – to the amusement of us watching from above on the ship.'

On 30 September, 3 RAR concentrated in Taegu, where Coad travelled to welcome them. Australian soldiers have not always operated happily under British command, but Coad impressed. 'He said simply, "I have always admired Australian soldiers and to have a battalion in my brigade is a dream come true,"' Robertson, recalled. 'He was a bloke you would follow down the barrel of a cannon – he would not have to look over his shoulder!'

Brigade HQ was relieved to have a third component. 'Apart from the pleasure of having Australians in the Brigade, they are all the more welcome as they form the third battalion,' 27th Brigade's War Diary noted on the day. On 1 October, the Diggers joined the brigade on clearing operations around Songju, and Coad formally renamed his force '27th Commonwealth Brigade'.[19] 'When you have Cockneys and Scots and Aussies together, it's a combination that's hard to beat,' said Diehard Ken Mankelow.

The Australians suffered their first casualties on 3 October. 'These Aussies drove a carrier into the minefield,' said Don Barrett. 'They were a bit careless.' Two men were killed, but at least one Digger proved to have a robust attitude to the loss. 'A big Aussie came up and said, "Platoon commander got his bloody head blown off!"' Barrett recalled.

The new arrivals immediately impressed the British soldiers. 'The Aussies were incredibly tough, they were outstanding,' said Second Lieutenant Owen Light. 'They had no time at all for anyone who was not really pushing it; luckily for us, I don't think we came under that category.' Corporal Harry Young encountered his new comrades when an Australian patrol strode over to his position to exchange cigarettes. 'They shouted, "Is that bloody Pommies up there?" and we shouted, "We're not bloody Pommies!" The Aussies said, "Jesus Christ! It's bloody Scotsmen!"' he recalled. 'The Diggers were great guys, great sense of humour. Were they good soldiers? By God – aye!'

With 3 RAR deployed, the hard men of the Korean War had landed.

* * *

27th Brigade received orders to move up to Seoul on 4 October; 3 RAR were first, the Middlesex last. The bulk of the men would fly from Taegu to Kimpo; the brigade transport would travel the 260 miles by road.

The road trip proved painful. In rural South Korea, there were virtually no metalled roads, but tracks of compressed dirt raised on bunds above the paddies. With most local transport being ox carts, the roadsides crumbled under the unfamiliar pressure of UNC convoys, creating hours of work for US engineers, who reinforced the shoulders with truckloads of stones.

27th Brigade's echelon and support vehicles had arrived from Hong Kong – and 3 RAR had brought theirs from Japan – though the brigade would still rely on US transport for battalion lift. The most notable vehicles were the Bren gun carriers, light armoured personnel carriers used by the mortar and machine gun platoons that resembled large tin cans on tracks. There were also three-ton Bedford trucks. 'Our three tonners had only two tyres at the rear carrying all the load; the Americans two-and-a-half-ton GMC trucks had eight tyres,' said REME Captain Jeffes. 'Their weight spread over the road so the thing held, but when our three tonners went over the edge of the road the road collapsed and they rolled over.'

The convoys halted at nights, sending out patrols and posting sentries against partisan attack. Diehard Edgar Green was sleeping in the rear of the Middlesex ammunition truck when he was woken by multiple explosions. The ammunition truck roared off, with Green believing that they were under guerilla attack. In fact, partisans had cached ammunition under a timber pile the men had lit for a bonfire. The ammunition had been ignited by the heat.

There were lighter moments. Roy Vincent, with the Argyll mortars, was amused to see one of the Australian carriers: Diggers had filled their vehicle with looted fowl. Further up, they passed a US truck convoy loaded with C-rations. An Australian leaped onto its tailboard, and flung boxes of the rations out to passing carriers. The long crawl up the peninsula would take a full week.

Meanwhile, foot elements were flying from Taegu to Kimpo. Waiting Diggers were astonished when the tail boom of one aircraft – a C119 'Flying Boxcar' – dropped off as it landed in front of them, trailing behind in a flurry of sparks and smoke. When the aircraft halted, the crew hurled open hatches and abandoned plane. Fortunately, it failed to ignite.[20]

Diehards entering the planes were handed parachutes and told to belt them on. Aircrew tightened straps. 'They said, "If we get hit, we drop the tail off and you run off the end and pull the ripcord!"' recalled Barrett. The Middlesex did not know what to think but had brought their own fortification: canned beer. 'They had (glassless) windows in the plane, and we found you could fit the empty cans through the portholes, and down onto Korea,' Barrett said. The flight proved uneventful.

One by one, the aircraft disgorged 27th Brigade at Kimpo, Seoul's airfield. Officers were impressed with the USAF: The transit of three battalions had been carried out without a single sheet of paperwork.[21]

Kimpo was being used to build up supplies for the next phase of operations. Filing off their aircraft, Diehards walked past a two-acre field of rations, piled about forty boxes high. 'The front of the column went over and each man picked up a box,' said Barrett. 'We thought we were supposed to do this; the guards did nothing as we were strung with ammunition and grenades. Later, we found we had been looting!' The US supply system was functioning with its customary profligacy. 'Kimpo was good because there were plenty of Yanks and they would do anything for you, compared to the British Army when you get bloody nothing!' said Spicer. Barrett acquired a sleeping bag and outer cover; he signed the chit, 'Lance Corporal Montgomery.' Officers drew .45s.

The brigade had already seen the human cost of war. At Kimpo, they would grasp its material cost, for the airfield was a vast scrap heap, littered with the carcasses of Russian and American aircraft. Among the acres of debris, corrugated iron huts and tents were sprouting. The brigade camped in this shantytown, building makeshift shelters and erecting two-man tents. The brigade could now have its first real rest.

A field sanitation unit was in operation, where Barrett had his first shower since arriving in Korea. The nights were turning chilly: Owen Light's platoon dug up peat and lit Highland fires. The Argylls received a visit from the 8th Army commander General Walton Walker. 'He talked about all the things we had done as a good general should – he was well briefed,' Light said. 'He seemed kind – a very sound chap.'

US marines, veterans of Inchon and Seoul, were in residence. 'They were jolly nice chaps and, I reckon, very, very good soldiers,' Major Dennis Rendell, the former paratrooper, said. 'We had a tremendous party with them and all got sick on their rye whiskey and peanut butter sandwiches.' One over-indulgent officer subsequently required resuscitation with an oxygen bottle filched from a wrecked plane.[22]

That was not the only cannibalised equipment. For his Company HQ, Rendell chose a wrecked cargo aircraft which, it was found, had its toilet intact. With field ablution facilities usually consisting of a cat-hole or, at best, a piece of crate straddling a slit trench, Rendell had the throne removed and secured to the back of his company jeep. Word of the innovation spread, bringing Rendell an unexpected daily guest: 'The CO always used to come and have a crap with us in the morning!' Rendell recalled. Whether Diehards saluted Man while he carried out his morning duty is unrecorded.

Green, meanwhile, was confronted with a disciplinary problem: Seven Diggers had deserted. It is a telling comment on 3 RAR that these men did not depart to escape combat; they had upped sticks to join the action. Bored at the brigade, they had travelled north to join the US First Cavalry Division, on clearing operations on the Imjin River, 30 miles north of Seoul. The men were welcomed by the Americans. Dubbing themselves 'Warrior Section', their presence was considered newsworthy and was widely reported.[23] Word got back to battalion. Desertion in war is a crime: A trio of Australian MPs arrived from Japan to deal with the miscreants. Green was at his CP shaving when the MPs, all spit and polish, appeared. Green took one look and ordered them out of his area. The guilty Diggers were fined, and reintegrated.[24] There was a precedent: In the Middle East in the Second World War, a similar situation had occurred. 'Green would have been familiar with that situation,' said O'Dowd.

Some men hitched rides from Kimpo into the part-ruined capital. The dead had not been cleared. 'The North Koreans had shot all the public servants, and then the South Koreans had shot another bunch, there were people lined up and shot everywhere,' said Sergeant Reg Bandy. 'It was pretty stenchy.'

Major John Willoughby, with a group of Middlesex officers, was impressed by the great, grey capitol building, but could not help noticing its 'backdrop of exceedingly hostile mountains'. They found the city's best hotel, the colonial-era Chosin. 'Matronly Victorian in its furnishings, it has already been taken over by US Army senior management,' wrote Willoughby. 'With the insignia of majors on our shoulders, we entered without challenge. The heavily padded armchairs took us by surprise . . . we bounced like children in pure delight.' Starved of information, the officers dived into periodicals. '*Time Magazine* offered the most authoritative guide to future events,' Willoughby mused. 'There is much doubt as to whether the crossing of the 38th parallel as an invasion of North Korea might constitute a political transgression exceeding the UN warrant.'[25]

The future course of operations was unclear. The NKPA had been crushed, the South liberated, but Kim Il-sung remained at large, his state remained intact, his army was regrouping. Would – should? – the UNC strike north and finish the job? This was the question being debated in Seoul and Tokyo, Washington and New York, London and Canberra. The outcome of their debates would also be of tremendous interest to Kim's jittery clique in Pyongyang, Stalin in the Kremlin and the guerilla strategist who presided over the great nation at the heart of Asia – Mao Tse-tung.

While statesmen mulled the future course of events, one UNC unit was already operating north – far north – of the 38th parallel.

Chapter Five
Behind Enemy Lines

Not by strength, by guile
Motto, Special Boat Squadron*

Approximately midnight, 5 October 1950. Chongjin coast, North Korea.

An autumn moon danced on the sea's silvery surface as the men perched on the inflatable dipped their paddles into the swell. White eyes in dark faces strained to see in the darkness ahead. To their front, an irregular black line was silhouetted against the starry sky: the enemy coastline.

The boat accelerated as the surf took it in. Foam boiled; the prow grounded. Paddles were shipped; weapons hefted. A single figure detached itself from the group and headed up the beach.

Lieutenant Peter Thomas – his green beret devoid of badges, his plain, dark uniform stripped of insignia – moved stealthily inland, a .45 pistol – waterproofed with condoms – at the ready.

For five minutes, he scanned the tracks leading off the beach. Nothing. Returning to the shore, he assessed the state of the surf. Positive. Reaching into his equipment, he produced a small, waterproof torch, masked with a red filter, the colour with the shortest wavelength. He raised it and flashed it out to sea.

Moments later, a long line of inflatables appeared out of the darkness beyond the surf and closed in on the beach. The recce party had done its job. The landing was unopposed.

The boats were dragged inshore. Men un-slung rifles and sub-

* The motto was changed in 2003 to *By Strength and Guile*.

machine guns, hefted 10-pound packs of explosives and spread out, advancing inland. The only sound was the waves of the Northern Pacific hushing onto the beach.

Some 130 saboteurs of 41 Commando, Royal Marines, were ashore in North Korea, 230 miles behind enemy lines.[1] The deep penetration raid was a high-risk operation – and an impressive feat for a unit that had not existed a month and a half previously.

*   *   *

While 27th Brigade in Hong Kong was preparing to deploy to Korea, a very different unit was activated back home. In discussions over the UK force package for Korea, the First Sea Lord suggested to the Chiefs of Staff that they dispatch the Royal Marine Brigade to Korea: He had been approached by the US Naval Commander-in-Chief to contribute to an amphibious raiding force, and was influenced by the fact that a US Marine Division was deploying. The Royal Marine brigade, however, was already operational in Malaya – a war which, due to its colonial setting, High Command considered a more important strategic geography than Korea.[2] Instead, on 16 August, a specialised force was raised in the countryside of Southwest England.[3]

This force was formed in response to a July request from MacArthur for a British raiding force. Originally, it was to have been Special Air Service troopers, but the SAS had been reduced to a single territorial regiment as the army slashed its various special operations outfits, post-Second World War.[4] The Royal Marines, however, had retained the elite outfits which had pioneered the ethos, training and techniques of modern special forces. These were, arguably, the most famed units thrown up by the greatest war in history; their name remains, seventy years later, a byword for the top-tier troops considered the pinnacle of modern militaries: 'commandos'.

In the darkest days of the war, with Nazism triumphant and the UK's back pressed against the wall, the commandos were conceived. In June 1940, Winston Churchill called for the creation of raiding units manned by 'specially trained troops of the hunter class who can develop a reign of terror down the enemy coast'.[5] The first commandos – the name, borrowed from the Boer War, referred to both the units and the men in them – were formed of army volunteers. In 1942, the Royal Marines – the naval force that guarded warships, manned naval guns and shore installations – joined the party.

Armed with weapons more common to gangsters and bank robbers than soldiers – explosives, submachine guns, black-bladed stilettos – the commandos launched night raids on enemy coastal installations, then disappeared seaward before sun-up. Their operations took them to Norway, the Channel Islands, the French Coast and the Greek Islands. Their ethos and operations – particularly near-suicidal raids on St Nazaire and Dieppe – captured the imagination of the world, and provided the benchmark and model for America's elite Rangers. When the tide of war turned and the Allies took the offensive in Europe and the Far East, commandos were used as shock infantry, taking out vital targets and spearheading offensives in Normandy, Northwest Europe and the Far East.

Commando training was longer, more rigorous and wider ranging than that of infantry. Commando School curricula encompassed the skills of rock climbing, navigation and stalking; on the tactical front, it covered not just light infantry warfare, but such esoterica as demolitions and close combat, with a specialisation in night fighting. No blanks were used on exercises, making night assault landings particularly risky: machine guns fired over boats – sometimes shooting paddles out of men's hands – while live mortar rounds crashed into the sea. 'Battle inoculation *par excellence*!' one commando called it.

Though dangerous – forty commandos were killed in training during the war – the regimen was humane in its way. There was (and is) competition between Britain's elite – paratroopers and commandos – but while the airborne selection course was designed to exhaust, humiliate and hammer a man down, commando training was engineered to build him up; unusually among military units, foul language was not used to belittle recruits.* In another break from

* No longer. During interviews, several 41 Commando veterans expressed surprise and displeasure when they saw instructors swearing at recruits on a TV documentary about contemporary RM commando training.

military convention, commandos were expected to be self-reliant, taking the initiative rather than blindly following orders.

A fetish was made of physical fitness. The grand finale of commando training would horrify an Olympian: Trainees had to complete a 30-mile cross-country speed march – at the killing commando pace of run 100 yards, walk 100 yards – with weapon and pack in eight hours; a nine-mile run with weapon and belt kit in ninety minutes; then a race over the assault course. Only after passing this test would trainees earn the title 'commando' and that prized icon, the green beret – a symbol of elitism since adopted by special forces worldwide.

The Army disbanded its Commandos in 1946; the Royal Marines did not. In 1950, there were two kinds of Royal Marines: fleet marines, posted on warships and naval gunnery installations; and commandos, manning specialist or training units or in 3 Commando Brigade, Royal Marines.* Comprising 40, 42, and 45 Commandos, each of approximately battalion strength, the brigade was hunting communist insurgents in the Malay jungle.

In response to MacArthur's request, 41 Commando ('Four One', not 'Forty First') was discreetly raised as a volunteer force among commandos at home stations or on other postings, and advertised on bases as heading 'for service in the Far East'. The new Commando, with a bayonet strength of approximately 250, would coalesce around three key members: Its CO; its second-in-command; and its RSM. Every man was personally interviewed for suitability by 41's commander a tall, stern-looking gent with a reputation as a disciplinarian.

Lieutenant Colonel Douglas Drysdale, 34, had served as brigade major of 3 Commando Brigade in the Far East in the Second World War, when, after a battle disaster, the CO of 44 Commando was sacked and he took over. 44 Commando was preparing to invade Malaya when the war ended. 'Drysdale liked his drink, and was incisive but jolly with it,' said Thomas. 'He was adored because he was charismatic: Some officers have it, some don't.' Despite being

*Today, all Royal Marines are commando-trained.

uncompromising, austere and a disciplinarian, Drysdale, nicknamed 'Dougie' was liked by his men because, as well as leading from the front, he always kept his troops informed.[6]

The unit second-in-command was Major Dennis Aldridge. Another Second World War Commando, Aldridge was a big, powerful officer who, despite his boyish face, was highly competent. The third member of the triad was Sergeant Major James Baines, universally known as 'Sticks' or 'Sticky' as he had joined the Corps as a boy drummer. His appearance – he combined the physique of an all-in wrestler with flashing eyes, bristling eyebrows and a thunderous voice – would have shaken Lucifer, but this murderous-looking man frequently had a twinkle in his eye.

The men volunteering for Drysdale's command were highly motivated. In 1944, Peter Thomas was about to be called up as a sapper, something he was not sure suited him: 'I wanted to be in a decent mob, a bit more operational,' he said. Having read about commando raids, he decided they were for him; an uncle in the Admiralty pulled strings and he was assigned to the marines. He was heading to the Far East when Japan surrendered. For 'six glorious weeks' he was military governor of Lantau Island in Hong Kong, then it was counter-insurgency in Palestine. But like all elite troops, the lieutenant felt left out: he had not fought in a big war. 1950 found him instructing at the Corps' NCO school. When his students learned of the new commando, most volunteered. Thomas did too, and took command of 41's Heavy Weapons troop.

As in infantry regiments, there were those for whom the marines was a tradition. Corporal Ron Moyse had had family in the marines since 1842; he, himself, joined up in 1943 as a boy bugler and was a physical training instructor at Bickleigh Commando School near Dartmoor when he was interviewed by Drysdale for 41. Despite his gentle West Country accent, the PTI was a big, hard-looking man, one of the unit's toughest.

In what would become a significant irony, another corporal, George Richards, joined 41 as he had previously done a tour of the Far East where he had been attracted by the Chinese, their food and their culture. 'I really enjoyed Singapore and Hong Kong, I thought it was a good chance to get back out there,' he said. 'I didn't realise Korea would be such a big conflict or I wouldn't have volunteered!'

One man was accepted against Drysdale's better judgment. Corporal Joe Belsey had recently married, but the CO had decided given the likely perils of Korean operations, not to accept newly-weds. After an initial rejection on those grounds, Belsey returned and pleaded his case strongly. Drysdale accepted him.[7]

Not all were volunteers. Marine Gordon Payne was on a heavy weapons course at Bickleigh when the entire course was assigned to the new commando. 'Volunteers? That's a fallacy!' he said. 'But nobody had their arms twisted.' Like every commando, he expected, even looked forward to, combat. 'You thought one day you would be engaged,' he said. 'It was par for the course.'

Another not-quite-volunteer was Marine Andrew Condron, a Scotsman from Bathgate, who had grown up reading about commandos, and, as a boy, had hiked the Lothian hills: 'I always had the attitude of setting myself against nature and setting myself physical tasks,' he said. Against his parents' wishes he signed up for twelve years with the marines in 1946. After earning his green beret, he adopted the arrogance of the elite. 'We did always feel that we were a bit better than anyone else,' Condron said. '*Esprit de corps* is inculcated.' He was hoping to go to signals intelligence in Kuala Lumpur, Malaya, when his name was posted for 41. 'I thought by the time we get there the war will be over ,' he said. 'What can the North Koreans do against the Americans?' At the unit interview, when asked, 'So Condron: Are you with us?' He replied, "Yessir!" ' .

And there were those who had 'been volunteered'. Corporal Dave Brady, a big, Anglo-Irishman, was by profession a commando assault engineer; by nature a comedian; and by (frequent) mischance, a troublemaker. Brady had been dispatched to 41 after an embarrassing incident in which an Egyptian military attaché to the UK had been 'accidentally' dunked underwater and nearly drowned during a demonstration of commando landing techniques; the exercise had been overseen by Brady. Arriving at Bickleigh for the unit interview, Brady – a self-professed coward – was impressed at the calibre of volunteers: 'Lots of old mates, characters all, and hard men indeed!'

as he put it. He changed his mind: perhaps his new posting might not be so bad.[8]

If 41 Commando needed signallers, engineers and heavy weapons experts, it also requested specialists of another kind – from the Corps' most shadowy arm. Jack Edmonds was a Londoner who had joined the marines in 1946 and served on warships when he heard about a special unit. He applied to the Special Raiding Wing, in 1949, the home of the Special Boat Squadron, or SBS, and was accepted for training. Even by commando standards, work was intense: canoeing; beach reconnaissance; diving using closed-circuit breathing apparatus; mining moored ships; raiding; parachuting; survival; resistance to interrogation. Of eight men on his course; two passed, including Edmonds. 'We got through, we were an elite,' he said. 'We were brainwashed that way.' A seven-man SBS detachment was assigned to 41.

Yet 41 Commando was so short of officers, it took on some who had not completed training. Second Lieutenant John Walter was on the commando course at Bickleigh when he saw 41 Commando mustering on the parade ground. Asked what he wanted to do after the imminent completion of his training by a senior officer, he mentioned his desire to join 41, 'because they were off to war'. Days later, during a field exercise on Dartmoor, a staff car pulled up and Walter was summoned to 41. 'I just went and collected a green beret from the store,' he said. 'I had not earned it!'

Still, there were not enough volunteers in the UK to fill 41 Commando's ranks. The troopship *Devonshire* was en route to Malaya with a fresh intake for 3 Commando Brigade in Malaya when, off Colombo, a signal was received that a new unit needed men. The troops on the *Devonshire* were the Royal Marines' youngest recruits, fresh from commando training. Marine John Underwood, a 19-year-old Bournemouth lad, was one of those on the ship who would be diverted from the jungles of Southeast Asia to the mountains of Northeast Asia. 'The Korean War had just broken out,' he said. 'At the time, it was so remote, it was an adventure.' Another 19-year-old was Marine Michael O'Brien from Pimlico, as was Marine Edward Stock, who was perfectly happy to join 41. 'This came out of the blue, it was something different,' he said. The news that they would come under American command was a plus: 'They had better food and everything,' he said. The contingent from *Devonshire* was unloaded at Singapore, from whence they flew to Okinawa and then to the Japanese mainland, 41 Commando's staging area for Korean operations.

Back home, a cloak-and-dagger operation was underway.

The UK-based contingent of 41 Commando would fly to Japan on BOAC civil flights via Rome, Cairo, Basra, Karachi, Rangoon and Hong Kong, but as this route took them over neutral nations, they would travel under civilian cover: 'a travelling football team'. The men who did not own one received a suit – 'which I am sure originated in prison discharge stores,' Brady reckoned – and would be issued a passport in London prior to boarding the first flight.[9]

The drama began at Waterloo Station where groups of commandos – hefting kitbags and dressed in ill-fitting suits – awaited contact with their handlers. 'It was quite humorous to see these "civilians" with military haircuts and army boots marching around trying to act nonchalant,' said one commando trained in real clandestine operations – Corporal Henry 'Harry Langton, a Liverpudlian and leader of 41's SBS cadre. Foreign Office bureaucrats played the game to the hilt. 'These guys with bowler hats and umbrellas came up and whispered, "There's a guy over there: If you go up to him, he'll give you a passport!"' Moyse recalled. He approached the man, and was surreptitiously handed a travel document; his occupation was listed as 'government official'.

41 Commando tripped its first ambush before departing British shores: At Heathrow, the men were caught in photographers' crosshairs as they boarded their flight. *The Daily Express* subsequently ran a cartoon of burly commandos in tight suits flying to war.[10] Then they took off. 'We travelled by Argonauts and stayed at fantastic hotels,' said Payne. 'I'd never been anywhere except Blackpool, so this trip was absolutely fantastic, it never seemed to enter our heads that we were going to fight a war.'

The flight east took five days. At stopovers, the farce continued. In the dining room of a Karachi hotel, a waiter asked Brady whether he and his party were footballers. Brady nodded. The waiter leaned in close, put his finger to his nose and whispered conspiratorially: 'Plenty fucking football teams come through here lately!' For once, Brady was speechless.[11]

*   *   *

41 Commando's advance party arrived at Camp McGill, a US 1st Cavalry Division camp near the port of Yokosuka on Tokyo Bay, on 5 September.[12] The unit's various separate components – 'Pounds Force', already in Japan; the UK men, flying out in relays by BOAC; the men from *Devonshire* flying in from Singapore, via Okinawa – trickled in.

On base, attired in olive drab American kit, the only thing that distinguished the commandos as British were green berets. The first priority was familiarisation with American weapons, compasses, radios and explosives. US marine NCOs were on hand for the training. 'They were great characters,' said Edmonds. 'Being a marine is everything to them; we were impressed.'

The eight-shot, semi-automatic M1 Garand rifle was an improvement over the bolt-action Lee Enfield, but the 20-shot Browning Automatic Rifle, or BAR, was considered inferior to the Bren. The lightweight M1 automatic carbine, with its automatic function, proved handy and popular, though the US fragmentation hand grenade was less lethal than the British Mark 36. Ammunition was plentiful. 'We were on the ranges day after day after day,' said Payne. 'In England, you were told each round cost thruppence – very sparse! – but over there, you'd fire as much as you liked.'

US barbers were a different matter. Walter had decided to get a US marine haircut – 'i.e. no hair!' – to make life easier in the field, when Drysdale heard about it. 'Don't be a fool!' he snapped. 'How will they pull you out of the water when you fall in?' Falling in became commonplace as commandos began training in amphibious raiding.

Their insertion platforms were ten-man, lozenge-shaped inflatables. Four men on each side paddled, perched on the gunwales, while a coxswain steered at the stern and another knelt in the bow.

Beach entry and egress through surf proved problematic. 'We went onto Chigasaki Bay, everyone paddling together to learn how to get through surf, keeping the boat straight on,' said Underwood. 'Myself, and all of us with weapons and everything, were flung onto the beach; we had taken the surf side-on. And one day there was a storm, but we paddled in – good training!' In marathon rows, the commandos learned to control their rubber steeds. Night-time navigation by compass and stars and capsize drills were ingrained.

Trained to operate in silence ashore, pre-briefings were essential: Each commando had to know the tasks of the rest of his section, RV points and extraction points. All became familiar with air reconnaissance photos of targets. Interspersed with amphibious and weapons training, speed marches built stamina.

Corporal Raymond Todd, the 'Pounds Force' veteran, was incorporated into 41 Commando. 'Because we were training with a professional unit, life was easier,' he said, but training was frenetic. 'It was 16–18 hour days, probably the hardest I ever worked,' said 18-year-old Marine Fred Hayhurst, a member of the *Devonshire's* youthful contingent. But living conditions were lavish. The US PX – the Post Exchange, the equivalent of a NAAFI – was a place of wonder. 'We had just left England and rationing, and the PX had things you could not imagine,' said Payne. 'I bought mostly chocolate and sweets, even through we were the most hard-up people in the camp.' American dining facilities were equally wondrous. 'When they gave you steak, you thought it was for four or five of you,' Payne recalled. 'Fantastic!' Some men requested tea, rather than coffee; they received a tureen of Southern-style iced tea.

After hours, commandos ventured out on the town. One group, Brady among them, entered a Japanese beer hall, where they were welcomed and stood rounds by US servicemen. Several gallons of Asahi later, Brady spotted a small US sailor being manhandled by burly MPs. Sense of justice heightened by lager intake, Brady waded in, fists flying, but his close-combat training proved unequal to the fists, boots and sticks of multiple MPs. The end result was the little sailor escaped, while the big commando was hauled into a US brig. Released the following morning, he returned black-eyed to the barracks where laughing commandos draped a sheet emblazoned with, 'Welcome Home Killer' from a window. Brady was 'severely reprimanded' by Drysdale but – as had been the case after the Egyptian military attaché incident – somehow kept his corporal's stripes.[13]

Brady's qualities were noted. On another night, commandos and US troops were watching a movie in the camp cinema when the film broke. Commandos shoved Brady on stage to tell jokes. When the movie was ready to restart, the audience insisted, instead, that Brady continue – although, in Thomas' words, 'it wasn't a bad film'.

In the canteen in the evenings, 41 Commando eschewed the jukebox and bawled songs. Musicality would become one of the unit's leitmotifs, with their unofficial march being, 'We're a Shower o' Bastards'. This proud addition to Britain's martial musical heritage began:

> She's a big fat bastard –
> Twice the size of me!
> Hairs across her belly –
> Like the branches of a tree!
> She can sing! Dance! Fight! Fuck!
> Fire a rifle! Drive a truck . . .

While hard training and off-duty bonding cemented unit cohesion, Drysdale and his officers were joining US Navy officers to pore over air reconnaissance photos of Korea's northeast coast, where the north – south rail line runs up to the Russian border – a strategic communications artery for the NKPA. Naval gunfire and air attacks could cut the line temporarily, but with peasant labour on hand, communist authorities easily refilled craters and re-laid rails and sleepers. To impact rail operations, bridges and tunnels had to be collapsed. Neither job could be performed by air or naval bombardment; what was needed were saboteurs to land and lay explosives. To ferry them to their targets, naval assets – the submarine USS *Perch* and the assault personnel destroyers, or APDs, USS *Wantuck*, and the USS *Horace A. Bass* were assigned, and began exercising with the raiders.

In the first week of October 1950, 41 Commando's active service in the Korean War began.

*   *   *

The commandos following Thomas had staged from the *Bass* and *Wantuck*; raid commander was Major Aldridge. All men had been briefed aboard on the positions they were to take ashore, the extraction plan, and pick-up points if left behind.[14]

As the sun sank over the Pacific, the commandos had quietly gathered on the destroyers' aft decks. Weapons were prepared, badges and insignia removed from uniforms and berets, dinghies inflated. As night fell, the ships blacked out. Commandos gazed at a glow on the northern horizon; they were informed the lights shone from the Russian port of Vladivostok.[15]

When the APDs were 3 miles off the target beach, landing craft were lowered over the side, then the commandos' dinghies. Each raider jumped up and down to ensure his equipment and weapons made no sound, then climbed aboard his designated inflatable. Ten-pound haversacks of explosives were passed down. The dinghies were hooked up to landing craft by cable, then water churned around their sterns as the landing craft aimed themselves for the North Korean coast. Half a mile off shore, the inflatables were released. The final stretch was paddled in silence.[16]

The sea was glassy calm but each time a paddle dug into the water, electric light danced in crazy spirals below the surface. 'The desperate thing was this swirl of luminescence,' said Walter. 'We thought, "Bloody hell, they are bound to see us!" But we carried on.' Raymond Todd could not help wondering if an ambush was lying in wait. 'If they know their business they'll wait until you are within a couple of hundred yards and mow you down.'

A red light winked four times from the shore: Thomas. Beach clear. The operation was on.

Thus far the pace had been sedate. Now, on the crest of waves surging inshore, the inflatables accelerated like surfboards. The beach raced toward them. As the waves broke, commandos hurdled out and into the foam, dragging inflatables ashore against the suction.

'Once you get feet on ground, it becomes a job,' said Todd. 'No stress, no fear.' Commandos were gripped with a quiet but intense excitement. 'As a youngster during the Second World War I'd heard about commando raids,' said Underwood. 'I had no idea I'd be participating myself!'

The beach was familiar; every commando had studied air recce photos. What could not be known was the purpose of a low concrete building halfway up the beach. Cautiously, commandos approached. It was deserted; it appeared to be used by fishermen. There was relief: if civilians had been discovered, their fate would have hung by a thread, for a streak of ruthlessness infuses commando operations. In the pre-raid briefing, Lieutenant Pounds had ordered: 'Civilians are to be left alone if they stay indoors; if they interfere, they are to be "rubbed out."'[17]

The demolition party, supervised by an American Underwater Demolition Team (UDT) officer, Lieutenant E. Smith, lugged the explosives to an embankment between two railway tunnels in the coastal hills. 'We had to manhandle about 2 tons of explosive up to the railway tunnel,' said Hayhurst, the 18-year-old. 'The American way is to think of the amount they want – then double it!'

Other commandos, responding to whispered orders and hand signals, fanned out and took up a defensive perimeter in the darkness, covering the engineers. 'We knew where our people were, any intrusion would be enemy,' said Walter. 'But there appeared to be no opposition.'

Tense hours – one, two, three, four – ticked by. The engineers carefully packed plastic explosive into a culvert. Finally, the job was done. Clock-style fuses – two in each stack of plastic – were set for 36 minutes. Extraction orders were passed from man to man. The commandos exfiltrated to the water's edge, passed through a checkpoint and were counted in to ensure that nobody was left behind. So far, the raid had gone perfectly. 'We'd been lucky,' said Thomas. 'They might've had the beach mined, guarded or enfiladed.'

Fortune would turn, however, in the final stage. The inflatables were being manhandled through the rising surf when a shot rang out. It was unclear what had happened. The commandos paddled seaward.

A couple of hundred yards offshore, the line of dinghies halted and turned inland: It was critical to face a detonation, so that evasive methods could be taken if debris blasted up by the explosion headed their way. Bobbing men counted down. 'Major Aldridge said, "If it does not go off, we'll have to go back in,"' recalled Marine Edward Stock, in Aldridge's boat. 'Then it was like the heavens opening.'

Violent orange flashed in the dark, accompanied by the near-instantaneous boom. 'It blew the whole hillside away and a lot of trees appeared to catch fire,' said Todd. 'Although my group must have been 800 yards away, debris – timber and rock – was falling down, making the water boil. I was really scared.'

No debris reached the boats. A relieved cheer went up. Then silence.

Out to sea could be heard the popping of the landing craft's baffled underwater exhausts. The commandos paddled out, and hooked up. Aboard the landing craft, 'Nancy' a night-vision device resembling a cine-camera, was aimed at the horizon to pick up an infra-red homing signal from the blacked-out destroyers.[18] Once their position was ID-ed, the boat and its train of inflatables got moving, commandos clinging on as their bows lifted.

The mystery of the shot was solved as the commandos were debriefed aboard. A man had been killed: SBS Corporal Ronald Babbs. The afternoon of the raid, he had told a comrade that he felt his luck had run out.[19] It had. Departing the beach, his boat had bucked in the surf, and a slung rifle had gone off. Babbs had survived seven the Second World War raids only to die by accident on his first Korean operation.

He was buried at sea in daylight. Commandos and US sailors gathered at the stern; the destroyer cut engines; a US trumpeter played 'Taps'; and Babbs was consigned to the Pacific. 'You don't realise how quiet the sea can be,' said Hayhurst. 'But we didn't have time to worry – we got orders at lunch that we were to do another raid that evening.'

The commandos were going in some 50 miles south of the first night's raid. The target was a railway tunnel and bridge south of the port of Songjin.

* * *

This time, Thomas swum in ahead while waiting commandos bobbed offshore. Dark, circular objects were spotted floating nearby. 'Mines?' someone whispered. After a few uncomfortable moments, the objects were identified: fishing floats.[20] The beach was clear. The commandos landed without incident, and again, spread out. This time, however, there were North Koreans nearby.

Marines Ralph Haine and Roger Tyack were scouting forward when they spotted a soldier and a girl locked in embrace in long grass to their front. What to do? Pounds came over their radio: 'Five minutes, then deal with them!' he ordered. Haines and Tyack stared at one another: Who would execute the girl? As they were deliberating, the lovers stood up, and holding hands, wandered inland – to the relief of the commandos.[21]

Situation resolved, the two demolition parties approached their targets: the bridge and the tunnel. Suddenly, firing burst out in the darkness ahead.

The demolition parties were preceded by Pounds, leading his troop up toward the tunnel entrance. Pounds spotted a sentry at the same time the sentry saw him, but the sentry had his rifle in his shoulder – he took aim – for a split second the commando officer could make out every detail of the sentry – pale face, light uniform, his baseball-type cap – then he fired. The round passed between Pounds and the commando beside him and ricocheted off the rail into the night. A commando fired a fast double tap – both rounds hit – the man went down – his rifle clattered to the ground.[22] Silence reinstated itself. Then, another shot: This time it was the unit's Korean interpreter, who had had a negligent discharge. Whispered swearing broke out.

Demolition work was well underway. O'Brien was under the wooden railway bridge, when the tracks vibrated: A night train was approaching from the tunnel. Commandos flattened themselves against the ground. 'We saw the lights from the train shining down, and there were all these soldiers and other people sat in this train chatting away and looking out,' O'Brien recalled. 'We thought they were all looking at us – and we were lying there looking at them!' Pounds, fearful that the train was carrying reinforcements, had a bazooka team sighting in. At the last moment, he yelled, 'Let it go!' The train thundered past, grit and dust from the tracks spitting into the faces of the commandos. They had not been spotted.[23]

Work resumed until another interruption: An enemy patrol approaching along the track. Commandos froze. 'We didn't want to give anything away,' O'Brien said. 'If we fired on a patrol, we were not achieving our task.' The patrol passed, but for a pair of stragglers bringing up the rear. The two halted over the prone figure of a sergeant. 'We thought, "They've spotted him!"' thought O'Brien, who carefully took aim. 'We knew we'd have to put 'em down.' In the gloom, he could not make out quite what was happening. After some moments, the North Koreans hurried off to catch up with the patrol. As soon as the two were out of earshot, the sergeant started cursing furiously. Something had happened, but O'Brien had no idea what. The patrol disappeared.

Job done, the commandos began extracting when, for the last time, the silence was ruptured as someone let out, 'a yell to wake the dead', Thomas recalled. It was Pounds. He had stepped on a live electric cable, cut earlier in the operation. His radio operator brushed the live wire off him with his rifle butt.

Despite the late hour, several civilians had been captured near the beach. One man, who had been wandering around inquisitively, was knocked out by a commando with his rifle butt, leaving tooth marks in the stock. Others were unharmed.[24] 'We could not take prisoners,' said Condron. 'So we just tied them up and gagged them, in a way that they could free themselves.' The locals were left as the commandos shoved off into the surf, running higher than the previous night.

The last boat out was Thomas', with Corporal Gersham Maindonald as the coxswain. Maindonald was particularly competent: A Guernsey man, he had been 'King's Badgeman', the best recruit in his intake. Now, he showed his worth. 'We paddled out when I heard a pathetic voice crying, "Wait for me!"' Thomas said. A commando had fallen asleep on the perimeter and missed the exfiltration. In darkness, amid breaking waves 6–8 feet high, Maindonald turned the boat –'no mean feat' in Thomas' words – and the commando was hauled inboard. The paddlers dug in, putting distance between themselves and the imminent detonation.

It was a little too close for comfort. 'We were just leaving, 50–100 yards away, when the explosive charges went off and the whole place went up in a great roar,' said Condron. 'Lumps of earth and dirt came down on top of us.'

There was no damage from the debris – then a machine gun on a promontory let rip.

'There were green tracers going over our heads,' said Underwood. 'We only had light weapons, it wasn't feasible to return fire.' O'Brien's impulse was to dive across his boat's rubber tubing: 'My first thought was, "I have to stop this boat being punctured, it's a long swim back to the ship!"' he said. The streaks, however, were well overhead; the North Korean gunners seemed to be probing. 'When the charges blew up, it lit up everything, so night vision was destroyed,' Underwood said. 'I think their firing was an automatic reaction.'

A rushing force hurtled over the heads of the furiously paddling commandos, and great white flashes lit up the promontory. From out to sea, the destroyers' 4-inch guns were shooting; the gun's tracers made it a target. 'They must have lowered that hilltop a few inches!' said Condron. The machine gun ceased. 'Whether it was hit, or whether it was discretion, I don't know,' Underwood said. 'But it didn't carry on.'

Once the commandos were back aboard, American sailors broke out 'medicinal' brandy and O'Brien heard why the sergeant had been cursing after the patrol passed. 'They had stopped with their feet within inches of his head to have a pee,' O'Brien recalled. 'He said, "First there's a bloody bloke up there, now it's bloody raining!" They were peeing all over his head and he could not do anything!' The story circulated to much laughter. Then the two ships headed east for Japan.

The two destroyer-launched raids had struck the furthest north but another raid had been carried out by the other half of 41 Commando. They had inserted from an unusual vessel: *'The Pregnant Perch'*.

* * *

On 30 September, the submarine USS *Perch* had slipped her moorings at Yokosuka Naval Base and headed northwest. The boat was specially modified. Her torpedo tubes had been removed and aft of her conning tower, a cylindrical hanger had been built; it was this bulbous feature that gave the *Perch* her maternal nickname.[25] In place of torpedoes were tiered bunks; the hanger housed raiding boats and their tow craft; *Perch* was a special operations submarine. Aboard, were sixty-seven men of 41 Commando under Drysdale's command.[26]

Inside, the *Perch* was well lit. Though she rolled on the surface, once submerged, she ran smoothly, the only mechanical sound being the hum of the motors, the whirr of ventilator fans and the creaking common to all ships. But she was cramped, and with water conserved for the 'heads' and the galley, dirty; pre-boarding, the men had been advised to pack talcum powder.

Moyse, the big PTI, found his bunk situated under an oil drip; when lying there, he covered himself in his waterproof poncho. Once submerged, air quality deteriorated. 'With 30 bods in one compartment, the air got pretty foul, so bad that you could not have struck a match, it would not have lit,' said SBS man Edmonds. But the American boat offered one advantage. 'We used to go down to the galley and the big black chef would say, "How d'you want your steak, buddy?"' Edmonds recalled. 'The food was fantastic! Having been aboard British subs, I couldn't believe it.'

Some 4 miles off the port of Hungnam, approximately 115 miles north of the 38th parallel, the boat came up to periscope depth. Her captain and Drysdale examined the scene. Satisfied, the *Perch* sank to a safer depth. Inside, the commandos rested. Soon it would be night.

After dark, an observer scanning offshore would have seen a great displacement of water and a huge, whale-like bulk breaking the sea surface. Then the *Perch* lay, virtually motionless, her casing awash and only her conning tower and boat hanger jutting above the waves.

Inside the hull, a long 'whoosh' was heard as the submarine blew her tanks to herald the ascent. In the commando compartment, white lights went off, red lights on, so eyes could pre-adjust to darkness. In the cave-like confines of the compartment, bathed in dim redness, the commandos – faces blackened, armed to the teeth – looked like a gang of fiends.

Sailors reached up. Hatches clanged open. An invigorating bouquet – the sea breeze – wafted down, penetrating the fug. Climbing up ladders and onto the slippery casing, the commandos, assembled near the stern. Swaying with the gently rolling submarine, breathing in the night air, they gazed out at the silvers, greys and blacks of the moonlit sea and sky.

Pressure hoses inflated dinghies. They were pushed overboard. Commandos climbed down, and hooked up to the powerboat. Then Drysdale was summoned. He quickly re-boarded and entered the control room. The radar had picked up a patrol boat contact. Abort! 'The skipper had a bit of a panic, they called us back on board, we had to rush down below decks again, down hatchways, closed hatchways, the alarm was going – we crash dived,' said Corporal George Richards. 'We left a chap, an American sailor, in the hanger – he was saved because it was airtight.'

The raid was reset for the following night. The commandos passed time doing what they could. 'You could not move on the submarine,' said Edmonds. 'We were confined to reading or playing crib, you don't want to disturb the stability of the sub.' Most men tried to sleep as the *Perch* rested on the seabed.[27]

The following night, 2 October, the *Perch*, again, rose to periscope depth. Clear. She breached. No patrol boat. The raid was on.

The commandos were decanted. Their boats hooked up to the P-boat, and were released half a mile out. Astride their inflatables' tubing like jockeys, the commandos paddled in, line-abreast. The target was a railway line running across a horseshoe-shaped beach.

'As we came into the beach there was the sound of the crickets and the sickly sweet smell they put on their crops – human fertiliser,' said Edmonds. 'We landed spot-on.' The demolition team headed for the railway line and the tunnel. Sections of commandos spread out to set up a perimeter.

'In position, we could see the civilian population further inland who were working on the land in the middle of the night, it was rather strange,' said Leslie Coote, the intelligence corporal. 'They were in white, and it was a fairly light night.' The white-clad peasants – who may have been gathering the harvest in darkness to avoid daytime air attacks – did not notice their visitors. Commandos kept a careful watch.

The railway line ran out of one tunnel in the hill, along a bank that crossed the beach, and into a second tunnel. Charges would be laid to destroy the embankment and anti-tank mines set inside one tunnel to ambush the next train.

Brady was one of the commandos in the tunnel. Suddenly, someone fired in the darkness, then Brady was sure he heard a rumbling: A train! If one arrived, the tunnel party would be crushed. They took off at a mad dash, with Brady exiting first, 'like a long dog'. He dove to the ground, taking up a firing position. A tense pause. Nothing. 'I can't hear a train,' someone whispered. 'No,' agreed another. Quiet chuckles. The panicked tunnel party climbed shamefacedly to their feet, returned to the tunnel and finished the job.[28]

A drainage culvert, some 3–4 feet high, had been found under the embankment. It was perfect for demolitions. Edmonds was engaged in ferrying the explosive packs up the beach. Some 2,000 pounds of explosive would be packed into the culvert and tamped with sandbags to channel the blast vertically. Captain Pat Ovens, the leader of the Assault Engineers, ordered Brady to pack the explosives in, then left to supervise some other work.

Brady peered inside. He sniffed. The culvert was about a foot deep in stinking rural ordure. With Ovens absent, Brady decided to use his rank: He ordered his section in. No movement. 'Come on, lads,' he hissed. Ovens re-emerged from the darkness. 'Get in there corporal, we don't have all bloody day!' Brady had no choice. Squatting down, he crawled through the filth and started to pack the charges.[29]

So far, so good. Time came to extract. In response to orders passed by a runner – 'walkie- talkies were few and far between, and we were observing radio silence,' said Moyse – the perimeter guards withdrew. Edmonds, at the culvert, was picking up his kit when there came a crackle of gunfire from the darkness: An enemy coastal patrol had blundered into the commandos. In confused shooting, Marine Peter Jones was hit.

Brady, on the beach, turned to the indistinct figure lying next to him. 'If I were Dougie, I think I'd piss off right now!' he whispered. 'Well, you are not, I am and we will,' the figure responded. It was Drysdale; a shocked Brady could see white teeth in the dark as his CO grinned.[30]

The commandos pulled back to the boats; Drysdale was the last to leave shore. As they paddled out, there was a tremendous boom: the charges placed in the culvert had gone off as planned, blasting the embankment. The detonation was followed by shooting as Korean shore patrols opened up in confusion.[31]

The *Perch* had been informed by radio of Jones' wound, but the surgeon was not required; Jones was dead by the time he reached the submarine. Sailors stowed the inflatables, commandos dropped through hatches, and the boat headed east.

Jones was buried the following day. The *Perch* cut her engines, US sailors lined the decks and the raiders stood hatless in the sunlight as a commando honour guard fired a volley. It was answered by gun salutes from the destroyers USS *Maddox* and *Thomas*, which had drawn alongside. UN flags fluttered at half-mast, then Jones slid into the sea under a white ensign. 'The sea was as calm as a millpond,' remembered Langton.

Some good news was announced: A rumble had been heard ashore, meaning the anti-tank mines laid in the tunnel had claimed a victim.[32] On the surface, the *Perch* headed for Japan. The crew had built a strong rapport with their passengers, who they invited up to the conning tower. Brady's imagination was captured. Lean sailors around the tower scanned with binoculars as the vessel's sharp bow sliced the waves, heading for an empty horizon. It was a warlike, cinematic tableau – then the corporal remembered that to the west, the peninsula they were heading away from was engulfed in a terrible war. Feeling guilt, he headed below.[33]

* * *

Ashore in Japan, 41 Commando were shown aerial photos of their handiwork: 'It was complete devastation,' said Maindonald. For those commandos who had not seen action before, it had been exciting. 'I did quite enjoy the raids,' said Condron, the Scottish commando. 'It was an adventure, what we had trained to do.'

The Americans were delighted. Vice Admiral Turner Joy, US Commander, Naval Forces, Far East, issued a press release: *British Marine Commandos Make Daring Raids*.[34] The US commander, Submarine Element, Western Pacific, wrote in an after-action report to the Chief of Naval Operations: 'The welding of American surface and sub-surface units and the indomitable Royal Marines into one assault group speaks volumes for the meticulous planning and "damn the torpedoes" spirit of all hands. It is an inspiration to serve with such fighting men.'[35]

Most unusually, a civilian had watched the raids from the *Bass* and *Wantuck*: The Right Honorable Tom Driberg, Member of Parliament and reporter. Though a leftist himself, he was impressed by 41 Commando: 'The most confirmed pacifist could hardly fail to admire these men's absolute dedication to their mission,' he wrote.[36] He penned a dramatic story that combined the two raids into one; it was widely syndicated.

The entire commando was invited to a British Embassy party. 'They gave us cakes, and people were pinching the cakes and signing the visitors' book, "Winston Churchill, RM,"' recalled Richards. 'We drank them out of all their beer, it was chaos – marines are good drinkers!' One commando, unable to locate a toilet, was discovered by a female embassy staffer as he eased springs in a sink.[37]

The raiding season was ending. Cold water complicated amphibious strikes, and with a UNC advance north imminent, there was no point in destroying infrastructure that would soon be needed by a unified Korea.

Drysdale set about retraining. Having been split into separate forces for the raids, the commando was re-organised along more conventional lines: Three Rifle Troops (each about forty-five men strong); Heavy Weapons Troop (armed with 81mm mortars and Browning .30 medium machine guns); Assault Engineers Troop; and Headquarters Troop. Training recommenced in ground warfare, including at ranges on the slopes of Mount Fuji. Transitioning from an amphibious raiding force to shock infantry, 41 Commando was mirroring, albeit in an accelerated timeframe, the experience of its wartime predecessors.

MacArthur had approved the release of certain ships and 41 Commando from theatre within November. This was premature, Drysdale wrote in a letter to General W.I. Nonweiler at the Royal Marines Office of the Admiralty. 'I personally am not convinced the war is over . . . it is <u>possible</u> that my appreciations will be unpleasantly correct,' Drysdale wrote. He had visited US Rear Admiral Arleigh Burke, Admiral Joy's deputy, telling him that he did not consider it 'morally right' for the unit to be withdrawn, suggesting that 41 could assume a ground role. Burke signalled the Royal Marines' American counterpart in Korea – the crack 1st US Marine Division – to see if they would accept 41 Commando. Yet Drysdale – an alpha male who exuded confidence – confided a nagging uncertainty to his superior. 'It was a difficult decision to make,' he wrote of volunteering his unit for further duties on the peninsula. 'I only hope it was right.'[38]

It was an understandable concern. While the commandos re-roled in Japan, the war in Korea had turned 180 degrees: The UNC had counter-invaded North Korea.

Chapter Six
Dust Clouds and Burning Towns

The die has been cast
Julius Caesar, crossing the Rubicon, 49 BC

13 October, 1950. 38th Parallel, near Kaesong.

Shrivelled eyes deep in hollow sockets gazed at Argyll Second Lieutenant Owen Light as he advanced. 'We were passing these trenches dug facing north,' Light recalled. 'And standing up in them were skeletons in uniforms; they still had their weapons.' The cadavers were the unburied remains of ROK units overrun on 25 June; a ghost force bearing silent witness to another invasion rolling across their frontier.

This offensive, however, was moving in the opposite direction of the one three and a half months earlier. Having successfully defended the south, the UNC was striking north.

On 27 September, President Harry Truman permitted General Douglas MacArthur to operate north of the 38th parallel. On 1 October, MacArthur broadcast a surrender message north. It went unanswered. The same day, South Korean President Rhee Syngman sent his forces north up the east coast. Rhee had made no secret of his ambition to unify Korea, hence earlier US reluctance to arm him with offensive weapons. Kim Il-sung's invasion, and the UNC response, had handed him the opportunity he had sought; the balance of power had tipped in his favour. Moreover, he had the support of MacArthur, who would settle for nothing less than total victory. What was absent was the approval of the wider world for an extension of the war northward.

Although Rhee had jumped the gun, Washington had been

gathering backing. On 30 September, a resolution, sponsored by the UK and seven other states, was placed before the UN. On 7 October, the assembly voted 47–5 – overwhelming a Soviet peace proposal – to pass UN Resolution 376(V). It called for a 'unified, independent and democratic government' with 'all appropriate steps' taken to ensure 'conditions of stability throughout Korea'.[1]

The invasion plan had already been laid out in a Joint Chiefs of Staff directive on 27 September. Its objective: The destruction of the NKPA. To avoid antagonising Peking and Moscow, only ROK troops would advance the final miles to the Chinese and Russian borders.[2] The line at which non-ROK troops would halt was some 50 miles south of the Yalu, the river which denoted the Sino-Korean frontier. This line was broadly demarcated by the town of Chongju in the west, and the cities of Hungnam and Hamhung in the east; it would be known to 27th Brigade as 'The MacArthur Line'.[3]

The UNC attack would be two-pronged. X Corps – comprising the US 1st Marine, the US 7th Infantry and the ROK Capital divisions – would advance in the peninsula's east. Divided from X Corps by the peninsula's mountainous spine, would be 8th Army. Led by US 1 Corps – 27th Brigade, ROK 1st Division and the US 1st Cavalry and 24th Infantry Divisions – 8th Army would strike north up the western axis. The brigade, the smallest unit in I Corps, would be commanded by one of the divisions. To I Corps' east, ROK II Corps would advance in parallel, just west of the mountains. Finally, IX Corps would mop up resistance in the south. The UNC in Korea now numbered almost 300,000 men.[4]

American reconnaissance units crossed on the 7 September; a full-scale US advance began on 9 October.[5] On 11 October, 27th Brigade was attached to 1st Cavalry Division.[6]

For some soldiers, the frontier was meaningless. 'We did not know about the 38th parallel or North Korea, we thought we were just going on to Pyongyang,' said Diehard Frank Whitehouse. 'We did not know if that was in the north or the south.' Others fretted that they were escalating beyond the UN mandate. 'We were under the understanding we were only going to the 38th parallel, then we were told we were going on,' said Middlesex Private Edgar Green. 'Chaps said, "How far are we going? Where's it going to end?"' Of more immediate concern was the terrain. 'Every day, the hills were getting bigger and higher and there were more of them,' Whitehouse said. The war was entering 'Tiger Country'.

These doubts, and the grim tableau passed by Light notwithstanding, the northward advance, the first Cold War invasion of a communist state, was animated by an almost carnival atmosphere. Middlesex Major Dennis Rendell was on a recce with Lieutenant Colonel Andrew Man when their jeep vehicle went over 'a hell of a bump' in the road. 'Somebody asked, "What the hell was that?"' Rendell recalled. 'The CO turned round and said, "That was the 38th parallel!"'

Planted beside dirt-track border crossings were signs advertising that fact. 'We crossed with a plethora of signs by the roadside saying, "You are crossing 38th parallel courtesy of 1st Cavalry,"' said Middlesex Major John Shipster. And behind American units – daubed in chalk or paint on makeshift road signs, mud walls, local cottages – was a bald, long-nosed head peeping over a wall. 'There was continual reference to "Kilroy" along the road,' Shipster said. 'Kilroy slept here'; 'Kilroy was here yesterday'; 'Kilroy has gone ahead'. It was appropriate that 'Kilroy' – the graffiti icon of the Second World War, the GI who 'always got there first' – had landed in Korea, for this campaign was beginning to resemble Northwest Europe in late 1944.

8th Army Commander General Walton Walker had served under Patton, the finest pursuit general of the war, as the commander of the XX Corps, known as 'The Ghost Corps' for its speed of advance;[7] 1st Cavalry Division's CO, General Hobart Gay, had been Patton's chief-of-staff.[8] In this headlong style of warfare, the priority is to advance so fast that the enemy, off-balance, has neither time nor space to consolidate and make a stand, so can be bypassed and surrounded. But in Korea, the *Wehrmacht* was not the enemy. While bypassed Germans could be wiped out, bypassed North Koreans ditched uniforms or melted into the hills.

Tactical issues aside, publicity-driven officers had individual agendas. With the NKPA apparently broken, US and ROK divisions were literally racing each other to seize prestige objectives. 'The speed of movement was terrific,' said Man: 'Let 'em roll! It was the American wild west all over again.'

* * *

Summer was over. Fall vies with spring as the finest season in Korea, and under clear, impossibly high skies, the countryside was painted in its autumnal palette: the trees and scrub on the undulating hillsides were a gorgeous riot of bronze, gold and copper, interspersed with jagged outcrops of pale grey granite and the evergreen of pines. In the valleys, the late rice harvest had been gathered; tall sheaves of bound rice straw stood among the paddies. Many of the mushroom-roofed villages sat among sprawling orchards, their well-pruned trees heavy with ripe apples. The days were cool, invigorating.

Under Japanese rule, the north of the peninsula had been the seat of industry, more well-off than the south. As they advanced into communist territory, some soldiers were surprised at how neat and prosperous it looked, compared to the war-ravaged hamlets of the Naktong and the corpse-strewn ruins of Seoul. 'South Korea I had found to be poverty stricken,' said Argyll Ralph Horsfield. 'In North Korea, the landscape seemed to change in the sense that the fields were all cultivated, there were trees, farms and orchards.' The two competing states were 'like chalk and cheese,' he thought.

Huge clouds of dust – in some areas, greyish yellow; in others a gingery red – billowed up from the miles-long tank and truck convoys, as, packed nose-to-tail, towing trailers and long artillery pieces, they ground up dirt tracks lined with empty ration cans tossed out by troops. Charging tanks dredged up bow waves of dust on the roads, but had to slow to a crawl to negotiate the sharp bends in villages. Recovery vehicles were overworked, hauling up vehicles that had tipped off raised tracks into the paddies.

Initial excitement soon dissipated. On 11 October, orders to move 3 RAR forward were impossible to carry out due to lack of transport. The following day, the Middlesex advance was held up, first by the tail of the US 5th Cavalry Regiment, then by 1st ROK Division crossing their front.[9] A furious Man planted anti-tank guns in the road as an obstacle so he was not bypassed, but on secondary roads that, with the poor maps issued, frequently led into *cul de sacs*, progress was grinding. 'It was a wild goose chase,' said Diehard Corporal Don Barrett. 'It was a farce.'

Insufficient transport, bad roads, and methodical flank clearances meant that 27th Brigade was not proceeding as fast as commanders wanted. 'Gay, the CO of the 1st Cavalry, told a liaison officer, "Tell that brigadier of yours to get off his ass!"' recalled REME Captain Reggie Jeffes.

Gay was a dynamo on the roads. Rendell was deploying his company when he sensed someone looking over his shoulder. It was the general, armed with a shotgun. 'I said, "Look general, why can't you leave me alone and let me fight my battle?"' Rendell recalled. This is not the way a major usually addresses a general, but Gay took it in good form. 'He said, "OK, if you feel like that,"' Rendell continued, 'So I said, "What's more, why do you carry that bloody shotgun?" He said, "You never know, you might see a 'phee-sant'." And he was right – there were a lot of game birds.'

While motorised Americans surged north, 27th Brigade was restricted to clearances in hills between Kaesong and Kumchon. This kind of work granted an intimate view of tragedies invisible from a speeding vehicle, for slowing the advance were enemy holdouts. 'When the Americans were leading, some sniper would start up from a hill and you'd see a whole battalion halted and there they'd be, waiting for airplanes to come along,' said Man. 'There was little idea of attacking with platoons, they just sat and waited. A lot of time was wasted and the odd sniper did his job quite nobly.' Such holdups invited massive retaliation. Rising above the dust haze, columns of smoke coiled slowly into blue skies. White marked phosphorous impacts; grey, burning wood or thatch; black, napalm. Fires had distinct odours. A burning village smelled of wood smoke; blazing pines had a strangely zesty bouquet; napalm reeked of petrol.

Private James Beverly's Middlesex platoon was tasked to eliminate an enemy position on high ground. 'We asked for an aircraft to strafe it, which they did. I must admit, I liked to see napalm go in – it sounds horrible – but they never retreated!' The following morning, the platoon took the ridge. The ground was still hot, the scrub was still smouldering – and so were the defenders 'They were like kamikazes! One was sitting at a machine gun, and he still had his hands on it, he was the colour of charcoal, and his head was nodding – it was the nerves or something,' Beverly said. 'They had stayed there and burnt . . . the whole country was burnt.'

Corporal John Pluck, the recent Middlesex reinforcement, cleared another village. 'The North Koreans liked to dig in around villages occupied by civilians,' he said. 'Americans passing by were fired on, they replied and blasted this village to hell.' Weapons at the port, well spaced, the Diehards advanced in a 50-yard line over open ground, warily entering the smoking settlement. It was heavily damaged; holed walls, sagging roofs, debris strewn between cottages. 'I heard a low moaning coming from one of these houses that had a shell hole in the roof,' Pluck recalled. He peered in. As his eyes adjusted, he could make out the prone outlines of a man, a woman and several children coated in thick dust. Another moan. Looking closely, Pluck registered a streak of red among the grey: A huge gash in the scalp of one of the children, a little girl, perhaps seven years old. Pluck lifted her carefully and carried her out. Helpless, he handed her over to an old woman in the next house. 'I was 23-years-old, a leader of men, but this disturbed me a great deal,' he said. Pluck continued the operation, vision blurred with tears. He later heard the child had died the same day.

Killings preceded 8th Army's arrival: it was simple for enemy to settle accounts with 'reactionaries', adopt civilian clothing and welcome the invaders. 'As you went into a village, men lined up and bowed low and said, "*Mansei, mansei!*" '* recalled Man. 'Not far away were bits and pieces of legs sticking out from under the earth.' Irish Diehard Frank Screeche-Powell recalled an old man and an infant lying dead in one village: 'I guess some of our men had laid them in peace with God,' he said. 'They'd been murdered by the Reds.'

Dispirited enemy troops, bypassed by the advance, dribbled in and

---

* *Mansei* – literally, 'ten thousand years' – is a Korean exhortation, similar to the European 'Bravo!' or 'Long live!' It is the Korean enunciation of the Chinese character that the Japanese pronounce as *banzai*.

surrendered, but there were occasional skirmishes. Around midnight on Friday 13 October, Phillip Bennett, the 3 RAR mortars officer, overheard a perimeter sentry shout a challenge. Bennett went over to find a Korean standing with his hands behind his back. 'I realised something odd was going on and heard the pin of a grenade being released – a large sound in the night!' Bennett said. 'He heaved it towards us, I shouted a warning and ducked for cover.' The grenade exploded, sprinkling the two Diggers with shrapnel. Bennett opened up: 'I tried to use my .38, but had three misfires out of six.' Still, at least one round struck; they heard screams as the Korean crawled into the darkness. Bennett's wounds, in his shoulder and side, were 'bloody painful' but not serious: he was dressed at the RAP. Bennett and the sentry were 3 RAR's first combat casualties. The battalion moved the next day. The wounded Korean was never found.

Transport was vexing. 'US sources could never provide us with more than a two-battalion lift, and so B Echelon had to be grounded to provide the third battalion lift,' wrote Coad. 'Most unsatisfactory.' The moving battalions were formed into semi-independent battle groups, with whatever supporting arms were available. The vanguard battalion – which changed daily – would lead up the road axis, the second cleared flanks and the third rested and moved forward in the evening.[10] This leapfrog style of movement, with the spearhead changing every day, set the stage for the actions to come. With the war fully mobile, little detailed planning was feasible. Coad, Green, Man and Neilson would have to plan and execute their operations on the run.

On 16 October, the brigade was ordered to pass through 1st Cavalry Division and seize Sariwon. Sariwon was particularly vital. Not only was it a key crossroads and reputed garrison town, it was also a prestige objective: 24th Infantry Division and 1st Cavalry Division had been told that whichever unit took Sariwon, would be given priority to capture Pyongyang.[11] Such things mattered to American commanders; Gay gave 27th Brigade the crucial task. After the frustrations of previous days, Coad was delighted. 'At last,' he wrote, 'we were going to get an axis!'[12]

* * *

At 06:35, the Argylls passed through the lines of 1st Cavalry and punched north into enemy territory. The countryside was idyllic: low, rolling hills; rich paddies and orchards; undamaged, peaceful villages.

Blazing the trail was A Company, led by that happiest of warriors, Major David Wilson. First were four M4 Shermans of the US 89th Tank Battalion, battened down; then another four loaded with a platoon of Jocks; a second platoon in trucks; a mortars section and a Vickers section in carriers; then the third platoon: 'Very like a the Second World War column going through France after Normandy,' Wilson mused. Behind, followed the rest of the battalion. Further back was a US general in a jeep, complete with obligatory press posse. Wilson was surprised to discover that he was there, not as a liaison, but as a referee to ensure 'fair play' between the 1st Cavalry spearhead – i.e. the Argylls – and 24th Division.[13]

The progress of the thrust was tensely followed by Brigade HQ. War Diary entries make clear the importance of pace.

At 07:45, the battle group passed its first objective, a range of hills, the Shermans knocking out an anti-tank gun. At 09:00, a bridge – un-demolished – was crossed. Snipers fired on the column from the village of Hungsu-ri. The lead platoon dismounted, rapid-firing into cottages on each side with their own weapons and the massive .50 calibre machine guns on the tank turrets, while tank gunners fired white phosphorous shells, igniting suspected sniper points. 'This was a noisy and effective way of clearing the main access and the snipers did not return,'[14] noted the A Company After-action Report.[15] There was one casualty of this short, violent action: Private Raymond Kinne,* was killed 2 yards from Wilson by a sniper in civilian clothes firing point-blank.[16] At 11:30, more snipers were encountered. The lead platoon deployed, killing four.[17] At 12:30, a key pass was cleared.

---

*Communist forces might, feasibly, have rued the killing of Kinne: Seeking revenge, his brother, Derek, volunteered for the Korean War. Captured at the Imjin in 1951, Derek was determined not to besmirch his brother's name; his extraordinary feats of resistance in the POW camps earned him a George Cross. (His story is told in the author's *To the Last Round*) Derek last visited the UN Cemetery in Pusan in 2010 to see his brother's name on the Commonwealth Memorial. Buried in North Korea, Raymond's body was never recovered.

Still no opposition. At approximately 14:00, in rolling country some 3 miles short of Sariwon, the inevitable happened.[18] Small arms and anti-tank weapons opened up from an apple orchard on the left of the road, at a point where it curved round the hill. The Argylls had tripped the NKPA defences.

The lead tank commander was hit, and, as men tumbled off trucks and tanks to deploy, so was one Jock, shot in the buttocks; the bullet exited through his chest. 'This chap was a bit lugubrious and one of the corporals had said, "Serve you right if you get hit in the arse,"' recalled his platoon commander, Ted Cunningham. 'The corporal came up to me and said, "Och sir, I wish I'd never said that."' Remarkably, the man was not seriously wounded: The bullet missed all vital organs.

It was clear to Wilson that enemy fire covered the road. This was a classic 'fire block' – i.e. a position parallel to a route, from which enemy could shoot anything that passed – a tactic the UNC would soon become unpleasantly familiar with. It would have to be eliminated. At this point, a spotter plane that had been over-flying the column chose to land on the track, separating the tanks from the Jocks of the lead platoon. To make matters worse, a US general, in a state of high excitement, arrived with his reporters.[19] 'They're in that orchard, rake 'em, blast 'em out of there!' yelled General Frank Allen, 1st Cavalry's assistant commander.[20]

Wilson issued orders. One platoon would hold the road; a second would assault; a third, on high ground, would secure the flank of the attacking platoon. The major then began directing tank fire onto the enemy in the orchard while mortars and Vickers prepared to engage.

The assault platoon was led by Light, the leader of the clearance patrol on the Naktong. By now, he and his men had fully gelled. 'I really thought my platoon were good guys, it wasn't long before you understood what made them laugh – danger, I think!' Light's sergeant was an Arnhem veteran. 'We would be advancing and he'd see someone hanging back and he'd shout, "Come up! How are ye gonna be killed back there!" and everybody would laugh.' On this, their first set-piece attack, there would be danger aplenty. 'This was a platoon attack,' said Light. 'What I'd trained for!'

Lining his men up in the monsoon ditch, he gave the order: Fix bayonets. 'It has two reasons,' Light said. 'One is psychological – it makes you feel better – and if your gun jams, you have something to fight with.' Snick, click: Jocks fitted the needle-like 'pig stickers' onto their muzzles. Ahead, the orchard rose up a gentle slope for about 200 yards: Light's attack would be at 90 degrees to the enemy position. As the platoon moved off, a five-minute barrage from mortars, tanks and Vickers ploughed up the enemy position. Light led his men silently though the orchard, deploying by hand signal – 'I wanted it done quietly,' he said. 'No nonsense!' – but due to the trees, could not see the effect of the support fire.

Their advance was so fast that Light worried they would walk into the covering fusillade – then suddenly, they were upon the North Koreans. All were in trenches, facing the column. Due to the bend in the road, Light's men had got behind them. The stealthy advance through the trees, combined with the tremendous cacophony of firing, had bought the Highlanders to within yards of the enemy undetected. 'The poor devils were facing the wrong way,' said Light. 'We sprang on them.' Jocks rapid-fired down into the trenches – enemy tried frantically to stand or turn – too late. 'They got up,' Light said. 'And they felt the kiss of death on them.' Only one got out of his trench after a corporal had a stoppage. The North Korean had the same problem; the two slashed and thrust at each other among the trees with bayonets, before the enemy was shot by another Jock.

It had been a massacre. 'We cleared them all out, we didn't get a scratch!' said Light. 'This is what we trained for, were good at, the Jocks were all laughing, they thought it was tremendous!' Light's platoon had killed seventeen enemy, capturing 10 LMGs; forty-two more enemy lay dead from the support fire.[21] The murderous attack won Light a nickname, the accuracy of which was confirmed by his company commander: 'The Jocks don't often get it wrong,' Wilson wrote. Light's nickname was a single word: 'Killer'.[22]

American reporters were impressed. 'The Argylls could have gone barrelling through,' wrote *Newsweek*'s correspondent, comparing the action to a Technicolour movie. 'They refused – partly because they hadn't seen much real combat (sic) and champed for a chance to show

how good they are . . . it was an impressive demonstration.'[23]

A Company's clearance had only taken about fifteen minutes, but impatience was brewing. The Deputy Commander of I Corps, the Deputy Chief of Staff of 1st Cavalry and an unidentified major general arrived and confronted Wilson, ordering him to remount and strike for Sariwon. This was uncomfortable; the major already had been ordered to go firm by Neilson, and his platoons were scattered over a square kilometre of countryside. 'Their presence and advice did not make the handling of the situation any easier,' noted the Argylls' War Diary. Then B and C Companies motored through; the generals and press promptly disappeared with the new vanguard.[24]

As A Company regrouped, 3 RAR rolled up. Seeing the carnage, a Digger leaned out of a truck and yelled, 'For Chrissakes mates, leave some for us!'[25] Wilson was ordered up to join an O Group in Sariwon itself, which was being secured by B and C Companies with barely any resistance. In the town, Wilson settled back in an abandoned barber shop as 3 RAR, meanwhile, rode through to establish a blocking position to the north.

It had been a remarkable day. It would be a more remarkable night.

*   *   *

Lieutenant Colonel Charlie Green led his battalion north of the town, establishing blocking positions well forward. 'He said, "We have got to get far forward so we can make a good start in the morning,"' recalled Lieutenant David Butler. 'It gave us a glimpse of Charles Green – that was the nature of him.' To his rear, B Echelon, together with elements of C Company, settled among an orchard as night fell; it was to be these elements, not Green's vanguard that would see action this night. Sergeant Reg Bandy of C Company and his section were digging into a dry paddy alongside a road junction as darkness fell. Three US tanks stood nearby.

Unknown to the Diggers, events inside Sariwon were out of control. The town had been entered by the Argylls at 15:20, and reported occupied by 16:20;[26] after dark, retreating North Koreans, driven by US forces pushing from the southwest, blundered into astonished Argylls. Close-range firefights were breaking out across the burning town, but not all enemy were so engaged, for Sariwon has two parallel roads running north–south.

Near 3 RAR's B Echelon came a burst of automatic fire. Then, from out of the gloom to their south, the Australians heard an unmistakable noise: The thump-thump-thump of marching feet. Ferguson, the mercurial second-in-command commanding the echelon while Green established his CP forward, immediately grasped the situation. 'Don't fire until I give the order!' he told Bandy and the other men digging in beside the track. Indistinct figures were tramping up the road, closer and closer. Ferguson ordered jeep headlights flicked on. In the sudden illumination an apparently endless column of marching enemy was revealed. 'They came in three ranks,' said Bandy. 'They thought the way was clear!'

Blocking the column stood a Sherman dominating the junction. With it stood Ferguson, together with men of B Company – sent back by Green to assist his second in command – and an interpreter. 'You're surrounded!' Ferguson roared, waiting for the South Korean to translate. 'Surrender or be massacred!' He gave the North Koreans two minutes to decide. Lying prone in the dry paddy just yards from the enemy mass, Bandy took first trigger pressure. 'There was dead silence,' said Bandy. 'It was the longest two minutes – it seemed like two hours!'

It was a risky bluff by Ferguson. In his exposed position, he would be the first man gunned down if the enemy went for broke. Soldiers on the track gaped, confused; Bandy reckoned they had spotted Australians in greatcoats – the night was cool – and, like the men in the town, concluded they were Russians reinforcing from the north. The NKPA vanguard seemed stunned. Some seemed to be taking firing positions, but on the track, had little cover. The clock ticked.

At the head of the column, weapons clattered to the ground. Hands rose. Like dominoes, the process was repeated down the long lines of men. Diggers cautiously emerged from cover, weapons levelled. On the faces of the enemy, surprise turned to anger when they registered the Australian numbers. 'They were pissed off when they realised there were only 120 of us!' Bandy recalled. Ferguson's bluff had worked. 'That's what made him a battle leader,' said Sniper Robbie Robertson. 'He turned that situation around.'

*   *   *

The enemy was – apparently – mastered. Ferguson ordered Butler to drive in to Sariwon to locate the ration truck, which had not arrived. Butler's young platoon sergeant, Alfred 'Jack' Harris, overheard Butler ask Ferguson what he was to do about enemy between the position and the town. Ferguson dismissed his concern, saying all enemy had 'probably' surrendered. Harris was less certain, but orders were orders. The platoon mounted a truck, Butler and Harris clambered into the cab and they started off south.[27]

Almost immediately, they found themselves driving between the marching lines of what appeared to be a North Korean regiment; Ferguson had not bagged the entire column. As they had with the Argylls, the NKPA mistook the Diggers for allies. 'There were people on either side of us shouting, "*Mansei* – Russki – *mansei!*"' said Butler. 'We went right through them and kept going.' The platoon in the back froze like statues; in the cab, Harris and Butler waved back. 'It was a bit dodgy!' Butler recalled

After passing the column, the truck was engulfed by smoke from burning railway carriages: the suburb south of Sariwon. The billowing clouds reflected flames 'like a stormy day' thought Harris.[28] Backlit by this hellish illumination, strode a devilish silhouette: A tall figure surmounted by a bonnet and carrying a crooked stick. Butler dismounted. 'Have you seen our CO?' the apparition enquired; it was John Slim, the Argyll adjutant, searching for Neilson who – unbeknownst to either man – had undergone an experience almost identical to Butler's. Butler could not help; Slim disappeared back into the night. Remarkably, Butler's platoon located the rations. Returning to B Echelon, they found the North Koreans they had passed had surrendered.[29]

With daylight, confusion evaporated. Ferguson's gambit had netted 1,982 prisoners – complete with machine guns, mortars and anti-tank guns.[30]

The Argylls had entered the town from the southeast. The enemy who had advanced in columns through the town had been pressed by 24th Infantry Division, advancing from the southwest. Meanwhile, the US 7th Cavalry had found a side road running parallel to the axis taken by 27th Brigade on the right. They had advanced northeast of Sariwon and trapped yet another group of NKPA, taking 1,700 prisoners, who they marched south toward 3 RAR in their headlights. Green had been preparing to launch up that axis at dawn; the American arrival from the north obviated his attack.

The Middlesex, bringing up the rear, saw only aftermath.

Sariwon was still burning as they drove through – a drive Major John Willougby found eerie. 'We jinked through the narrow streets and the smoke and flames of burning houses,' he wrote. 'Passing through the main square were a number of civilians leaning against the walls or crouching in doorways and it was only in looking back that I realised that they were all dead – dreadful.'[31] The Koreans had been either asphyxiated by napalm or killed by a blast in the high altitude bombing that had preceded the Argyll attack, leaving no external wounds.

Amid the chaos floated hundreds of banknotes. 'Someone had flushed a North Korean paymaster and in our brief halts, bundles of crisp new banknotes were distributed up and down the column in their hundreds of thousands,' Willoughby noted.[32] Men eagerly stuffed their packs, but it was soon discovered that an egg could not be had for less than one million won.[33]

* * *

27th Brigade's seizure of Sariwon secured 1st Cavalry's claim on Pyongyang.[34] Delighted, Gay wrote to Coad on the 'sensational drive through enemy territory,' which had 'sped 31 miles in 12 hours to deal the enemy a disastrous blow'.[35] But though 27th Brigade had opened the gates of Pyongyang, it would not drive through them.

'We were diverted away from the main route by no less than the diminutive figure of the general himself clad in a US Air Force flight jacket and with a belt and pistol at his waist,' recalled Lieutenant Alf Argent, 3 RAR's intelligence officer, of Gay. 'He halted Lieutenant Colonel Green in his carrier and directed he and his battalion to another route to the west.' Green was amused at a general directing traffic, but his Diggers watched sourly as 1st Cavalry rumbled past. It was a bitter pill for 3 RAR, as they knew the division – 'MacArthur's Palace Guard' – from Japan. 'We did not like 1st Cav: on guard duties in Japan, they got everything they wanted and others didn't,' said Mortar Sergeant Tom Muggleton. 'There were 18,000 of 'em, all in vehicles,' said Bandy. 'It was like a circus, nobody walking, all swinging from .30 calibres and .50 calibres.' The choking dust in their wake was like a sandstorm: soldiers could not see each other across the width of the track they were marching up.[36]

With the UNC victorious, Koreans were appearing at the entrances to their villages as the columns drove through, waving South Korean flags; Ken Mankelow wondered where they had got them, but given the brutal consequences of being seen to support the wrong side – by now, right-wing ROK paramilitaries were arriving – it was prudent for civilians to have two sets. Apples were thrown into passing vehicles, leading some men to worry about grenades. Many North Koreans were genuinely grateful toward their liberators. Signals Lieutenant Peter Baldwn was doing foot reconnaissance up a track for an overnight location, when a little boy appeared and wagged his finger. Baldwin thought he was being 'cheeky' but the child ran ahead of him, pointing to a tripwire leading to a hand grenade. Baldwin was 'eternally grateful'.

The western route Gay had assigned 27th Brigade was, 'an atrocious axis as usual,' Coad thought.[37] Much of 18 October was spent hauling trucks out of ditches; making matters worse, heavy rain fell. But there were still operational enemy. On 19 October, Len Opie's section, leading 3 RAR, was marching alongside a US Sherman when a haystack in a paddy suddenly opened fire. Opie's section deployed. The lead Sherman spun on its tracks – catching a man's foot in its treads –and returned fire, hitting the 'haystack', a camouflaged T34. The tank stood motionless, its crew stunned. One of Opie's men leapt onto its hull, and banged on the top hatch. An NKPA soldier opened it and was shot. That ended the action. Another tank and SPG were captured, unmanned and out of fuel.[38]

Meanwhile, 1st Cavalry was launching a set-piece assault on Pyongyang. Reginald Thompson, a highly experienced correspondent for the *Daily Telegraph,* watched big guns firing and infantry formations spreading over the plain; it reminded him of a nineteenth-century battle portrait. The attack hit air. The enemy had fled.[39] Ahead, among wooded hills, nestled Kim's capital on the Taedong River. On 19 October, 1st Cavalry and 1st ROK Division entered the city from different directions. Bar snipers, there was little resistance. For 1st ROK's commander, General Paik Sun-yup, it was tremendously satisfying: He was a native of Pyongyang.

The following day, 27th Brigade rolled in. First were the neat houses and tiny gardens of the suburbs; then the tram lines up broad city-centre avenues, over which loomed great concrete government buildings hung with enormous placards of Stalin and Kim. Many men were impressed by their glimpse of Pyongyang.* 'As a youngster I couldn't believe what I was seeing, because you heard about the terrible communists, and they had these marvellous big buildings,' said Diehard Ted Haywood; the football stadium 'made Wembley look second class,' he thought. Locals were restive, Willoughby noted. 'The population were tentatively beginning to loot and bales of cotton were being carried home.'[40] Diggers filled 3 RAR's water bowser at the brewery and drove it round the companies to fill everyone's water bottles, but it proved to be weak beer.[41]

Grimmer events were also underway for advancing behind the 8th Army, Rhee's paramilitaries were rooting out hardcore communists. 'I remember how terribly cruel the South Koreans were to the citizens, I think they had broken into some liquor stores, were quite drunk and were shooting people in the streets and marching them off,' said REME Captain Reggie Jeffes. 'It was really an awful business, but there was nothing we could do.'

Pyongyang was largely intact, though much infrastructure – public transport, the water mains, sewage pumps and the great iron bridges over the Taedong River – had been destroyed by retreating NKPA.[42] 'It seemed that the experience of Seoul had taught the

---

* The same holds true today: Pyongyang, as the author can attest, is a fine advertisement for the Democratic People's Republic of Korea. Few defectors who escape the impoverished and isolated nation, alas, support the contention of success and comfort that their showpiece capital represents.

Koreans not to defend their towns,' wrote Thompson.[43] He and fellow journalists were free to wander. They feasted on caviar and champagne in the empty Russian embassy; it, and adjacent diplomatic housing, showed signs of being recently abandoned, with bottles of beer unfinished on the tables. Then, guided by a local, they entered Kim Il-sung's lair, the presidium. It was set on a commanding hill, Moran-san, overlooking the city. From above, it was camouflaged with netting and foliage, but inside, the dictator's inner sanctum proved magnificent. Kim's office was thickly carpeted, hung with crimson-lined black silk curtains and dominated by a massive, carved desk. But at least one souvenir hunter had arrived before the reporters: A plaster cast of the North Korean leader had been decapitated.[44] The office would subsequently be occupied by General Walker, who did not bother removing its large portrait of Stalin.

Kim himself had flown. On 11 October, he had broadcast a radio address urging last-ditch resistance: 'Let us defend every inch of our motherland at the cost of our blood!'[45] While his men surrendered or were cut down, the ex-guerilla decamped for the mountain town of Kanggye, in Korea's distant north, 20 miles south of the Yalu. The dictator's distress at this stage of the war may be imagined: on 14 October, he had admitted to his army that he had not expected US forces to cross the 38th parallel.[46]

While Thompson rifled through Kim's bunker, 27th Brigade officers met a very different leader. Willoughby happened to be at Pyongyang airfield on 20 October where camera crews and press had gathered: 'something big was in preparation'. A transport aircraft with 'a cloud of escorting fighters' landed. Boarding steps were positioned. 'One got an impression of pressure within and sure enough, this door suddenly burst open and down the steps rushed the perfectly trained team of photographers, halting at their designated stations and immediately turning round to focus on the doorway,' an impressed Willoughby wrote. 'There was a long pause and suddenly there he was standing motionless in the doorway: MacArthur in majesty.' As the supreme commander was greeted by Walker, press closed in. 'Hands were shaken, full face; hands shaken again, right profile; then left profile and finally full face again for luck and up the steps went the great man and back to Tokyo,' noted Willoughby. 'Just like that.' [47]

MacArthur had every reason to beam. Still flush with his Inchon victory, he had conferenced with Truman at Wake Island on 15 October. Truman posed the big question: What if China intervenes? MacArthur assured him that if they did, US air power would ensure 'the greatest slaughter'. Victory in Korea was, essentially, won.[48]

Brigadier Coad, his radio link down and unable to locate Divisional HQ, led his brigade into the northern suburbs. 'We then went firm just outside the town and hoped that we should be allowed a rest,' Coad wrote. 'But that was not to be.'[49]

Chapter Seven
At the Tip of the Spear

The gates of mercy shall all be shut up,
And the flesh'd soldier, rough and hard of heart,
In liberty of bloody hand shall range
With conscience wide as hell
William Shakespeare

Early afternoon, 30 miles north of Pyongyang.

Ahead shone a rectangle of brightness. Men ran toward it, tumbled out, disappeared. AP photographer Max Desfor was last in line: He ran along the vibrating metal floor, through the door and into nothingness. 'I felt the jerk of parachute, then all of a sudden I saw the ground coming up to meet me and I was there,' he said. 'It only takes 30 seconds to land from 700 feet, I landed fine and remembered to bend my knees!'

Remembering to bend knees upon landing is basic for a trained paratrooper, but not for a civilian who had never jumped before – even less so for one whose sole pre-training was a verbal tip delivered by a paratrooper sitting opposite Desfor as the aircraft was flying for its drop zone. Even for the adventurous photojournalist, this was high risk.

The day previously, Desfor had been accompanying 27th Brigade – 'they were well trained and there was a feeling of safety with them, it was the same thing with the marines; they were safer than the 24th Division or the ROKs' – when he had heard of a parachute operation being planned. A sympathetic British officer jeeped him to Kimpo, to join the first jump of the war.

Now, on the ground behind the North Korean front line, Desfor

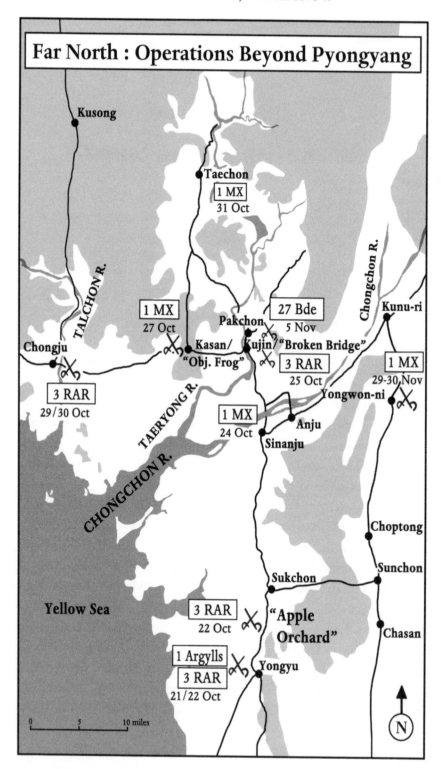

Far North : Operations Beyond Pyongyang

Kusong

Taechon

1 MX
31 Oct

TALCHON R.

Chongchon R.

Kunu-ri

1 MX
27 Oct

27 Bde
5 Nov

Pakchon

Kujin

"Broken Bridge"

Chongju

Kasan/
"Obj. Frog"

3 RAR
25 Oct

1 MX
29-30 Nov

3 RAR
29/30 Oct

Yongwon-ni

TAERYONG R.

1 MX
24 Oct

Anju

Sinanju

CHONGCHON R.

Choptong

Sunchon

Sukchon

Yellow Sea

3 RAR
22 Oct

"Apple
Orchard"

Chasan

1 Argylls

Yongyu

3 RAR
21/22 Oct

0   5   10 miles

N

ditched his harness. The second wave was coming down, lines of parachutes blossoming as planes droned by. Desfor raised his lens: 'It's a beautiful picture, the sky filled with paratroopers.' The first incident on the ground was a wounded trooper. Desfor ran over for a picture – to find a rival correspondent for United Press. 'I said, "Gee, I'd take your picture if you were AP, but you're UP!"' he said. In fact, six correspondents had joined the drop. Paratroopers regrouped and moved on their objectives.

The 187th Airborne Regimental Combat Team, 4,064 men, had landed on two drop zones around the towns of Sukchon and Sunchon – watched through Ray-ban sunglasses by MacArthur himself, circling above in his personal Constellation. The towns, 15 miles apart, were 33 miles north of Pyongyang.[1] The mission, Desfor was told, was to cut off retreating NKPA and recapture American POWs being conveyed north by train. This latter mission was critical, for on the UNC advance north from the Naktong, along with over 7,000 civilian victims, some 485 American and 1,002 South Korea POWs had been discovered killed.[2]

The sky soldiers had achieved surprise, landing in the rear of a retreating enemy regiment. But airborne troops are light troops. Prompt relief by ground forces is essential.

* * *

Soon after dawn on 21 October, orders were received that 27th Brigade was passing from the command of 1st Cavalry to 24th Infantry Division. The 24th was still south of Pyongyang, but an American liaison officer arrived at Coad's HQ, carrying a map trace and orders:[3] 27th Brigade was to strike north, securing the town of Sinanju and its river crossings on the Chongchon River.[4] This was a significant thrust: Sinanju was over 50 road miles from Pyongyang. The 1st ROK Division would be advancing on a parallel axis east of the brigade. Complicating matters was a circle drawn around the town of Sukchon with the words '187th ACT', yet the brigadier had no information about the drop.[5] In short, Coad was to spearhead the UNC drive north on the western flank, and relieve, en route, an airborne unit about which he had no information, all while under command of a division which lay south of Pyongyang – a division, moreover, of which Coad's brigade had unpleasant memories from the Naktong breakout.

27th Brigade started north at 12:00 the same day. It was slow going. 'All the bridges had been demolished and we forced our way though churned-up fords,' Willoughby noted. 'We passed the remains of the Pyongyang fire brigade – virtually new fire engines which looked as if they had been driving nose to tail when they were caught by the USAF.'[6]

Once clear of the suburbs, the advance accelerated through open countryside with the Argylls leading. A series of phase lines – Cat, Dog, Rat, Mouse, Elephant, Lion, Tiger – were passed without incident. The country was getting hillier, but there was no contact until they closed on the town of Yongyu, some 21 miles north. The leading company dismounted; the enemy fled. The whereabouts of the American paratroopers were still unknown, and it was dusk. Coad ordered 27th Brigade to 'go firm for the night and curl up.'[7]

As darkness was falling, Lieutenant Colonel Neilson briefed Second Lieutenant Alan Lauder, the recently arrived reinforcement, to reconnoiter forward and fix the location of the paratroopers. The subaltern and a section of Jocks mounted a Sherman, and trundled warily into Yongyu. All went according to plan; they linked up with Americans dug in on the north edge of the town. 'We had no problem getting in,' Lauder said. 'An American officer there said, "Great, we're pleased you're here."' With these Americans of K Company, 187th Airborne located, and the main battalion some 2 miles north, Lauder's little force returned to the Argylls, half a mile distant.[8] All was quiet; a link up could be made at dawn, then 3 RAR would pass through and take point.

At 23:30 firing broke out.[9] A retreating North Korean force from the 239th Regiment had blundered into the airborne and were trying to break through. In confusion, some assaulted the Argylls' A Company.[10] Flares fizzed above; muzzles flickered in the blackness. Light's platoon were in cover behind a scattering of oval Korean grave mounds. Light heard grenades go off, and a man in a neighbouring platoon cry out. The platoon commander shouted,

'Where are you hit?' The Jock replied, 'In the arms, the chest and the legs, sir!' Light came under intense fire – 'bullets were going everywhere' – so told his mortar man, McCardy, that it was time to move. Light gave him a push; the man fell over, dead, one of two Jocks killed that night. 'There was terrible fighting going on and we could hear Korean voices around us in the dark,' said Lauder. 'Very tense!' The Argylls held, but clearly the airborne were under pressure.

At dawn, Lauder was again assigned to contact the US positions by Neilson; he took his platoon and three tanks. By now an American colonel had appeared. 'He insisted we follow this retreating North Korean regiment through the town; this seemed a bit ambitious to me, so I said we were a recce patrol and had to report back,' Lauder recalled. 'He said it was an American tank and it would do what he told it.' The Sherman gunned its engines; Jocks clung on as they entered, again, Yongyu's main street. It was just a couple of hundred yards from end to end but by now, 'there were lots of dead enemy bodies around, some still dying in the road – not very nice! – and bullets whizzing past your ear,' Lauder recalled. At the north of town, Lauder told the tank commander that he and his men were dismounting, adding that it was not a good idea for such a small force to pursue the enemy. The tank commander – after speaking to his battalion CO on the radio – agreed and halted.[11] K Company were firm, north of the town, but beyond Yongyu, Lauder could see heavy enemy forces moving through orchards.

Neilson, having heard from Lauder over his battalion net, reported to Coad on the presence of the US colonel. Coad was fuming – the small force could easily have been overrun in the town. He drove forward to confront the officer himself and in a sharp exchange, ordered him back to Corps HQ. The colonel departed.[12]

3 RAR would take vanguard and link up with the main body of the airborne, somewhere north of Yongyu, after Argylls secured the town. It proved a nest of snipers, presenting a tricky tactical problem: While snipers could not prevent combat units like 3 RAR from motoring through, they could pick off rear and command elements. Relief of the airborne was urgent, there was no time to clear Yongyu,

house-by-house. The solution had been discussed on the Naktong within days of the brigade's landing: 'Subject to the urgency of the situation and there being no civilians present', Middlesex officers had decided, 'the only suitable action will be . . . bypass the village and burn out the defenders'.[13] The Argylls put this ruthless tactic into practice. Yongyu would be put to the torch. 'Burn them out!' Wilson ordered.[14]

Some troops had misgivings. 'When you are told to burn a town, it first causes some concern that you should do such a thing – then you wonder how to start it,' recalled Peter Jones, the Argyll who had been aboard HMS *Jamaica*. 'The houses were mainly wood, and a match to the ceiling straw had amazing results.'[15] When phosphorous grenades were bought into play, the blaze caught, racing from roof to roof. 'I threw a grenade on this thatch and it went up,' said Light. 'The brigade major came up-column and said, "What are you doing and who gave you these orders?" I said, "Major Wilson!" and he said, "Oh!"' The men grew enthusiastic. Jocks set to 'with great dash and relish, and soon had some good fires burning,' Coad noted approvingly.[16]

3 RAR drove through choking smoke. 'When we were through the town, it was like coming into a spotlight, it was so bright,' said Butler. Before long, the Argylls were being asked to douse their conflagration; accompanying US artillery could not pass through the searing heat.[17]

Brigade HQ, south of the town was deluged with refugees from the town; sympathetic soldiers gave up their own rations and provided straw to sleep on. 'Some of these civilians will long remember the help given by British troops outside Yongyu,' the War Diarist noted on 22 October. As there is no mention of the firing of the town in the diary, the diarist was presumably ignorant of the fact that it was British troops who ignited the homes – albeit due to the exigencies of war. It was yet another in a series of tragedies suffered by the Koreans of 1950. Worse ordeals lay ahead.

* * *

None of this was on the minds of Diggers advancing to contact with the support of 18 US Shermans. North of Yongyu, the first troops

Green's CP bumped into were Lauder's recce patrol, halted following Coad's intervention. 'The Aussie colonel was very interested to know what we had seen, and he immediately put in an attack on the orchard,' recalled the Scotsman, who decided he had better swiftly return to his own battalion, otherwise, 'I could see myself getting involved in this too; they were quite a gung ho bunch, the Aussies.'

At Sariwon, 3 RAR had been the anvil. In this operation, they would be the hammer, but Green would have to wield it judiciously, as, apart from the company still dug in north of Yongyu, the exact location of 3rd Battalion, 187th Airborne, was not demarcated. All that was known was that 5 miles north was the town of Sukchon, the drop zone. This complicated Green's task as he could not use artillery; it might hit friendly troops.

Diggers were especially keen to advance as they had recently been issued, not with individual C-rations, but B-rations: large tins, designed to be heated in field kitchens. Many had labels missing, with the result that platoons found themselves issued with tins of sauerkraut, turnips, carrots and tomato juice. In the orchards ahead, huge apples beckoned. Other Australians were keen simply to fight.

In the vanguard was C Company, commanded by Alamein veteran Captain Archer Denness. The Kalgoorlie native neither drank nor swore – an unusual distinction among the Diggers, not noted for restrained drinking or genteel language – but was fit and aggressive; his troops nicknamed him 'Armour-piercing Archie'.[18] Mounted on Shermans and trucks, Denness' men probed northward up a road running through a broad valley. Some 500 yards to the east was an apple orchard climbing up gently rising high ground; to the west were paddy fields among which stood wigwam-shaped sheaves of harvested rice straw, each slightly over the height of a man.

Action started from the orchard. 'We were passing this cutting and this sentry stood up – he must have been asleep – and shot,' said Bandy. 'Someone shot him, we all jumped off the tanks, and Denness shouted, 'No artillery! Bullets and bayonets!'

Lacking support weapons, C Company would rely on old-fashioned infantry tools: gunpowder, sharp steel and testosterone. Two platoons surged into the orchard and up the slope.

'This ridge line was about 200 feet high, covered with apple trees, and when you fired these apples fell off the trees,' Bandy said. Most of C Company were young soldiers who had not seen action; Bandy was so busy controlling them that, 'I did not fire a bloody shot myself.' Enemy were in trenches and foxholes, and many – presumably exhausted by the previous night's action – were asleep. Moreover, they were deployed north, facing the airborne; they were unprepared to repel an assault from the south. They panicked.

'A lot of enemy got out of their fighting pits, they were so untrained,' said Butler, whose platoon was firing cover from the road. 'They were killed for their trouble.' Any unit that panics and breaks in action is ripe for massacre, and so it was for the NKPA: C Company's body count was even more spectacular than Light's assault south of Sariwon. 'It was all over in 15 minutes, it happened so quick, it bamboozled them,' Bandy said. 'They thought they would get a warning, but we were on them and killing them, they panicked and were all over the place.'

On the low ground, Denness ordered Butler's 9 Platoon to head north, straight up the road, raised on a dyke, that ran toward the suspected American positions. The terrain was flat and open: Butler deployed his men in waist-deep monsoon ditches flanking the road and started advancing. At a culvert under the road, Sergeant Jack Harris' men fired a round through – directly into the leg of another Digger advancing on the other side. Harris dashed over to the man and ripped open his trousers with a bayonet. The damage was hideous: 'The exit hole was bigger than my clenched fist, with splintered bone and blood making a gruesome mess.' Harris fumbled for his gauze and dropped it in; it disappeared into the wound. Butler arrived and ordered Harris to get moving; medics would clear casualties. Gasping, the man begged Harris not to tell anyone he had been hit by friendly fire – then handed over his the Second World War Luger. Harris was assigning men to clear the next culvert when a Digger emerged from it, a tiny Korean child in his arms and a family following him: He had been about to grenade the culvert when two children – followed by their twelve-member family – scurried out. Escorting them to the rear, the grinning Digger, a huge man, looked, 'comical but magnificent,' Harris thought.[19]

The next obstacle was a bloodied horse and its overturned cart, surrounded by six dying enemy soldiers, blocked the road. As they attempted to heave the obstacle out off the track, Butler's platoon came under fire from enemy dug in on hills. 'Most of the enemy continued to focus north' – toward the GIs – 'and were not aware we were there, but as we got closer, more would turn around,' Butler said. Bursts zipped overhead; Diggers returned fire at enemy in plain sight. 'The sheer weight of opposition was getting too much for us, when suddenly the company commander marched down the middle of the road!' said Butler. 'He was in full view, his signaller was going up and down dodging bullets, and I had to get out of the drain to talk to him!' Denness had bought support: two Shermans. Their main armament, shooting into enemy positions less than 50 yards away, retrieved the situation. 'Their battle power was enormous,' Butler recalled.

The tanks finished the horse. The leading Sherman rolled over the creature – a leg caught in the tracks – the tank shuddered, its engine strained – the helpless animal was hurled up, off the road and into the paddy. The loud 'thunk' it made as it landed in the dry paddy prompted one enemy to peer over a bund: Harris nailed him with one round. The horse raised its head once, looked at the advancing soldiers, then died.[20] The path was clear to advance the final few hundred yards to the American positions.

Distant paratroops could now see Australians closing. An airborne officer watched with astonishment the butchery inflicted by a single, fearsome Digger, 'Bluey' – so called because of his red hair – Smith.[21] A giant of a man, Smith 'loved the army, and he had guts,' Bandy reckoned. Smith lunged into a North Korean trench, bayonet fixed. He emerged soaked in crimson. Asked if he was wounded, he replied, 'You should see the other jokers!'[22] In the trench lay eight dead enemy.[23]

Sniper Robbie Robertson, with Green's Command Post behind C Company, had watched Denness' men go in. 'They just overran the enemy, kept them off balance, they did not give a shit that they were outnumbered,' he said. The CP was moving through an uncleared section of the orchard when they hit a line of trenches and bunkers – two- or three-man dug-outs, with top cover, still occupied by live enemy. NKPA charged out; a melee surged around the CP. 'It was close combat, we were three to four paces from these bunkers,' Robertson said. Diggers threw grenades through openings, then fired in: 'You follow up with fire as they might burst out, away from the grenade.' Robertson was passing one when another soldier dropped a grenade it. It was hurled back out. Robertson dived down – the grenade went off – an enemy soldier sprang out of the bunker, firing a burp gun. His burst barely missed the sniper: 'All three rounds went into the ground under my chest, and I fired three shots as I scrambled to my feet,' he said. 'You can fire just as quickly with a bolt as a semi-auto; the rifle bucks anyway, so you have to re-aim.' The enemy soldier went down. Robertson was trained to kill at 1,000 yards; this target had been at muzzle-to-muzzle range. Even though combat was whirling all around, the marksman in Robertson could not help noting his group: Three tight rounds through the North Korean's cheekbone. 'In a position where you're being gunned to death – well, it makes for accurate fire!' he said.

Signals Sergeant Jack Gallaway was impressed at his CO's behaviour: Green, ignoring the fighting, was scanning map boards and controlling the battalion action. Panicked enemy were running around in the open. Over open sights, Robertson fired again and again. 'I was a sniper and when we place a shot we don't miss – down he goes!' he said. D Company was summoned to assist the headquarters troops in finishing off enemy survivors.

While C Company cleared the orchard, Private Stan Connelly of B Company was covering their flank when a North Korea leapt out of a rice sheaf at him. 'He jumped out, he had a fixed bayonet and took a poke at me,' Connelly recalled. 'I reflexively parried the thrust with the Bren, and my number two shot him dead.' Connelly was slashed across the hand, but continued advancing.

C Company had reached a treeline at the end of the broad valley. It was approximately 14:00.[24] 'I was talking to David Butler, who had a bullet hole through his web belt, when we saw movement in the scrub,' said Sergeant Tom Muggleton, the Mortar Fire Controller. 'So we approached, and could see this great scrape of red earth, and in it were several paratroopers.' 'By God, we're pleased to see you!' they told the Diggers. The Americans – bar a couple who attempted to surrender to C Company, wearing Russian-looking greatcoats – were relieved. A staff sergeant approached Bandy. 'Nobody can tell you what it's like to come back from the dead!' he said, in tears. A US officer presented Gallaway with his .45 pistol. 'I said, "You can't just give me that!"' Gallaway recalled, 'And he said, "Ah – I just lost it!"'

The Australians had overrun the NKPA and linked up with the Americans. Job done, Butler and his platoon sat down and cracked open ration tins for lunch. Their surroundings hardly impelled appetite. 'There were dead all around us as we ate,' he said. 'God knows how many bodies.' But the butchery was not over yet. Enemy holdouts, bypassed during the narrow-front advance up the road, were sniping from rice sheaves. Butler was ordered to sweep through, clearing the paddies. The lieutenant ordered his men to form extended line and fix bayonets. Then they strode forward.

Unlike the British bayonets – the needle-like 'pig stickers' – the Australians carried the old pattern 'sword bayonets' with their broad, 18-inch blades. Though no more lethal than the British weapons – in edged weapons combat, the stab is deadlier than the slash – they were more fearsome looking, and unlike the dull, blued steel of the British bayonets, the Diggers' blades were bright. Seeing the inexorable advance of the tall figures in slouch hats, their bayonets reflecting the crisp sunlight, the hidden enemy panicked, breaking cover and running. The resultant drama awed spectators.

Coad was passing up the road. Fascinated, he stopped to view a scene that was more hunt than battle. 'An Australian platoon lined up in a paddy field and walked through it as if they were driving snipe,' Coad wrote. 'The soldiers, when they saw a pile of straw, kicked it and out would bolt a North Korean. Up with a rifle, down with a North Korean.'[25] Viewing everything from high ground had been a young war correspondent from the *Melbourne Sun,* Harry Gordon. As overnight copy editor, he had been following the war closely since its outbreak, so when an Australian press pool was assigned to Korea, he was his paper's top choice. Gordon had not covered the Second World War; Korea was his first conflict, and he was keen to see it up close. 'It was an amazing experience to see,' he said. A bullet shattered the windscreen of a jeep nearby from which a photographer was shooting; Gordon stayed put. 'Diggers were stabbing and kicking into rice bundles, enemy would run out and be cut down,' he recalled. 'It was close-range, brutal stuff.'

Butler's action finished the fight.* In one of the most lop-sided battles of the war, 3 RAR had lost seven wounded; the enemy had lost 150 dead and 239 prisoners.[26] 'It was a turkey shoot,' said Muggleton, the MFC whose mortars had been redundant. 'It was a one-way affair.' The action, a masterpiece of old-fashioned infanteering, became known simply as 'The Battle of the Apple Orchard'. Those there knew they had set a standard. 'After that, you couldn't hold the Diggers!' said Bandy. 'We thought we could take on the world!'

Middlesex passed through 3 RAR and linked up with the main body of the airborne late in the afternoon. 'It was one of the worst sights I saw: All along the road were dead North Korean soldiers in ditches,' said Green. 'They must have been some mothers' sons at one time. We were looking at them from the height of a lorry and they looked a mess.' Still, they delighted in the fruit. 'There were beautiful apples, we stuffed our uniforms, they would have absorbed a bullet!' reckoned Stafford volunteer Ray Rogers.

The first airborne operation of the war was over. Some airborne – such as the group Desfor, the photographer was with – barely saw any action. Those relieved by 27th Brigade were a different story. The NKPA 239th Regiment, which had been deployed to overrun the 3rd Battalion of the 187th, had been effectively annihilated.

The trainload of US POWs was a different matter. Bandy later witnessed their fate. 'They were massacred in this tunnel, they were hanging out of the carriages and on the ground,' he said. 'That kept us going – a bit of spite.' Seventy five POWs had been murdered north of Sunchon; twenty-one survived.[27]

---

* For the day's work, Butler won a US Silver Star; Denness, an MC.

Diggers assessed their post-battle reactions. 'It was just a day at the office, no after-effect or anything,' said Connelly, who patched up his bayonet wound with tape. 'When you're young, you can live through anything – we were envious of C Company!' Others were more stirred. 'Afterward, you did get the shakes a bit,' said Robertson. 'You tended to be full of adrenalin, so when you stopped, you shook, but it did not last long, you settled down.' It had been a good day for the sniper: 'I think I got about twenty-four in that fight, though I don't announce it with a megaphone,' he said. Word of his lethal accuracy spread, earning Robertson a nickname: 'The Hitman'.

One Australian was more thoughtful. Sergeant Jack Harris had seen scores of enemy dead littering the battleground, but the memory that stayed with him from that bloody day were the soft brown eyes of the horse as it lay dying in the paddy field. [28]

* * *

On 23 October, Argylls drove up to modern-looking apartment blocks: This was Sinanju, the city on the Chongchon River, 27th Brigade's limit of exploitation. Having spearheaded 8th Army's advance 55 miles from Pyongyang, the brigade had hit no resistance in the mountains between Sukchon and Sinanju, but as they closed on the river, leading Argylls came under ineffective fire from the north bank.[29]

Sinanju itself was clear of enemy, but smashed up. The road bridge that carried the main Pyongyang highway north had been blown; the rail bridge marked on maps did not exist.[30] Coad ordered the Middlesex to prepare to cross. 'This river was understood to be our final objective,' wrote Willoughby. 'We were very tired, but our orders for a rest were crushed by orders to cross the river tomorrow morning by daylight.'[31]

US engineers would provide thirty boats. How fast did the river flow and when was high tide? A frightened local was found; using sign language and drawing in the dust with a stick, he conveyed that high tide was at 18:00.[32] Coad wanted to cross that evening, but that left little time for reconnaissance, and Man wanted to see how the river looked at high tide. A dawn crossing was planned.

A river assault crossing is one of the riskiest operations of war. Barrett was nervous when he heard orders: 'The expectation is that the crossing in assault boats will be opposed and casualties heavy'.[33] There were only enough boats to lift two companies at a time. A and C would lead, followed by Tac HQ and B Company; finally, Willoughby's D. The major was as worried as Barrett: 'There could hardly have been a site less likely to offer surprise,' he wrote. 'There is nothing to do but wait and morosely speculate on news that the rise and fall of the tide at Inchon was 36 feet.'[34]

Coad was equally concerned. A 'very agitated' US engineering officer had arrived at his HQ, telling him that he could not guarantee patching up the bridge, meaning the Middlesex – assuming they made it across the river – would be isolated on the north bank, without transport or heavy weapons. 'The situation was now serious,' Coad wrote; he had had no personal contact with a senior commander for ten days. [35]

The crossing would take place 4 miles downstream from the town. At the crossing point, Diehards were ordered to stay off the skyline until darkness, and not to show any lights. At dusk, Barrett and his mates lay flat and looked over at their objective. There was a 1,000-yard approach to the river, with no cover; then the Chongchon itself, approximately 800 yards wide. Beyond, everything was overlooked by foothills that tumbled down to within 400 yards of the northern bank. 'The Aussies were moved up behind us,' Barrett said. 'Coad expected us to take heavy casualties.'

October 24 dawned with a hard frost. This was soon burned off by bright sunshine, but the autumn chill had been noted by higher command; two days earlier, the Diehards had been issued with an American field jacket to wear over their lightweight tropical kit. The crossing did not begin until 08:30.

A Company hefted assault boats – each carried an eight-man section – down to the river, splashed in, and set off for the opposite bank. Ray Rogers, with A Company, was apprehensive: 'There were these moth eaten oars, and I had the radio: If I went into the water, I was not going to get out!' Oars slapped water. Men panted. Minutes passed. 'The closer we got to shore, the tenser we got,' Rogers said.

Left: 27th Brigade's leaders pose for the camera 'somewhere in Korea'. From left: Lieutenant Colonel Leslie Neilson, 1st Argylls; Brigadier Basil 'Aubrey' Coad, 27th Brigade; Lieutenant Colonel Andrew Man, 1st Middlesex. *Courtesy of Barry Reed*

Below: Lieutenant Colonel Charles 'Charlie' Green and Major Bruce 'Ferg' Ferguson; commander and second in command of 3 RAR. Both men are wearing the slouch hat favoured by Diggers in the early phase of the fighting. *Australian War Memorial 146876–1*

Above: With the NKPA laying siege to the 'Pusan Perimeter' the UN Command have their backs to the wall. Men of 27th Brigade – the first non-ROK, non-US reinforcements – site a Bren gun overlooking the Naktong. The spiral stakes in the foreground are for barbed wire.
© *AP/Press Association Images*

Left: Bleeding out and unconscious, Lieutenant Jock Edington is evacuated as disaster unfolds across the summit of Point 282.
Argyll and Sutherland Highlanders Museum

Left: In one of the most extraordinary war photographs ever taken, AP photographer Max Desfor spun and clicked at the moment US marines gunned down a North Korean sniper (in his pavement hide, right). Desfor's image captures the extreme close range of much Korean War combat. © *AP/Press Association Images*

Left: UNC Supreme Commander General Douglas MacArthur oversees the Inchon landing; X Corps Commander General Ned Almond stands at his shoulder. The triumph made the Truman administration and US Joint Chiefs reluctant to question MacArthur's strategy thereafter, but it would be the great general's last victory. © *AP/Press Association Images*

Below: The UNC charges north. Jocks of Major David Wilson's A Company assault dug-in NKPA positioned in hills south of Sariwon. *Time & Life Pictures/Getty Images*

Above: Two children sit next to their dead mother, killed as Argylls advanced on Sariwon. The population would suffer terrible fallout from the fighting.
© *AP/Press Association Images*

Left: Argylls carry a child back to safety from the front.
Australian War Memorial

P00675_065–1

Right: Cheerful Diggers ride through the ruins of Sariwon on a US Sherman while Jocks clear the streets. After dark, the town would be the scene of one of the most extraordinary encounters of modern warfare.
Australian War Memorial

P00675_057–1

Left: A North Korean soldier lies dead in the paddies as a US Sherman prowls in the background after the 'Apple Orchard' battle. The slaughter 3 RAR wrought in their first action delighted Coad but shocked some troops following behind. *Australian War Memorial* P01813_656–1

Right: Robbie 'The Hitman' Robertson. The rabbit hunter and 3 RAR sniper was trained to shoot beyond a thousand yards; his first kill in Korea came at handshake range. *Australian War Memorial* P03732_001–1

Below: In a burning village, an Argyll Bren gunner prepares to engage snipers. He is wearing the knit cap comforter widely worn by British troops in preference to helmets. *By Arthur Gulliver/Courtesy of the State Library of Victoria*

Above: With 27th Brigade spearheading the UNC advance, an Argyll officer, mounted on a Sherman of the US 89th Tank Battalion, scans through binoculars. The landscape is typical hill country north of Sukchon and Sunchon. *Time & Life Pictures/Getty Images*

Above: The corpse of a North Korean civilian, two limbs blown off by a grenade, is gruesome testimony to the killing power of high explosive. *Australian War Memorial* 147015–2

Left: A Middlesex Bren Gun Carrier clatters past a burning thatched cottage – possibly fired in anti-sniper clearance. Note the Bren mounted in the cockpit visor. *By Arthur Gulliver/Courtesy of the State Library of Victoria*

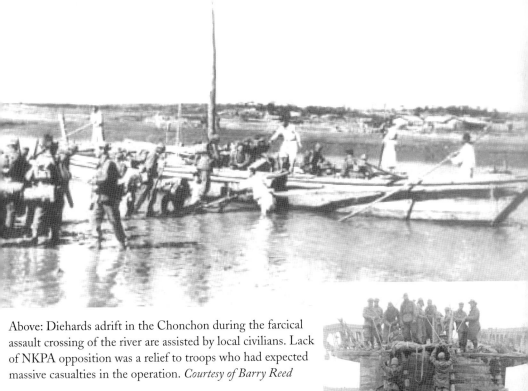

Above: Diehards adrift in the Chonchon during the farcical assault crossing of the river are assisted by local civilians. Lack of NKPA opposition was a relief to troops who had expected massive casualties in the operation. *Courtesy of Barry Reed*

Right: The 'Broken Bridge' at Kujin, with the makeshift ladders Diggers used in their advance.
Australian War Memorial HOBJ1646–2

Below: Diggers on the west bank of the Taeryong after the battle of Kujin. In the distance can be seen the hills through which a new enemy would soon strike in an attempt to surround 27th Brigade. In the foreground lie bazookas and captured enemy weapons.
Australian War Memorial P01813_660–1

Above: Diehards bypass an NKPA T34, knocked out by napalm during the fight for 'Objective Frog'. Some soldiers would be haunted for decades by the sight of the incinerated tanks' crews. *By Arthur Gulliver/Courtesy of the State Library of Victoria*

Left: 30 October: 27th Brigade has reached Chongju, its limit of exploitation in North Korea. The Korean War appears won, but some Argylls, dug in overlooking the blazing town, sense a strange menace as darkness falls. *By Arthur Gulliver/Courtesy of the State Library of Victoria*

Right: A wounded Digger is treated south of Pakchon. The medic is Sergeant Thomas Murray, winner of the George Medal for heroism at 'Broken Bridge'. *Australian War Memorial* *146958*

Below: China has struck; the battle of Pakchon is on. 3 RAR mortars fire over a US Sherman as Diggers attack to retake an overrun hill dominating 27th Brigade's line of retreat. *Courtesy of the State Library of Victoria*

Below: 27th Brigade troops use a US Sherman for cover as they fight past an enemy fireblock in the race to reach the Chongchon before the enemy. *Time & Life Pictures/Getty Images*

Above: China's 'human wave' rolls south. The bugles used to signal units during the assault create a cacophony that terrifies many UNC troops. Note the quilted uniform and ration bandoleer of the bugler. *Courtesy of Korea National War Memorial*

Below: UNC forces are crumbling. Lacking transport, 27th Brigade is ordered to march 20 miles south into the unknown. 'We led with the pipes,' said Captain John Slim. 'The locals loved it and it let the enemy know we were coming!' *Australian War Memorial* 148889–2

Left: D Company Diehards advance warily into hills south of Kunu-ri to cover the US 2nd Infantry Division's desperate breakout. Their facial expressions reflect the gravity of the tactical situation. *Courtesy of Barry Reed*

Below: CPVA advance through the junkyard/slaughterground that mark 2nd Infantry Division's graveyard in 'The Gauntlet', south of Kunu-ri. *Courtesy of Korean National War Memorial*

Left: Refugees – homeless, dispossessed or fleeing communists; mostly old people, women and children – flee south. This was painted from memory by artist Kim Song-hwan for a collector who presented it to his wife, a former refugee. On first viewing, she burst into tears. *Courtesy of Kim Song-hwan*

Left: This tiny girl waiting to cross the Taedong is just one of 630,000 North Koreans who swarmed south in the war winter of 1950/51. © *AP/Press Association Images*

Below: Bundled up against the freeze – photographer Max Desfor could barely operate his camera – desperate civilians clamber over Pyongyang's twisted Taedong bridge. The iconic shot caught the tragedy of the war and won Desfor a Pulitzer.
© *AP/Press Association Images*

Right: Commandos rig explosives on a North Korean rail line; note that their berets and uniforms are stripped of all insignia. (The shot dates from 1951. 41 Commando's 1950 raids took place at night and were not photographed).
Courtesy of US Navy

Left: Commandos head for the Hamgyong highlands to link up with the crack 1st US Marine Division for the UNC's final offensive. They are motoring unknowingly up into the Korean War's most harrowing battlescape: Chosin Reservoir.
Courtesy of Les Coote/ Royal Marines Museum Image Collection

Right: View from a Koto-ri observation post, up-valley toward Hagaru-ri: the route of the doomed Taskforce Drysdale in Hellfire Valley. The refracted light is typical of the strange atmospheric conditions at Chosin.
Courtesy of Les Coote/ Royal Marines Museum Image Collection

Above: With Chinese besieging the airhead at Hagaru-ri, marine artillerymen fire their 105mm howitzer over medevac C47s on the makeshift landing strip into the surrounding hills. *Courtesy of US Marine Corps*

Below: The breakout is underway. US marines at a dismantled roadblock watch as a Corsair (visible in the smoke) napalms Chinese in the hills. The column would generally have 15-20 minutes to pass before enemy re-commenced shooting. Commandos were astounded at the precision of marine close-air support. *Courtesy of US Marine Corps*

Right: The frozen corpses of US marines and British commandos, recovered from Hellfire Valley, await burial at Koto-ri. The frost was so impenetrable that their burial pit was blasted into the ground with explosive. *Courtesy of US Marine Corps*

Below: 41 Commando regroup at Koto-ri. From left: Captain Pat Ovens, Major Dennis Aldridge, Lieutenant Colonel Douglas Drysdale. *Courtesy of Les Coote/Royal Marines Museum Image Collection*

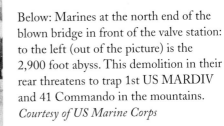

Below: Marines at the north end of the blown bridge in front of the valve station: to the left (out of the picture) is the 2,900 foot abyss. This demolition in their rear threatens to trap 1st US MARDIV and 41 Commando in the mountains. *Courtesy of US Marine Corps*

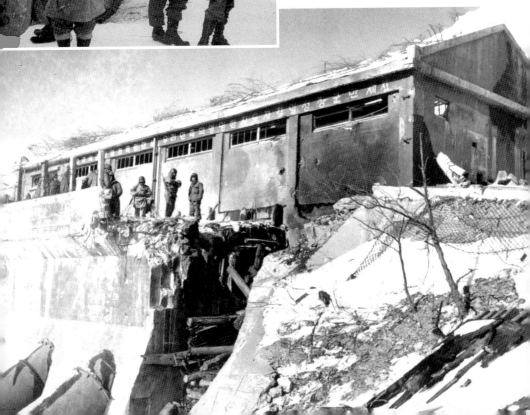

Above: Commandos and US marine engineers head south through the soaring Funchilin Pass, across the air-dropped treadway bridge. The wounded Lieutenant Colonel Drysdale marches in the center of the photograph. *Courtesy of US Marine Corps*

Below: Christmas Eve, 1950. The USS *Begor* stands offshore as Hungnam docks are blown into oblivion in the most spectacular manifestation of 'scorched earth.' It is an apocalyptic finale to the ill-fated UNC foray into North Korea. © *AP/Press Association Images*

Watchers on the south bank held their breaths, waiting for the rip of automatic fire. Across, Rogers jumped out of his boat with the company CP – to sink knee deep in freezing black mud. 'Are they waiting till we are stuck?' he wondered desperately. 'Have they got a bead on us?' Nothing. The sections advanced inland. Still nothing. 'It was relief – sheer relief!' said Rogers. The NKPA had abandoned the Chongchon.

The following companies did, however, face opposition – from the river itself. The tide had turned and assault boats were swept away. Willoughby found his company being tossed along, 'at an alarming rate, our progress toward the far side seemed minimal and there was no sign of the rest of the battalion'.[36] The situation was not aided by lack of propulsion. 'Each section got into a boat, but it was where are the paddles?' recalled Private Ken Mankelow. 'We were told, "Use your rifles" but you can't use a rifle to paddle.' As the tide retreated, mud islands appeared mid-river, on which several boats grounded. Whitehouse leapt overboard to push his boat off; he sank to his waist in freezing black mud. 'This was 20–30 yards from shore, I thought it was solid, but it was mud all the way,' he said. 'It was a bit of a shambles, nobody knew where anyone was going, boats were going by left, right and centre.'

Across the river, a reception committee waited. 'There were civilians pulling us out, it was comical!' said Barrett. 'They were all in their Sunday best, old men with black hats, running up and down to welcome us.' His platoon advanced inland from the riverbank to a little fenced-in village. A striking woman – 'very tall, wearing a khaki siren suit and speaking English'– threw her arms around the Diehards, thanking them for saving her. Barrett was bemused.

A local junk was commandeered to help move some of the boats; it too went aground on an island, to be shifted by Diehards who jumped over and shoved it off. Finally, Man's men were across. They regrouped and advanced.

While the riverine drama was underway, Brigade HQ received fresh orders. Sinanju and the Chongchon had been their original target line; now they were to advance 10 miles further north to Pakchon, then wheel left for the town of Chongju, a further 20 miles northwest.[37] Chongju marked the western flank of the 'MacArthur Line', the line at which non-Korean UNC forces would halt. Only ROK troops would continue to the Yalu River, the China frontier. 24th Division signalled Coad, indicating the imminent end of operations: 'One more stroke will do it.'[38]

Local developments seemed to support this optimism. Sixty-six POWs were collected from around Sinanju, including a beautifully dressed officer, who had, however, little information to impart. 'One would hazard a guess that his desertion was not a great loss to the North Korean Army,' 27th Brigade's War Diarist commented.[39] The problem of how to get the rest of the brigade and its transport across the Chonchon was solved when orders were received to head 5 miles east to the town of Anju: 1st ROK Division had secured a crossing, a sandbag bridge.[40]

Over the Chongchon, Diehards had occupied the high ground by evening. There was relief at the bloodless – if embarrassing – operation. 'It was chaos, and if anybody had been opposing us, they would have wiped us out laughing,' said Mankelow. 'Later we had a tea and a fag, everybody said, "What a screw up!"' The battalion – the very tip of the UNC spear – in the hills without supporting arms, spent an uncomfortable night without blankets. For the first time, the temperature dropped below freezing;[41] the Argylls water bowser froze solid. [42]

The brigade spent 25 October entering and enlarging the Middlesex bridgehead. Late in the afternoon, 3 RAR broke out and advanced upon the village of Kujin and the town of Pakchon, 5 miles north of the Chongchon. They were not the first brigade members into Pakchon, however. The pace of the advance and the axes taken were now confusing members even of Brigade HQ. Two MPs responsible for traffic direction were posting brigade signs – codename 'Nottingham' – on the outskirts of Pakchon when someone opened fire on them. Enemy was still in residence; the pair was ahead of the vanguard. 'Two crestfallen and somewhat indignant MPs were soon returning to the sanctity of Brigade HQ,' the War Diarist noted.[43]

* * *

North of the Chongchon, Kujin and Pakchon both lay on the east bank of the Taeryong River. For 27th Brigade to thrust west for Chongju, the Taeryong would have to be crossed. The 3 RAR's advance company, together with Shermans of the US 89th Tank Battalion, made Kujin at 16:00. NKPA engineers had dealt with the massively-built, 300-yard long brick bridge spanning the river: Its central span had been blown and dropped 20 feet into the water, making it impassable to vehicles. 'It looked like the gap of a large, missing tooth,' thought Gordon.

Yet the fallen span might provide a base for infantry to climb up onto the un-demolished section: Men began knocking together two rough scaling ladders. Two sections of B Company would go over on initial reconnaissance. Still, this did not solve the problem of a vehicle crossing; transport would not be able to cross this bridge. Green ordered D Company to advance up to Pakchon, where there was a ford.

The recce patrol from B Company was first up the scaling ladders and across the bridge. There was no enemy fire. On the west bank, the patrol – fully exposed, and well forward of the battalion – were proceeding warily, when some fifty enemy appeared on a ridge to the right, hands held high. As the would-be POWs approached, firing broke out from further up the high ground – apparently to discourage surrenders. Meanwhile, a US light observation plane, buzzing overhead, reported at least two companies of enemy dug in the high ground. The patrol, with ten POWs, prudently withdrew east.

At 17:30, a brace of US Shooting Star ground attack jets thundered over the Australians, making strafing runs on the enemy positions. Few of the Diggers were impressed; the jets simply moved too fast to be accurate. After their departure, Green ordered mortar and artillery fire. The high ground over the river was churned up in great smoke and dust clouds.

At 18:30, D Company returned from Pakchon to the battalion area with a haul of 225 prisoners. American engineers with them had discovered a damaged ford, and would work overnight to make it passable for vehicles. A platoon of D remained with them as escort.[44]

His right flank secured, determined not to allow enemy to reinforce the crossing – and perhaps encouraged by collapsing North Korean morale – Green made a decision. 'The CO said, "If we don't get across that bloody river tonight, we will never get across,"' recalled Bandy, who overheard the orders. Green would thrust A and B Companies across the river to seize a bridgehead on the west bank. It was an aggressive plan. The companies would take a while to negotiate the ladders in the dark, and if heavily attacked, would have the river to their backs.

Among the point platoon was journalist Harry Gordon. 'The sun was sinking, there was a deep pink glow as we went up the ladder to engage the enemy and establish a bridgehead,' he recalled. 'Nobody seemed to know more than that B Company was going over.' The platoon waited for orders to launch them across. Some men were smoking, others talking in low voices. 'One man beefed about his underwear, one wanted a T-bone steak,' Gordon, armed only with his notebook, recalled. 'There was a mood of tense expectancy; this was the nervous talk before battle.'

'OK! Time to move!' the platoon commander, Lieutenant Eric Larson, told his men. Cigarettes were scrunched out, packs shouldered, greatcoats buttoned and weapons cocked. The evening was chilly: Frost covered the ground, puddles were iced over. Up on the concrete bridge, Larson's men advanced into the dying glow of the sun.

The crossing of the felled span proved easy enough, but it was time-consuming getting over. The first man reached the west bank at 19:00. The sunset had almost faded, the moon had risen. Gordon moved forward with the 'congestion of slouch-hatted silhouettes' to the west bank, where there was a brief huddle. 'Alright, let her go!' Larson whispered. A flare went up in an orange burst. The platoon advanced toward their objective, a low, scrub-covered hill.

The men, Gordon noted, had unconsciously adopted a semi-crouch. 'You'd pay two bob to see this at the pictures,' whispered a private. 'But we're getting it for nothing!' Nobody answered. The platoon crested the first ridge without contact. There were signs of enemy: a clutch of burp guns, abandoned uniforms. 'The North

Korean troops had turned peasant,' reckoned Gordon. The platoon continued for a second hill.

A burst of automatic fire ruptured the chill silence. Larson, in the lead, had opened up with his sub-machine gun. 'There was a heave in the shrubbery, and a body slumped out,' said Gordon, 10 yards behind. A North Korean, wounded in the air strike, had tried to throw a grenade. 'There were several of these living booby traps,' said Gordon. 'Larson had seen movement and did not hesitate, though it shocked the wits out of me!' Moans emanated from the scrub; advancing Diggers, 'put them out of their misery'. Stay-behinds on suicide missions were ominous. Clearly, despite earlier surrenders, courage had not deserted every enemy soldier.

All around, voices started talking – voices speaking Korean. 'Someone fired into the voices,' Gordon recalled. 'Suddenly, it was awfully noisy.' The reporter found himself in the midst of a close-range, night firefight. All around were blue and orange winks of burp gun muzzle flashes; Diggers fired back into silhouettes. 'There were North Koreans in far greater numbers than anticipated, and they were fanning out,' said Gordon. He dived and weaved, trying to stay in sight of Larson. The platoon seemed to have the enemy on three sides. 'We were like a pointing finger,' said Gordon. Larson, realising that he had exploited too far forward, led his men back toward the bridge. Sporadic mortar fire was now landing. 'We were jumping, running and scrambling,' Gordon recalled. They tumbled back to where A and B Companies which had crossed over behind Larson's platoon, were digging in.

Private Stan Connelly had advanced with his platoon when his officer disappeared over the side of the ridge: He had been tackled by a North Korean. There was the sound of a struggle than the lieutenant re-appeared, shouting, 'He got my rifle!' The platoon took up defensive positions, expecting a charge. None came. They started digging into the gravel-hard earth. The two companies were deployed along a ridgeline parallel to the river, separated by the cutting through which the Chongju road led onto the bridge. A Company was on the left; B, the right. At 19:30 they came under ineffective fire: the shells, probably armour piercing, simply buried themselves in the earth rather than exploding. Ineffectual mortar fire also began landing. From 10:30, firing picked up.[45]

Lying prone on the A Company perimeter was Private Mick Servos; he had not been able to dig a slit trench. He registered an odd zinging sound: Behind and above his position was a steel electricity pylon and enemy rounds were hitting it. The noise was comforting: 'We were not frightened,' Servos said. 'They were firing too high.' But these were not shells, they were bullets. The enemy was closing into small arms range.

On the eastern bank, the men of C Support and Headquarters Companies could hear the rising crackle in the darkness over the river. At 23:00, Green sent Sergeant Reg Bandy's platoon across to reinforce A Company. Bandy's mate, Jack Harris was anxious; he warned the big NCO to keep his head down; Bandy promised to hug the ground, slapped Harris on the shoulder, and set off over the bridge into battle.[46] Reaching A Company, Bandy's men dug in.

A chill drizzle fell. Through it, small arms fire intensified steadily. At 04:00, Diggers lying in cover made out a new sound: A squeaking and clanking approaching through the darkness. A heavy gun cracked. In its momentary flash, the Australians saw what they were facing: A pair of enemy tanks – the feared T34 – along with a force of some sixty infantry, including a motorcycle sidecar and a Russian jeep.

Like the rest of 27th Brigade, the Diggers had been issued the 3.5-inch bazooka. Crews loaded rockets into their 'stovepipes', carefully aimed and – nothing. The weapons would not shoot. Nor could fire be called in from over the river; the mortar fire controller, Sergeant Tom Muggleton with B Company, was having radio problems. These equipment malfunctions left the Australian infantry defenceless. The T34s continued to advance. Obviously they were not going to stand off, they were going to drive right through the 3 RAR companies and on to the bridge.

Armour at close range appears so fearsome, so indestructible that a term has been coined – 'tank fright' – to denote the panic it can spark. If a unit breaks and runs, it can be slaughtered, either by tank gunfire, or – horribly – by thrashing steel tracks. With the river at their back, the Diggers had nowhere to run. But a tank has its own problems at night. Unless it has infantry spotters calling in targets, crew vision is highly restricted. And the infantry were vulnerable, for the North Korean force was being lit up, both by the flashes of their tank guns, and by their accompanying motorcycle, which had a slit in the cover of its headlight.[47]

Thus far, the Diggers had not returned fire; to do so, would give away their position to the tanks. Now, with the enemy between 100 and 150 yards off, A Company let loose. 'We let them into the trap and hit them with everything we had,' said Servos. 'We could see them going down all over – it was a hell of a play!' The enemy infantry were decimated by the Diggers' opening volley, but some took cover and returned fire. A runner next to Bandy was shot through the skull. 'One of my guys saw the muzzle flash and got him at about 150 yards,' the sergeant said.

The tank fire was less accurate. One of Bandy's men was lying behind a burial mound: the T34 blasted the top two feet of it off, but did not get the Digger in its cover. The power pylon took further punishment from the tank fire. 'They were just blasting away,' said Bandy. 'They did not know where we were, there were no flares, the tank could not lay on us.'

Although their infantry escort had been wiped out, the T34s continued to prowl within close range of the Diggers' positions; one actually lumbered into the cutting between the two companies. 'They were practically on top of B Company HQ,' said Muggleton. 'It was a very tense night, they came down and blew a bloke's head off at Company HQ, 40–50 metres away.' The mobile fortress halted some 10 yards from a foxhole occupied by a pair of Diggers; up close, it looked 'about the size of the Taxation Building, and equally fearsome'. The two spent the night huddled in their hole, listening to the tank crew's fire orders.[48]

Wounded were being evacuated across the broken bridge. It was a desperate business. By the light of gun flashes, under sniper fire, stretchers were secured with rope, lowered some 20 feet over the edge onto the broken span resting in the water below, then transferred to folding boats waiting to be hauled to the RAP on the east bank by ropes. After his adventure with Larson's platoon, Gordon had retired across the bridge to write up his adventure. From there, he witnessed the biggest drama of the night.

In one of the first boats was a corporal, Jim Delaney, and a soldier wounded in the buttocks. The latter had just been transferred to the boat when things went wrong. 'The boat hit some rubble, skewed in the swift current, banged into a pylon, swerved and capsized,' recalled Gordon. Both men were spilled into the icy river, and seized by its six-knot flow. Delaney, a non-swimmer, floundered. His wounded companion shoved him toward one of the bridge pylon supports, where a rope was thrown to him, but was swept away himself.

Overseeing the evacuation was 3 RAR's Drum Sergeant Tom Murray. He stripped down and dived off the bridge into the frigid black water. Reaching the casualty, Murray clutched him in a lifesaver's embrace and swam him to the east bank. Gordon was amazed. 'I had covered hangings and plane crashes, so I had seen some bad things, but this was inspirational, the casual heroism,' he said. 'I was transfixed, it was a privilege to see it unfolding before your eyes.'* Murray re-clothed himself and continued directing operations on the bridge.

A grey dawn broke. Chilled Diggers looked around to see the damage. In Connelly's section, one man was dead, another seriously wounded with a head shot. The light also illuminated more enemy – for Muggleton, targets. 'It was the best mortar target I've had in my life!' he said. 'Two tanks, and about a company of men on a little crest.' Excited, he radioed back to the baseplate position – to no avail: His set was 'as dead as a doornail'. The MFC was apoplectic.

His target, did not tarry: Vulnerable to airpower, the enemy were retreating. Servos' section was ordered up the road to where the mechanised attack had been halted. Enemy dead had been evacuated, but the track was covered in debris and bits of uniform. The jeep – a Russian model – was recovered intact and put into use by the battalion.[†] It had had a senior occupant, because a briefcase was recovered.

---

* Murray was awarded the George Medal for his actions that night.
† The jeep was later shipped to Australia. It is still used on Anzac Day parades.

It proved to be the property of one Lieutenant Colonel Kim In-sik, commander of 17th Tank Brigade's reconnaissance unit. In it, were documents including the brigade's War Diary, which detailed its movements all the way from the Naktong. Other papers stated that the brigade had twenty operational tanks and six artillery pieces, and was planning to defend Chongju, 27th Brigade's limit of exploitation, 20 miles west of Kujin.[49]

While Servos' section cleared the road, Muggleton stormed back across the bridge to the mortar platoon, ranting about the 'bloody useless SCR 536 radio'. 'The OC said, "You should be court martialed for leaving your post!" I said, "What the hell am I going to do if I have no radio?"' The sergeant calmed down when he was given a better set, but could not forget that perfect target.

Green's gamble had paid off. His battalion had bounced the Taeryong; established a bridgehead; broken counterattacks; faced down – without support – enemy armour; and driven it into retreat. 'After that, they can send them by divisions,' the elated CO told his HQ staff. 'This battalion will hold them!'[50]

There was an immediate investigation into the failed bazookas. It was discovered that the battalion had been given new models, and their electric firing mechanisms were still packed in grease. Solvent was applied and the bazookas made ready.[51]

For 3 RAR, it had been a more expensive battle than the 'Apple Orchard'. The fight for Kujin – or, as the Diggers dubbed it, 'The Battle of Broken Bridge' – had claimed twenty-two wounded and eight killed, plus an American forward observation officer dead; one hundred North Koreans had died, fifty were captured.[52]

Among the fallen Diggers was an A Company NCO, Sergeant McDonald. Lengthy books have been written about the last words of famous persons; McDonald's are unlikely to appear in any such work, but speak volumes about the Spartan spirit of Charlie Green's men. Hit in the groin, McDonald was informed that there was nothing that could be done to save him; femoral artery severed, he was bleeding out. The NCO digested this information, then spoke. There was no self-pity, no melodrama. 'Oh, fuck it,' he said. 'Give us a smoke, will you?' McDonald was handed a cigarette.

He sat and smoked, bled and died with the lit cigarette dangling from his lip.[53]

* * *

At dawn on 26 October, the Argylls crossed the Taeryong to widen the 3 RAR bridgehead. They met no opposition. At 13:00, the Middlesex piled onto the 89th Tank Battalion's Shermans and drove over the river crossing at Pakchon.[54] Clusters of Diehards stood on the hulls, clinging to the turrets as the tanks churned across the shingle riverbed, leaving broad wakes. On the far bank rose great, fog-like banks of smoke from artillery preparation. The Middlesex dug in near a village, their start line for an attack the following morning. After dark, the Diehards came under tank fire: Armour piercing shells tore through the houses of the village with a high-velocity 'whoofing' sound.[55] Willoughby was convinced the enemy were shooting at silhouetted Shermans; he instructed the American tanks to take hull down positions below the ridge crest.[56]

Given the heavy fighting the Australians had encountered, the proximity of enemy armour and the intelligence from Colonel Kim's documents, Coad shortened his bounds toward Chongju. The Middlesex objective on 27 October was just 5 miles west: the high ground overlooking Kasan crossroads on the Kujin-Chongju road: 'Objective Frog'. The urbane Major Roly Gwynne – Man had been taken sick – orchestrated a textbook attack: A single company would deploy to secure a phase line – a village or ridge. There, it would go firm, to be leapfrogged by the next. Air support was on call. Tanks would shoot from the road.

The first phase line was the village of Yongsong-ri. At dawn, US air reconnaissance had identified this as the source of the previous night's shelling and an air strike had gone in. At 09:00, as the Diehard spearhead approached, it was blazing furiously and erupting with irregular explosions; it had been used as an ammunition depot.[57] C Company attempted to enter; but was repelled by the heat. In the confusion, a Sherman reversed into the OC's Bren Carrier: the major's legs were crushed.[58]

Once the fires died down, C Company secured the ashes of the village, while A Company moved through into open country. Beyond the village, waiting enemy tanks and infantry opened up. One shell scraped along the hull of a Sherman and ricocheted off into a paddy, killing two Diehards taking cover. When the ambush was sprung, signaller Ray Rogers was riding on a trailer towed by his company commander's jeep. The trailer was covered with a tarpaulin, and as the jeep accelerated along the road, Rogers clung on for dear life. He could plainly see an un-camouflaged T34 standing about 250 yards off, its turret traversing, its gun following the racing jeep. A Sherman fired, scoring a direct hit. The T34 brewed up. A burning enemy crewman leapt out of the vehicle; machine guns finished him.[59] Two T34s broke cover; they were set upon by aircraft. Enjoying the battle's spectacular developments was a BBC reporter, though he cursed when his recorder broke down just as US artillery 155mm support fire howled in.[60]

D Company passed through A. Ahead was a circular valley, surrounded by low ridges. Small arms erupted from high ground to the right, where A Company had been fired at. The gruelling pace of operations was telling: Willoughby was distressed to see his soldiers trudging along, 'too weary to take any reaction either to the crack of the bullets or the platoon commander's orders'. Willoughby roared – 'maybe I had a louder voice' – and led his men into action.[61] 'Major Willoughby said, "Walk, don't run", as if it was a training exercise,' recalled Whitehouse who was feeling particularly vulnerable – he was carrying a bright yellow air recognition panel. 'As we got near to where we thought they were, the order came, "Charge!" and we started running like mad dogs, shouting and screaming.' Some 300 yards ahead, a platoon of enemy stood up and started, 'running like hell'. None of Willoughby's soldiers reacted: 'They were young men from decent families and no-one fired until, in desperation, I let off my rifle and missed, then the rest opened fire in a half-hearted way and also missed,' the major wrote. 'We were simply punch-drunk, strained and fatigued.'[62]

B Company leapfrogged D Company to carry the next ridge. Mankelow was advancing when tanks were spotted ahead. 'We were not sure whose tanks they were – we thought they were Yanks – then suddenly they opened fire,' he said. The brigade was well supported; an air strike went in almost immediately. The US ground attack jets gave no aural warning of their approach; part of their deadliness was that they were only heard when they had thundered overhead. 'They came straight down firing cannon, we cheered 'em on, you could see explosions going up and then they dropped napalm,' said Mankelow.

There was a pause in the attack, as the battalion consolidated. The next objective was a ridge running across the road some 1,000 yards forward: Objective 'Frog' itself. D Company advanced. Tanks, artillery and air strikes blasted up a maelstrom of dust in the dry paddies. Willoughby's men took the ridge without casualties. All that now remained was digging in and clearance patrols to secure the area.

Corporal John Pluck was sweeping with his platoon in skirmish line when someone shouted, 'There's a Gook!' Pluck turned – an enemy cap was bobbing above the scrub – Pluck brought up his Sten and released a two-round burst. The target went down. Pluck examined his kill. 'I'd put two rounds in his chest, but the chap was already wounded by a shell splinter, he had had a little fire going, he was cooking some meat, and his rifle was stacked beside him, he was no danger whatsoever – I saw his head move and fired, it happened in a second.' Pluck realised the man was helpless, and probably wanted to surrender: 'It was so unnecessary.' The battalion dug in around Kasan crossroads. It was approximately 16:30.

In what Coad considered 'a very sticky action',[63] three Middlesex were dead and four wounded; an estimated seventy-five enemy had been killed and twenty POWs taken. Ten tanks and two SPGs had been knocked out, most by napalm air strikes.[64] While a tank – essentially, a box of armoured steel – may not appear combustible, it is: paint burns, fuel and oil blazes, ammunition explodes. Moreover, if napalm pours into, or splashes up into air intakes, it creates a hellish conflagration inside. All this makes fire the bane of tank crews; a burning armoured vehicle turns red hot, roasting those inside.

Curious soldiers wandered over to examine brewed-up T34s. Corporal Harry Spicer and his mates found a roll of material on one of the hulks. With bitter nights now descending, they cut it up and distributed it. Perched upright in the turret of his smoking machine watching the looting Diehards, was the charred cadaver of the enemy tank commander, blackened like a fossil. It was a sight Spicer would never forget.

* * *

While Diehards had been fighting for 'Frog', Brigade HQ received unsettling intelligence; some 400 enemy were advancing on Pakchon from the north. With his three battalions all across the Taeryong, this placed Coad in a dicey position: If the enemy retook Pakchon and Kujin, the brigade echelons would be overrun, its fighting elements cut off on the wrong side of the river. The Argylls were being warned to cover the town when the US 5th Regimental Combat Team appeared from the south. The Americans had caught up with the brigade. It was a timely relief.[65] While 27th Brigade continued its attack westwards, 5th RCT would strike north for the town of Taechon.

On 28 October, the Argylls passed through the Middlesex. Overflown by a spotter plane, they advanced nearly 15 miles; one SPG was knocked out by an air strike. An officer of the 17th Tank Brigade was captured; he told interrogators that he had been tasked to defend the approaches to Chongju, but his brigade had taken severe losses on the Taeryong – i.e. fighting the Australians.[66] Chongju is an important road and rail junction, though for 27th Brigade, of more import was the fact that it was their final objective, on the west bank of the River Talchon. A ridge of high, wooded hills on the riverbank afford strong defensive positions. On 29 October, 17th Tank Brigade would meet 3 RAR on these hills for a last battle.

The Diggers passed through the Jocks for the drive on the town. D Company led 3 RAR up the highway to where it passed into a cutting through a pine-covered ridge. There, spotter aircraft radioed that there was enemy infantry and armour dug in on both sides of the highway: a massive roadblock. Green halted his advance to soften up the positions. For three hours, air strikes – launched by screaming F80 jets and droning P51 propeller fighters – pounded the area with bombs, rockets, napalm and machine guns. Nine enemy tanks were reported knocked out.[67] Then Green unleashed his bayonets.

D Company would attack left of the cutting; once they went firm, A Company would take the right.

At 14:30, D Company advanced. It immediately came under fire. An American Sherman was knocked out by a dug-in T34; clearly the air strikes had not been as effective as claimed. 10 Platoon seized high ground on the right, enfilading enemy firing into the other two platoons as they strode across the paddies. As the Diggers fought up through the trees, Private Jack Stafford spotted a camouflaged T34. Though he had no anti-tank weapon, he could see that the vehicle had an external fuel tank attached; unlike the rest of the vehicle, the barrel was not armoured. Crawling into position, he fired from 20 yards with his Bren. The fuel ignited and the tank brewed up.* [68] At 16:30, D Company had secured the left of the road.[69]

At Battalion HQ, a message was received: D Company was being sniped. HQ dispatched its own human hunter. 'Being a sniper, when you went to a company because they were in a bit of bother, nobody spoke to us,' said Robertson. 'They were silent, I thought, "What's this about?" But we were hit men, a different breed to them.' Robertson and his spotter were shown the direction the enemy sniper was believed to be shooting from. Moving carefully – ensuring they had foliage behind them, not breaking skyline – the pair sunk into camouflage, and slowly scanned likely firing points. 'You have to study for a while – you have to make sure he is not studying you!' said Robertson. Then he noticed something: 'In a tangle of leaves and branches, there was a straight bit.' The North Korean's rifle had given him away. Squinting into his telescopic sight, Robertson lined up the crosshairs, the thick, blunt aiming post – 'I would have liked a sharper aiming post' – on the head of the sniper in his hide. He squeezed the trigger. The result was unspectacular: no leap, no scream, no red mist. 'We just saw him collapse,' Robertson said. 'That's about it.' The target had been 'switched off'.

It was A Company's turn to assault. The company commander, Captain Bill Chitts, approached American tankers, asking them to

---

* Stafford received the US Silver Star for this action. In fact, the tank was, according to Len Opie and 3 RAR's War Diary, abandoned at the time.

support his attack. Perhaps rattled by the earlier hit on the Sherman, they declined. Chitts was furious. 'Get your fucking tanks out of the fucking road, I'll do it myself!' he snarled.[70] The advance began. 'This was a normal infantryman's job,' said Mick Servos. 'Go in and kill the enemy!' Moving just behind the assault platoons in Chitts' Tac HQ was MFC Muggleton and an American FOO. Ahead, a rolling barrage of 155mm US artillery and Australian 3-inch mortar fire was churning up the front face of the ridge, blasting clouds of smoke and scrub into the air ahead of the leading platoons. 'Mortars are more frightening than artillery they spread all over the place,' said Muggleton. 'The barrage was about 100–150 yards ahead, and as we got up the hill, it fired on the reverse slope.'

Daylight was dying as A Company fought through the enemy positions. The MFC heard unfamiliar explosions: he later found out they were bazookas. The weapons that had misfired at 'Broken Bridge' were now working fine: Three dug-in tanks were destroyed as A Company assaulted the ridge. 'They thought they would blow us off the face of the earth with the tanks, but A Company knocked them out!' Muggleton said. Both D and C Companies were secure on their objectives. Green moved B Company astride the road, placed his HQ behind them and C Company for rear protection. It was about 18:00.

At Brigade HQ, a collection of tents and stationary vehicles under camouflage netting, officers were monitoring the battle over the crackling radio net. The Diggers were being counter-attacked. At that moment, Coad was summoned to 24th Division for a command conference – a 35-mile road trip.

On 24 October, MacArthur had unilaterally extended the line beyond which non-ROK UNC forces could operate: All UNC troops, not just ROKs, were now to strike north for the Yalu River. The US Joint Chiefs of Staff requested an explanation for this change of plan. MacArthur responded that he had latitude under existing directives, and following the Wake conference with Truman on 15 October, to issue the order. With ROK II Corps attacking through central Korea, it appears that MacArthur wanted X Corps in the east, and I Corps – spearheaded by 27th Brigade and ROK 1st Division on their right flank – in the west to accelerate the pace.[71] Regardless of Chinese sensitivities, the 'MacArthur Line' had evaporated, the UNC was going all the way: The Yalu, not the Chongchon, would be the final frontier. This was behind Coad's summons.

Upon arrival at 24th Division, General John Church asked Coad if he wanted 27th Brigade relieved. 'A difficult question, I thought, as the relieving Regimental Commander was also present,' Coad wrote. 'I pointed out that we were alright to go to the Yalu, but we were slowing up and as speed was essential, fresh troops would obviously go faster.'[72] The decision was made to pass 24th Division's 21st RCT through to make the final dash to the Yalu.

East of Chongju, battle raged on. In darkness, North Koreans counter-attacked D Company furiously. 'This one fellow, we called him "Horace", he was about six feet five, he wouldn't die,' said Opie. 'He just kept carrying on, he was moaning . . . it took me half a mag to finish him off.' The enemy made it to Battalion HQ, but were repulsed by the defence platoon. Unable to break through, they had to return the way they had come. Under Lieutenant David Mannett, Diggers of 10 Platoon held their fire until enemy were within yards, then opened up. By 21:00 it was all over.

Unable to overrun D Company, enemy attention shifted to A. At 21:30, waves of NKPA charged in. Noise and confusion. 'We could hear them – *mansei, mansei*! all night,' said Muggleton. 'We could not see them, all we could see was the flash of rifles.' Gunnery was called in. 'Chitts said, "Bring it as close as you can!"' Muggleton, working with the American FOO, recalled. The shocking red and white detonations of the 155mm shells flashed in the blackness, their impacts dangerously close – within 10 yards of Digger slit trenches.[73] Prone behind a burial mound, Muggleton, his back teeth reverberating from blast, wondered what the mound's occupants thought: 'They were buried sitting up and I don't know what they were thinking, looking down on us from heaven – or up from hell!' The MFC was impressed by the US 90th Field Artillery FOO: 'He was only a little fellow, it was a marvellous shoot!'

At Battalion HQ, Captain Ben O'Dowd watched Green in action, verbally calming one company commander and keeping the guns firing. 'We had trouble keeping the American artillery firing all night, they would stand down,' he said. 'We reckoned Charlie couldn't sleep without guns firing!'

Just before midnight, Coad returned to Brigade HQ, where he learned that 3 RAR had not advanced beyond its first objective – the ridgeline bisected by the highway – but had gone firm.[74] At D Company, fighting had died down. Gallaway was sent forward with a can of coffee and discovered exactly how close the combat had been. Gallaway poured Opie a mug, then, noticing another man in the trench next to him who appeared to be sleeping, asked Opie, 'What about your mate?' 'I dunno if he wants any,' Opie replied, grabbing the man by his hair and holding up his head. The 'mate' was a dead North Korean. 'Len was a very cool customer,' Gallaway said. 'He just knew no fear.'

Morning found 3 RAR in full possession of the ridge; they had seized it from a battalion 500–600 strong, supported by dug-in tanks; an estimated 150 enemy were killed, including thirty-four in front of Mannett's platoon. Nine Australians had been killed, thirty wounded.[75] It was 27th Brigade's stiffest battle since the Naktong.

With resistance cracked, Chongju lay open. 3 RAR exploited forward, while the Middlesex advanced to take hills to their north. By now, even officers were feeling the strain. At Man's O Group, one company commander was reduced to tears; Willoughby took him aside, guaranteeing that he would support him 'at the first sign of trouble'. The attack swept through a forest. Willoughby urged his men to stay in close visual range and remain silent. From their flank came heavy burp gun fire: Shipster's C Company was using captured weapons to shoot into anything suspicious. 'A waste of ammunition and it tells the enemy exactly where you are,' thought Willoughby crossly.[76] There was no opposition.

The Argylls passed through, crossed the Talchon River and entered Chongju. Under the guns of Shermans, files of Jocks penetrated the ruined and empty streets, past the burning telephone exchange. The only opposition was sniper fire. The town was secured at 17:15.[77]

There was an air of finality. 'We thought this was the end of the party, we thought there might be a parade in Pyongyang,' said O'Dowd, anticipating a possible occupation role. His CO agreed. 'We are unlikely to be in any more big battles,' Green told his signals officer. 'We have made it.'[78]

Diggers picked over what many expected to be their last battlefield. Argent, examining destroyed T34s, was surprised to find one with a British radio, presumably sent to the USSR during the Second World War. The tank was a veteran: Its logbook showed it had been serviced in East Germany. Sniper Robertson recovered his opposite number's weapon. Looking it over with professional interest, he discovered that the short Russian scope had a light-gathering lens, but its sharper, thinner aiming post was so fine, it was impossible to make out against a dark background. The thicker post on his own rifle, however, could even be used by moonlight.

But there were pockets of danger. As the Diehards dug in, a section was sent to recce a village at the base of B Company's hill. Barrett heard the section shout up that there was enemy in the settlement. His platoon commander, Lieutenant Gus Sander, a Jewish refugee from Germany, did not believe it. He went down the hill. Kicking open the door of a cottage, he walked into a burst. Barrett's section was summoned. The corporal hurriedly stuffed pouches with all ammunition available and led his men down to the village. In the dimness behind the open door of one cottage, he made out an armed enemy hiding behind a woman holding a child; he could not shoot through the human shield. A sudden brrrrrrppp: Barrett was under fire from another burp gunner. His section hit the ground, returned fire. Sanders and another wounded man were dragged out. Barrett backed out of the village, covering the with-drawal with a Bren.

Sanders was dead. Padre William Jones was appalled to see him. 'He was a marvellous kid,' Jones said. 'Any mischief in the mess, he was in the middle of it.' Jones oversaw a field burial and returned to Battalion HQ, when two soldiers approached him. They told him that they were Jewish and so was Sanders – a fact Jones had been ignorant of – and asked to say a prayer over his grave. Jones consented. They drove to the grave, under a roadside tree. In that lonely place, the two Diehards intoned a Jewish prayer. Meanwhile, a strong fighting patrol had stormed the village. The burp gunner in the house was killed, the sniper armed with an anti-tank rifle was flushed out of a rice sheaf and gunned down.

3 RAR Sergeant Jack Harris had played no role in the previous night's battle. He was sitting with his platoon on high ground, when an agitated American dashed up, reporting an enemy SPG digging in below Harris' position. A skeptical Harris took a bazooka team and descended into the valley to investigate. As the patrol neared a ruined village, Harris spotted movement, then was spun round: A bullet had gone through his left hand. Seconds later, agony struck: the round had carried away his knuckles. Harris' bazooka operator took aim at the nearest cottage and pulled his trigger. Flame erupted from the back of the launcher – the rocket shot out – explosion – the house was obliterated. The action was over. A medic hurried down, shooting Harris with morphine and evacuating him. At the RAP, the CO appeared, telling the sergeant that he should not have gone after the gun; it could be destroyed by air strike. Then Harris was stretchered off to the US MASH at Anju.

Leaving his battalion, the sergeant wept, but a thought nagged him. He had not seen the reported SPG, and was sure it had not been destroyed.[79]

*   *   *

Gloom was settling over the high scrubby ridges overlooking the Talchon when a 16-year-old boy returned to 3 RAR Battalion HQ east of Chongju from an errand. His name was Choi Yung. In the chaos of war, he had fled his North Korean home, hoping to reach Seoul, but become lost. Scrabbling around the Kujin battlefield some days earlier, he had been adopted by 3 RAR's medical section. Now, he found the Diggers uncharacteristically hushed. He was told why.[80] 'The Boss' had been hit.

Exhausted by the previous day and night, Lieutenant Colonel Green had stayed awake to visit his companies,[81] file casualty reports and prepare a telegram for his wife, Olwyn, regarding the possible purchase of a farm – the couple's dream.[82] With the Argylls having

234 | SCORCHED EARTH, BLACK SNOW

leapfrogged 3 RAR, Green was at last able to retire. Battalion HQ was in a re-entrant. On the ridge above, C Company was digging in, under desultory fire from a hidden SPG. Green's tent had been pitched near a single tree that stood in the HQ area.[83] At around 18:10, he retired.

The tall Australian had been lying in the tent when a single SPG shell hit the top branches of the tree and detonated.* A piece of shrapnel scythed down, ripped through the canvas and into his abdomen. His batman rushed into HQ to report. HQ personnel, medics and reporters crowded around as the colonel was stretchered off on a jeep for the Anju MASH. Few men held out any hope. The RAP had barely enough bandages to staunch Green's wound.

Everyone there claims to have heard Green's last words. 'He was disemboweled; the last words I heard him say were, "Can I have another blanket?"' Gordon remembered. 'Who is going to look after my men,' was what his batman recalled, but others heard it differently. 'They say he said, "Who is going to look after my men?"' recalled Robertson. 'But what he said was, "Who is going to look after Olwyn?"' Only later, when the sniper learned the name of Green's wife, did he understand his CO's words.

Diggers were devastated. Their quiet, unsmiling CO had not been an easy man to know, but all recognised his cool competence: It was Green who had forged their battalion into such a fearsome war machine. There was bitterness toward an unjust fate: The only man hit by a fluke shot. 'Just his flaming luck,' said Gallaway. 'The war is over and he buys a farm!' In an echo of Trafalgar, O'Dowd passed judgment: 'Kismet.'[84]

Lieutenant Colonel Charles Hercules Green died the following day. Coad, who attended his funeral, would keep a photograph of the Australian colonel to hand for the rest of the campaign. 'Coad described him as the finest battalion commander he had ever known,' said Gallaway. 'That was our sentiment, too.' MacArthur and Australian

---

* Was it an SPG? Most accounts agree that it was, but Gallaway is convinced it was a drop-short US mortar that had been firing in the vicinity earlier. 'I watched the thing explode, and it was black powder, like a mortar,' he said. 'I know what I saw.'

Prime Minister Menzies sent their regrets.[85] The following day, MacArthur's headquarters awarded Green a Silver Star, the second highest US medal for gallantry, for the 'Apple Orchard' battle.* [86]

The battalion's seasoned second-in-command, Major Bruce Ferguson, was expected to take over. Instead, a familiar face arrived. 'We'd got rid of him once already,' spat O'Dowd. 'He was completely useless!' Lieutenant Colonel Floyd Walsh – originally passed over by Canberra for lack of combat experience – was 3 RAR's new commander.

*   *   *

Coad's men were halted 50 miles south of the Yalu, their nine-day rampage through North Korea over. They had led the UNC advance 70 map miles up North Korea's western flank, crossed three rivers, relieved an airborne battalion, won four battles and forced four rivers.

It had been an exhilarating charge. 'I loved it, I loved all the fighting, it was thrilling, exciting,' said Servos. 'It is an exciting and invigorating experience to participate in a full-scale pursuit of a beaten enemy,' Shipster added, musing. 'Perhaps these primitive feelings have their origins in man's early background as a hunter?' [87] 'There was a feeling of satisfaction, a feeling of elation,' Captain John Slim said. 'We'd almost done the job.'

The final push was underway. US formations would exploit north to seize the town of Sinuiju, the key river crossing on the Yalu. Across the front, other UNC formations were closing on the border. The end seemed near. On 22 October, MacArthur had diverted arriving ammunition ships back to the US. 1st Cavalry started turning in equipment; the 2nd and 3rd Infantry Divisions, Tokyo High Command was informed, would soon redeploy to Europe.[88] With combat dwindling and reconstruction pending, a Civil Assistance Command was activated on 30 October.[89]

* Although both Man and Neilson received DSOs for the Naktong Crossing battles, Green received no British award. Given the performance of 3 RAR, it seems odd that he was not granted a bar to the DSO he already held. Some Diggers are bitter about this to this day, though it should be added that a number of British soldiers complain that 27th Brigade's awards for the campaign were parsimonious.

27th Brigade became 24th Division's reserve. With 29th Brigade's arrival from the UK imminent – its commander Brigadier Tom Brodie was due to visit Coad on 31 October[90] – happy expectations circulated around 27th Brigade, for 29th Brigade was their relief. Jocks and Diehards were told they would soon be sailing for home base.[91] 'We were looking forward to seeing the night spots in Hong Kong!' recalled Light. Willoughby was simply relieved. 'It is a wonderful feeling knowing that peace is so near, for we really have had enough,' he wrote.[92]

In their outposts, awaiting official news of war's end and transport to Hong Kong, men scanned the sere landscape stretching toward the frontier, gazing into bleak infinity. North of Chongju, the terrain is relatively gentle, corrugated only by rolling hills; northeast, it ascends into mountains. The gold and crimson mantle of autumn was now fading from their slopes, laying bare a winter undercoat of grey and umber. Over this stark vista hung an immensity of brooding sky, its heavy clouds presaging an early winter.

North lay the Yalu and the wilds of Manchuria, but the river's southern bank was the limit of exploitation. Once UNC forces reached it, Kim was finished, Korea reunified and the fighting over. Was the beast of war satiated with the peninsula's brief – it had lasted just four months – but intense bloodletting?

Perhaps not. The late Colonel Kim's diary, captured by 3 RAR, was portentous. 'The time for the overall counter-plan is here before us now . . . to change the tide of battle from defence to attack,' it read.[93] Moreover, UNC air reconnaissance was reporting increasing two-way vehicle traffic across the Yalu, as well as the appearance of new aircraft in Manchuria.[94]

This intelligence did not percolate down to 27th Brigade's men, shivering in their slit trenches, nor had many dwelled on the strategic significance of the 'MacArthur Line's' evaporation, but some soldiers were picking up sinister feedback from the frosted scrub and jagged horizons beyond their gun sights. Some of this may be put down to rational signs: In recent contacts, resistance had stiffened, and, unlike the population further south, who had turned out in numbers to greet the UNC, waving flags and throwing apples, those locals in the north who had not fled into the hills were cold, unfriendly. But other signals were being detected by more primitive antennae, for frontline soldiers develop a near-supernatural sixth sense.

Late on 30 October, Shipster was informed that the US 21st RCT would pass through Chongju. 'I was relieved to hear this because I had a premonition that things were not right,' he said. Watching the Americans driving through the burning town in a cloud of dust, headlights blazing, he was amazed to hear that they had got 20 miles unopposed.

The same evening, the Middlesex were ordered to return east, to hold the town of Taechon, backstopping the US 5th RCT heading north. Lieutenant Colonel Man was unhappy with what he found. 'There was a nasty smell about the village we found ourselves in, it was pretty ominous,' Man said. 'When you have been fighting a war, you get a pretty good smell of what is happening.' Shipster's instinct persisted. 'I remember meeting Colonel Man on the roadside and he said, "There is something odd going on,"' Shipster recalled. 'And I said, "Colonel, I think there is something odd going on all around us!"'

The Highlanders, – those fey fighting men from the north – were also sensing the invisible malevolence settling over the wasted land. 'It was beginning to feel slightly hostile, the natives had got more sullen, you got the feeling they knew something we didn't,' said Lauder. 'I had a feeling – I wasn't even discussing this with other officers – this uncomfortable feeling that we were too far north.'

Dug into a ridge above Chongju, Second Lieutenant Ted Cunningham gazed out of his trench as daylight faded. At his feet, the empty town presented a disquieting sight: Its grid of streets was blazing in the blackness, but there were no inhabitants to put the fires out. 'We were overlooking the town, it was going up in flames, and it was very clear that we were out on a limb, just us,' Cunningham said. 'It was quite eerie; there was an unreal feeling.'

31 October 1950 dawned with a chill: Halloween, the 'Feast of the Dead'. In austere Britain, children recalled tales of ghosts and witches. Eight thousand miles to the east, their brothers, fathers and uncles were about to encounter something far more terrifying, a force

that would stun the world as it struck with shock suddenness out of the winter descending over the Korean killing grounds.

That day, a Middlesex patrol brought in two prisoners. One was North Korean. The other was Chinese.[95]

Part Two
Tragedy

Oh! Wherefore come ye forth in triumph from the north,
With your hands, and your feet, and your raiment all
red?

Thomas Babington Macaulay

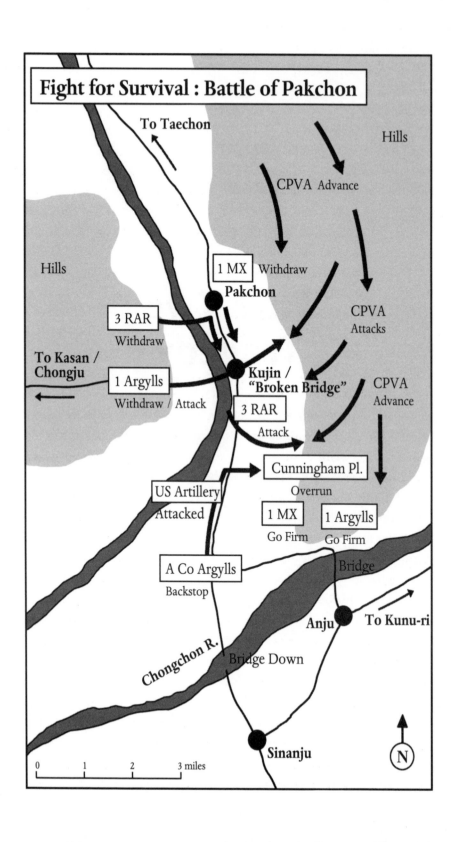

Fight for Survival : Battle of Pakchon

To Taechon

Hills

CPVA Advance

1 MX Withdraw

Pakchon

3 RAR Withdraw

To Kasan / Chongju

1 Argylls Withdraw / Attack

Kujin / "Broken Bridge"

3 RAR Attack

CPVA Attacks

CPVA Advance

Cunningham Pl.

Overrun

US Artillery Attacked

1 MX Go Firm

1 Argylls Go Firm

A Co Argylls Backstop

Bridge

Anju

To Kunu-ri

Chongchon R.

Bridge Down

Sinanju

N

0   1   2   3 miles

Chapter Eight
North Wind

She goes ten thousand miles on the business of war
She crosses mountain passes as if flying
Northern gusts carry the sound of army rattles
Cold light shines on iron armour

Anon, 'The Ballad of Fa Mu-lan'

08:00, 5 November. South of Pakchon.

Breakfast beckoned Major David Wilson: A nearby American unit had invited the ever-cheerful Argyll major to join them. A hot meal was welcome. Wilson and his Jocks had spent the previous night shivering between taped-together blankets, for the barren paddies, the scrub on the hills to the east, the dirt road and the rail line that ran through this stark desolation were all dusted with frost. To the west, glittered the icy Taeryong River; to the south, the Chongchon.

As he wandered over to the Americans – a clutch of tanks and an artillery echelon –Wilson could see, several miles to his north, smoke from what looked like shell impacts. Given that the commotion was between the bulk of 27th Brigade and his own A Company, some 5 miles south of the three battalions, and given that nothing had come through on his radio – telephone lines to Battalion HQ seemed to be down – he assumed it was inconsequential. The morning was frigid but clear, and he could hear no gunfire.

The meal proved outstanding: hot cakes, syrup, bacon, scalding coffee. Wilson was shovelling it down when he was called over to one of the tanks; his CO was apparently on the radio. Wilson leaned into the Sherman and picked up the mike. It was, indeed, Lieutenant Colonel Neilson. He sounded agitated. An unidentified enemy force had infiltrated between Wilson's company and the brigade. The major was ordered to 'get as many characters as I could' and eliminate a 'roadblock' on the brigade's line of withdrawal. Air support was en route. Wilson rallied his Jocks. 'It was a pity about the breakfast,' the major thought.[1]

The briefing was swift. One platoon would remain to guard the American detachment. Wilson would lead two platoons to attack up the road. The two platoons, with a section of Vickers and a section of 3-inch mortars, mounted trucks and Shermans and clattered north up the frozen track.

27th Brigade had seen no combat over the last five days, but there had been unsettling rumours, menacing sightings and a rushed redeployment. Now, the Highlanders would meet a new enemy in battle. 'The Chinese invented fireworks,' mused Private Eric Gurr who, in Second Lieutenant Ted Cunningham's platoon, was in the assault force. 'We should've guessed they'd do something on November the Fifth!'

For the slightly built Scottish orphan, Guy Fawkes Day, 1950, would be the most traumatic day of his life.

*　*　*

The history of Western military entanglement in twentieth-century East Asia is, to a great degree, a history of disaster. In 1905, a shockwave rippled across the globe when Japan defeated Russia, the first significant loss inflicted on a European power by an Asian nation. In late 1941 and 1942, Imperial Japan bloodied the US Pacific Fleet at Pearl Harbor, defeated US forces in the Philippines and shattered British prestige in Malaya, Singapore and Burma. In October 1950, French units were wiped out in jungles south of the Chinese border in Indochina – the first major offensive by Ho Chi Minh's Vietnamese communists that would culminate in the bloodied mud of Dien Bien Phu in 1954. America's agony in Vietnam lay far ahead. Even by these standards, the experience the UNC would suffer in North Korea in winter 1950 ranks high as a catastrophe for Western arms.

The architects of that catastrophe were an army of ghosts. They were invisible: Under cover of darkness, low cloud and the smoke of burning forests, their drab columns had been marching south since 19

October — two days after 27th Brigade took Sariwon – unseen by
UNC air reconnaissance. In frost, they draped themselves in white
sheets. In daylight, they lay up under camouflage or in villages; at
night, they forged deeper. And they were inaudible: They used no
radios, meaning UNC signals intelligence were entirely ignorant of
their presence Their leader had set up shop in a disused mine shaft on
19 October. He was a marshal in China's People's Liberation Army.
His name was Peng Te-huai.

The son of peasants who had died when he was nine, Peng, fifty-
two, had lived with his beggar grandmother and worked as a child
miner before joining the army as a private. Built like a bulldog, his
strong back and shoulders bespoke his harsh early life. During the
Chinese communists' Long March, he had risen to one of two key
military commands, beside Marshal Lin Biao. While the latter
specialised in feints and surprises, Peng favoured frontal assaults and
battles of annihilation. For Peng, a battle was not won unless he
replenished from enemy dumps.[2]

Peng's commander, Communist Party Chairman Mao Tse-tung,
had donned military uniform when the Korean War broke out.[3]
Having forced the US-supported Chiang Kai-shek to retreat to
Taiwan and proclaimed the People's Republic in October 1949, Mao
was in contact with fellow communists in Pyongyang and Moscow.
In July, following Kim Il-sung's invasion, Mao had beefed up troops
in Manchuria, for Stalin had undertaken to build forty-seven
industrial enterprises in China, thirty-six in the northeast – adjacent
to Korea.[4] As the war turned against Kim, Peking began considering
intervention: A fortnight after Inchon, Premier Chou En-lai publicly
warned that China would act if UNC forces crossed the 38th parallel.
London fretted; Washington brushed it aside.[5]

The best place to defend a frontier is well forward of it, and Mao
was convinced that Korea's rugged landscape provided the ideal
terrain in which to fight America in a confrontation he considered
inevitable.[6] Peng agreed. Comparing the US to a tiger, he wrote that
it is the nature of a tiger to consume humans; its time of attack
depends only upon its appetite.[7]

While many at the time saw Chinese intervention as ideologically

244 | SCORCHED EARTH, BLACK SNOW

grounded, Peking had abundant historical precedents for a defense of Korea, a traditional tributary state and geo-strategic buffer on China's northeast flank.* Chinese armies had battled Japan in Korea in the sixteenth and nineteenth centuries. In 1931, Japan used Korea as a springboard for the invasion of Manchuria, which then became the base for the 1937 invasion of China. China's rationale to buttress North Korea was encapsulated in a proverb: 'When the lips are destroyed, the teeth feel cold.'[8]

And Mao was not averse to force. He was massing troops opposite Taiwan, and on 7 October, had invaded Tibet. On 8 October – seven days after ROK troops had crossed the 38th parallel – Mao decided to commit. On being informed, Kim clapped and shouted, 'Excellent!'[9] When Stalin – preparing to wash his hands of the defeated Kim – read, on 13 October, of Mao's intentions, the dictator was moved. 'The Chinese comrades are so good!' he declared.[10]

But there would be no open declaration of war; Mao's expeditionary force would operate as a 'volunteer' legion, similar to the international brigades which had battled Spanish fascism. In reality, the 'Chinese People's Volunteer Army' or CPVA, were regulars of the People's Liberation Army. Mao was not gambling only with the other men's children: His own son, Captain Mao Anting, joined Peng in his mine shaft HQ, where he would become among the CPVA's first KIAs.

Chinese troops were immunised to harsh terrain, austere rations, endless marches. This could have been said of Chiang's nationalists – who had impressed neither British nor American observers in the Second World War – but Mao, recognising the potential of peasant soldiers, had instituted reforms. PLA troops were not physically abused by officers; equality was emphasised; rations were adequate; discipline was fair; a system existed for handling complaints; and corruption was eradicated.[11] Given the brutal injustices of traditional Chinese life, these were radical innovations. Moreover, political

---

* Many pundits today wonder why economic dragon China supports basket-case North Korea. A shift from economics to geopolitics and a reading of Northeast Asian history is instructive. Strategically, North Korea, a buffer state against US-supported South Korea and ancient foe Japan, remains as vital for China today as it was in late 1950.

officers indoctrinated troops in fighting for 'the honour of the Chinese'.[12] For a nation which boasted an ancient and sophisticated culture, but which had suffered over 100 years of foreign humiliation – the Opium Wars, the loss of treaty ports, the Boxer Rebellion, two Sino-Japanese wars – nationalism was a significant spur.

The NKPA had been a conventional, Soviet-style force; the CPVA had a different *modus operandi*. Equipment was primitive, but effective. Warm, quilted cotton uniforms were reversible: drab on one side, white on the other. A bandoleer of rations, usually ground soybean flour, was slung around torsos. Re-supply came via trucks, mule train, coolie labour, or captured dumps. Weapons were a mix of Chinese, Japanese, Soviet and Western small arms, mortars and light artillery. Many assault troops had no firearms, carrying instead sacks of hand grenades. Camouflage, concealment and night movement were highly developed. If spotted in the open by aircraft, men were trained to freeze, making them appear like trees. They could cover 18 miles cross-country per day – a pace comparable to the 20 miles of Caesar's legions, but over far rougher terrain than Roman roads.[13]

Pre-combat CPVA tactics – infiltrating enemy lines to set up machine guns inside perimeters; moving behind enemy positions; establishing ambushes on lines of communication – were those of the guerilla. But what the UNC would find most terrifying was the assault. This was unleashed, usually at night, in Napoleonic fashion: In response to bugles, gongs and whistles, attackers – massed as close as possible to UNC positions – would break cover and surge forward in waves.

The CPVA formations deploying secretly into Korea in 1950 were the PLA's elite: 'iron troops'.[14] Their guerilla tactics, their shock arrival in theatre, and their numbers – China, with 475 million people, was the world's most populous nation – granted tremendous psychological advantages. Though the CPVA had crossed the frontier on 19 October, they would wait another week before revealing their presence: The enemy was being lured in deep, a strategy summarised in a brutal saying: *Open the gate – beckon in the dog. Close the gate – beat the dog.*[15]

While the UNC could boast approximately, 300,000 men,[16] its frontline strength in North Korea was around 130,000: four US divisions, six ROK divisions and 27th Brigade.[17] By the last week of October, the crumbling NKPA, numbered perhaps 80,000,[18] probably including some 40,000 guerillas.[19] Now they were joined by some 210,000 Chinese in nineteen divisions, poised to crush the spearheads approaching the Yalu.[20]

China's covert deployment into North Korea ranks as the most successful mass infiltration of modern warfare. And dating back to antiquity, every Chinese knew the reality of warfare. Eighth-century poet Li Bai had written of the endless burning of beacon fires, of desert battlefields strewn with bones, of ravens pecking out the entrails of dead soldiers and draping them in the branches of wasted trees. Twentieth-century 'People's Volunteers' had been fighting their entire lives. Early modern China had been wracked by warlords; in 1937, Japan invaded; after 1945, it had been civil war. For the guerilla columns, North Korea, China's ragged edge of empire, was just the latest front in a war without end.

And Peng's soldiers had few illusions. The wiry men marching south called themselves 'human bullets';[21] the Yalu crossings into Korea were dubbed 'The Gates of Hell'.[22]

*   *   *

At 11:15 on 1 November, Brigadier Basil Coad had received orders. His brigade was to hold Taechon, but withdraw from the hard-won town of Chongju. This seemed odd: The final US and ROK advance to the Yalu was underway. At 21:30, Coad was summoned to 24th Division HQ. He found it full of 'excitable American staff officers, all chattering'. Divisional Commander John Church was at the maps. His words were explosive: 'Coad, the Chinese are in! the Second World WarI has started!'[23]

On 26 October, 8th Army had driven into . . . something. A reconnaissance platoon of ROK 6th Division reached the Yalu that day. They were wiped out by unknown forces. Next was ROK 7th Regiment, shattered the same night. Two ROK regiments drove north to assist. On 28 October, they too were annihilated. To the left, the ROK 1st Division ran into trouble at the mining town of Unsan. On 30 October, US 1st Cavalry were sent north to assist 1st ROK. Its lead regiment, 8th Cavalry, was surrounded. Two battalions managed to escape; the third was wiped out in an action that shocked media compared to the Little Big Horn massacre. In four days, two ROK divisions and an American regiment had been virtually destroyed. And on 31 October, enemy jets flashed into action over the border: MIG-15s.[24]

Faced by an unknown foe, High Command was losing its nerve. 'It was order, counter-order,' said Argyll Adjutant John Slim. 'The disorder was beginning.' 3 RAR remained at Chongju – there was only enough transport for one battalion – while the Argylls joined the Middlesex at Taechon. There, on the 2 November, the 5th US RCT came barrelling south 'in a hell of a hurry'.[25] The following day, 21st RCT pulled back through 27th Brigade

On the 3 November, after two days of confused orders, 27th Brigade was told to hold bridgeheads over the Taeryong River at Pakchon so 8th Army could resume its offensive – something that seemed a distant possibility given the overall situation. For officers plotting movements on maps, it was clear the fighting was burning across the front, from east to west. The unit furthest west was 27th Brigade; in Coad's words, '25 miles out in the blue'.[26]

* * *

First came the refugees:[27] Terrified streams of Korean peasants, telling of the approach of massive enemy forces. Then US aircraft were fired on from hills to the brigade's southeast.[28] Orders were received at 08:00, 3 November, to abandon Taechon and retire south on Pakchon, but 27th Brigade knew that transport might not be forthcoming. Sure enough, no trucks arrived. The situation was so confused, that Coad drove to 24th Divisional HQ for clarification, where he intercepted an American officer carrying an air recce report. The report stated that heavy enemy forces were converging on Taechon from north and northwest. The Argylls and Middesex were completely exposed. There was no time to wait for transport; Coad ordered immediate withdrawal.[29]

Middlesex Major John Shipster had earlier taken a patrol north of Taechon, where he had discovered a group of strange-looking dead enemy: All were bigger than North Koreans; all were wearing odd uniforms. 'We had not seen a Chinaman before, he was beautifully turned out,' said Lieutenant Colonel Andrew Man. 'He had a lovely pair of fur-lined boots – which my drum major purloined for his own use – a lovely hat and nice clean uniform and he was dead on this hillside.' As the major and his CO were discussing the find, 'The radios burst into activity, saying that China had entered the war and orders were given immediately to about turn!' Shipster recalled. Coad's 'immediate withdrawal' orders were received at around 11:00.[30] At the Argyll HQ, the news was phlegmatically delivered by the CO. 'The colonel came in,' recalled Captain John Slim. 'He said, "There's a problem: The Chinese have intervened."'

By now, Diehards and Jocks on hilltop outposts scanning the swathe of mountains to their north, were seeing astonishing sights.

'In the distance – I don't know yardage, but beyond firing range – the hills in front of us just changed colour,' said Middlesex Private James Beverly. He started when he realised what he was seeing: The uniforms of huge numbers of enemy swarming down the slopes. 'God!' Beverly said. 'There were more Chinese than any other country, and I reckon half of them came over the fucking border!'

'I was on a mountain top, we had a great view across this valley about a mile away, and I could see them,' recalled Argyll Second Lieutenant Owen Light: silhouette after silhouette marching past a gap on a distant ridgeline. He began counting. 'I stopped at 3,000,' he said. 'I had 33 men!'

Word spread. 'People were talking: "Bloody Chinese are in,"' said Diehard Private Edgar Green, in rear echelon. 'One bloke said, "We're not going to get out of this now!"' Even Diggers were unnerved; one told Signals Sergeant Jack Gallaway, 'We'll run out of bullets before they run out of soldiers!'

The road between Taechon and Pakchon winds 12 miles through hills and ridges, ideal ambush country. Instead, brigade columns would head southwest for the Kasan crossroads, where 3 RAR were pulling back from Chongju to hold the junction, then turn east to Pakchon. Ahead of the British battalions, Sergeant Paddy Redmond was tasked to mark the route. With a truck and three soldiers he was halted, signposting, when he spotted an enemy squad moving among trees just across the road. At the same moment, the Chinese spotted the Diehards. Redmond froze. 'They did not interfere with us, and we did not fire,' he said. 'It was a tense moment; they were the width of a road away!' In one of those remarkable incidents of war, it had been 'live and let live', neither side willing to fire the first, fatal shot.

The Argylls led. As Middlesex saddled up, one soldier accidentally brushed one of the hundreds of rice straw sheaves standing in the paddies. It fell, revealing a carefully hidden crate of Russian artillery ammunition. Diehards were astounded. A fast check was made. All around, the endless stooks concealed identical caches.[31] The arsenals indicated a clandestine preparation for an imminent offensive; but there was no time to destroy it.

Previously, the under-equipped brigade's reliance upon insufficient US transport had been a frustration. Now it was a peril. The Middlesex left dangling from any vehicles available, including that of a US mortar unit swept up in the retreat.[32] 'Our company jeep carried about eight, the company truck a further dozen, and the rest of us clung to the guns of the US Army,' wrote Major John Willoughby. The withdrawal came not a moment too soon. The brigade rearguard – Middlesex carriers and Shermans of the US 89th Tank Battalion – fired on Chinese entering Taechon from the north as Diehards cleared it from the south.[33]

Confusion and poor signals held dire implications for some units. Willoughby's trucks rolled past a relaxed American outpost. 'They seemed disinterested in their circumstances, making coffee, spreading out bedrolls and so forth,' he wrote. 'It was not till long after that it struck me that perhaps they were unaware of the changed circumstances. Poor chaps.'

By 16:00, the brigade was redeployed around Pakchon. The Taeryong crossings they were covering were the ford at Pakchon, and 2,000 yards further south, the broken bridge at Kujin, where 3 RAR had fought on 25–26 October. The Middlesex held an arc north and east of Pakchon; the Argylls and 3 RAR covered approaches to the bridges on the west bank. The Shermans of 89th Tank Battalion and the 105mm guns of the US 61st Artillery Battalion were leaguered south of Pakchon, east of the river.

27th Brigade now came under 'Taskforce Davidson' named for the deputy commander of the US 24th Infantry Division, Brigadier Garrison Davidson. This was unsatisfactory to Coad: taskforce commanders lacked command and control infrastructure. 'The Americans used taskforces quite a lot,' the brigadier noted. 'My experience was they are mostly unsatisfactory, and practically always disastrous.' A six-mile gap yawned between 27th Brigade and Davidson's 19th RCT to the east. Coad asked Davidson to position a battalion on high ground between the two units. 'He said he would try, but never did,' Coad wrote.[34]

Coad's position was precarious. Over half of his brigade was deployed west of the Taeryong, yet every indication was that an attack would come from the north or east. Moreover, the brigade had the Chongchon, behind it, 6 miles south. 'The position was an extremely bad one and asking for envelopment,' Coad wrote.[35] As insurance, Wilson's A Company was deployed as backstop, securing 27th Brigade's rear.

By 01:00 on 4 November, the last US units had pulled back through 27th Brigade from north and west.[36] Coad's men were anchoring the left flank of the entire 8th Army. The fourth was quiet, but an unsettling battle indicator was the swarm of refugees fleeing across the Chongchon: some 20,000 crossed in two days.[37] After dark, combat was heard in the east: 'We saw a lot of fireworks,' said Captain Reggie Jeffes at Brigade HQ. 'They were obviously being heavily attacked.' One of 19th RCT's battalions abandoned its equipment and vehicles, and fled across the Chongchon. 27th Brigade's right flank yawned open.

* * *

At 09:00 on 5 November, the Middlesex, deployed furthest north, had been warned to prepare for 'any eventuality'.[38] It was not long in coming. Shipster was huddling with his C Company in a dried riverbed when his CSM pointed eastward. 'I looked over and there was a seemingly endless column of Chinese passing us about half a mile away, all with their headdress spiked with cut-down branches, and their uniforms spiked with vegetation,' recalled Shipster. He was reminded of Shakespeare's line that sealed the doom of Macbeth: *Fear not, till Birnham wood./Do come to Dunsinane.* 'The only thing was to sit tight,' the major said. 'I don't know how many thousands were in that column, it seemed endless, it was part of the main Chinese army moving southwards.'

Argylls, too, were learning the gravity of the situation. 'There was something wrong because these huge mortar bombs – much bigger than North Korean mortars – were landing in front of our positions: You hear a wsssssh, then a crump, then frost flies up,' said Argyll Corporal Harry Young. 'At that stage, we noticed a lot of movement behind us.' Robert Searle was with the Argyll mortars not with Wilson's force when fire orders came. The direction was ominous: 'We were firing back the way we had to go.' A sergeant major doubled past Corporal Richard Peet's section: 'Conserve your ammunition!' he advised. 'We're surrounded!'

For Coad, assimilating reports of enemy and learning of the plight of the US artillery in his rear, 'the anticipated had obviously happened': Enemy were striking deep into his echelon, through hills to the east. 'It was now obvious that the Chinese were in strength behind us,' the brigadier fretted. 'Air reported an entire division.'[39]

Coad called Davidson – mercifully, rear phone lines had not yet been cut – requesting orders. 'He had no idea at all,' Coad wrote. 'He left it to me to do the best I thought.'[40] Coad made a fast decision. 27th Brigade would redeploy south, seizing high ground overlooking the Chongchon crossing. He could count on no assistance from US ground forces: A brigade ration truck driver was at 24th Division HQ where an American general[*] told him, 'We think the world of your brigade and wish them luck!'[41]

To reach the Chongchon, the Argylls and Australians would have to cross east over the Taeryong; the Middlesex would march south. Coad's plan was in three phases. 3 RAR would attack southeast of the Argylls and go firm on high ground to the east of the road,

[*] According to Willoughby, the general said: "Gee, I've done all I can for them!"

screening it. The Middlesex would then pass south through 3 RAR, take the hills overlooking the Chonchon and dig in. Finally, the Argylls would pass behind both battalions and hold the Chongchon crossing at Anju. 27th Brigade's rat-run was a single track across the paddies east of the Taeryong.

HQs were all business. At brigade, Lieutenant Peter Baldwin and his signals troops hurriedly packed. 'We were due to bug out, we knew we were having to pass through the enemy and the camp commandant called everyone together and gave a great lecture about the traditions of the British Army and don't let comrades down,' he recalled. A fellow signals officer cursed; the speech had put the fear of God into the HQ personnel. At the Middlesex Battalion HQ, Padre Jones arrived for his Sunday service. 'Keep away from us, Padre,' an officer snarled. 'There is enough trouble without you as well!'[42] Radios crackled. NCOs bawled orders. Soldiers buckled on gear. Vehicle engines coughed into life.

27th Brigade was in a race for survival: A 6-mile fight past or over any enemy in its path. If the Chinese halted them or beat them to the Chongchon crossing, they would be cut off from their rear, surrounded and destroyed. To hold open the road behind his battalions, all Coad had was David Wilson's scratch force.

* * *

Wilson's little battlegroup – four US Shermans, two platoons of Jocks, including carriers with two mortars and machine guns, the major himself in his Land Rover – rolled north for the battle smoke, reaching a situation reminiscent, Wilson thought, 'Of older and better days': C Battery of the US 61st Artillery had formed their six guns into a semi-circle and were firing point-blank into Chinese who had infiltrated under cover of paddy bunds. 'As men of the guns were hit, other men would come forward to take their place,' Wilson noted. 'A most inspiring sight!'[43] Lacking anti-personnel rounds, the howitzers were shooting down, bouncing their shells off frozen paddies into enemy just 30 yards away; this unusual method explained, presumably, why Wilson had heard no firing.

The Shermans buttoned up and rolled forward, turrets swivelling for targets. Jocks dropped from their hulls, deploying into skirmish lines. The dry paddies around the battery came suddenly alive: Enemy, realising they were being counter-attacked, broke cover. 'Gooks started up like quails or partridges, in all directions,' Wilson noted. 'Excellent shooting was had over the LMGs and 3-inch mortars. At the same time, the four tanks were having excellent practice at Gooks moving north along the railway line to Pakchon.' In twenty minutes, the battery position was cleared.[44] The artillery was secure, but had fired most of their ammunition.[*] The question was now how to hold open the road. 'I was told, "for God's sake, hang on where you are!"' Wilson recalled. Some 800 yards to the east, a low range of hills dominated the track. Wilson ordered Second Lieutenant Ted Cunningham's platoon to seize a key hill, while he deployed the rest of his force along the road.

Henry 'Chick' Cochrane was with the mortar half-section. 'Major Wilson came along – he was mad! – and said, "Jock, there's Gooks up there! Put a couple of mortar bombs on top!" I said, "Right ye are!"' Cochrane's crew dropped bombs into the mouths of their tubes. The bombs thunked up and out. Seconds later, puffs of black smoke erupted on the low, brown hill. With the barrage on target, the mortar men began walking explosions along the ridge.

Cunningham's platoon skirmished eastward, two sections moving, a third firing cover. Crunching over the frosted paddies was Gurr. 'Bullets were buzzing around and hitting the ground round about,' he said. 'It was pretty nerve racking.' He could not see who was shooting at him, but the marksman vacated as the Jocks closed. The hill was taken without casualties. Cunningham deployed his three sections – not nearly enough men to cover the position – into a fragile perimeter. The summit was bare but heavy scrub and pines covered the slopes.

From the hill, enemy movement was plainly visible, 300, 400 yards to the east. 'I said to my mate, "I think the Chinese have pulled us

---

[*] The rescue of the 61st Artillery generated letters of commendation for 27th Brigade from no less then four American generals, as well as Major Joseph Knott, the 61st CO, who wrote that his men were, 'greatly impressed by the discipline, coolness and workmanship of the British under fire'. See 27th Brigade War Diary, Appendix C.

into a trap,"' Gurr said. He was deeply uneasy: He had fought North Koreans, but there seemed to be many, many more Chinese. Then movement ceased; the swarm of brown uniforms vanished. Gurr relaxed. 'We thought that was that,' he said.

It was approximately 10:30.[45]

*   *   *

While Wilson was attacking from the south to pinch out the enemy force in the brigade's rear, Neilson ordered his remaining two companies to head east over the Taeryong – across the 'Broken Bridge' 3 RAR had fought for a week earlier – and attack from the north. B Company clambered across first. Rounds cracked overhead. Major Alastair Gordon-Ingram, who had survived Point 282 and Sariwon, went down, a sniper bullet through his shoulder. Doctor Douglas Haldane evacuated him by light US aircraft that landed on the dirt road.

B Company, across by 10:00, advanced on an enemy-occupied hamlet. Captain Colin Mitchell led a platoon, as Argylls 'pepper potted' forward – one man firing, the other manoeuvring – a style of advance that confuses defenders, granting no clear targets. The attack took its objective; in the settlement, sprawled some twenty enemy dead. As his Argylls consolidated, Mitchell kicked one body over to take a look. It opened an eye. Mitchell fired with his Luger, roaring, 'They're alive!' Argylls shot down into the 'corpses'. It was over in seconds. The Chinese had been playing dead, waiting to be bypassed, so that they could take the Jocks from behind.[46] The dead were rechecked. An officer picked up one Chinese by his belt. The man was hit in the stomach: Undigested rice spilled out of his belly.[47] B Company exploited eastwards another mile, taking up positions behind a prominent paddy bund, covering the road so vehicles could pass safely southward.

A Company had saved the American artillery from the south. B Company had attacked north of it and gone firm. C Company was crossing the Taeryong. The situation in the Argyll sector seemed stabilised – then reports of a fresh emergency arrived. Slim was at Tac HQ when Wilson came over the radio. The major kept a cheerful face in front of his Jocks, but did not hold back from higher ups. 'He was saying, "Come and help me!"' Slim recalled. Wilson needed it. At 11:00, Cunningham's lone platoon, on the hill dominating the brigade's line of withdrawal to the south, had been overrun.

*　*　*

'Overrun'. The word itself cannot convey the terror it would hold for the men of the UNC in North Korea in 1950. What does it mean in actuality?

'You felt really exposed, there was a feeling of isolation,' said Cunningham, on his thinly held hilltop. 'And you had not met the Chinese in battle before, you had no idea how they went about things.' The teenage subaltern was about to find out.

Gurr, who had thought the Chinese had retreated, was on one knee in Cunningham's forward, eastward-facing ten-man section, peering into the distance when things happened with heart-stopping suddenness: An enemy emerged from scrub directly in front of Gurr. 'He was on top of me – right on top of me! – I could have put my hand out and touched him,' Gurr said. There was no space even to raise his rifle to fire. 'I thought, "This is it, I've had it!"' The enemy fired his burp gun – bullets passed between Gurr's legs – the barrel rose – a round tore into Gurr's thigh with the force of a hammer strike – another went through his thumb. Beside Gurr was fellow Argyll John Meighan. A Chinese rammed his bayonet into his chest – Meighan raised his rifle, fired – the man jolted back, dead – another enemy dashed past, shooting. Meighan was shot through the wrist. The force of the bullet – possibly a dum-dum – splintered the bones. Meighan lost consciousness.[48] More Chinese surged over Gurr; he played dead. He could hear intense gunfire and a sound UNC soldiers would come to dread: the discordant notes of a bugle. The Chinese had leveraged their excellent fieldcraft to close up tight below the hill. Their earlier disappearance had not been a retreat; they had ducked behind paddy bunds and crawled alongside them. Making dead ground at the bottom of the hill, they had infiltrated through ground scrub.

In the centre of his platoon, Cunningham's first indication of action had been automatic fire hammering from his forward section over the crest. Then he saw the shadows flitting through the scrub and pines all around. 'We had a perimeter but they were coming round the contours on three sides of us,' Cunningham said. 'There seemed an awful lot.' As his CP was engulfed in chaos, Cunningham's stress levels went hyper. He was speaking on the radio to Wilson – Wilson urged him to hang on, the hill was critical – while trying to keep a grip on events all around, redeploying men from his rear section to the forward sections. Individual gunshots coalesced into a relentless crackle. Intra-platoon communication was by shouting.

Bullets kicked up dust. Argylls tumbled. 'Suddenly, our numbers dropped,' Cunningham said 'We were losing a lot of men, we were being decimated.' His sergeant was hit in the head. 'He fell on top of me, it was one of the most unpleasant experiences . . . ghastly, blood everywhere . . . I would not wish anyone to have to hold somebody who's had their head blasted away.'

Below, on the road, the mortar section heard disaster unfold. 'All I heard was shouting through the wireless, "Five rounds rapid!" in a sort of a panicked voice,' recalled Cochrane. 'The last words were screaming for mortar fire.'

The platoon was finished. 'They came over the top, they were in among us, it was the end,' Cunningham said. 'I told people to get out, then I got myself out as fast as I bloody well could.' Scrambling and weaving down the western slope, bursts whipped over his head as Chinese shot down. 'The firing was gratuitous,' he said. 'The noise of it, the pinging, was like a cowboy film.' At the base of the hill, stunned survivors tumbled into a ditch in dead ground, out of sight of enemy above. In mere minutes, the thirty-strong platoon had lost five killed, six wounded.[49]

On the hill, Gurr lay still. The bullet in his thigh stung; the top of his thumb dangled from a flap of raw flesh. Chinese were consolidating. A few feet away, a wounded Argyll sang 'God Save the King'. 'I think he was delirious,' Gurr said. He hissed: 'For God's sake! Play dead!' The singing soon stopped; the man had died. A Chinese soldier approached and stood over Gurr. Terrified, the

Argyll froze as the man kicked him over and started rummaging through his pockets. Gurr was carrying a fountain pen, a birthday present. The enemy removed it, examined it, then – noting that the Scotsman lived – replaced it, motioning at him to place his hands on his head and lie still. Gurr did so. The soldier left.

Another burst – probably from a Chinese who had spotted movement and fired instinctively – tore into Gurr. One round grazed his head, another ploughed into his shoulder, another his chest. Riddled; bleeding out from five bullet wounds; the Scotsman's pain numbed in the chill air. Consciousness slipped away.

* * *

South of the Argyll B and C Companies were 3 RAR. Unlike the Argylls and Middlesex, who had seen the enemy numbers beyond Taechon, 3 RAR, the last battalion to retire from the west, had not yet met any Chinese. Diggers had been infuriated by the 2 November order to evacuate Chongju, the town they had fought for where Lieutenant Colonel Green had been killed. 'We were shocked, we were not used to this,' said Sergeant Tom Muggleton. 'You stood your ground!'

Now, on 5 November, they were retreating again, but action was clearly imminent for it was Sunday, and the battalion had been in action on the three previous Sundays, at Apple Orchard, Broken Bridge and Chongju.[50] The battalion crossed the Taeryong without resistance at 11:30 and mounted US trucks, which began heading south. As they rattled toward the Argyll mortars on the road, they came under fire from the east.

The mortar men, having heard Cunningham's platoon being overrun, now saw enemy skirmishers heading for them. 'I said to the bloke on my right, "Take the mortar sights off, wait till they are within 100 yards, then dump it in the water and I will see you in Pusan!"' Cochrane recalled. He was relieved to see approaching Diggers. 'These Aussies came and said, "Alright Jock?" and we said, "Yes, but no ammo!"' The Australians, setting up their own mortars, handed over a few cases. 'The party was going to start!' reckoned Captain Ben O'Dowd.

SCORCHED EARTH, BLACK SNOW

Massive air attacks had been laid on. For the first time in support of 3 RAR, this included the elite Mustang pilots of Australia's 77 Squadron. An ACT turned their radio volume to maximum. 'You could hear the pilots saying, "There he is, get that bastard on the left!"' said Sergeant Reg Bandy. 'It was like being at the pictures!' Huge clouds of smoke and dust billowed over the hills as rockets and napalm did their work.

3 RAR would attack eastward and retake the hill lost by Cunningham's platoon. In this, his first action, Lieutenant Colonel Floyd Walsh deployed two companies – A on the left, B on the right. Diggers dismounted, shook out into extended line, fixed their long bayonets and waited. Walsh radioed Coad. 'When you want me to launch the attack, I only have to press the button,' he reported. 'Well, press the bloody thing!' the brigadier snapped.[51] The attack was on. It was 14:00.

With their objective some 800 yards across open ground, the long line strode forward, each man spaced at least 10 feet from the next to minimise the effect of enemy automatics. 'We were not told how serious the situation was, it was just another big attack,' said A Company Private Mick Servos, who had so enjoyed earlier combat. The line came under fire immediately. 'A machine gun nest was on the hill firing at us, I could see him firing, see bullets landing,' Servos said. Bursts were hitting just ahead of the advancing line; Servos watched spurts of dust arrowing towards him from the right as the gunner swivelled. 'I thought I had better jump – then it felt like the wind had picked up a house and the house had hit me.' He collapsed. Five rounds had punched right through his thigh. 'I almost got a DSO – dick shot off!' he said. 'I was lucky, it shot all the muscle out of my leg, but did not hit bone.'

Other men were falling. Next to Private Stan Connelly in B Company, the company clerk went down. 'His head exploded like a watermelon, he dropped dead beside me,' Connelly said. 'This upset me, but the attack had to go on.' The Diggers could not lose momentum to care for casualties. Wounded and dead lay behind in the paddy.

Mortars Lieutenant Phillip Bennett, the victor in the grenade-pistol duel in one of the Diggers' first actions, watched keenly. 'We could see our fire going where it was being asked for, on the enemy side of the hills,' he said. 'You see lots of bursting ammunition, clouds of dust, smoke and God knows what – pretty good for morale!' Once the companies entered scrub at the hill's base, he lost visual.

Another officer had a uniquely privileged perspective. 'The Aussies attacked – a full battalion attack!' said Cunningham, at the foot of the hill. 'One was amazed that they were doing this with the fire coming off the hill, it was awesome – a lot of people, the full monty! – I was in a position that you would never see it from unless you were enemy.'

Diggers passed through Cunningham's clutch of Argylls and ascended. Connelly, hefting a Bren, was exhausted as he approached the crest, but joined the final charge. 'We surged up,' he said. 'I saw a couple of enemy, threw the Bren up on my shoulder and fired from there, using it like a rifle.' The Chinese had watched the big Australians stride through their machine gun fire; as they closed for the kill, the enemy broke. 'We could see their backs and were picking them off as they went,' Connelly said. Now, the Chinese were overrun.

The firefight jolted Gurr back to consciousness. 'Aussies were coming up the hill, bayonets fixed, throwing phosphorous grenades,' he said. Blood-spattered from five wounds, shaven headed and slight in stature – like a Chinese – Gurr was mistaken for enemy. An Australian levelled his bayonet and charged. 'I yelled, "I am an Argyll!"' he said. He was recognised. Lying nearby was the wounded Meighan. As he was being tended to by two Australians, a Chinese leapt from cover, aimed at the three soldiers and pulled the trigger of his burp gun. Click. The enemy, with an empty magazine or a stoppage, froze, helpless. Lieutenant Noel 'Chick' Charlesworth, the platoon commander, took aim and pulled his own trigger. Click. The officer's magazine was also empty. The Chinese fled.[*52]

* In 1997, David Wilson put Meighan in contact with the Australian platoon commander, Charlesworth. Meighan phoned him from Scotland, thanking him for saving his life. See Gurr, Eric; Charlesworth, Chick; Meighan, John; *A Hill in Korea*, www.britains-smallwars.com

The position was secure by 15:00, the survivors' ordeal over.[53] 'I was glad to be alive,' said Gurr.[*] Among the Diggers' dead was Lieutenant Eric Larson, who had led the vanguard over 'Broken Bridge'. On the hilltop, men began digging in immediately, including D Company on an adjacent ridge. The effect of the napalm attacks – 'heat treatment' in Digger parlance – was appalling. Private Len Opie found a Chinese with his arm burned off; Opie grabbed him to hurl him into a pit and his arm came off, '... so I achieved what very few people had, I beat him over his head with his own arm.' C Company and Battalion HQ dug in on the low ground, holding the road.

Fire continued to come in. 'We had one bloke, on the skyline like a ballerina, he said, "I can see them," then he said, "I've been shot!"' recalled John 'Lofty' Portener. 'He dropped his tweeds, he'd been shot through the scrotum, we could see a white testes. We bandaged the bastard up, we used a towel – just the bag was torn! It was a bit of a laugh.'

Crumps and explosions of dirt began walking along the ridges: The Chinese were using mortars. A Company's CP took a direct hit, its forceful commander, Bill Chitts being severely wounded in the legs – a development that would have serious consequences. Argylls and Diggers helped wounded down the slopes.

In the paddy, Servos, his thigh bleeding heavily, lay helpless. 'I'd got left,' he said. 'High and dry.' It was late afternoon when two walking wounded spotted him and lifted him. The three supported each other, hobbling toward the road, when a tank approached from the north. One of the walking wounded said, 'If that's an enemy tank, we're finished!' It was a Sherman.

The commander leaned out of his turret and invited the three bloodied Diggers aboard, warning them to hang on. 'There's a roadblock ahead!' he said, 'I'm gonna knock through and shoot shit out of it!' Pockets of enemy were scattered all along the east side of the road; the Australians clambered behind the right of the turret.

---

[*] Also in 1997, Wilson wrote to Gurr, giving him details of Paterson's grave – the corporal whose radio message was abruptly cut off was evacuated alive from the hill, but died of his wounds in hospital, and was buried in Singapore – and apologising for sending him into battle so badly briefed. Gurr, letter to author, 2010.

All were in a bad way: Servos' damaged leg was agony, the second man's hand 'was hanging off', while the third's arm 'looked like a butcher's shop'. The engine revved and the Sherman barrelled down the track, dust blasting up behind. The Diggers clung to the vibrating hull. As the tank passed enemy shooting from the side of the road – a fire block, not a roadblock – its turret rotated left and it let rip with its heavy machine guns. Then they were past.

Up in the hills as afternoon faded, two Diggers probed forward of B Company. 'One guy, Ron Tully, said, "Come with me, I want to get some souvenirs" – he wanted pistols or something,' recalled Connelly. The two walked cautiously to the forward edge of the feature where a re-entrant was packed with dead Chinese 'lined up almost head-to-toe'. Connelly was apprehensive, but Tully went down among them and was busily searching the first 'body' – when it produced a grenade. 'I don't know if it was to commit hara-kiri or to get Tully, but he failed to throw it,' said Connelly. 'It exploded and spattered Tully with his brains.' The two dashed back inside the perimeter. Tully 'went to pieces,' and Connelly was rattled. Was the pile of enemy actually dead, he wondered, or were they lying doggo, to rise and attack after dusk?

* * *

While the Diggers took the high ground, the rest of the brigade, to the north, had been moving. Second Lieutenant Alan Lauder, with the Argylls' C Company, was leading his platoon eastward over the broken bridge where a US officer greeted them grimly with, 'The shit's hit the fan!' Jocks burst into laughter. The American was astounded by their amusement, but it was his phrase: No Argyll had ever heard it before.

Laughter dried up when Argylls, high up on the bridge, got their first look at the battlefield. 'We began to see enemy, they appeared to be in vast numbers swarming all over the hills within half a mile, like ants,' Lauder recalled. With a lurch, he realised that what was happening was contrary to all experience in Korea thus far. 'This was the first time we'd seen a large body of enemy coming toward us rather than running away.'

C Company joined B in its holding position east of the road. 'We were told to stand and hold at all costs,' said Ron Yetman. 'This was my worst time in Korea.' As brigade vehicles passed behind the prone Argylls, something started to happen on the high ground. 'All the bushes across the valley on the hill opposite started moving,' said Yetman. 'I didn't believe my eyes! There were hordes of them, and just two companies of Argylls!' Even the ferocious Mitchell wondered if the end had come: The Argylls were now, 'a thin red line indeed'.[54]

Evening the odds, was the unprecedented pounding from the air. Lauder watched astonished as Australian Mustangs, flying at almost zero feet, raced *under* power cables in strafing runs on the ridges.

The Middlesex had been alerted to move at 12:50, but had not started until 14:00.[55] 'We received orders to concentrate on the main road as quickly as possible. A truck company arrived . . . with them were three US liaison officers, who, having decided that the time had come to rejoin their formation south of the Chongchon, had run into a roadblock blocking the escape route, and brought us news that we were cut off,' wrote Major John Willoughby. 'However, come what may, we had to occupy those formidable hills overlooking the river crossing before the Chinese got there.'[56]

Jammed together on trucks, the battalion headed south through Pakchon's ruined streets, before emerging into open country. 'I thought, "Peking here were come!"' recalled Frank Whitehouse. Every man knew this was a different kind of battle to previous experience. 'You were not fighting for king and country,' Beverly said. 'You were fighting to stay alive.'

Skirmishes erupted along the roadside as Diehard dismounts fought past pockets of enemy. 'We were told to head for a point down the road, so we fixed bayonets and marched down,' Corporal Bob Yerby said. 'Anyone who popped up we shot at them, there were bullets whistling over your head.' Dead enemy were passed. 'We just kicked them to one side and carried on; we had to get out.' It was clear the Chinese meant business. 'They were not going to turn and run, they were going to fight,' Yerby reckoned. 'Your hearing intensified, your nerves intensified tenfold; something big was happening all around us.'

As the Middlesex bore down on 3 RAR, the Diggers were attacking eastward, their Vickers and mortars beside the road shooting cover. 'We drove through this attack at right angles, through the dust and smoke,' wrote Willoughby, whose D Company were leading. 'Machine guns were obligingly holding their fire while we passed in front of them.'[57]

The Middlesex continued until they reached their objective southeast of 3 RAR: the ridge overlooking the Chongchon. As Diehards debussed preparatory to attacking upward, Willoughby ordered his CSM to keep the trucks nearby for any eventuality. The NCO obliged, threatening to shoot any driver who left without orders. As his men took up assault positions, Willoughby scanned his objective through binoculars. He could see figures, apparently wearing Australian slouch hats, waving at the Diehards to come up. However, they were running. 'Australians never walk or run, they stride across anything,' Willoughby thought. Focusing in, he saw they were Chinese: Twigs in their headgear for top camouflage stuck out horizontally.[58]

A US FOO arrived, and the hills fountained up as his barrage landed. Middlesex advanced upward. Their objective was taken without fighting; seven enemy lay dead on the ridge. Diehards dug in. Thanks to US transport and firepower, Man's men had beaten the Chinese to the ridge.

At 15:00, relieved Argylls watching the camouflaged enemy mass in motion to the east, got orders to head south, B Company on trucks, C on tanks. 'It was almost like hitching a lift,' recalled Haldane. 'Get me back!' Neilson's Jocks passed behind the Middlesex, and dug in on the hills directly opposite the crossings over the Chongchon River at Anju. Along with brigade administrative elements, the US 61st Artillery crossed south over the river and set up their guns facing north.

By nightfall, 27th Brigade had given up the Taeryong, but was holding a three-mile bridgehead north of the Chongchon. The Argylls were on the east of the line, the Middlesex in the centre and

3 RAR to the west, a mile north of the other battalions. The Battle of Pakchon had been a touch-and-go series of fast moves and repeated crises: 'An exciting enough day for anyone,' Coad noted dryly.[59] 'The Brigade today, by forceful action, extricated itself from a difficult position,' the War Diarist wrote with understatement. Demolitions equipment was discovered on dead Chinese; they had been planning to blow the bridge, trapping the brigade.[60] This realisation prompted some unpleasant business at the crossing. 'Civilian casualties came down the road that night, a lot had been hit in cross-fire, and blood was dripping from their hand carts,' said Captain Reggie Jeffes. 'Of course, you had to inspect every one very carefully because the Chinese were quite likely to try and get through this way.'

And 5 November 1950, was not yet over.

* * *

The western slopes of the low ridgeline the Australians were occupying were bathed in the orange glare as the sun dissolved in the Yellow Sea. 'I don't want to see that old sun go down,' sang Gallaway as he hacked into frozen ground at Battalion HQ. His sentiment was shared by many. A, B and D Companies were on high ground. C Company was astride the road covering Support Company and Battalion HQ.

To the northeast, the mountains turned purple as darkness fell. Bugles sounded in the east: enemy companies were manoeuvering. Mortar flashes lit up the Diggers' positions. Firing began crackling along the ridges.

3 RAR's mortars – firing rapidly in response to DF requests – had been set up near Battalion HQ. Chinese counter-mortar fire, seeking them, now began to impact around Battalion HQ. Walsh ordered O'Dowd to relocate the headquarters 1,000 yards south. This was a significant movement, at night, and would necessitate the loss of telephone lines to the rifle companies. O'Dowd protested. Walsh insisted. Listening in on the net, Coad permitted the withdrawal of Battalion HQ, but insisted the rifle companies stay put. The operation – requiring the striking of tents and loading of vehicles with

equipment – to an undefined location, in the dark, under enemy fire, proved chaotic.

Then at 20:00, Walsh ordered the rifle companies to withdraw.

'We had just got it under control, when the CO gives orders to move back half a mile,' Bandy said. 'Everybody was pissed off, we knew it was stupid.' Gallaway heard it all happen. 'We knew from radio traffic that something bad was going on, we could hear officers arguing, Major Wally Brown abused Colonel Walsh wholeheartedly, he was not pleased with life at D Company,' Gallaway remembered. 'When we got orders to pull out we were down that road like Brown's cows, it was black dark, we didn't know what was going on.' Walsh's decision was extraordinary. His companies were in contact, they had no clear rear areas to head for, there were no timings, no planning data.[61] In his first battle, 3 RAR's new CO had lost his nerve.

B and D Companies were commanded by veterans: In firm positions, neither obeyed Walsh's order immediately. C Company, on the road, under the tight control of 'Armour Piercing Archie' Denness complied. 'We were in some strife,' recalled Lieutenant David Butler, whose platoon had cleared the 'Apple Orchard'. Enemy probed towards the company from the west, trying to make the Australians give away their position. Denness' men held their fire. Then a heavy machine gun let loose from across the river. A .50 calibre machine gun can shoot down an aircraft or demolish a brick building; Butler found being under its arcing tracers, 'Very, very uncomfortable.' When the command came to break contact, Butler was too busy to be frightened: He had to make sure all his men were with him during the withdrawal. In silence, the company moved down the road in single file toward the supposed location of Battalion HQ, every man primed to utter the password, 'Acid Bath' when challenged.

It was A Company, on the left flank, who would suffer the worst for Chitts, wounded, had passed command to an inexperienced 22-year-old, Lieutenant Algy Clark. Clark's orders over the radio were to regroup on the road, where he would be met by Walsh. Clark's training told him that withdrawal in contact requires units to be thinned out, check points established in rear, and an RV established. None were apparent, but he obeyed. As Clark was planning the move, Chinese assaulted his CP. Two privates were shot, his CSM killed, a man lost his head to a grenade, and Clark took shrapnel in the face. Control disintegrated.[62]

Among A Company was Don Woods, a Vickers gunner from Tasmania who had joined the Army after hearing what a cushy posting Japan was. Earlier, as the enemy stormed up, he had been firing into Chinese – visible in his muzzle flash – from about 15 feet: 'They were close, you could see the whites of their eyes!' he recalled. One Digger nearby was bayoneted in his foxhole, but Woods' position seemed to be holding. Then things went wrong. The machine gunners heard movement from slopes above and behind them. 'We said, "It's A Company!"' but it was not: A shower of stick grenades landed among the two machine guns. Woods was lifted by blast – shrapnel thudded into his thigh. Amid the company's disorderly withdrawal, enemy had infiltrated above them. 'We were left on our own,' Woods said. 'There was a breakdown in comms, it was bloody frightening – we knew we had to get out.' The gunners feverishly whipped the locks out of their weapons, disabling them. Woods, in pain but mobile, hurled a grenade behind him to slow down pursuit as they set off. Other men did the same: their withdrawal was covered by the detonations. One Digger, badly wounded by shrapnel, was dragged along by his webbing. Woods snap shot at shadows. In darkness, in utter confusion, surrounded by enemy, he wondered if he would see his family again. The group reached level ground. Ahead, they heard an unmistakable clanking, and moving lights. It was an American tank on the road. The survivors climbed aboard, and were carried south to Battalion HQ.

Charlesworth, meanwhile, had ordered his platoon back and was counting men through when he reached thirty-five; he was counting enemy. He shouted a warning to his Diggers and opened fire. Then he too came under fire from the abandoned high ground. His platoon broke up; small groups of men fought their way along to B Company or down to the road.[63] Clark, wounded but still effective, was leading survivors of Company HQ through the darkness. Shadowy enemy were blundering around everywhere, but seemed as disorganised as the Diggers. 'By acting boldly and confidently', Clark discovered that enemy avoided his group. He led his men south.[64]

By the early hours, only D Company was in position. The remaining companies were, in Butler's words, 'in a blob', on the low ground, locations unknown to Battalion HQ. An enemy attack to finish off 3 RAR seemed inevitable. From the dark hills echoed a haunting sound: A bugler piping 'The Last Post'. Men wondered if it was a wounded Argyll or Digger left behind.* [65]

Coad learned of Walsh's disastrous conduct in person. 'Bruce Ferguson arrived at Brigade HQ with another officer to complain and say the battalion was in chaos,' recalled Reggie Jeffes. Shocked, Coad ordered the Middlesex to establish roadblocks to their west in case of an enemy breakthrough. This was done. The Diehards were not under attack, but were tense. 'During the night the Americans had obviously bought a great deal of artillery to positions south of the river,' recalled Willoughby. 'The noise of shells passing overhead was continuous.'[66]

Dawn. A chill mist wreathed the frosted countryside. All lay eerily silent. Coad drove straight for 3 RAR to see for himself what had happened. In the shambolic Battalion HQ, wounded were being treated; a medic plucked shrapnel from Woods' leg with pliers. The brigadier bumped into O'Dowd. Shoving a map in front of him, Coad asked the captain where the rifle companies were. O'Dowd had no idea. Coad stabbed his finger on the map, telling O'Dowd exactly where he wanted them deployed. Then he drove off to locate Walsh.

Sergeant Tom Muggleton was nearby when the two met. 'I didn't know why Brigadier Coad was there,' said Muggleton, who sensing the imminence of something dramatic, made himself scarce. 'I was hiding in a bush and there was a lot of hand-waving going on.' Muggleton did not overhear what was said, but the result of the meeting was summed up by 3 RAR's War Diarist. 'Lieutenant Colonel F.S. Walsh was re-posted to the Australian Operational

---

*They never found out; the piper's identity remains a mystery.

Research Team attached to 8th Army Headquarters.' Coad had sacked him on the spot.

It was a dicey thing for a British brigadier to do to an Australian colonel in mid-battle, but no Digger complained. 'We never liked Walsh, we didn't think he was competent,' said Muggleton. 'All the decisions he made were wrong.' 'That night was not the best effort of the battalion,' agreed Bennett. 'But it was the entire responsibility of the CO who didn't have the strength of character to handle it.' In Walsh's place was appointed an officer who was, in Bennett's opinion, 'A man's man and a soldier's soldier': Second-in-command Major Bruce Ferguson.

Pakchon had been a bloody affair: Twelve Diggers had been killed, sixty-four wounded.[67] A Company was decimated. With the Australians at their mercy, why had the Chinese not finished them?

* * *

Supported by Shermans, patrols advanced cautiously into the mist to answer this question. They found nobody. 'The Chinese had disappeared, it was incredible,' said Woods. 'Our boys went back and got our machine guns.' On 7 November, patrols probed further. Leading one, up a nameless valley and into nameless hills, was Cunningham.

'My platoon were in front again – I don't know why, because we were depleted,' he said. 'We were going across this paddy, and I remember watching this extraordinary barrage walking along this hill – puffs of smoke and earth flying up in a straight line.' His luck had held on 5 November; now it would run out. 'Suddenly, I found I could not walk,' he said; an invisible impact had flung him violently to the ground. Wilson pelted over, took one look and stabbed him with a morphine syrette. Cunningham feeling no pain, looked down. 'My legs had been shattered by shrapnel, they were at funny angles, I had a head wound, but could not know how bad that was, and I had stomach wound that looked very gory, there was a lot of blood,' he said, 'I was messed up, but didn't know the implications.' He went under, coming round in the brigade dressing station. There, he was thrust into a US ambulance that bumped off south over the Chongchon.

Cunningham and five of his ill-starred platoon had been wounded by mortar fire, but it was not an enemy bomb: it was a 'drop short' from their own battalion.[68] The Chinese had broken contact completely.

All patrols discovered were bodies of enemy dead, some buried, others not. 3 RAR patrols skirmished and captured three North Koreans, but there were no major engagements. The story was identical across the entire front. After a week of action, the Chinese had not simply disengaged, they had disappeared.* 27th Brigade had reacted effectively at Pakchon, but was fortunate to have been attacked on the final day of the enemy offensive.

The next twenty days remain the strangest period of the Korean War. Across the entire front, as cautious units retook terrain lost in the shock onslaught, fighting dwindled away to patrol skirmishes. 27th Brigade advanced in line with ROK and US troops, who the brigade sometimes found slow in keeping up – a big change from the lightning charges of October.

The Brigade War Diary captures these operations. 9 November:

> The day was quiet in the Brigade sector. 11 November: Progress was held up and the ROKs did not appear to be getting on . . . [1st Cav] were reported to be advancing, but were not up to the line by the end of the day. 13 November: Apart from patrolling, no other operation was carried out today. 16 November: Advances carried out along the whole divisional front with no opposition reported.

They were strange days. To the northeast, magnificent mountains faded into the blue distance; in the foreground, the landscape bore the imprint of war. Beside bare paddies lay charred villages. Here and there sat trackless tanks and trucks, stationary beside the road,

---

* Some sources, including 27th Brigade War Diary and the Australian official history, mention 3 RAR scouts seeing an 'estimated 800' enemy retreating north on 7 November, and calling in air and artillery strikes, caused 'heavy casualties'. However, there is no mention of this incident in 3 RAR's War Diary, nor in any Digger interviews that this author conducted.

telling the story of the earlier retreat. Bridges and viaducts were twisted, broken skeletons. And everywhere lay death. Digger patrols came across atrocities: men and women with their hands wired together and shot.[69] Encased in ice on the edge of the Chongchon, a civilian body lay frozen near the riverbank, ignored by all.[70]

Far above could be seen one of the twentieth century's most apocalyptic spectacles. Trailing long, white vapour trails across the icy blue sky were massed formations of glinting silver crosses: B29 Superfortresses, heading for the Yalu Bridges.[71] On 8 November, Sinuiju, the border town was visited by 77 B29s. Two thirds of the city was devastated.[72] MacArthur, his confident prediction that the Chinese could not intervene disproven, was upping the ante.

Wounded were treated. Servos and Gurr made it to a US MASH. 'It was well organised, on the go, lots of wounded coming in,' said Gurr. 'There was shouting and some screaming, people in agony,' recalled Servos. A minor operation was performed on his leg, and it was drained. Then he was flown to Japan, as was Gurr. All his bullets were removed, but for one in his chest.

The mangled Cunningham, in a morphine daze, spent two days bumping south in an ambulance before being flown out. In Osaka, a decision was made on the youth's legs. 'They thought that if they amputated one, they would have a better chance of saving the other,' he said. 'A lot of people would have advocated a double, so I said almost casually, "You'd better do it, and do your best on the other one."' The operation was carried out, but Cunningham was not sorry for himself. 'The deepest feeling was the disappointment of not being able to hold the hill,' he said. 'And I seem to have lost a lot of people I'd got to know.' He was moved to the British hospital at Kure in preparation for a long rehabilitation.

Back at Brigade, a disappointment was overcome. After the announcement of an imminent return to Hong Kong in Chongju two weeks previously, it had been rumoured that 10 November would mark relief day. 'In the morning, the colour sergeant said, "I want a list of how many people want to draw Hong Kong dollars on the boat,"' recalled Lance Corporal Don Barrett. 'At 12 o'clock they said, "It ain't going to happen."' Following Chinese intervention, and at the suggestion of Air Vice Marshal Cecil Bourchier in Tokyo, the Imperial General Staff in London had agreed, on 6 November, that 27th Brigade would remain in theatre, regardless of 29th Brigade's arrival.[73] Willoughby broke the news to his company, moving from section to section. 'They all took it marvellously, no complaints, a few wry smiles and silence thereafter,' he wrote. 'It is a bitter disappointment. Only ten days ago, we thought this war had been won.'[74]

Battered units were reinforced. O'Dowd took over the 3 RAR's decimated A Company, 'kidnapping' Muggleton as his CSM. Among his reinforcements was the Australian Army's first Aboriginal officer, Lieutenant Reg Saunders.

But there was no action. On 11 November, the Argylls commemorated a solemn Remembrance Day – every man had lost a recent comrade[75] – and the RSM put the men through some foot drill, impressing a passing US colonel, who halted his jeep to watch.[76] Captain Robin Fairrie kept his Jocks amused, patrolling the riverbanks and bagging duck. 'He had this shotgun which had been his grandfather's,' recalled MacKenzie. 'Well, his bivvy caught fire and the shotgun got ruined, so he took it out, dug a hole and gave it a burial.' Shipster's C Company scattered corn kernels soaked in alcohol near the river; drunken pheasants were subsequently scooped up for the pot.[77] Correspondent Harry Gordon and some Diggers went grenade fishing in the Taeryong; after C-rations, the stunned fish proved delicious. 3 RAR's intelligence officer, Alf Argent, was startled when a British officer asked if he had bought a shotgun: The mountains, apparently, offered excellent bear hunting.

In the regimental journal, nameless Middlesex wags jotted down the terminology of the campaign for posterity:

Many enemies – Reported by all civilians. An uncertain number of possible enemy seen in an unspecified area at an unspecified time. The basis of all intelligence reports.

Patrols – Military excursions for the purpose of collecting firewood.

Prophylactic fire – Designed to give an operational atmosphere to an advance up an unoccupied valley.

Pinned down by fire – 'Say! Was that a shot?'

Perimeter – To be held at all costs. Only to be abandoned if attacked.

Change of plan – An eventuality inseparable from any operation.

Situation fluid – 'Hold on to your hats boys! Anything can happen!'

Fire for effect – This means any forward troops may expect to be shelled at any time from the rear.

Harassing fire – This is designed to keep friendly troops awake all night. It is no inconvenience to the enemy.

Let's get the hell outta here! – Vide Chapt 1, Para 1, of the American Military Manual 'Actions to be taken in the event of an emergency'.

Let 'em roll – Op. order for the advance. Only alternative to [previous].

Air support – A two-edged weapon.

The big picture – A nebulous panorama of the strategical situation, mainly derived from air survey.

Your difficulties are appreciated – 'Sorry, we cannot help – carry on!'[78]

On 13 November, a gift arrived from Prime Minister Clement Attlee: A UN flag previously flown over Trafalgar Square. Coad planted it at Brigade HQ. Three days later, Brigade HQ established itself – for the third time – in Pakchon. By 17 November, the town was showing signs of normality as the populace began to reappear.[79] In the mornings, women crouched on the Chongchon's bank, doing the endless laundry.[80]

The first light snows had fallen on 12 November.[81] 'The joy was watching the Aussies when the first snow came,' said Argyll Intelligence Officer Sandy Boswell. 'They were like children, they'd never seen snow before, they leapt out of their trenches and had snowball fights and it was great to see these big tough fellows playing around like that.' The snow did not set. Soon it would.

On the morning of the 14 November, Willoughby was sitting in his jeep eating 'a miserable breakfast of cold beef stew' when he registered an ominous, unidentifiable sound: 'I gradually became aware of a distant, drawn-out moan.' For microseconds he could not work out what it was, then he was buffeted by a freezing blast: 'The most ghastly wind I have ever experienced descended upon us from the North.' The morning temperature was a few degrees above freezing; it plunged 22 degrees in two hours. By noon, all food had frozen it its tins, water bottles solidified. Willoughby, eyes streaming, feared for his ears. 'There was no escape; all our wintry yesterdays were gentle,' he wrote. 'Mother-in-law's breath!' cursed a passing Digger.[82]

The wolfish wind was carrying the Manchurian winter down the mountain passes. That day, a number of vehicles suffered cracked cylinder blocks and heads; British, US and captured Russian antifreeze all seemed ineffective.[83] By now, most men were wearing jungle greens, British battledress and a US parka, but the cold was piercing. Soldiers, shivering uncontrollably, lined slit trenches with rice straw torn from paddy stooks and cottage roofs, and with quilts from looted homes.

By late November, most men were outfitted with US gear. 'We got winter clothing – long johns, hoods, pile hats, pile jackets – jolly good,' said Barrett. 'The British contribution was a dish cloth about the size of a handkerchief, they said, "Tie it round your neck" but it didn't reach!' 'You'd never recognise them as Scottish battalion,' said Argyll Quartermaster Andrew Brown, who used his initiative to ensure his men got the best. After being offered a drink of medical alcohol by a US supply colonel he realised that the British had a valuable currency. 'The military attaché from Japan arrived and I said, "If you could get a case of whiskey it would sort out a lot of problems!" The going rate for a bottle of whiskey was 100 pairs of slacks or 50 pairs of boots.' But cold weather gear was not waterproof. On 17 November, rain fell, soaking men, who rapidly froze.[84] On 25 November, 27th Brigade was assigned to Corps Reserve and moved into Pakchon. Thankful Diggers dubbed the move 'Operation Defrost'.[85]

* * *

Amid these low-intensity operations, men reflected on their experiences. 27th Brigade had only been in North Korea since 11 October, but the period seemed like a dark dream, for this was war in enemy territory in an era predating the concept of 'hearts and minds'.

Looting was commonplace. 'I regret to say some Americans would, if they saw someone with a watch on, take their watches off,' recalled Cunningham. But it was not just the Americans. Brigadier Coad drove past a Middlesex patrol which had clothed themselves with drapes and clothing from nearby homes for extra warmth. He sent back a lighthearted order: 'No more pink tea towels!'[86] By the time rations arrived at forward units, local houses had been raided for anything edible as poor villages proved larders for hungry men.[87] 'Once we stopped at this location in North Korea and one of the lads killed this pig,' said Argyll Ralph Horsfield. 'I remember this guy cooking pork in this big Korean dish, in the fat of the pig itself.' It might not have occurred to brigade soldiers, but for a Korean peasant family, loss of livestock could be disastrous. Destruction, verging on vandalism, was frequent, with houses being torn apart or even burnt for soldiers' warmth 'I felt privately that it got out of hand,' admitted Woods. 'People knocked down homesteads for fire, I felt it was excessive.'

By now, most soldiers had been confronted by the gruesome effect of various munitions. Some sights would haunt men decades later. Barrett passed the victims of an airburst: 'They were laid out like stars, stripped of clothes and dotted with little red dots on the edge of their slit trenches, just splattered with red blodges.' Argylls rolled into a village where an enemy column lay smoking: 'The main street was dead bodies, all burnt to cinders,' recalled Corporal Richard Peet. 'We got on to tanks and just ploughed straight down.' Mixed up with the scores of human corpses were bullocks and the debris of carts. 'The North Korean unit had been annihilated by air strike, it was just appalling,' Lauder said. 'There is not a nice way of fighting a war.'

That was particularly true given the almost indiscriminate application of air power permitted following the Chinese offensive.

'Various sources of information have revealed that enemy troops are in the habit of putting on civilian clothes and living in the villages by day. By night they once again become soldiers,' 27th Brigade's War Diary noted on 7 November. 'A policy has now started to strike villages by day and buildings which might be harbouring enemy troops. When planes are in the area and cannot find a target, they are to attack *any likely looking village*.' [Author italics]

Napalm caused the most horrific deaths. At Pakchon, Barrett's patrol encountered a hideous naked cadaver. 'I came across this body all burned – there were no extremities left at all, everything was gone; no fingers, no toes, no eyes or ears – but the hair was still in place and the pubic hair was still in place,' he said. An evil curiosity filled him. 'I touched it with a stick and it just crumbled; I could not tell if it was man or woman.'

When snipers fired from villages, the brigade didn't bother with risky infantry clearances. 'Villages that resisted were burned,' said Lauder, who had been told by veterans of the raid/counter-raid campaigns along the Northwest Frontier, that guerillas hid weapons in thatch. So it proved in Korea. 'When we set fire to North Korean villages, the thatch exploded like firework displays.'

Collateral damage was immense. 'When Yanks use their artillery, they don't mess around,' said Gallaway. 'They obliterate the bastards.' While some officers and reporters professed distaste for profligate American force, others preferred to wield firepower rather than risk manpower. 'Given the option of going in with a bayonet and having bombers going in and flattening it, I'd prefer the latter,' said Lauder.

Absent rules of engagement, civilians in the path of the advance were at immense risk. Reporters Max Desfor and Reginald Thompson were behind advancing Argylls during the dash on Sariwon when firing broke out ahead. They hurried forward, to find Jocks standing above an overgrown ditch. In it was a bundle of white bedding and a young mother, shot dead. With her were two toddlers. One sat in silent shock; the other, tinier child, was tearing at its mother's hair, screaming. Desfor clicked his shutter. 'It was heart rending,' he said 'Why did I shoot it? Because it was there, this was war; this is what should not happen.' A medical corporal removed the orphans. Their mother was left in the ditch.

Then there was the behaviour of allies. Reporters were shocked to see GIs stripping North Korean POWs naked to humiliate them, and some Australians had seen US paratroopers roughing up POWs after the 'Apple Orchard' battle.[88] At a US medical post, a wounded Digger watched a group of Americans sitting round a stove, periodically poking a badly wounded North Korean on a stretcher, making bets on how long he would live.[89] And with South Korean anti-communist paramilitaries roaming behind the front, brutality was rampant. 'I was walking though a village at dusk and heard screaming,' recalled Digger Stan Gallop. 'There were South Koreans beating North Koreans with wooden rods, breaking their arms. We could imagine what was going to happen.'

Yet it was not just Koreans and GIs who were guilty of brutality. One of the most sensitive Diehards, Julian Tunstall, was struck by two aspects of the campaign: 'racial discrimination' and 'brutal destruction'.[90] He recalled three NKPA prisoners lashed to a jeep trailer, cord cutting deeply into their flesh. One was beaten around the face by a British NCO, then they were forced to strip naked and wash while a mob mocked them.[91] Thompson remarked with disgust of correspondents hefting weapons and talking of killing 'Gooks' but for soldiers the temptation was stronger, the opportunities broader.[92] The cruel gift that war grants men – to destroy and kill, free of moral and judicial restraints – was taking effect. Australian and British soldiers had entered a heart of darkness, for in a conflict tainted with racism and coloured with atrocity, amid a landscape upon which massive destruction had been unleashed and in which mutilation and death were commonplace, ethics eroded and the devil beckoned. In the South, British soldiers had shot wounded enemy. In the North, some brigade members would descend further.

Barrett had bypassed 3 RAR at Yongyu. A Digger corporal had a silenced Sten gun for mercy killings of badly wounded, and discussion was underway as to whether he ought to finish an enemy who had lost most of his face. Then, from the paddy came a burp gun burst. 'Out in field was an Aussie and he'd had two Gooks – he'd taken their burp gun – and he motioned and they started walking away,' Barrett remembered. 'It misfired, so he called them back. One came back and fixed it. They walked away, then he mowed them down.' The prisoners had been shot in cold blood. 'I spoke to one Aussie, and said, "We have difficulty telling North from South,"' Barrett recalled. 'He said, "We don't care. North, South, they're all dead."' Len Opie concurred. 'We used to rush through villages firing into bunkers but half the time we didn't know until later that they were probably civilians,' he said. 'In those days, nobody worried too much.'

POWs were not the only victims of unsanctioned, but sanction-free killings. Frank Screeche-Powell, the Irish corporal, was with the Middlesex Mortars Platoon who had just finished a shoot on the edge of a ruined village, when an elderly Korean appeared among the rubble. 'This old man came through fossicking, I think he was just looking for something, he was not armed,' he said. 'One of our guys – he was a bit gung ho – shot him.' Screeche-Powell was stunned. 'The old man was unarmed, he was not a threat,' he said. 'Most mortar men never get to shoot their rifles, that was probably the only time he used it.' The corporal was tempted to shoot the soldier himself, but did not. Nothing was said; the killer did not even face a reprimand. The murder of the old Korean would replay across Screeche-Powell's memory for the rest of his life.

* * *

The Chinese offensive, unannounced by Peking and discrediting MacArthur's assurances to Truman, had administered a terrific shock to the UNC. Moreover, the B29 offensive against the border bridges – 12 spanned the Yalu and Tumen rivers – had failed: The two rivers would soon be totally iced over. And the disengagement on 6 November was a puzzle. Had China's attack simply been a warning? Did the sudden disappearance of the enemy indicate his defeat? Were the Chinese regulars or volunteers?

While these questions were being debated in Washington, MacArthur remained welded to total victory. After the Chinese evaporated, he demanded a resumption of the UNC offensive on

15 November but concurred when 8th Army Commander Walton Walker argued for a delay.[93] Still, MacArthur stuck to his previous aims: destruction of enemy forces; unification of Korea. He refused to countenance a defensive line along the 40th parallel, just north of Korea's 'waist' – the narrowest part of the peninsula – a strategy promoted by Washington's Joint Chiefs and London's General Staff that would deliver control of most of Korea, bar a buffer zone south of the China border.[94] MacArthur's planned final offensive would be on a wide front, for the peninsula broadens in the north: The Korea–China frontier is twice as wide as the 'waist'. Like the fingers on a hand, advancing UNC units would spread out the further north they penetrated.

D-Day was set: 24 November. Convoys crawled through the grey hills, trucking supplies up to the front. Innumerable artillery barrels pointed north. Tanks squatted under traditional gates in ruined village courtyards, engines idling to keep from freezing. Muffled troops stood around fires burning in 44-gallon drums. The days counted down.

But before the attack could begin, an obsession had gripped the Americans: They were determined to celebrate Thanksgiving on 23 November in grand style, and with typical American generosity, every UNC unit would eat its fill. The logistic feat which delivered prawn cocktail, turkey, cranberry sauce and pumpkin pie to units across Korea astonished soldiers from less prosperous nations.

'In the midst of all this mayhem, we got turkey!' said Butler. 'They'd gone to endless trouble, they're a different race.' Morale climbed. 'We got stuff we'd never seen, certainly not in post-war UK,' Mankelow recalled. There was a poignant scene at 27th Brigade HQ. A courtyard had been cleaned, a table set with linen, and the black American truck drivers invited to be seated. In the British Army at Christmas, officers serve men; this tradition was transferred to Thanksgiving. The GIs were first embarrassed, then entered the spirit of it.[95] The banquet was remembered by most as the best rations they would have in Korea.

24 November dawned icy, clear, brilliant. MacArthur flew from Tokyo, landing in his Constellation at Sinanju on the Chongchon,

then jeeped for I Corps and 24th Division. There, he uttered the words that would brand this offensive. 'Home by Christmas!' he said, telling General John Church, 'Don't make me a liar, fellow!'[96]

The UNC attack would be a 'massive compression envelopment' between the pincers of 8th Army in the west, and X Corps in the east. 'If successful, this should for all practical purposes end the war' MacArthur's communiqué read. The man himself was then flown slowly along the Yalu Valley, peering out at the terrain below, assuring himself that no enemy was there in force. Indeed, MacArthur's Tokyo intelligence unit estimated less than 100,000 Chinese had joined the first offensive; the CIA estimated CPVA inside North Korea at 30–40,000.[97]

H-Hour was 10:00. 'Today marked the opening day of the offensive which it is hoped would reach the Manchurian border and finish the Korean War,' 27th Brigade's War Diary noted.[*] Assault units crouched on their start lines. The 8th Army attack – the US 2nd, 24th and 25th Infantry divisions, the ROK 1st, 7th and 8th divisions – jumped off as planned. From west to east, 8th Army advanced in line abreast: I; IX and ROK II Corps. Across Korea's mountain spine, X Corps was also in motion. The offensive rolled north. Keen to get the job done, to be 'Home by Christmas', to be out of this freezing waste, many soldiers were still replete with Thanksgiving treats.

They had been fattened for the kill. MacArthur's intelligence estimates were woefully inaccurate, for China's early November disengagement had been for logistical, not tactical reasons; the CPVA's primitive supply lines could only sustain an offensive for a week. Peng's 'human wave' had not receded into Manchuria; in the past eighteen days, ever more CPVA had poured through 'The Gates of Hell'. Unseen, unheard, thirty-six Chinese divisions – as many as 388,00 men,[98] lay 10–12 miles ahead of the 8th Army, waiting for their enemy to enter the killing zone.[99] Not only did they outnumber the 342,000 strong UNC, they were heavier in combat troops, lighter in logistic troops, and in the days to come, would concentrate.[100] And

---

[*] Curiously, the WD gives the wrong date – 25 November, not 24th.

this would not be a limited offensive, this would be a massive counter. Brilliantly camouflaged; invisible to the eyes of reconnaissance pilots and Douglas MacArthur himself; they stood poised to annihilate the advancing imperialists and drive them far from China's frontier.

The United Nations Command was driving blindly into the jaws of the twentieth century's greatest trap. Over the great, grey mountains of North Korea, the perfect storm was about to break.

Chapter Nine
Scorched Earth

Grenadiers of my Guard! You are witnessing the
disintegration of an army!
Napoleon Bonaparte, the retreat from Moscow

Evening, 26 November 1950. Pakchon.

For the first time since Seoul, Middlesex Major John Willoughby relaxed. His D Company was stood down, 'without a care in the world'. A mobile bath unit had arrived and filled a cut-down 44-gallon drum in the courtyard of the house that Company HQ had requisitioned with hot water. The major wallowed happily.[1]

27th Brigade, in I Corps reserve, had pulled back into Pakchon on 25 November.[2] From there, Willoughby had watched the juggernaut roll by. 'MacArthur's offensive has begun – almost too good to be true. All day long, the American Army has poured past along the road to the North. Vehicles of every variety and tanks in a nose-to-tail procession winds on without end.' He was pleased to see the cautious speed: Unlike the October charges, the GIs were advancing at the pace of infantry patrols clearing the path.[3]

Willoughby was half asleep in his bath when he was called to the field telephone. Had his company seen anything? Four men on white horses had been reported reconnoitring brigade positions at a nearby crossroads. A dark vision flashed across his mind's eye: War, Famine, Pestilence, Death: The Four Horsemen of the Apocalypse. His reaction was two words: 'Oh God'.[4]

* * *

At approximately the same time, 19:30, Brigadier Basil Coad was signalled by 8th Army, who warned him to prepare to move to another front. At 23:15, further orders arrived: 'Army ordered us to pass to IX Corps earliest, obviously things were not going well there.' The brigade would move early on 27 November.[5] IX Corps, east of I Corps and west of ROK II Corps, was commanded by General John Coulter. 8th Army Commander Walton Walker had been dissatisfied with Coulter during the Pusan fighting due to his insistent calls for help. After the breakout, Coulter took command of the newly activated IX Corps, which had been guarding supply routes against NKPA guerillas.[6] This corps was now the centre of 8th Army.

Earlier the same day, *Daily Telegraph* reporter Reginald Thompson had visited IX Corps. The first two days of the advance had gone as planned, but at HQ, Thompson found 'anxious tension'. The US 2nd and 25th Divisions had met enemy in the north and were holding, but the town of Tokchon to their east – which should have been miles in the rear of ROK II Corps, on the 8th Army's right flank – seemed to have fallen. Clearly, 'something had happened'.[7]

At 07:45 on 27 November, Coad raced off. The brigadier was shaken by what he found at Corps HQ, a mess of tentage penetrated here and there with chimneys for space heaters. 'The hysteria was quite frightening,' Coad wrote. 'This day and the succeeding ones were extremely difficult for the brigade as a succession of pretty impossible tasks were handed out by Corps HQ, which required a good deal of diplomatic arguing to avoid the brigade, without supporting arms, being hopelessly committed.'[8]

His brigade mounted trucks at 10:00. Under heavy overcast, 27th Brigade rumbled over the Chongchon, where ice floes were grinding against the bridge pilings, then along roads down which a stabbing wind was blasting clouds of yellow dust,[9] arriving at their new concentration area at 15:00.[10] The battalions dug in near the mining village of Kunu-ri, a road and rail junction among gaunt hills. Officers discovered what had rattled Coad. 'The ops map showed the dispositions of three US divisions . . . each bearing the note "exact location unknown" or a query mark with menacing red arrows jabbing at them indicating that they were under mass attack.' Willoughby noted:

To their right... there did not appear to be any UN forces at all, but instead a large arrow curved north to south towards 8th Army communications. It was a particularly large thick arrow, bearing the figure, also in red, 'two million'. The military situation depicted was quite dreadful even allowing for the ridiculous overestimate. A force of 20,000 across the line of communications would be bad enough, even 2,000 would probably have done it.[11]

While US divisions thrusting north had hit Chinese holding attacks, Marshal Peng had launched his main effort against the ROK troops holding 8th Army's east flank on the night of 25 November. The ROK 7th and 8th Divisions were shattered, the 6th crumbling. ROK II Corps, Walker's right flank, was now a 25-mile void. By 21:30, general withdrawal was being discussed by IX Corps. That night, the US 2nd and 25th Divisions began retreating.[12] MacArthur's war-ending offensive had lasted just three days. 27th Brigade was placed at one hour's notice to move.[13]

*   *   *

Dawn brought no relief. 'At 05:00 hours, the situation was described as critical,' the Brigade War Diarist noted. Six enemy divisions were advancing in a broad envelopment through the wreckage in the east: 8th Army faced being rolled up from the right flank.[14]

Coad was again summoned to IX Corps HQ. Coulter proposed a number of counter-attacks – though he could lend the brigade no support arms.[15] One was to strike east towards Tokchon, to cauterise the evisceration of ROK II Corps. Coad, expecting to be cut off, and with Corps unable to provide locations of either friendly or enemy units, resisted strongly, saying he could see no useful purpose in taking his brigade there.[16] He counter-suggested that 27th Brigade would be most usefully employed holding open the Kunu-ri-Sunchon-Chasan route, the easternmost of the two main roads running south to Pyongyang, a critical line of communications. Coulter agreed.[17] Officers were relieved at Coad's insistence. 'This was considered to be a pretty good order, because by now, "Blind

Freddy" could see that High Command had lost its grip,' reckoned 3 RAR Captain Ben O'Dowd.

Men were equally relieved, for the rumour mill was spinning in overdrive. 'News came that 250,000 Chinese troops had crossed the border, heading straight toward us,' I said to Roy Vincent.' 'If they are coming toward us and are moving at 4 miles an hour and are 20 miles away, in four or five hours time they will be overrunning us,' recalled Argyll Henry Cochrane. 'In the morning, we got ordered to move.'

The distance to Chasan was 23 miles, down a road flanked by hills and mountains. Transport would be provided for the brigade only after Corps HQ moved south.[18] No trucks arrived. 'They gave you vehicles to move forward,' said 3 RAR Sergeant Tom Muggleton. 'But they were not that plentiful when you wanted to move back.' Crucial hours passed. The battalions – first the Argylls, then 3 RAR, then the Middlesex – would march.

Briefings were terse. At Brigade HQ, a captain told his men: 'There's no transport, so we go on foot. There's a roadblock reported five miles behind us. We fight through that and proceed to our new positions. Remember what I've told you: we fight as a team!'[19] Paddy Boyd, the Argylls' giant RSM told his Jocks, 'You'll carry full magazines in your rifles and Bren guns. If the road is clear, you'll march to Sunchon. If the road is blocked, you'll fight through to Sunchon. But you will go through to Sunchon.'[20]

With light snow falling, the infantry deployed into alternate tactical files, covering both sides of the track, 50 yards between platoons. Vehicles were in the centre of the column. At 13:45, music skirled as Wilson's A Company, in the lead, stepped off into the unknown. 'We led with the pipers,' said Argyll Adjutant John Slim. 'The locals loved it and it let the enemy know we were coming!'

A tented US field hospital was bypassed. 'We wanted to say, "Get out! Go!"' recalled Middlesex Lance Corporal Don Barrett. 'Lorries went past, stacked with bodies piled up, off to a mass grave.' Retreating vehicles showered the marchers in dust. A US artillery battery, guns firing in all directions – including south – was passed next.[21] The road climbed into a pass through the hills. Through a gap, men saw a distant train, sitting abandoned in the east.[22] Hours passed;

miles too. Heavy breaths in, out. One foot in front of the other, again and again. A watching reporter, David Walker of the *Daily Express*, wrote, 'There was something about the spirit of these troops as they followed the pipes, whose music curled contemptuously through these hard, unfriendly hills, that seemed to raise them far above ordinary men.'[23]

Feet were suffering. The nails driven through the soles of ammunition boots channelled the chill into marching feet; boots did little to soften the impact of the frosted, iron-hard track. Roy Vincent, in a mortar carrier, picked up suffering Jocks with blood welling out of their lace holes, tears frozen on their cheeks. Laggards were encouraged by a CSM's warning: 'If you don't keep up, the next man you'll find coming down this road will be Joe Stalin!'[24]

Darkness fell. The temperature, too, began its night-time plunge. The occasional convoys that had passed earlier dwindled until the brigade was alone in the rugged hills south of Kunu-ri. Machine gun fire echoed somewhere to the southeast.[25] The long snake of soldiers trudged on. On either side, ridges loomed sinister and indistinct in the darkness; the forlorn wail of the bagpipes echoed from the crags. With the fall in temperature, the sky cleared. Far above, the black vault was sprinkled with a storm of stars. Among their chill glitter, Major David Wilson sensed an other-worldly presence.

If the profession of soldiering has a spiritual side, one vehicle to that state is the night march. This is when exhausted troops, lulled by the trancelike rhythm of the plodding column, switch over to autopilot and half-asleep, half-awake, leave behind bodily aches and retreat deep into thoughts and dreams. So it was for the major that night. The pipes keened. The hills were a perfect ambush site – though nobody yet knew it, the pass would be an abattoir 36 hours hence – but Wilson sensed spectral allies: Ranks of Argylls long dead, looking down upon their descendents in their hour of need, guiding them out of peril. Years later, Wilson would come across a line in a poem that captured his feelings on that march: *Those soldier stars/That pace the beats of heaven.*[26]

The Middlesex's D Company was marching down a narrow pass when Sergeant Paddy Bermingham was almost deafened by a rifle report beside his ear. A flurry of shots rippled along the side of the column. In the muzzle flashes, the silhouettes of his platoon were briefly illuminated, freezing the scene for an instant. The fusillade ceased. The column continued; nobody had been hit, returned fire or even taken cover. Bermingham was mystified; he could only guess it had been a hit-and-run squad, who, seeing the strength and tactical disposition of its intended prey, decided against prosecuting the ambush.[27]

Brigade transport, reaching the harbour area near Chasan, unloaded and, with extra US vehicles, returned to carry the infantry, most of whom had marched 15–20 miles. The last to be picked up were the Diehards, arriving at the harbour area at 03:15.[28] Men collapsed onto frozen paddies, rolling in rice straw under blankets and ponchos. The brigade had made it through Kunu-ri Pass.

While the brigade night marched, 8th Army Commander Walker and X Corps' Commander Almond were summoned to Tokyo for an emergency evening conference. Even MacArthur was now forced to admit reality: The UNC faced 'an entirely new war . . . conditions beyond its control and strength'.[29]

Victorious Chinese had broken cover: Air reconnaissance reported thousands of enemy flowing through the hills.[30] While Peng's soldiers were close to their dumps, MacArthur's were in enemy country, at the end of long, tenuous supply lines. More critically, 8th Army, burdened with artillery, tanks and vehicles, were funnelled into a single, narrow dimension: the roads. The unhampered CPVA, traversing the terrain cross-country, could appear on ridges above the roads, in villages beside them, in ditches below them. For the UNC, the entire countryside beyond the dirt roads had become hostile territory.* 27th Brigade was a cog in the machine of total war – a machine that was now spinning wildly out of control.

* * *

* In 1941–2, the British Army had faced a similar situation in Malaya and Burma: The Japanese had mastered the jungle; the road-bound British had not.

Men were shaken awake at dawn. IX Corps had given 27th Brigade three tasks. 3 RAR were to hold the Taedong River ferry at Chasan. The Argylls were in reserve; they were later given two further roles, which were both cancelled, indicating the state of staff work at Corps.[31] At 07:00 orders came for the Middlesex to advance back up the road they had marched down the night before, to the village of Yongwon-ni, where it was reported that the enemy had cut the road. There were no tanks, no artillery, no trucks. Repeated requests were made. Finally transport – but neither guns nor armour – arrived at 10:00.[32]

Orders were to secure the pass area; send a patrol through it to contact the US 2nd Infantry Division, or 2ID, in Kunu-ri; and search villages, bringing in any suspicious characters.[33] Chasan to Yongwon was 15 map miles; Yongwon to Kunu-ri was a further six, but the winding route and rising contours made it longer. 2ID were fighting north of Kunu-ri. If the enemy held Yongwon, their escape route south was cut. Diehards saddled up, attaching bed rolls to the backs of belts, slinging small packs and 100-round canvas bandoleers over parkas, filling pouches with Bren magazines and clipping braces of hand grenades to belts. 'We lined up inside the trucks trying to look warlike,' said Lance Corporal Don Barrett. 'This was now enemy territory.'

The track winding into the hills, with their pine forests spilling down onto the road, was devoid of life, the roadside villages empty. Even the ubiquitous refugees had disappeared. A radio message crackled through: enemy ahead. The warning was shouted from truck to truck. Suddenly, lead vehicles halted. Men jumped out, deployed. Ahead, lay a bullet-riddled jeep in a ditch; sprawled in it was a dead US colonel and his driver.[34] A tense silence. 'Nothing stirred, and all at once the mountains about us seemed much higher, more inaccessible, more menacing,' wrote Shipster. 'The valley ahead and the pass beyond were absolutely silent. Nothing moved except for the shift of elbows supporting binoculars, scanning every ridge and crevice above us.'[35]

A group of male civilians in dirty white clothing appeared. The tension cracked. D Company rounded them up. With the convoy halted, Man made his dispositions. C Company would hold hills overlooking the road above Tac HQ. D Company would seize the first hill feature to the north, then A Company would take a hill overlooking the mouth of the pass. B Company was held back to exploit.[36] An abandoned artillery truck was parked against the railway embankment on the left, still full of shells. Kit bags and various bits of gear littered the roadside, indicating a hasty withdrawal. 'It looked a bit ominous,' said Barrett.

Willoughby's D Company advanced up-valley. Directly ahead, the road climbed into the hills, disappearing for a few hundred yards, reappearing as it curved on a shoulder round the western contour of the slopes, then disappeared from sight again into the pass at the top. His men scrambled up a grassy ridge on the left of the road to cover A Company's advance. 'Five American fighters came in low over the hills behind us and machine gunned the wooded slopes above the pass and little figures could be seen running about.' Willoughby noted: Enemy.

Movement was spotted to the north. 'In the distance at the top of the pass, a small cloud of dust appeared and a solitary jeep careered down, jinking and bouncing from one side of the road to the other,' Willoughby remembered. 'The slopes above it came to life with flashes of rifle fire and still the jeep came on.' It disappeared behind a shoulder and was seen no more.

D Company was watching A Company preparing to attack when suddenly 'fire was opened on us from the hills on our flanks, every ridge and peak appeared to be occupied and mortar and machine gun fire began to be intense,' the major noted.[37] Black mortar bursts blossomed, followed by the distinctive ripping of a Russian machine gun. The slower Middlesex Vickers hammered back. Battalion mortars thunked.

B Company, ahead of D but behind A, was poised for a jump forward. Barrett was in cover next to the railway line that curved to the left of the hills; behind was an old tunnel and about 1,000 yards away, he could see Chinese milling around – 'most peculiar!' Two Mustangs dived into the attack. 'One came and fired on A Company's hill and a burst went between my LMG section and the rest of us, ground was spurting up about a meter high with a whoosh!'

A Company continued for its objective. The lead platoon crested the summit to be swept with a violent fusillade of machine guns, mortars and grenades. The platoon commander, twice wounded, was killed and nine men hit.[38] The company reeled back.

Man, seeing the Chinese movement on the hills, realised he was facing more than he could handle, but radio communications with the Brigade were down. Willoughby was ordered to hand over control of his company and report to Brigade HQ in person, 'informing them that the battalion would have to disengage if it could'. He jumped into a jeep. 'As I drove along the deserted road I didn't know whether I preferred the loneliness of this journey to the fireworks display amongst my friends.'[39]

The fighting was about 75 yards ahead of B Company. Barrett could see A Company retreating; as they came through, he was ordered to bring up their rear; this was a leapfrog retrograde movement, company covering company. As Barrett's section withdrew, bullets were knocking bits of what looked like cotton off trees all around. They took cover beside the road. When shooting halted, Barrett led his men up onto the track. Firing resumed, rounds from unseen marksmen whipping between the dispersed Diehards. 'I thought, "What a fantastic section, they never ran, they just marched on,"' Barrett recalled. Then someone shouted, 'Run, you silly bastards!' They did. Passing through the RAP, Barrett saw a lot of jackets covered in blood: 'I remember thinking, "What a bloody mess."'

US trucks were waiting; radio contact had been re-established and Coad had ordered Man to extricate before dark. IX Corps was furious, until Coad explained how precarious the situation had become.[40] 'Coad was not everybody's cup of tea but he was mine,' said Man. 'He was responsible that his little British contingent was not left out; there were occasions when one or more battalions under his command would have been left out to no good event.'

Exactly how precarious the position was would be discovered by the last sub-unit to extract, D Company.

Sergeant Paddy Bermingham had been withdrawing, when Man himself appeared. There was confusion; the CO told them that B

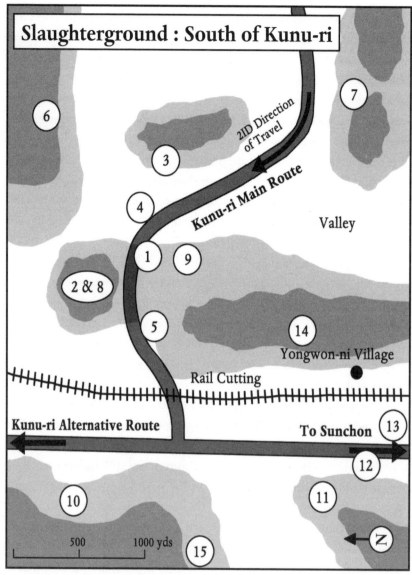

Slaughterground : South of Kunu-ri

1 Middlesex : Holding Actions South of Kunu-ri

November 29 : ① Abandoned jeep with dead US colonel
② D Co position ③ A Co abortive attack ④ B Co position
⑤ Mortars / Tac HQ ⑥ CPVA position ⑦ CPVA position
November 30 : ⑧ D Co position ⑨ C Co position
⑩ B Co position ⑪ A Co position
⑫ US artillery position (weapon pits used for dead of 2 ID)
⑬ Tac HQ ⑭ A Co rearguard platoon
(attacked by CPVA, who took hill) ⑮ CPVA position

Company were not through yet. (In fact, they had come through right behind A Company.) Bermingham and his men redeployed on their ridge and faced north, the sergeant worrying about shooting up B Company as they approached. It was now around 17:00. The pre-dusk gloom was settling. A column of vague figures, in company strength, advanced toward Bermingham. The combination of dull light and dusty binoculars prevented the sergeant from identifying them until they had closed to within 100 yards. Enemy. Bermingham yelled at a nearby Bren gunner to fire a full magazine. The man let rip, but to Bermingham's 'absolute horror' the Chinese did not take cover: They stormed forward, firing submachine guns and screaming 'Sha! Sha!'*41

In the urgent intensity of combat, some men pulled off feats that observers might consider heroic, but were in fact due to adrenalin creating tunnel-vision concentration that shut down peripheral awareness. 'I was up on one knee firing, my blokes were lying down firing, and one says, "Harry! Get down!"' recalled Corporal Harry Spicer. 'Bullets were hitting bushes all around, but I was so engrossed I hadn't noticed. If you saw it in a movie, you'd say, "What an idiot!"'

The Chinese charge lost momentum as it hit the bottom of the hill, but around one flank, one enemy got behind a Diehard, grabbed his weapon and shot him with it. The soldier, one of the battalion's best boxers, was just grazed. He leapt up – the Chinese did not know how to operate the Lee Enfield's bolt to reload – decked him with a punch, retrieved his rifle and fled, helter skelter, with the rest of the platoon to the bottom of the hill. To Bermingham's surprise and relief, the Chinese did not pursue. Trucks were waiting 50 yards down the road. The sergeant, counting all his men in, was dragged over the tailgate of the last truck, whose black driver, a the Second World War GI, had been calmly firing his rifle from the bonnet. The trucks rolled off, past a rearguard of Vickers machine guns in Bren carriers. Once again, Bermingham was surprised that the enemy did not fire after the retreating Diehards.

* 'Kill! Kill!' though none of the British knew it at the time. The war cry dates back to the 1900 Boxer Rebellion.

Ahead of the withdrawing trucks, the reverberation of heavy firing of a calibre Bermingham did not recognise, evidenced Chinese in their rear. Round a bend was a US truck mounted with twin anti-aircraft guns, firing at just 40 yards range into a ridge parallel to the road. Sky-lined enemy, infiltrating along it, were perfectly aligned as the mounted Vickers platoon rolled up and opened fire. The CPVA were 'hosed off the ridge'. Then the convoy was clear.[42]

The Middlesex harboured 8 miles south at the railway station of Choptong-ri, alongside the reconnaissance company of 1st Cavalry Division, 8th Army's reserve, which was deploying on the eastern flank. Given the chaotic nature of the fighting, Diehard casualties proved lighter than feared: one killed, twenty-six wounded. But this meant the battalion was down one platoon, and no replacements were expected.[43]

There would be heavy work on the morrow. A US RCT was tasked to pass through the Middlesex the following day and strike north; around midnight, word arrived that it was unavailable.[44] At 02:40 on 30 November, Corps HQ told Coad that 2ID would be coming out in daylight; the Middlesex were to advance back up to the pass, and deploy south of grid line 85 at Yongwon, covering the Americans as they broke out south. Coad requested guns and armour to beef up the Diehards. After 'a good deal of argument' these were allotted.[45]

Meanwhile, a group of bedraggled Turks had arrived at Brigade HQ, attempting to converse with Coad in French. 'They had a reputation as fierce fighters,' Baldwin said. 'If they were in disarray, then God help us.'

*   *   *

The Turks were, indeed, in disarray. On 28 November, they had been sent to restore IX Corps' right flank following the erosion of ROK II Corps – the operation Coad had prudently resisted. The brigade lacked radios and trucks, and their US liaison group lacked language skills. In their first engagement, they ambushed ROK stragglers. Then they came under massive attack. In conditions of utter confusion, the Turks, with their preference for the bayonet, forged a legend, but were unable to hold; the 5,000 strong brigade suffered over 1,000 casualties. 2ID, in Kunu-ri was under attack from the north; now its eastern entire flank was totally exposed. If the division did not get out, it faced annihilation.

D Company, with five US tanks under command, would lead the Middlesex back up to their limit of exploitation on grid line 85, Yongwon, to cover the division's southward breakout. Diehards were told 2ID would be 'pushing the Chinese in front of them, it would be like shooting fish in a barrel'.[46] Willoughby found the commander of the US Patton tank platoon, Lieutenant Robert Harper 'cheerful and enthusiastic'. The risk, as Willoughby saw it, was how soon they would make enemy contact. He plotted the move carefully, showing Harper on the map where he wanted him to slow and proceed cautiously. Then D Company clambered onto the tanks, which set off north 'at a terrifying speed'. The bend in the track where Willoughby wanted to slow down was passed; the tanks did not de-accelerate, until reaching the positions of the previous day. 'We leapt off our transport and flung ourselves in the nearest defensive positions,' Willoughby noted. 'Nothing happened . . . my heart had been in my mouth for those last few minutes.' Enemy had disappeared. A light aircraft swooped over, dropping a sack of red-silk squares. Assuming these to be recognition signals for 2ID, Diehards passed them around.[47]

The remaining companies arrived and deployed. A Company took positions overlooking Tac HQ south of the empty village; C and D on hills to the south of the pass, with B in the left rear. At 11:00 enemy were sighted and fired upon by battalion mortars. As D Company was deploying along a ridge facing north, there was an explosion on the south slope: A US 105mm artillery battery had arrived and fired a ranging shot directly into D Company's hill.[48]

Given the previous day's communications problems, Lieutenant Peter Baldwin had been dropped off to establish a hilltop signals relay between the Middlesex and Brigade. He and his section set up a transmitter on high ground. 'It was very mountainous with the MSR winding round the edges of mountains, when this black bomber appeared and started circling,' Baldwin recalled. Suddenly, it swooped in on an attack run. Signallers took cover as bombs detonated, while Baldwin stood, frantically waving a fluorescent marker panel. 'It was frightening, but being an officer one is meant to show leadership,' he said. 'Luckily he made only one run.' Nobody had been hit; Baldwin later discovered it was a carrier-based aircraft with no information on the marker panels. A massive air support operation was gathering to support 2ID's run south.

Ahead of D Company of the Middlesex, noise of firing broke out, then five American tanks appeared through the pass. Willoughby was on the road when the leader skidded to a halt, and an officer jumped out. 'Gee, that was a hot ride!' he said, climbed back inside, and trundled off before Willoughby had a chance to ask him 2ID's status. The remark, however, led him to believe all was well.[49] Diehards waited. Shipster wondered whether 2ID's infantry sweep would appear over the eastern or western shoulder of the pass.[50]

Willoughby was scanning through binoculars at the distant gap in the hills when he saw a 'bumper to bumper' column of vehicles appear slowly on the visible stretch of road, the shoulder cut into the mountainside. The Chinese 'had done another disappearing act,' he concluded. But a distant crackling grew in volume and urgency: gunfire. The major could see occupants jumping out of vehicles, while others tipped over the edge and rolled down the mountainside.[51] The Diehards were capturing a shock glimpse of 2ID's death agony as it retreated from Kunu-ri.

* * *

Even the name has a hollow, foreboding reverberation: Kunu-ri. A village among hills; a crossroad; a rail junction. South of it, the road – down which 27th Brigade had marched – wound between barren slopes. At its high point, 'the pass' was a narrow, 450-yard stretch of road enclosed by steep embankments, 50 feet high. Here, the US Army would face its most hideous ordeal since the Battle of the Bulge.

2ID had been under mounting enemy pressure from the north since the start of the Chinese offensive on the night of 25 November. Now, it was the most exposed unit of the 8th Army. Its depleted and exhausted men had a 6-mile stretch of road to cover to reach safety –

the Middlesex covering the position south of the pass. 2ID's CO, General Laurence Keiser, knew there were Chinese in his rear, but not their strength. A tank platoon had passed down the road on 29 November, reporting that it had come under fire, but there were no physical obstacles, no roadblock.[52] Early infantry attacks by Keiser's exhausted men and ROK units with 2ID to clear the Chinese from the heights had failed, but Keiser believed – due to the fog of war, faulty radio communications, and confused command and co-ordination between the 8th Army, IX Corps and 27th Brigade – that he could bounce any ambush. Adding to this belief was his under-standing that the Middlesex, with whom he lacked communications, were attacking north to link up with him about one mile down the road; in fact, the Diehards were deployed at grid line 85 awaiting 2ID and unable to support it in the pass.[53] Instead of attacking in a divisional sweep clearing the ridges, Keiser's division would drive south through the pass in series of column. It would prove a catastrophic mistake.

With 2ID's right flank wide open, a full Chinese division, the 113th, was infiltrating the hills overlooking its line of withdrawal. Throughout 30 November, they would, in the classic military maxim, 'reinforce success' feeding in more men, more weapons. Mortars, and as many as forty machine guns would create a fire block, that, by the evening, would cover at least 3 miles of 2ID's 6-mile escape corridor – a route soon to be named 'The Gauntlet'. So it began.

One by one, units motored into the enfilade. As vehicles drove under the Chinese guns, men were shot off tanks and trucks. Wrecked vehicles created blockages, further funnelling the retreat into kill zones. Progress was stop-start as GIs leapt from vehicles, which often then drove on without them. Unit integrity was collapsing, and with Keiser fighting his way south, firing an old Springfield rifle, command evaporated. Dead lay in the road; wounded piled up in the ditches. Roiling clouds of dust spoiled the Chinese aim, but they had laid their sights on the road, so could barely miss. Diving aircraft, trying to eliminate emplaced weapons on the ridges, added to the maelstrom with bombs, rockets and napalm, some of which poured onto the road. The 8th Army commander

Walker, overhead in an observation aircraft, cursed at the confusion, shouting ineffectually at the men to fight.[54]

*　*　*

It was survivors of this carnage who began appearing at Yongwon around midday. A clutch of jeeps piled with wounded and dead, their tattered tyres flapping wildly on the road, passed through the Middlesex position. In the distance, Willoughby watched another vehicle column appear, attempting to double-bank the first. 'There were some simply dreadful scenes up there,' he wrote. 'A long stream of survivors now started to reach us from below the pass, first in twos and threes, then a steady stream, many wounded, utterly forsaken and in tears.' Willoughby wondered if the spectacle would affect the morale of his young soldiers; it seemed only to strengthen their resolution. 'One of the saddest aspects of this human tide was they were all themselves lone, solitary refugees hoping for sanctuary,' Willoughby noted. 'Many were wounded and dragging themselves along, but never did I see a comrade helping another, I don't believe this was lack of humanity, but total bewilderment.'[55]

'It was just a massacre,' said Frank Whitehouse. 'You don't forget it, it is still a memory I carry with me.' Further south, watching splintered 2ID trucks pass with crimson streaming down their sides, Wilson was reminded of descriptions of naval battles in the age of sail, when blood poured from the scuppers of shot-up warships.[56]

Tanks arrived, driving at full throttle. 'They came roaring down the pass, through this gully and back onto the road, firing with their main armaments and .50 calibres,' said Barrett, on low ground with B Company. Two men were hit next to Private Ken Mankelow. 'One of my platoon members got a 50 cal through both cheeks of his buttocks,' he said. 'It tore a terrible wound in his bum, but he did survive.' The second Diehard was killed.

Lieutenant Colonel Man, seeing what was happening, planted himself in the middle of the road; when the first Patton rocked up, the little officer icily asked the tank commander to stop killing his men. The situation was tense; a senior NCO stood beside Man, rifle at the ready.[57] Hundreds of wounded were treated, swamping the battalion aid post. Keiser arrived, conversed briefly with Man, then headed south. Shocked survivors streamed through.

By 16:00, the pass ahead had become still and silent; through binoculars, officers could see vehicles locked together and immovable; the stream of survivors seemed to have stopped. Man had been in contact with Brigade HQ, who had ordered him to use his own judgment when to disengage.[58] But by now, some time after 16:00, enemy vanguards, debouching from the hills, were infiltrating around the Middlesex as they mounted their vehicles.

The US 105mm battery, near Tac HQ, opened fire directly into the Chinese. 'We could see them down below firing over open sights,' said Spicer. 'We couldn't see the Chinese, they were shooting into the hillside, the enemy were in the scrub.' Diehards pulled back, clambering onto trucks, jeeps and land rovers. The Americans were 'fighting their guns magnificently,' Willoughby thought, but bullets were zipping in from several directions and the road was enfiladed by machine gun fire. 'I don't know why none of D Company were hit because from my land rover I could see the dusty road ahead being churned up by bullets we drove through.'[59]

The artillery was moving, too; Barrett could see bodies lying in their gun pits. (In fact these were the dead from 2ID.) 'By now, the Chinese had got to the edge of this hill, maybe 50 feet up, peeping over,' said Barrett. 'One man was hanging off the back of the artillery vehicles and was shot off. I went out on the wing of a truck with my legs dangling over.'

Last out were A Company, covering Tac HQ. Rogers saw dust spots around his feet: 'Half the Chinese Army were shooting at me!' The enemy had taken over positions vacated by the Diehards, to the north and southwest of the road. Rogers was pinned down in low ground. CSM Danny Cranfield – a black soldier from St Helena – yelled 'Stay down!' 'I'm sleeping!' Rogers shouted back. In a pause in the fire, Cranfield leaned in, grabbed Rogers and dragged him back. An enemy grenade landed – Cranfield picked it up to hurl it back – it detonated in his hand. Though the Chinese used percussion, rather than fragmentation bombs, it still caused a horrific injury: the flesh of Cranfield's fingers was 'peeled back like a banana'. In shock, he was evacuated south.

At Tac HQ – by now under both mortar and small arms fire – Man had been furiously busy, overseeing evacuation of US casualties, arranging American tanks to fire cover, directing traffic. Now, amid frantic noise and movement, he exercised leadership. 'Colonel Man was sitting on a shooting stick, reading a map,' Rogers said. 'It was for the sole purpose of steadying the blokes.'

Corporal Bob Yerby's platoon found itself rearguard. Suddenly – as so often in this war, as if from nowhere – a crowd of Chinese appeared and ran right into the Diehards. Then it was close combat. 'We turned round – we had bayonets fixed, we nearly always did – we were hitting with rifle butts killing anything in front of us, just berserk,' Yerby said. 'It was intense, like a melee in football, you were shooting at anyone who was not one of your chaps.' After perhaps seconds, perhaps minutes – as if by mutual agreement – the two forces broke breathlessly away from each other. Yerby's platoon pulled back.

Speeding vehicles were laden to the limit with Middlesex clinging on and American wounded piled in the back. Drivers drove furiously, knocking down roadside cottages[60] and plunging through creek fords, sending up great sprays of water.[61] As they passed Choptong-ri, Willoughby glanced across to the RAP manned by the Middlesex medical sergeant: He had treated 250 men, exhausting all his morphine and dressings.[62]

At Chasan, MO Stanley Boydell was working frantically to stabilise casualties; his stress was so great, that Boydell himself was subsequently evacuated to Japan. The shuttling of casualties caused problems, with some drivers reluctant to return north. 'This was dealt with by an order to put a man with a gun on each truck,' Boydell recalled. 'Until we were on board he was not to allow that truck to move.'

Heading south, Yerby found himself shuddering uncontrollably following the hand-to-hand action. 'Afterwards it was scary, but at the time, nothing; I suppose something takes over, you are not rational,' Yerby recalled. 'When it is over, you look at your hands, they are shaking like the leaves on a tree, it was, "God! Did that really happen?"'

At Brigade HQ, Thompson watched a dust-coated Coad listen as a young 2ID officer explained why they had tried to bounce rather than fight through the enemy fireblock. Coad's gaunt, lined face looked grimmer than the journalist had ever seen it.[63]

Yet some 2ID units were still coming through well after nightfall, hours after the Middlesex withdrawal; the silence and lack of movement noted by the battalion at around 16:00 must have been the gap between one serial moving through the pass and the next. And the division's rearguard, the 23rd RCT under one of the 8th Army's most effective officers, Colonel Paul Freeman, did not run south: it took the western road from Kunu-ri toward Anju, escaping almost unscathed. Freeman's departure, however, left remaining elements exposed from the rear. There were poignant scenes as the 2nd Engineer Battalion, realising they were finished, burned their colours.[*]

The massacre in Kunu-ri pass cost 2ID 4,037 casualties and 114 artillery pieces lost.[64] Keiser was relieved of command,[†] though it was IX Corps' General Coulter who had ordered him to take the southern road, despite an offer from I Corps that 2ID take the Anju road – the route taken by Freeman.[65] On the day of the disaster, Coulter was moving his IX Corps HQ to Pyongyang.

The disastrous turn of events compelled ludicrous self-justification An 8th Army communiqué on 29 November claimed: 'The assault launched by 8th Army five days ago probably saved our army from a trap which might well have destroyed them. Had we waited passively in place . . . from beyond the Yalu, [the enemy] would have undoubtedly brought the 200,000 troops known to be assembled there

---

[*] Every year on 30 November, the 2nd Engineers – still stationed in Korea – burn their colours in remembrance of the 1950 tragedy.

[†] Some US historians have been critical of 27th Brigade at Kunu-ri, but Keiser did thank the brigade for their assistance that day. In a letter to Coad on 5 December, he wrote: 'I personally wish to express my sincere appreciation to you and your command for your valiant efforts . . . your assistance in helping our forces open the KUNU-RI – SUNCHON road resulted in the safe passage of a large portion of the 2nd Infantry Division through the blockaded area.' See 27th Brigade War Diary

. . . The timing of our attack was indeed most fortunate.' Some correspondents thought it a joke.[66] It was not. The 'massive compression envelopment' announced less than a week previously had been conveniently forgotten.

On the same day as 2ID's ordeal – but a world away in Washington – the catastrophe was reflected in talk of the most ominous kind. President Harry Truman, in a press conference, refused to rule out atomic weapons. A shaken Prime Minister Clement Attlee departed for talks with Truman. There could be no conventional reinforcement of the UNC from Washington. So flensed had the US military become, post-1945, that no divisions would become available for Korea until 1952.[67]

The disintegration of ROK II Corps, the savaging of the Turks and the 2ID catastrophe had established Chinese mastery of the battlefield. High Command's grip slipping: Orders were given that shipping in Pusan was to stand by, as evacuation of the peninsula might become necessary.[68]

This opinion rapidly prevailed among the 8th Army. Awed by the landscape, stupified by the cold, horrified by the carnage and stunned by the reversal of fortune, the morale of an army expecting to be 'home by Christmas' flickered and died. Headlights glared through a great haze of dust as miles-long columns – bulldozers, artillery prime movers, tanks, trucks, jeeps – drove frantically south, away from the 'enemy hordes'.

8th Army was unmanned. The longest retreat in US military history –'The Big Bug-out' – had commenced.

* * *

At Brigade, signs of decontrol were alarming. Turks – 'hellish good soldiers' in Slim's opinion – straggled into the Brigade HQ area: Argyll subaltern Owen Light watched survivors marching grimly with wounded and dead strapped to their backs. They were in a dangerous mood. 'The Turkish brigade commander arrived at Brigade HQ and said, "I will not fight under American command any more!"' said Captain Reggie Jeffes, who heard reports of Turks assaulting GIs. 2ID remnants still arrived: A tank rumbled by carrying an agonised soldier with his arm trapped under the turret, an injury that would probably necessitate amputation if a working MASH could be located.[69]

'American command was very dicey indeed, issuing orders and counter orders continuously,' Jeffes added 'Absolute panic stations.' December 1, Willoughby thought, was 'a day of confusion and everything except us were driving for all they were worth southwards – where? No one knew.' 27th Brigade was now attached to 1st Cavalry Division, covering the northeast as 8th Army rearguard. The brigade was ordered to establish blocking positions. 'The situation is vague and confused,' the Brigade War Diary noted. Without authorisation, 1st Cavalry units withdrew from a position that day when enemy soldiers were seen on high ground.[70] On 2 December, reports came of heavy enemy movement. The Brigade Operations Log was skeptical: 'It is the opinion that certain units are giving this information in order to extract . . . orders for premature and quite unjustifiable withdrawals.' Meanwhile, communications was lost with 1st Cavalry HQ.[71]

3 RAR was dispatched to cover the Yopa-ri bridge across the Taedong River. They deployed below forested hills. Captain Ben O'Dowd's A Company skirmished with a Chinese patrol, capturing their bivouac – hollowed-out rice stooks, laid out with bed rolls. It was torched. After dark, there were occasional bugle calls and the rumble of UNC artillery in the hills to their front. It was a bright, moonlit night; O'Dowd fretted that his Diggers' dark uniforms would make them easy targets against a fresh snowfall. But no attack came. The following morning, the Australians retreated across the bridge, blowing it behind them.[72]

At Brigade HQ, Jeffes heard that Lieutenant Colonel Bruce Ferguson's land rover had stalled. He did not get along with the fiery Australian: During the advance, 'Ferg' had ordered him to recover vehicles 50 miles back. Jeffes replied that was too far, he could only do that if they had gone off the road. Ferguson replied fine, he would push them off. Now, Jeffes pulled up at Ferguson's vehicle, next to two US tanks shooting into the hills. Ferguson looked up from his map. 'Christ! King fucking bluebell himself!' he spat; Jeffes' call-sign was 'Bluebell'. Ignoring the abuse, Jeffes cleaned the land rover's points, the engine caught, and Ferguson was delighted. 'I could do nothing wrong after that,' Jeffes recalled. 'The fact that I had gone, and not sent a fitter.'

Meanwhile, the Argylls had been dispatched into rugged hills with a taskforce of the 1st Cavalry. A withdrawal order came late in the afternoon. A Company was ordered to head south down a craggy ridgeline, onto a road, to be met by transport. In vain did Wilson complain that the route was 2 miles off his map, and night was falling; orders were orders. He led A Company cross-country on the basis of verbal descriptions – and remarkably reached the RV. There he was told that orders had changed and he and his exhausted (and furious) men were to return the way he had come. It was 02:00. The US FOO attached to the battalion was ordered to leave, but Wilson was impressed and touched when the young subaltern sought out Lieutenant Colonel Neilson to apologise for leaving the Argylls without artillery.[73] Marching through the night, Wilson and his men exfiltrated over a frozen river without enemy contact.[74] Even so, the isolation and scarce intelligence were giving even the Argyll's fiercest men the jitters. Slim dreaded the hourly turnover of vehicle engines to prevent them from freezing: 'That told the bloody Chinamen where we were.'

On 3 December, Willoughby's D Company of the Middlesex was adjacent to a company of 1st Cavalry covering the road to Pyongyang. He introduced himself, and was told by an officer, 'If during the night you see two red Verey lights, collect together everyone you can and go in that direction' – south. That, Willoughby mused, would leave both D Company's flank and the road wide open. Returning to his men, he heard reports from air reconnaissance of 20,000 enemy approaching. Ahead, under a heavy sky, lay fir forests and grey mountains. An air strike roared over, machine gunning suspected Chinese. 'We watched with some awe their bullets striking the ground and floating away as ricochets into the gloom,' wrote the major. Bombers followed, until the light failed. 'In the unreality of almost total silence, we settled down to make what we could of the night,' Willoughby noted. 'There seemed to be every prospect of our having to fight it out to gain time for the UN army to extricate itself from this appalling muddle.' Over the radio, he listened to the BBC: Attlee was claiming that the UK had no quarrel with China. Camouflaging their positions with pine sprigs, the Diehards hoped that air's estimates of enemy numbers were exaggerated. No contact. The next morning a patrol recced a ford where the USAF claimed to have wiped out a Chinese battalion. All that could be found were two dead civilians and a slaughtered ox. The flanking 1st Cavalry sub-unit appeared to have disappeared in the night.[75]

The brigade would follow. Coad had considered the rearguard operations 'pointless', but was 'astounded' when at Divisional HQ on 3 December he was ordered to withdraw 135 miles the following day.[76] But the brigade, the last 8th Army unit to drive south, was pleased with a US unit newly attached, the 2nd Chemical Mortar Battalion. 'They were great guys, all West Point,' said Argyll subaltern Alan Lauder. 'Very able, always up beside you.'

The pullback was a ramshackle affair. As usual, there was insufficient transport; as usual, the Middlesex rode on mudguards of trucks, with other men lying in the trailers of the mortar battalion, clinging to each other. 'In this manner, we reached the junction with the main road ahead of the enemy,' said Willoughby. 'By how much, we shall never know; the wind had returned and it was a fearful journey.'[77]

Some officers maintained morale: Wilson sounded his hunting horn to rally his company and Jocks responded appropriately, barking like hounds.[78] But many soldiers wondered just how far behind the Chinese were. 'There was fear that at any second you could be pounced upon,' said Yerby. 'You were constantly jumpy.' 'I was quite relieved to be going southward but was not relieved in the style in which we were doing it,' added Shipster. 'We knew that survival depended on cohesion, keeping together and strictest discipline.'

As the brigade joined the southward rush, 8th Army seemed to be disintegrating. 'We could rely on each other, but we did not know about anyone else,' said Spicer. 'Covering the withdrawal was worse than going forward, you were waiting for the enemy, and you knew if they came, there was nobody to help.' After Pakchon and Kunu-ri, the brigade had learned to respect US artillery, but even gunner officers were flagging. 'Three times I personally met the observation officer in his jeep coming back,' said Man. 'We were stationary, but he was terrified of being left out, he was certain we were going to go without him.'

There were scenes of near mutiny. 'This truck came down, and on its front was written "Pusan!"' Man recalled. 'The officer sitting beside the driver got out and rushed up to my policeman who was trying to clear the road, and this chap said, "You can't hold me up, I'm an officer!" and my soldier knocked him down. The RSM of the Argylls was so delighted, he turned his back and of course did not see it.'

Panic could be infectious. 'The American transport troops allotted to us – very nice fellows – had only one intention: Get back as early as possible, and we had to put guards on transport,' said Shipster. 'I remember two drivers had taken position to cover the transport, and their conversation went, "Did that bush move?" All three in unison said, "Yes, let's get the hell out of here!"' A Digger story circulated of a truck driving at 40 mph being overtaken by a running GI – who was still in his sleeping bag.[79] 'The Americans were not trained for this kind of warfare,' said Argyll Harry Young. 'It was a bloody shame, because they were hell of nice guys.'

Paddies were filled with burnt-out vehicle carcasses shunted off the road. 'I remember passing an American tank which was broken down and I told the American chap, "We're the last troops, you'd better burn that before the Chinese get it,"' said Man. 'Some weeks later I got a rocket from Japan, saying, "British officers will not give orders to Americans to burn their tanks!" It didn't worry me.' But not all machines were effectively destroyed. 'One of my drivers joined the convoy driving this mobile crane!' recalled 3 RAR Signals Sergeant Jack Gallaway. The huge vehicle was later blown up.

It was a good time to learn how to drive. 'It didn't matter if you bumped into someone, or another vehicle,' said Argyll MO Douglas Haldane, getting to grips with his ambulance jeep. 'I was not really an acceptable driver when I came back; I had to get proper lessons!'

By now, the brigade's remaining vehicles were in a parlous state. One Argyll mortar carrier clanked to a halt. It was swiftly unloaded, and the Jocks jumped on a truck after opening the fuel cocks for the last unit to set fire to. 'It must have made a hell of a show,' said Roy Vincent. 'Sixty six high explosive, six smoke bombs and two petrol tanks – quite a bang!'

At the rear of 27th Brigade's column trundled Jeffes' REME Scammel recovery truck, dragging eight clapped-out vehicles.

* * *

The retreat's backdrop was the cruelest winter in memory. The frosted countryside undulated and rose up into mountains that were hard and jagged. Some days were dark and overcast; the coldest ones were bright and clear. At night, a full moon – 'Chinese moon' in UNC parlance, referring to the enemy's mastery of darkness – reflected off snow and frosted ruins with a ghostly, silver splendour. 'Cold hurts, when you can't get out of it,' said Boydell. 'The cold was worse than anything.'

The first heavy snow had fallen after dark on 3 December. 'I was in a slit trench with my poncho on top of me and I woke up and wondered what this weight was,' said Lauder. 'It was 4 inches of snow.' Lauder could not open his eyes; his lids had frozen together. Jeffes, sleeping under a jeep in an Arctic sleeping bag bartered from an American colonel for whisky, woke to find his nose attached to the chassis by a stalactite of ice. The warm-weather Australians suffered most. 'You'd be stuck, crammed in a hole, and in the morning you'd be lifted out and get your legs straightened out and start walking,' said Sniper Robbie Robertson. 'But the Diggers did not complain, you didn't say, "Ah it's cold" – you knew it was bloody cold.'

Men piled on whatever clothing they had. Boydell wore several pairs of pyjamas under his uniform, and a long coat taken from a dead American officer over it. Some British winter gear was decent: String vests kept sweat from freezing on the skin; 'woolly pullies' with neck drawstrings captured body heat. But most US winter kit – pile waistcoats, parkas and caps – was far superior to its British equivalent. Mitten gauntlets, which hung on a cord around the neck, were good, but needed a hole cut for the trigger finger. By now most men looked like Americans – though Man insisted on wearing his peaked cap and was once spotted with a pile cap and his peaked cap on top.[80] If men removed their boots when they wrapped themselves in blankets or sleeping bags, the footwear would be frozen stiff in the morning. 'You'd put your feet in the fire to warm them up, and your boots would shrivel up a bit,' said Young.

Rations froze solid. 'You could not put a pick through a tin of beans, you had to thaw it out,' Young recalled. Tins were cooked over spirit stoves, but cold proved insidious. 'When a can of, say, pork and beans was heated, the outside would bubble tantalizingly, but when you put the spoon in, it met a frozen centre,' said 3 RAR Intelligence Officer Alf Argent. Diggers discovered a unique way to heat food. 'If you dented a can and threw it in a fire, when the dent was blown back out, it was time to pull it out and eat,' said Stan Connelly. 'It was like a pressure cooker.' While driving, Willoughby heated rations by wiring tins to his vehicle's exhaust manifold. But war scenery ruined appetites. Jake Mutch and his mates were about to eat a tin of meat noodles when they noticed a nearby dead enemy nearby with his head split. 'His brain looked exactly like the bloody stuff in the tin,' Mutch said. 'None of us could eat it.'

Water bottles were carried inside clothes or they solidified. Men melted snow for water, but found it took long minutes to produce a single cupful. In barracks, men avoided sergeant majors, but now they tracked them down: CSMs were in charge of rum rations, doled out with a large spoon. It helped keep the cold out, especially when added to hot tea.

Ablutions were problematic. 'You tried to shave, you'd have this mess kit of water, you'd put your razor in and it would freeze into a block,' said Argyll Lieutenant Owen Light. 'One soldier had this funny moustache, and half of it broke off!' At night, men lit small fires at the bottom of their slit trenches, looting villages for charcoal braziers. 'We used to put them in trenches or carriers to keep our feet warm,' said Argyll Adam MacKenzie.

Vehicles froze to the ground when, during the day, the sun

thawed the top layer of frost. Caution was necessary with vehicles and weapons; exposed flesh stuck to metal, leaving painful strips. Weapon oil froze; rifles and Brens were cleaned dry. When riding tanks, men put their boots on the exhausts until they began to char. The worst was being exposed when the wind howled in. 'Crossing frozen rivers, the terrible winds were so sharp, they were like spears,' said Yerby.

With 27th Brigade being rearguard, most villages it entered were abandoned. Men tore apart ruined homes for firewood; if cottages were standing, men piled in for the night. Flues ran from kitchen stoves under floors, creating highly effective central heating; that system, and the *kimchi* pots, which kept vegetables frozen for the winter, impressed the technically minded Jeffes: 'Very, very clever!' But fires had to be stoked judiciously. By now, even Coad was carrying a carbine, and one evening, in a Korean home, he put his weapon and magazines on the hot floor. In the middle of the night, the weapon cooked off. 'There was a certain degree of chaos when that went off, I can tell you!' said Jeffes. Argyll Intelligence Officer Sandy Boswell went into one where shivering men overloaded the stove and the house burst into flames. Argylls tumbled out, but the battalion war diary did not survive. Neilson ordered Boswell to re-write it from memory.

As the retreat continued, there would be fewer houses but more fires, for as 8th Army exited North Korea, it was leaving nothing standing in its wake.

*   *   *

Previously, devastation had been incidental: Collateral damage from bombs and guns as the front steamrollered up the peninsula, touching a village or district here, bypassing one there. Now it would be deliberate. On 2 December, 8th Army ordered all food stocks to be burnt, bridges destroyed, boats sunk. Locomotives, carriages, signals, rails, port facilities, oil tanks, cranes – all would be denied the enemy. This was 'scorched earth'.[81]

'Every village we went through we set fire to, it was, "Get out and burn it,"' said Whitehouse. 'This was official policy: "Don't leave anything!"' Men struggled for words to describe the scenes. 'It was like walking through a film set, when you describe it to people, it seems far-fetched,' said Yerby. 'The hills, the mountains, the hovels destroyed, the snow . . . it was something you don't see every day of your life.' Destruction extended for mile after mile. 'You'd see Americans with zippo lighters, lighting up the eaves of buildings,' added Gallaway. 'I was told to find a village to camp in, I was driving down this road looking for one, and I just couldn't find one that was not destroyed.'

Some men took part almost joyously in the arson. 'The Aussies had a load of beers and were dishing them out, they had a big fire and we were all dancing around,' said Argyll Quartermaster Andrew Brown. 'There was this North Korean barrack full of stuff, and eventually I thought, "We'll deny them this," and got a driver to go along with his jerry can, set a match, and up she went. Nice!'

Others felt guilt at the vandalism. 'You used to wonder, "There's a nice home here, like a croft, and we went and destroyed it,"' Mutch said. 'As a country boy, I was concerned with the animals and cattle walking about unclaimed.' Much livestock was killed. 'Dead animals were everywhere beside the road,' said Digger John 'Lofty' Portener. 'There were cattle – everyone had a cow in Korea – with their legs sticking up, frozen stiff, I imagine they were shot by airplanes.' There were worse sights. 'During the retreat, I saw some enemy soldiers who had been crushed by tank tracks and these pigs, which were running loose, were eating their remains,' recalled Australian correspondent Harry Gordon. 'That is something I have not been able to get out of my mind.'

Incidents were surreal, nightmarish. 'We did a night march through a forest on fire beside this river,' recalled Light. 'It was not a pleasant thing, we thought we'd get burnt alive.' The Argylls walked warily along a track through the trees, pines crackling and popping all around them, sparks flying. 'I have no idea why it was on fire,' Light added. Perhaps it was the work of the CPVA, who used smoke as top cover; perhaps the USAF, who napalmed forests to light the way for units moving at night.

Those youngsters who had been curious to experience war in

Hong Kong now recognised their naivety. 'When I went, it was for the excitement of getting somewhere,' mused Private James Beverly. 'Now I thought, "Am I ever going to get out of here?"'

The spectacle of a nation put to the torch was lurid, Biblical. In daytime, the orange glow from innumerable blazes was diffused through the dust haze and reflected in the snow clouds, illuminating the holocaust with a dull, evil light. When twilight settled over the mountains, scrub on their slopes, blazing from napalm, flickered like a lacework of amber against the blackness.*

* * *

If the dead were a terrible sight on the long, long retreat into South Korea, the living were pitiable.

A Korean winter is the season of retreat inside cottages; of thick quilts on warm floors; of heavy, pungent stews; of the companionship of three generations living together under beamed roofs. Not in the burning winter of 1950. Between 400,000–650,000 refugees swarmed onto roads and tracks, fleeing with the UNC from their wasted land.[82] Many – Christians; those who had welcomed or assisted the 8th Army – feared communist retribution. Others – their homes destroyed and livestock dead – had little choice but to join the freezing *Via Dolorosa*.

Down wind-tunnel valleys, through blackened villages, across broken bridges, the suffering tide rolled south. With the armies having appropriated young males, the refugees were old people, women and children, and with military traffic dominating the roads, they were forced onto secondary tracks. Bundled up, they piled their

---

* 'Scorched earth' was rescinded in January. Even senior US officers considered the destruction excessive. (see Appleman, 1989, pp. 356, 361–2). In the House of Lords, Lord Strabolgi asked whether a scorched earth policy was in effect in Korea, and if so, whether the British government had been consulted. Lord Henderson, Undersecretary of State for Foreign Affairs replied that UNC forces, 'have not adopted any such policy in Korea . . . particular care has been taken to ensure the safety of public utilities.' (See Hansard, 23 January, 1951) This was either ignorance or disingenuous. Even US Department of Defense broadcasts used the term. Discussing the demolition of Hungnam Port (see Chapter 11) the voiceover of *Combat Bulletin 106* states: 'In the UN's new scorched earth tactics, few buildings are left in which Chinese Reds will be able to hide from observation or air attack'.

possessions on A-frame backpack carriers and carts. Babies were strapped to backs, little children scurried alongside carrying pathetic parcels from homes they would never see again. 'When everything they have is on their backs and it is snowing and they are in a long line to get away from battle and there is nothing you can do and the odds are they will probably die in the cold . . .' said Boydell. 'These things are horrendous.'

This was a procession not just of two cultures but of two centuries. UNC soldiers rolled by in vehicles; Koreans stumbled along on foot or in bullock carts, the latter often rolling on tyres salvaged from abandoned jeeps. With civilians lacking road priority and amid a commonly expressed racial contempt for the 'Gooks' there was frequent abuse. 'The American drivers were not kind to them,' said Barrett. 'They would try and scrape along the side of the bullock carts just for fun. If I'd been braver I'd have reprimanded 'em, but they were driving me.'

Making matters worse were orders to halt refugee columns to prevent infiltration. 'At night you had to get very tough, you had to block the roads and shoot at them,' said Wilson. 'You can't hold a position at night with people wandering around in all directions. It was not funny.'

Some soldiers resisted orders to fire on refugees. MFC Henry Chick Cochrane was ordered by Captain Colin Mitchell to bomb a bridge. 'He said, "I want a bomb down there," I said, "Right, I'll plot it on the map,"' Cochrane recalled, but when he looked, the bridge was crawling with refugees. He refused the order. Captain Fairrie, the mortars officer arrived and talked with Mitchell. Then Fairrie told Cochrane, 'You'll be alright now.' Mitchell returned and asked if Cochrane could hit the bridge. 'I said, "I'll knock any brick you like off it – but not at the moment."' Mitchell left.

There were countless tragedies. 3 RAR Intelligence Officer Alf Argent passed an old man mutely standing beside the track with a dead child in his arms, hit by a truck or tank, tears glistening on his cheeks. Willoughby noted the silence of the refugees; even children were mute. Passing a temporarily halted convoy, he saw ROK troops assisting some refugees, who had just thrown their bedding and bundles into the truck, when, before they could clamber aboard, the column started up again. The refugees – two children, a mother and a baby – were left standing helplessly, watching their only possessions disappear in the dust.[83] In utter despair, some mothers abandoned offspring. 'You'd see women on the edge of iced rivers, they'd take babies off their backs, put them in a hole in the ice and let them go,' recalled Mankelow. 'Others put babies on the side of the road and kept walking, just walking...'

The plight of children was most heart-rending. 'Argylls are good at helping people, when we gave the children chocolates and sweets, they were over the moon,' said Mutch, 'Poor wee mites!' At other times, kindliness was overturned. 'The Jocks were kind to women and children, but there were times when we completely ignored them, we were quite rough getting them out of the way,' admitted Slim. 'Like all people in that sort of situation, the refugees were mesmerised, in shock. They were smart to get out of the way.'

Yet desperation was a spur. Thompson watched a boy with a smaller child on his back, climbing the skeletal girders of a downed viaduct, leaping gaps with a 50-foot drop below. Silhouetted against a slate sky, the reporter thought him, 'a heroic figure, greater than tragedy'.[84]

On 3 December, with Washington apparently considering nuclear options, South Korea's defence minister opined that his people would rather die in an atomic blast then become communist slaves.[85] Whether the electorate concurred is uncertain, but the passengers of one of the last trains south had no opinion. Man saw it chugging into a station: it was so packed, that desperate refugees had lashed themselves to the locomotive and its carriages. In the sub-zero temperatures, wind chill had done its work: Every one of the external passengers was frozen dead.

The retreat rolled on.

* * *

Pyongyang was ringed with fire. Many units had already retreated when, with enemy forces sweeping down from the northeast, Walker had given official evacuation orders on 3 December.[86] With transport so congested, it was impossible to evacuate all UNC dumps in the city: Most were to be destroyed in place. Massive detonations sounded as huge stores of equipment, food, clothing, ammunition, explosives were blown. The resultant fires were so fierce that units of the US 24th Infantry Division, ordered into the city to salvage left-behind equipment, were unable to enter;[87] conflagrations actually raised the air temperature despite the freezing weather.[88] Great columns of black smoke rose thousands of feet.

Wastage was immense. A US engineering battalion destroyed 185 of their own railway flatcars.[89] One newly-arrived unit, however, refused to follow suit: 27th Brigade's latest addition, India's 60th Field Ambulance. Having disembarked in Pusan in late November, 60th Field arrived in Pyongyang on 3 December with six months of supplies to find chaos and destruction. In defiance of orders from US Transportation Command that he abandon the six months of medical supplies, the unit CO, Lieutenant Colonel Rangaraj, concentrated his men and equipment in five carriages of a train, de-coupled it from the rear, and had two of his soldiers, former railwaymen, get up a head of steam. With armed soldiers, including paratroopers of the US 187th Airborne Brigade – the 60th Field ambulance was parachute-trained – standing on the footplates, the hijacked train chugged south, against the protests of transport officers.* [90]

On 4 December, 27th Brigade approached the capital. 'The Brigade, having led the UN forces out of Pyongyang . . . now performed the duties of rearguard into Pyongyang,' Coad noted. 'Very fitting.'[91] The city resembled a painting by Hieronymus Bosch. 'Coming back, everything was on fire, Americans were blowing everything up,' said Rogers. 'You felt the blast from 2 miles away, then this mushroom cloud went up.' The brigade detoured round the

---

* US Transport Command subsequently demanded a court martial for Rangaraj. When US General Matthew Ridgway approached Colonel Frank Bowen of the 187th Airborne to learn details, Bowen said if he court martialled Rangaraj, he would have to do the same to forty of his own paratroopers. The matter was dropped. Details in correspondence from Smallbridge to Gandevia, 1992. The Indian Field Ambulance married up with 27th Brigade on 14 December.

suburbs. Some soldiers had witnessed such destruction before. 'I'd seen Manila after MacArthur finished with it,' said Gallaway. 'I thought this was the normal thing you did with cities: you demolished them.'

North of the city, 27th Brigade met what was to have been its relief: the newly arrived 29th Brigade, deployed north of the city as covering force. There was, in fact, no imminent exit from Korea for British troops. After four days of meetings with Truman, Attlee was reassured by Truman on the atomic question (though the allies remained divided over policy toward Peking). In return, Attlee promised that British soldiers would stand alongside their American allies in Korea. Men from the two brigades roared and jeered at each other as they passed. 'We were shouting, "Where you been? What took so long?"' recalled Spicer. 'But we also said, "Good to see you, mate!"' The 29th, having looted American dumps, hurled booty into the 27th's vehicles as they passed.

29th Brigade had not yet seen action and appeared beautifully equipped. 'They looked frightfully smart in their quite useless British winter kit,' said Wilson. 'We were dressed like tramps in American kit which was much better, but we were absolutely filthy.' The approaches to the Taedong bridges were defended by 29th Brigade's massive Centurion tanks. The pontoons sagged under their trucks as 27th Brigade rattled across. 'I could see nothing at all of Pyongyang, just a blaze from beginning to end,' said Lieutenant Peter Baldwin. 'We were passing through at night, the sense was that the Chinese were right behind us.'

Much of Pyongyang's populace was fleeing. With military sand-bag and pontoon bridges guarded for the exclusive use of troops, refugees waded the ice-rimmed Taedong, or took scarce boats. There was one more option, and that is what photojournalist Max Desfor – engulfed in the retreat like everyone else – encountered. He was photographing refugees in boats, when something caught his eye. He walked round a corner of the riverbank to a promontory and there he saw it: a felled bridge sticking out of the water, its twisted girders alive with refugees. 'They were scurrying along the girders with what little belongings they had on their shoulders, just inching along, hanging on, it was an awesome effort,' Desfor said. 'It was heart-rending, I had to wind my mechanical camera, but my hands were so cold I could only make eight exposures.' He climbed into a jeep to rejoin the pullback, not knowing he had taken the iconic photograph of the Korean War.

UNC rearguards exited Pyongyong on the evening of 5 December. The area of North Korea south of the capital would not be defended. On 4 December, the US Joint Chiefs had been informed that 8th Army was retreating south of the 38th parallel.[92] On 6 December, air reconnaissance reported Chinese units, complete with supply camels, entering Pyongyang.[93] The only communist capital captured by free world forces in the course of the Cold War had been held for less than two months.

*　　*　　*

South of Pyongyang, the endless military traffic crawled in a stop-start column at less than 2 mph, barely faster than the plodding refugees.[94] Open vehicles were freezing, but the brigade was under-supplied with transport; some days, the battalions marched.

During night halts, men dug in, as much for cover from the vicious wind as from the enemy, hacking into permafrost with picks. 'Boots on the ground,' said Lauder. 'You don't control it unless you are there with a gun.' The ground was doubly dangerous: North Korean guerillas, as well as Chinese regulars, were now appearing. 'In the hills we'd often come across holes; you couldn't turn your back on them,' said Argyll Ron Yetman. 'Somebody would fire or drop a grenade down, because you didn't know if there was a Korean in it.'

On 5 December, a company of Diggers was sent to relieve a US unit under attack. They arrived to find nobody at the scene, but equipped themselves from the litter of abandoned American kit, including two jeeps.[95] In this jittery atmosphere, brigade units were assigned as close protection for Corps HQ. At sunset on 7 December, a bugler sounded retreat, sparking a minor panic among some echelon troops, for whom a bugle at dusk meant only one thing. They later conceded it was 'kinda jazzy'.[96] Yet the guerillas were no mirage. At dawn on 9 December, the vehicle column came under automatic fire from a pine-covered ridge.[97] The guerillas had chosen their time and place well: The rising sun was at their back, blinding those trying to spot and fire on them. But it was a hit-and-run raid; the ambush was brief.[98]

On 6 December, it was announced that King George VI had awarded Coad an OBE for services in Korea. The following day, Man was summoned to Brigade HQ. 'The brigadier was leaning on his jeep, absolutely played out,' Man said; the lonely strain of command had caused a breakdown. Coad was evacuated to the rear for a rest; Man temporarily assumed command.

On 11 December, 27th Brigade retreated across the 38th parallel – two months to the day it had advanced in the opposite direction. As he re-entered South Korea, 3 RAR Lieutenant Alf Argent's eye was caught by a new road sign parodying those of the advance. It read, simply: 'You are crossing the 38th parallel Courtesy of the Chinese Communist Forces'.

The brigade deployed in the hills above the town of Uijongbu, astride the key attack route to Seoul, 15 miles south. Uijongbu was an empty ruin, the gaunt hills surrounding it deep in snow. The temperature was now minus 20 degrees, but at last, a defensive line was being formed. 27th Brigade hacked through the permafrost into concrete-hard earth.

What lay behind them? The twisted steel skeletons of girder bridges, half sunk in iced-over rivers. Brick chimney stacks marked the graves of houses; charred piles of straw were all that remained of cottages and huts; downed telegraph wires lay in tangles. Shards of brown glaze – smashed *kimchi* pots – jutted from the ground, alongside the upturned carcasses of dead cattle, rigid hooves pointed skyward. Here lay a silver chopstick, there a piece of broken lacquerware. And against the frozen grey ash of ruins, a flicker of white: a calligraphic scroll blowing on the winter wind.

* * *

There would be no close pursuit. The Chinese lacked vehicles, but more germanely, had no reason to fight: 8th Army was fleeing North Korea of its own accord. Peng had aimed to take a line from Wonsan to Pyongyang, across the 'waist' of the peninsula.[99] In fact, his offensive had liberated all of North Korea on the western flank. It was an astonishing victory for under-armed troops from a nation whose martial ability had been derided since the Opium War of 1842. A new superpower was striding the global stage. Red China had stood up.

The final act in North Korea, however, had yet to play out. While 27th Brigade had been operating south of Kunu-ri, even more dramatic events had been underway 80 miles northeast. There, 41 Commando, attached to the crack 1st US Marine Division, had deployed deep into Korea's most hostile terrain. Bored into that terrain was a strange, amoeba-shaped water feature known to Koreans as 'Changjin'. On the colonial-era maps the troops were issued, however, it bore its Japanese name.

It was this name that the fascinated and horrified American and British publics would learn as they unfolded newspapers to read of an impending catastrophe, an Asian Stalingrad threatening the annihilation of their crack troops, surrounded 70 miles inside freezing highlands by a force three times their own number.

That pairing of Japanese nomenclature with English common noun still echoes through history, denoting the coldest, darkest, most harrowing clash-of-arms of the Korean War. Chosin Reservoir.

Chapter Ten

White Hell

Storm'd at with shot and shell,
Boldly they rode and well,
Into the jaws of Death,
Into the mouth of Hell
Alfred, Lord Tennyson

Mid-morning, 28 November. Hamhung, Northeast Korea.

From a distance, the bundled-up men slinging packs and equipment onto truck beds, then clambering aboard themselves, looked like US marines. On their feet were the high 'shoepac' winter boots; they were clad in the bulky, knee-length khaki parkas; and slung from their shoulders were: M1 carbines, M1 Garands and BARs. But a distinguishing feature stood in the tactical drabness: Under the parka hoods peeped green berets. Drivers gunned engines; gravel crunched; then the long convoy – twenty-two trucks and one weapons carrier – jolted off. 41 Commando was moving out.[1]

The commando, 235 strong, had arrived at the northeastern Korean port of Hungnam from Japan on 20 November, then proceeded 8 miles inland, to the industrial city of Hamhung. A rear-party stayed in the city: 217 men would move up to the front. Now, they were *en route* to join their American brethren, the powerful, 13,500-strong 1st US Marine Division, or 1st MARDIV.

The US marines, following the Inchon and Seoul operations on the west of the peninsula, had been re-embarked and landed for operations in Korea's northeast. This was the province of X Corps,

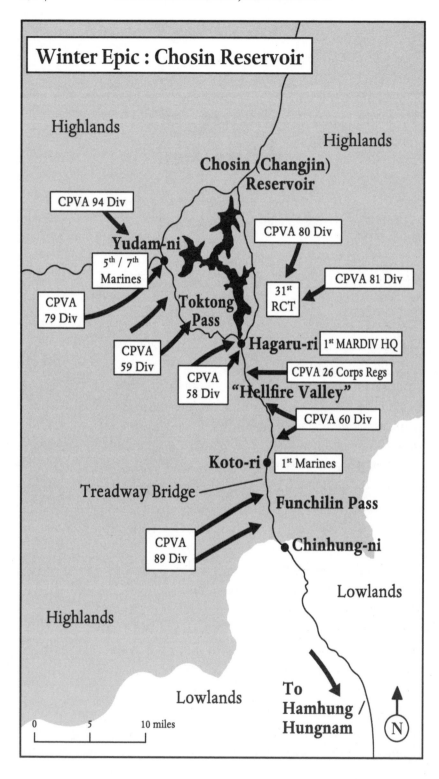

separated from General Walton Walker's 8th Army in the west by
Korea's mountain spine. The commandos were to take on a
specialised role: They would join X Corps' spearhead, 7th Marine
Regiment at Yudam-ni, as a reconnaissance unit screening the
Americans as they advanced northwestwards over mountain tracks
to link up with 8th Army.

Having enjoyed Thanksgiving, some of Lieutenant Colonel
Drysdale's men were expecting combat to sputter out. 'A few stray
guerillas' was what Corporal George Richards had heard of
expected enemy. 'We wanted to be in at the kill,' said Lieutenant
Peter Thomas. 'Like so many wars, it was, "Home by Christmas,
boys!" This was the last operation before the collapse of North
Korea.'

Not everyone was gung ho. 'I enjoyed the commando raids but
had misgivings about going in as infantry and being involved quite
heavily,' said Marine John Underwood. 'I had a different mental
attitude.' Underwood's CO also had (private) doubts: Unconvinced
by victory forecasts, Drysdale had anticipated, just five days
previously, that his men would be embroiled in 'a long and very
unpleasant winter campaign'.[2]

Still, morale was high. 41 Commando was the only non-ROK,
non-US unit in X Corps. As their convoy left Hamhung, GIs outside
the city shouted, 'Who are you? Turks?' Commandos yelled back
identifying themselves.[3] Soon, the factories, warehouses and railway
yards were behind.

They were heading away from the sea, the customary refuge of
marines. The road took them through the skeletal orchards of the
agricultural lowlands – much of it churned to a morass by vehicles –
then, some 30 miles from the coast, began a steep ascent to the snow-
covered highlands, 4,000 feet above sea level. This was where 1st
MARDIV was deployed around Chosin Reservoir in Hamgyong, the
Korean province abutting Siberia.

*　　*　　*

The high country of Hamgyong is the peninsula's most forbidding landscape.* Here, the bones of Korea – 'the dragon's back' – break through the land's crust and climb skyward in their most dramatic fashion: Viewed from the sea, the great grey mountains present a castle-like wall. In summer, Hamgyong's highlands are a sparsely populated, alpine landscape runnelled by crystal streams, roamed by deer and over flown by eagles. In winter, the terrain is unearthly: A moonscape of frigid rock and frozen water, scoured by bitter, 35 mile per hour winds whipping up blizzards from Siberia.

The area's reputation dates back to the Dark Ages. 1st MARDIV's rear echelon at Chinhung-ni, the township squatting at the base of the high country, was the limit of exploitation of a sixth-century warrior king whose conquests laid the groundwork for Korea's unification: Advancing from the south, Chinhung prudently halted his march at the foot of the highlands.[4] More recently, Hamgyong was where the Japanese were rumoured to have carried out atomic weapons research during the Second World War.

It was a fitting location for such activities, not just due to its isolation, but because the height of the reservoir, deep inside the highlands, made it ideal for hydro-electric generation. The mighty pumps of three turbine stations had supplied fully one third of the electricity generated across Hirohito's empire, feeding the hungry factories in Hamhung which were, by some accounts, the largest industrial complex in East Asia. Because of the war, these facilities now lay abandoned. They were also glittering with frost and dusted with snow, for on 14 November, a cold front had descended. Temperatures after dark plunged to minus 24 degrees Fahrenheit.

Past Chinhung, 41 Commando's line of vehicles shifted gear as they laboured upwards. As the altitude increased, the temperature dropped. On the open trucks, commandos huddled into parkas, but the bitter winds, glaciated with snow flurries, lashed their faces.

---

* Hamgyong retains its dark reputation today. Lacking arable land, it is customarily among the hardest hit by the shortages and famines that have ravaged North Korea since the late 1990s, and was the site, in 2006 and 2009, of underground nuclear tests. It is also the location of one of the most feared places in Asia: 'Reeducation Facility No 15', the Yodok Labour Camp. Holding an estimated 30,000 inmates charged with political crimes, it is one of the largest facilities in Kim Jong-il's gulag.

Icicles of mucous dangled from nostrils; lungs were seared; back teeth ached. Numbed men shivered – and not just from the cold. Beyond the lurching tailgates of their trucks, the frosted lowlands, dotted with villages and towns, spread under the gaze of awed commandos like the map of a winter fairytale.

Soon, however, the vista was lost, obscured by soaring granite shoulders as the track wound round 'switchbacks' – crescent-shaped hairpin turns curving round the mountain contours. The convoy was now crawling under battlement-like ridges, for this was the 10-mile pass that guards both the highlands: Its name, Funchilin means 'Yellow Grass Pass' for from here on, the weather is so extreme that green no longer appears. The road itself was enough to turn a driver's hair grey. On one side, it was overshadowed by rocky cliffs and slopes, stubbled with scrawny fir saplings; on the other, it dropped away into an abyss hundreds, then thousands of feet deep. Yet this track – a shelf chiselled into the cliffs – was the Main Supply Route, or MSR, for the entire 1st MARDIV. Running parallel to it, and crossing it at one point, was a rail line, complete with cable to haul trains up. No trains ran; the track had been put out of action earlier in the war. The dead communications artery was somehow portentous.

Drysdale considered the terrain 'poisonous'[5] and many troops would use an identical adjective to describe it: 'god-forsaken'. 'I had not been in a landscape like that before,' said Underwood. 'It was absolutely bleak.' Compared to the heights they were now penetrating, the commandos' rugged training grounds on England's southwestern moors were like nursery gardens. 'It was big country,' said Corporal Ron Moyse.

Commandos of literary bent might have recalled American Civil War writer Ambrose Bierce's grim line, *No country is so wild and difficult but men will make it a theatre of war*, for their trucks were now rolling over shapeless, blackened humps lying in the road. Only their tattered uniforms gave these objects away as enemy bodies, left, unburied, from fighting weeks earlier.[6]

Before long, came signs of a very-much-alive enemy. Pairs of Corsairs – the navy-blue, gull-winged USMC close-support fighters – were wheeling, diving and strafing invisible targets over distant ridges. 'They were going over, you saw a plume of napalm and thought, "Oh, something's happening,"' said Lieutenant John Walter, the officer who had not completed his commando course. 'Then we started stopping. This was totally unexpected.' The route from the coast to 41's destination, the combat base at Koto-ri, was supposed to be friendly territory. With no resistance anticipated, the commandos were engaged in an administrative, not a tactical move. All heavy weapons were crated; the only operational concession had been the stripping away of the trucks' canvas tarps.

During unexplained halts, frozen men dismounted to brew up. The reasons for other stops were clear: To let ambulance jeeps loaded with bloodied bundles pass them southward, heading for the coastal lowlands. Rumours spread. A US marine heading south warned the commandos to prepare for enemy cavalry.[7] Apprehension rose. 'There were explosions in the mountains, shell bursts going up and we were thinking, "What're we going in to?"' said Richards. The drive continued.

Just below the head of the pass, squatted a bunker-like concrete construction: The hydroelectric valve station. In front of it, spanning a plunging chasm, was a concrete bridge, and under the bridge, diving down the mountainside for 2,900 feet like roller coaster tracks, were four parallel water pipes. The trucks rolled across. Beyond the pass, the road continued onto a hilly plateau. At 16:30 the convoy arrived inside the Koto-ri perimeter.[8]

* * *

The marine combat base, built around the little mountain village, guarded the entrance to Funchilin Pass. Early winter darkness was already settling as the commandos began unloading. Amid grey and white mountains, the drab base with its crated supplies, bundled up men and snow-covered tentage reminded many of a Klondike gold mining camp – albeit one bristling with weaponry. Large, bell-shaped canvas tents, clearly stencilled 'US Marines' – for the corps jealously differentiates itself from the US Army, a force marines despise – clustered everywhere. Marines had pioneered 'warm-up tents' containing space heaters and lit by petrol lanterns, through which squads were rotated to thaw out. Other tents had other purposes. Commandos chuckled when the downdraft from a helicopter whipped away one tent, revealing four marines, trousers round their ankles and buttocks blue with cold, squatting over a pit containing brown stalagmites of frozen excrement: a field latrine.[9] Between the tents, gunnery, tanks and vehicles, bonfires were flickering here and there, indicating that the base was not anticipating an attack, but Corporal Dave Brady noted with some foreboding that artillery barrels were not pointing north, but toward every point of the compass: all-round defence.[10]

In command at Koto was a living legend: Colonel Lewis 'Chesty' Puller, commander, 1st US Marine Regiment. A born marine, the Virginian had, like the other commanders of 1st MARDIV, won his spurs in the tropical carnage of the Pacific campaign, winning four Navy Crosses. By 1950, he was revered throughout the Marine Corps,[11] and famed for his off-the-cuff quotability; on first espying a flamethrower, he is reputed to have asked, 'Where do you fix the bayonet?'[12] He was a cigar chewer and whiskey drinker – perhaps explaining Koto-ri's callsign: 'Whiskey One' – whose men took perverse pride in serving under the toughest marine of them all. 'Puller was like Patton: It takes a bastard to be a good leader,' said one. 'But he was a loving bastard.'[13] This was the warrior Drysdale joined in conference as 41 Commando deployed for the night around the perimeter.

Puller was the archetypal US marine. Founded in 1775, the corps had won a global reputation in the Second World War. In close combat, the corps had blended headlong assaults with maximum firepower to steamroller fanatical Japanese as it traversed the Pacific, island by bloody island. Some US soldiers criticised marines for their simplistic tactics, but while the corps made heavy call upon its men's aggression, it also pioneered an innovative system of close-air support. In defiance of the post-the Second World War watering-down of America's armed forces, the corps maintained brutal training, the arrogance of an elite and a swaggering machismo. In Korea, the division was composed of professional officers and NCOs; the Second World War veterans called up for Korea; and young volunteers and reservists. Many marines hailed from the South – America's prime martial recruiting ground. In Korea, they had proven their mettle at the Pusan Perimeter, the Inchon landing, and the Seoul street fighting. Here in the east, they had briefly met the Chinese during their 'First Offensive' and defeated them. The enemy had since vanished.

Royal Marines had only served alongside their US brethren once previously – in 1900, as part of multinational forces fighting China's Boxer Rebellion – but they shared a common heritage. At Koto, a US marine examined the cap badge on Brady's beret. The British badge featured a globe of the eastern hemisphere; the American, the western. 'Yup, you got one half, we got the other,' the marine told Brady.[14] While 27th Brigade were unimpressed by the US Army, the commandos soon gained tremendous respect for the marines. It was mutual. Corporal Don Saunchegrow, a weapons-carrier driver assigned to the US marines' bath and shower unit in the lowlands before being tasked to convoy 41 Commando up to Koto, found British accents and slang difficult to comprehend, but was impressed: 41 were, 'a hell of a rough unit', he thought, 'like a bomb waiting for a place to go off'.[15]

Yet the two corps had divergent approaches, and in the days to come, the tactical differences between unorthodox, fast-moving, lightly-armed commandos, versus orthodox, firepower-reliant, shock troops would be highlighted as they faced a trial of ice and fire that had no parallel in their combined histories. Oddly, in their second shoulder-to-shoulder campaign, the two corps would be fighting the same enemy faced in 1900.*

1st MARDIV was a component of the 84,000 strong X Corps, commanded by US Army General Edward 'Ned' Almond. Almond had not enjoyed a distinguished the Second World War career, but in the Far East, had become a privileged member of MacArthur's inner circle, where he was known as 'The Big A', 'Ned the Dread'

---

* By an eerie coincidence, a ceremony took place in the Royal Marine Barracks, Portsmouth, on 28 November, in which the 'Canton Bell' – captured by Royal Marines during the Opium Wars – was presented to US Marines. It was announced at the ceremony that 41 Commando had just joined 1st MARDIV in Korea. (See Hayhurst, p.108.) Given the time difference, the ceremony was underway at the same time Taskforce Drysdale was fighting toward Hagaru-ri on 29 November.

and – thanks to his closeness to the supreme commander – 'The Anointed One'.[16] On assuming command of X Corps, he had proven to be a highly aggressive commander, as keen as his master to finish the war speedily, who flayed subordinates when they did not meet timetables. He also had a taste for generals' privileges: His command caravan contained a hot shower and flush toilet, while his table was supplied with fresh rations from Japan.[17]

* * *

In late November, X Corps was scattered across Hamgyong's mountains. The US 7th Infantry Division – and its large contingent of half-trained ROK troops – had reached the Yalu at Hyesanjin, while the ROK 3rd and Capital Divisions were striking north up the coast. But the unit deepest in the mountains was 1st MARDIV, deployed in a 34-mile string of positions that stretched from below the highland plateau, to the western flank of the frozen reservoir itself, 65 miles inland.

The rearmost battalion of Puller's 1st Marines was in reserve at Chinhung-ri. Eight miles further north, through Funchilin Pass, lay his regimental base, Koto. Eleven miles further north was his third battalion, at the village of Hagaru-ri, just south of the frozen reservoir. Hagaru was where 1st MARDIV's commander, Major General Oliver Prince Smith, was busily establishing supply dumps. The bulk of Smith's fighting men – the 5th and 7th Marine Regiments – were deployed at Yudam-ni, 14 miles northwest of Hagaru and west of the reservoir. Smith's 'devil dogs' would be X Corps' spearhead as it wheeled left to link up with the 8th Army. Completing the X Corps' deployment were two infantry battalions and one artillery battalion: the 7th Infantry Division's 31st Regimental Combat Team, east of the reservoir.

Smith – commonly known as 'OP' for his initials and sometimes as 'The Professor' for his patrician manner – was almost the diametric opposite of his subordinate, Puller. The silver-haired, 57-year-old Texan was a Christian Scientist who neither drank nor swore, but was greatly respected for his combat command record from the Pacific.[18] Yet as winter settled upon the reservoir, Smith, far from

leading the kind of surging advance so beloved of marine commanders, was behaving with an almost un-corps like prudence. The
subdued, pipe-smoking professional was deeply concerned at the
headlong strategy dictated by MacArthur and Almond.[19] Making
matters worse, the wary Smith and the thrusting Almond had clashed
as early as Inchon.

Their disagreement at Chosin was professional, not personal.
Marines are seaborne troops, but Smith's vanguard at Yudam was 78
road miles from Hungnam Port. 1st MARDIV's MSR was a single
road. Should things go wrong, this rat-run was enfiladed for half its
length by hills and mountains. Although there had been, since the
puzzling Chinese disengagement in the first week of November, no
major contacts, Smith had deliberately slowed his advance to about
one mile a day. Moreover, he had engineers hacking an airfield out
of the frozen soil at Hagaru. So worried was Smith about his
deployment, that he had taken the highly unusual step of complaining to the Marine Corps Commandant in Washington. But in
Korea, there was no over-ruling Almond. The advance would
continue. The war was all-but-finished.

The strategic fragility of his positions was not the only thing
troubling Smith, for his organic air asset, the US Marine 1st Fighter
Wing, based at Yonpo Airfield near Hamhung, was flying
reconnaissance. What they were reporting in the high country was
sinister in the extreme.

Just prior to 41 Commando's arrival at Koto-ri, Marine Captain
Lyle Bradley had been patrolling in his Corsair fighter-bomber south
of the Yalu. The Minnesota native was, like most 1st MARDIV
officers, highly experienced: He had flown combat in the Second
World War, then been recalled from reserve to join the 'Black Sheep'
squadron – a unit so famed from the Pacific that it inspired a TV
series – in Korea.

It was one of those intensely bright, late November days. The sky
was a translucent blue; the crystalline clarity of the air magnified
vision. Bradley and his wingman were comfortable in their cockpits,
for their rugged, propeller-driven ground-attack aircraft included
heaters. They droned over a landscape that unfolded below them like

a rumpled blanket of grey and white. Controlling their aircraft lightly, they scanned the terrain.

'I was scanning, and could see trails on top of the mountains – hundreds of footprints,' Bradley said. 'Who could be out there hiking in large numbers?' Although low-level flying was risky – pilots had been briefed that enemy were stretching cables across valleys to shred aircraft – Bradley wanted a closer look. Swooping down to 20 feet, he skimmed over the ridgeline, close enough to 'even see the types of shoes'. At stalling speed and minimum height, he followed the ridge and its trail of footprints down to where they terminated, at a mountain village. In the village were 'hundreds of guys in uniforms, all squatting around'. Then he was past.

Alarmed, he banked for a second pass. Nothing. Every man in the village had disappeared. Back at base, he filed his findings. Another pilot in a different squadron, Gerald Smith, had reported the same. For Bradley, what was particularly significant about the tracks in the snow was not just their numbers but also their direction. They could not have been made by fleeing enemy stragglers for all the footprints pointed south – heading for the marines.

* * *

The spoor Bradley had spotted in the snow represented only a tiny fraction of the force secretly massing in the frost-bound mountains.

The CPVA's crack 3rd Field Army – all 120,000 of them – had been infiltrating northeastern Korea for weeks. Now they were poised to strike. Half of this force, the CPVA's 9th Army Group – comprising the 20th Army (58th 59th, 60th and 98th Divisions) and 27th Army (the 79th, 80th, 81st and 94th Divisions) – was heading for the reservoir.[20] The two armies totalled some 60,000 men. The coming battle would pitch eight Chinese divisions against the marines' one; in manpower terms, with 13,500 marines and 4,500 soldiers facing them, the Chinese would have 3–1 odds in their favour.[21]

And this would be no ordinary battle. Commissars ensured men were fully indoctrinated against the foe. A pamphlet read: 'the Wall Street house-dog, General MacArthur, demanded that the American so-called "marines" be immediately placed at his disposal . . . [the marines] have abundantly covered Korean soil with the blood and tears of hundreds of thousands of Korean women, old men and children'. The Royal Marines also came in for a propaganda broadside. A Tass broadcast spat: 'The basic training of Royal Marines is aimed at making bandits and killers of them . . . in addition, they are steeped in the murderous traditions which have been established in the corps during its more than 300 years of bloody history'.

In his eve of battle address, 3rd Field's commander, General Song Shi-lun, finished with a demand for ruthlessness that made clear to his troops that the struggle to come was to be less a battle, more a cull: 'Kill these marines as you would snakes in your own home!'[22]

*   *   *

None of this was known to commandos settling in for the night as darkness descended on Koto. American C-rations were issued. 'Pork and beans are things I see in my dreams; iced tea's rotten, seems like hot tea can't be gotten; it's chicken all the time,' hummed Brady, ever the joker.[23] Some American rations, however, were received wonderingly by troops from a nation still suffering wartime rationing: One young commando told the US marine who had presented him with a can of cocoa that it was a delicacy that 'even the bloody king himself don't get!'[24]

Commandos were allotted sentry positions on Koto's northern perimeter. The foot-and-a-half deep permafrost proved impossible to dig into; men scratched what holes they could with bayonets. Everyone was heavily bundled up – underwear, long johns and string vest; shirt, one or two woollen pullovers, battledress top and trousers; combat jacket and trousers, pile-lined parka; gloves and gauntlets – but at night, the cold became shocking, and the commandos had not been issued Artic sleeping bags. Duty was one hour on, one hour off. In off-hours, commandos piled into the warming tents where mess tins of coffee bubbled on petrol-burning stoves, and cans of rations defrosted.

Most commandos would find it a tense, sleepless night – and not just because of the cold. Something was underway. Throughout the hours of darkness, Koto's guns thundered. The booms reverberated, for the mountains around the base made it a quadraphonic acoustic arena, and on distant ridges, the shells detonated with split-second white flashes. But no attack came.

* * *

Dawn, 29 November, Koto-ri.

From the rim of the distant North Pacific, a pale sun rose and peeped over the frost-glazed ridges. Deep-frozen commandos stamped feet, rubbed animation back into numb limbs, slapped frost from parkas. As the landscape took shape, they were astonished to see what daylight revealed: The opposite ridge was alive.

'The place was swarming with Chinese – about 300 yards away – among these steep-sided fir trees, you could see them moving, and some were walking around the bottom of the valley,' recalled Walter. 'They were not in military formation, they were just walking about.'

Marine Teddy Allen heard a hiss past his head, but it was only when he saw a nearby twig break that he realised he was under fire. Either because of the ammunition the Chinese were using, or because of freak acoustics caused by the temperature, the sound was not the ballistic crack that Allen, one of 41's best shots, was used to from the range.

Action had begun. The order was passed: fire at will. 'It was just excitement, so I put my shooting skills to work,' Allen recalled, as he settled down and began sniping at upper bodies sky-lined along the ridge. For the first time, he was shooting live enemy, but felt nothing. 'The thing is, the enemy are not human, they're targets; you don't think of them as fathers or as children.' His marksmanship was successful. The popular Captain Ralph Parkinson-Cumine arrived at Allen's position, cheerful as ever. 'I hear you got one – well done!' he exclaimed.

Walter was less pleased. Remembering the road trip of the previous day, he was appalled at the enemy's proximity: 'It was an administrative, not a tactical move!' he said. If the Chinese had arrived earlier, they could have wiped out 41 Commando in their vehicles.

41 Commando was not to know that 8th Army in the west was already reeling from Peng's great counter-offensive, launched late on 25 November. Here, in the east, Song's had struck on the night of 27–28 November. The 5th and 7th Marines at Yudam had been hit hard, as had 31st RCT. After a night of confused fighting, enemy melted away to avoid air strikes. Still, their presence did not entirely evaporate in daylight. On the afternoon of 28 November, Drysdale, jeeping well ahead of his commando, had attempted to drive forward to the 7th Marines at Yudam, but was halted at a roadblock; he returned as his men arrived at Koto. X Corps, however, did not grasp the gravity of the situation. While 41 Commando were trucking up from Hamhung, General Almond had helicoptered into 31st RCT's perimeter.

Almond's Korean command had started during the war's most successful phase: the Inchon landing in September. Then and since, everything had gone the UNC's way. Perhaps this was what made him slow to realise that these assaults were not a last-ditch enemy counter, but the first wave of a mass onslaught.

Facing officers of 31st RCT, Almond did not order withdrawal, or even consolidation. Instead, he told stunned GIs to resume the advance. His words, to a unit that had spent the previous night fighting desperately, and now stood on the brink of destruction, have gone down in history. 'We are still attacking and we are going all the way to the Yalu,' Almond said. 'Don't let a bunch of goddamn Chinese laundrymen stop you!' A battalion commander, Lieutenant Colonel Don Faith, protested that 31st RCT was under siege from two enemy divisions. Almond shot back: 'There aren't two Chinese divisions in all North Korea!'[25] It was a disastrous underestimate. Before departing for his headquarters on the coast, Almond handed out three silver stars, America's third highest award for gallantry. Faith hurled his into the snow in disgust. Less than 48 hours later, the 32-year-old colonel would lie dead among the wreckage of his command. As darkness fell on the 28th the troops around the reservoir braced themselves for night.

Now, on the morning of the 29 November, to the amazement of commandos like Allen and Waters, Chinese vanguards had reached

Koto – 25 miles south of the marine spearhead at Yudam. X Corps in the reservoir area had been broken up into four separate pockets. The 5th and 7th Marine Regiments were bottled up at Yudam. The 31st RCT was in dire straits east of the reservoir. The central marine base at Hagaru was surrounded, while Koto was screened by light forces. General Song's enemies were isolated on four 'islands'. Blocking the 'bridge' connecting these islands – the single-lane road that led to the coast – was a simple matter, since the Chinese held the 'sea' – the rugged countryside. For UNC forces around Chosin Reservoir, extinction loomed.

The coordinated assaults all the way along his deployment confirmed Smith's worst fears. His division was vulnerable to being consumed piecemeal; the only unit not in imminent peril was his reserve battalion in the lowlands, at Chinhung. The immediate priority was to cling to Hagaru in the centre, his Divisional HQ. Hagaru was essential, for if the marine regiments west of the reservoir, and the army regiment east of it were to withdraw, they had to pass through Hagaru; it stood on the road junction that was their only viable line of retreat. Problem: The garrison defending it comprised only a single, under-strength marine battalion, 3rd Battalion, 1st Marines, as well as *ad hoc* formations from the dozens of support and echelon units engaged in the building of the airfield and administering supplies piling up there. A full Chinese division, the 58th, had already attacked on the 28 October, though having arrived late, had not had the advantage of a full night to fight through.[26] If the 58th reorganised and attacked again, it could overrun the lynchpin of Smith's command.

Never before – not even in the darkest days of the Second World War – had an entire marine division faced destruction. Urgent reinforcement of Hagaru was critical. The senior combat unit available to fight north stood at Koto: 41 Commando, Royal Marines.

* * *

Puller and Drysdale had spent the night conferencing. A composite force, led by 41 Commando, would knife through the 11 miles to reinforce Hagaru. German soldiers in the Second World War had called units patched together to cope with desperate situations 'alarm units', but in Korea the practice was to name them after their commander. Thus was born 'Taskforce Drysdale'. It comprised 41 Commando, Royal Marines; Captain Carl Sitter's George Company, 3rd Battalion, 1st Marines, joining the rest of their unit beseiged at Hagaru; Captain Charles Peckham's Baker Company, 31st Infantry Regiment, 7th Infantry Division; and various marine headquarters and service units. The force's 922 men would mount 141 trucks and jeeps.[27] Drysdale had only received his orders and the makeup of his scratch command at 20:00 on 28 November [28] and knew none of his subordinates, yet delivered orders to sub-unit commanders briskly and concisely – orders that Sitter considered the best briefing he ever received.[29]

Taskforce officers then departed to brief their own men. In the frosty morning, Drysdale held a parade inspection of 41 Commando, checking that each man was shaved, his weapon cleaned. This was not spit-and-polish discipline, it was a calculated move: the colonel wanted his men feeling fresh.[30] Michael O'Brien, the 19-year-old commando, was impressed with his stickler of a CO. 'He was a harsh man, a kind man, a leader,' he said. 'I would have followed him to hell.' Watching US marines – mostly unshaven due to the cold – were astounded to see a unit parading before jumping off into combat.[31]

The convoy assembled. Drivers gunned freezing engines. Men's steaming breath mingled with exhaust smoke. The line of march was sorted out, sub-units assembled, troops assigned to transport. Vehicles were loaded with equipment and ammunition, mortars and machine guns prepared for rapid deployment. Individuals checked and rechecked personal weapons. Gloved fingers pressed shining cartridges onto the springs of magazines, pouches were stuffed, hand grenades primed. 41 Commando's RSM, 'Sticky' Baines – who one US marine considered, 'the roughest, toughest, most lethal-looking son-of-a-bitch I ever faced in my life',[32] – stalked past his commandos. 'Good luck, lads!' he said with an encouraging wink.[33]

It was an unusually kindly gesture from that baleful man, but an appropriate one. The sudden, drastic change in situation had scratched 41's original mission – recce over the mountains – for good.

Even with the flimsy information available, it was obvious to every commando that this breakthrough operation was a desperate one. Men steeled themselves.

'We knew we were going to get into the thick of it and we were going to have a job to get through,' said Marine Gordon Payne. 'Word had got round that the Chinese were up there in their thousands, waiting for us. I suspected we were going to be hammered, but strangely enough you had no fear, you think, "It's not me who's going to get hit, it's him; I'm alright, it won't be me."' Two days earlier, Brady had been utterly convinced of UNC superiority: 'Here we were, part of a magnificently equipped, huge, international group of armies, armed to the teeth with the latest weaponry . . . we were on a collision course with an enemy we could piss all over!' Now, about to cross the start line, the jocular corporal faced reality: 'We were deeply in the shit!'[34] His commander was less vulgar but equally laconic. Drysdale told his taskforce officers, 'This won't be a walk in the sun.'[35]

Eleven miles is no great distance, and the road connecting Koto to Hagaru was not nearly as dramatic as that through Funchilin; it was a track wending through reasonably level ground, albeit commanded on both sides by hills. Herein lay the problem. Fighting up a ridge-dominated route is a devilish business. Given the necessity for speed and the taskforce's lack of numbers, a broad front sweep to clear terrain and secure the road was not feasible. Instead, it would be a narrow front, motorised thrust – a mission more suited to panzer grenadiers than commandos and marines. The tactical imperative was to seize commanding heights, securing the convoy so it could pass safely below. Drysdale's plan was for 41 Commando to take the first ridge, then for George Company to leapfrog and seize the next. Meanwhile, the US Army's Baker Company would advance along the track, dismantling roadblocks.

Yet this was no mailed fist striking north. With air and artillery support, the column packed a formidable punch, but its forearm – the soft-skinned trucks and jeeps conveying the troops – was unprotected. Air reconnaissance had reported nine roadblocks[36] and several patrols on the road the previous day had simply vanished into thin air.[37]

Song had assessed the importance of Smith's lifeline, and deployed accordingly. Awaiting the battalion-sized relief column in the hills were three Chinese regiments of the 58th and 60th Divisions.[38] Taskforce Drysdale was driving into odds of nine-to-one against.

Under a low, leaden sky, the snowscape beyond the perimeter was bathed in dense, yellowish light. Ahead of the drab, olive-green vehicles lining up inside the base, the grey road twisted through white lowlands and snow-covered hills. The only signs of civilisation in this melancholic wilderness were the telegraph poles lining the road and the parallel rail track. At 09:30, 29 November, Taskforce Drysdale's lead elements rolled out of Koto.

Eleven miles to Hagaru-ri.

*   *   *

Things started well enough. Brady was at the head of the column on foot with other members of Captain Pat Ovens' assault engineer troop, checking for mines with electronic detectors and metal probes. Just 100 yards beyond Koto was a knocked-out American tank. As the convoy moved past, bursts of small arms fire cracked down from the hills – to be answered immediately by a 15-minute barrage from marine artillery.[39]

Then came the first of what would be greeted by many commandos as their saviours: a USMC air strike. The enemy position, east of the road, was just a mile outside Koto. SBS Marine Jack Edmonds, in the fourth of 41 Commando's vehicles, watched the stubby fighter bombers shriek overhead in shallow dives. Barrels tumbled from the Corsairs' bellies and ploughed into the snow. 'The position where we were coming under fire from was enveloped in a massive ball of flame –100 yards long and 100 yards wide,' Edmonds said. When the oily black smoke cleared, he was surprised to see Chinese ahead in sitting positions: 'There was not a mark on them, no sign of burns on them, at first you thought they were alive, as some others were lying there burning; napalm is a terrible weapon.' Those not roasted alive had been asphyxiated. Commandos concurred with Edmonds' horror of napalm, but were impressed by the Corsair pilots. 'They flew so low, you could see their faces, their accuracy was fantastic,' said O'Brien. After the strike was a momentary silence – then the resumption of shooting from the hills.

On the road, engineers tried to ignore the shots as they continued probing for mines when a US marine beside Brady gasped, 'Look at those motherfuckers go!' Brady looked up. Charging up the hillside to the right of the road – bayonets fixed, green berets standing out against the snow – was 41 Commando in skirmish line. The men were firing and manoeuvring, sections leapfrogging each other at speed, up the slope. Brady felt a surge of pride and affection for his unit.[40] This was the core commandment of mountain warfare: Clear the heights.

In the leading wave was Walter. 'This was the first real attack I'd been involved in and the opposition did not look too formidable, so off we went,' he said. Higher up the hill, the slope steepened. Commandos were scrambling up on hands and knees, when a voice to Walter's right yelled, 'Look out sir!' A rifle was jutting out over a crest just above his head. It was so close, Walter grabbed the barrel and looked into a slit trench with a tiny, one-man tunnel for protection against air burst dug into its wall. A Chinese lay curled in the bottom. 'I called out, "It's alright, he's dead"– then he winked! He'd been feigning death! At that point I should've shot him, he could have had grenades or anything, but he came up looking like Dick Whittington – he had a little hanky on the end of a stick! He did not want his rifle.' The enemy soldier, 'meek and mild', had had enough. He climbed out, and was motioned off down the hill a prisoner. What next?

In the face of airpower and the fast-moving commando assault, enemy resistance had crumbled. The job was done, the hill cleared. SBS Corporal Harry Langton was consolidating, when he was called for a quick O Group. Langton sat down on a boulder. 'It turned out to be a Chinese who had been hit by napalm – he had rolled himself into a ball, he was just a gooey mess, unidentifiable as a human,' said Langton. 'Napalm was effective but very, very bad.'

Commandos filed back down to where B Company was clearing the first roadblock as George Company went in against the second hill. Resistance had stiffened. With sergeants roaring and positions being blasted with a bazooka, Corporal Raymond Todd was reminded of a John Wayne movie. But marines were going down, shouts going up for 'corpsman' – marine medics. One commando considered the marine tactics clumsy. 'The Americans depend a lot on firepower and suffer a lot of casualties,' said O'Brien. 'By going to ground and picking targets, we suffered fewer casualties.' Still, George Company took its hill. As firing died down and dirty smoke drifted up, one incident astonished the men on the road.

41 Commando had overrun an enemy machine gun position in their attack when a single Chinese appeared near George Company and raced toward the crewless weapon. George Company opened fire. The man ran through the fusillade, oblivious. Then he was running across the front of 41 Commando, who also opened up, to no more effect. Hundreds of eyes tracked the lone enemy soldier through rear-sights as he reached the machine gun. When he stopped, commandos found the range. The Chinese jerked violently as he was cut down. A dozen commandos all claimed to have killed him, but Todd admired the lone enemy: 'He was a brave man,' he said.

Though renowned for their camouflage, enemy on the hills were easy to spot. 'We could see the Chinese,' said Payne. 'Some were wearing white camouflage suits, some were in dull khaki. There were a lot of them.' Their visibility meant that Heavy Weapons troop could duel enemy sharpshooters and machine gunners from the road, where Thomas set up a Browning machine gun and bought a position 200 yards up a slope under fire. 'You could see puffs of snow, so you could adjust fire from there,' Thomas said. 'We got the better of them.'

But however inspiring the hillside attacks had appeared, their effectiveness was limited. The taskforce lacked men to remain behind and picket the ridges, so enemy simply rolled with the punches: Walter watched the enemy filtering back after his men had taken the first hill. 'The Chinese were very sensible: They just drifted down, another 500 feet or so,' he said. 'They were not there to hold a position, just potting at us and being in the way. They did not have to chance their arms.' And the attacks had eaten valuable time. 'It had not worked, so we got back down on to the road,' said the big

PTI, Corporal Ron Moyse. 'We realised it was not going to be easy.'

On the road, Brady was dealing with a 'box mine' – a simple wooden box packed with explosives and a pressure detonator, which was crude but effective, for it could not be picked up by a detector and would blow the wheels off a vehicle – when snow around him spurted up. It took him a second or two to realise he was under fire. He dropped prone. Though he could not see where the shooting was coming from, he fired his carbine in the general direction: 'It made me feel a little better to be doing something slightly aggressive rather than just lie there and think of England.' He was astonished when a US marine stood up next to him, and started rapid firing from the hip. 'Get down, you fucking idiot!' Brady bawled. The American looked down at Brady, and informed him that in his position, the only place he could be hit was the head – the most fatal spot. Faced with this logic, Brady was dumbfounded: Had all his tactical training been mistaken? Seconds later, there came a 'fleshy smack' and the American crumpled, his lower leg a tangle of crimson muscle and white bone. He was dragged away, leaving a pool of frozen blood on the snow. 'I had just witnessed the perfect example of a self-inflicted wound administered by the enemy!' thought Brady. The mine dealt with, he remounted. In the truck, Brady was surprised to notice, as he lit a cigarette, that his hands were shaking.[41]

The convoy rolled forward, leaving the hills to the enemy. Shunted off the road was an abandoned truck, victim of an ambush the previous day. Sprawled on its back beside the truck was the corpse of a US marine sergeant. The dead man's face was turned toward the ashen skies, his eye sockets full of snow. 'This was the first time I'd seen a US marine abandoned,' said Todd, who had seen the corps in action at Inchon. 'Usually they would take ridiculous risks to get their dead back. It struck me with some force that we were in a difficult situation.'

* * *

The hill assaults and the stop-start motion as the road was cleared of mines and obstacles ate time. By midday, just 2 miles had been covered and the column was 'still meeting steady opposition from the front and right flanks,' the Commando War Diary stated. Drysdale postponed an attack on the third hill along the road, Hill 1182, and radioed Puller.[42] Puller told him to sit tight: A company of marine tanks had become available. This would grant punch. The armour comprised the seventeen tanks of Captain Bruce Clarke's Dog Company, 1st USMC Tank Battalion. Drysdale would spread the armour in pairs throughout his column, providing both firepower and protection to the soft-skinned vehicles, hopefully keeping adventurous Chinese at a distance.

When the tanks arrived at 13:30 however, Clarke – imbued with cavalry spirit, despite the fact that he was operating in an infantry support–convoy escort role – insisted that his armour operate massed. This was 'a grave tactical error, but since they were not under my direct command, I had to accept the decision,' Drysdale stated.[43]

The tanks clattered up to the column's head. As progress resumed, the order of march was the tanks; George Company; Drysdale and his CP in a jeep; 41 Commando; Baker Company; and the marine support and echelon units. No further attempts would be made to clear the ridges, for the column had to break through by 17:00, when daylight would start to fade. Taskforce Drysdale would use its armoured snout to bludgeon aside the roadblocks, and dash through the enfilade.

With their enemy in plain view, barely fighting back, Chinese fire was getting accurate. 'You'd hear this awful wail: "Corpsman!"' recalled Thomas. The cry would summon an ambulance jeep, threading through the column. 'Bullets were whistling over the top and through the trucks, jeeps were going backward and forward trying to get back with stretcher cases,' said Richards, who had so liked the Chinese he had met in Singapore and Hong Kong. 'It seemed a bit frightening, sometimes they tipped a stretcher over the side – the body was dead.' Payne was unsettled by the increasing racket. 'Bullets would zip here and there, they would rattle into the lorry,' he said. His preconceptions about what combat would be like were off the mark, he realised: 'War films do no justice to the real experience of coming under fire.'

And a new sound was now being heard. A distant thunk; a pause;

then a booming crump, accompanying a fountain of dirty white erupting along the track. Bracketing the convoy, these geysers pelted the men in the back of the trucks with snow and frozen clods of dirt. The Chinese were bringing mortars into action.

At the head of the column, tanks were continually halting – they could not fire accurately on the move – traversing turrets and blasting away at targets moving on the ridges. But every time the tanks stopped to shoot, the entire, three-mile long column behind them concertinaed, with unpleasant results for vehicles that halted opposite an enemy firing point. 'If the tanks stopped to do any shooting it would be the luck of the draw whether your truck stopped in front of Chinese 25 yards away or there were no Chinese there at all,' said Todd. The repeated stops were generating a sense of apprehension and urgency. 'Things had gone pear-shaped,' thought Payne, in the middle of the convoy. 'The front of the convoy was encountering roadblocks, it would stop and start and we were saying, "What the hell? Let's get going!"'

Payne was in the back of an open truck loaded to the gunwales with gear – bed rolls and packs – as well as mortars, machine guns and ammunition. Rounds from the hills cracked overhead and pinged as they ricocheted off the metalwork. Although the shots were sporadic, they were taking effect; men were being hit. Payne glimpsed a casualty, an American sitting beside the road: Half of the man's face had been shot away. 'He was alive – just,' said Payne.

The effect of the temperature on the badly wounded was just one horror Chosin Reservoir had in store. In the cold, blood froze more quickly than it could coagulate, with the result that hideous wounds, which would normally prove fatal did not kill outright. Men with limbs blown off might survive until they reached warmth. Then, once blood started flowing, they had little chance.

Though under constant fire from tanks and Corsairs, the enemy had had plenty of time to dig in and zero his weapons on the road. In the trucks, radios were being wrecked, and units mixed up as men dismounted to take cover, then remounted. Cohesion, command and control – hardly strong points of Taskforce Drysdale, which had been patched together in a matter of hours – was disintegrating.

At 16:00, Drysdale's radio communications broke down completely; not only were his signals put together at short notice, the cold froze the chemical processes that generated electrical current inside the batteries.[44] The column was a mile south of the roadside hamlet of Pusung-ni. Ahead, the valley narrowed. West of the road was the frozen River Changjin, then frosted countryside rising up to hills. To the east, was a railway embankment running parallel to the road, then high ground undulating up to more hills in which the enemy had embedded machine guns and mortars. Over this bleak landscape, daylight was fading and there was not much more than an hour remaining until dusk.

Given imminent darkness, increasing casualties and tortuous progress, Drysdale made the decision to withdraw. At about the same time, a liaison officer from Koto arrived bearing a message from General Smith. It was unequivocal. The relief force's arrival was 'imperative', the message made clear. The column was to break through to Hagaru, 'at all costs'.[45]

'At all costs'– Smith's order was an unusual one for a general commanding troops of a democracy. It dictates, quite simply, that the mission takes precedence over men's lives. It was an order Smith did not deliver lightly, but he had no good option. If Taskforce Drysdale did not break through to Hagaru . . . if the Chinese launched a big attack . . . if Hagaru was overrun . . . the bulk of 1st MARDIV and 31st RCT were doomed. These were stern facts; Drysdale understood them. His response was terse. 'Very well, then,' he said. 'We'll give them a show!'[46]

Word was passed that the taskforce would press onward, smashing its way through every obstacle, hell or bust. 'Our orders were to get on any truck that was moving and get through, we have got to save those at Hagaru,' recalled O'Brien. 'Save them? We were in a bit of a problem ourselves!'

And the protective air patrols were becoming ineffectual: Lacking night-vision equipment, the Corsairs, whose overflights had done so much to keep Chinese heads down, could no longer remain on station. The enemy moved ever closer. 'They potted at us while the light was there,' said Walter. 'But as the light dimmed they got more and more adventurous.' In the gloom, O'Brien could see the Chinese gathering on the hilltops.[47] This alarming development was noted by air reconnaissance, who reported huge enemy units converging upon the road. To the pilots, skimming over masses of Chinese in their white camouflage, it looked as if entire hillsides were in motion.[48]

Night fell over the mountains. The moon rose, glittering on the snow. 'It got dark,' said Moyse. 'Things started to happen.' Ghostly hosts were descending the hillsides, infiltrating the villages, infesting the monsoon ditches beside the road. The death of Taskforce Drysdale – thus far a gradual process of attrition, as a man was picked off here, a truck crippled there – began to accelerate to manic speed.

For the commandos, marines and soldiers, the true nightmare was now beginning.

* * *

What would take place was not a battle, but a 6-mile running night fight, as a series of close-range ambushes flared up at different points along the flanks of the column. The Chinese held all advantages. First, they outnumbered their prey. Second, they were shooting from static positions on the ground – more accurate platforms than moving vehicles. Third, they were low; their enemies on trucks were high. Fourth, they had enfilade; the slow moving, stop-start column was a virtual shooting gallery. Survivors would liken the after-dark action to the massacre in a Western, with settlers firing from covered wagons but being relentlessly whittled down by swarming Indians.

The spearhead of the column – its powerful armoured ram of tanks, followed by the marines of George Company, who retained their cohesion, with Drysdale in his open jeep among them – was fighting furiously as it drove into the first ambushes. A grenade landed in the vehicle of US Marine William Baugh; Baugh dived onto the explosive, sacrificing himself in an act that earned him a posthumous Medal of Honour (one of seventeen to be awarded at Chosin Reservoir).[49] The lead vehicles bore down on a cluster of tents: the marines thought they had finally reached American lines, but the tents were occupied by the Chinese: Another ambush.[50] Drysdale was hit in his jeep when a Chinese hurled a grenade from a ditch, wounding him in the arm.[51] At 19:30,[52] the vanguard of the taskforce crashed into Hagaru: the leading tank rolled over a jeep owned by the marines holding the perimeter roadblock; a second ran out of fuel on the spot.[53] Devoid of armoured muscle, the bulk of 41 Commando and the units further behind, would now bear the full fury of the enemy attacks.

Tripping multiple fire blocks, men were constantly leaping over the sides of trucks to return fire from ditches; one commando landed on top of a group of Chinese, who got up and ran.[54] The priority was to keep moving, even though the road surface was liberally strewn with box mines and satchel charges and grenades were being hurled under passing vehicles. 'It was confusion, chaos, if there was any control at all, it was junior officers and NCOs,' said Moyse. 'People had got on and off trucks, so it was a mix. When you saw a moving truck, you'd try and get on. In the confusion, all you could do was reactionary, firing back, everyone did that on an individual basis.' Yet however shredded their tyres, however, riddled their bodywork, however bent out of shape their chassis, the drivers' task was to keep rolling, squeezing past or shoving aside wrecks in the road.

Visually, the scene was a kaleidoscope of flashes and movement. Muzzles winked and flashed. Green tracers streaked through and over vehicles, ricocheting off bodywork; red tracers zipped back into the darkness, split-second explosions detonated a performance of flashing chaos. 'Lots of explosions, tracers flying about, things on fire, trucks on fire, people running about, people trying to get on trucks,' said Moyse. 'You could see muzzle flashes, and grenades, the blur of somebody running by.'

The cacophony was hellish: the clatter of gears; the roar of engines; the screams of wounded; the boom of explosions; and the relentless crackle of firing. 'I can't put into words the noise, I remember a group of us singing, "We're a shower o' bastards" and firing,' said O'Brien. 'We could see 'em running and darting, blowing bugles, shouting, screaming.'

The taskforce had one advantage: the Chinese, in their white quilts, were more visible in the darkness than the dark khaki of the UNC troops. The enemy were yelling at each other, Moyse noted, but most commandos were keeping quiet, neither panicking nor giving away their positions, just firing away individually. The night fighting training was paying off.

Yet 41 Commando was being gunned down. Moyse was in the back of a truck when it passed a fireblock that let rip as his vehicle passed just 5 yards away. One commando, Royston Woolidge, was immediately killed; others wounded. 'I was sitting on the right-hand side of a truck which was loaded up to the gunwales with kit. We were sitting on the edge, and I was kneeling, and as a result, avoided getting shot through the legs. They raked the side of the truck. D Troop commander Captain "Daddy" Marsh, who had both legs over the side, was shot through both thighs and the guy next to me, "Tanky" Web got shot through the eye; it came out the back of his head he was a mess, an absolute mess.' Moyse attempted to administer morphine to Marsh who was in severe pain, but the officer blew up. 'I'm in charge!' he roared. 'While I have control of my senses, I'll command the situation!'

Walter was in the same truck. 'It doesn't take many wounded in a truck to focus the collective intention to try and help with bandaging and treatment – you rather lose interest in what is happening outside.' Walter's interest was reignited when the vehicle juddered to a standstill; its driver – a prime target – had been hit. Walter was impressed at the man's reaction: 'The truck came to a halt – the US marine driver was extremely good, he halted the truck rather than going into the ditch, and dove into the passenger seat.' But he could not continue driving. Walter crawled into the cab. He had never driven a vehicle before in his life – let alone a truck full of wounded commandos in a close-range, night-time firefight – but this was no time for reticence. 'The driver said, "That thing on the right? Put your foot there and keep it down!"' Walter recalled; he stamped on the accelerator. 'We roared off into the night.'

The commandos were discovering that the opposition's light machine guns and submachine guns were more effective than their own. 'We had a bloke named Claridge who stood in the front of the cab firing a BAR, blazing away, but it was attracting fire to him,' said Edmonds, near the head of the commando's vehicles. 'The Chinese had burp guns and Brens, and the Brens proved better than the BARs.' The enemy was so close that it was possible to make out the details of their weapons; Richards could see Chinese firing a short-nozzle Bren, a more advanced design than the commandos had ever been issued.

Other men were finding that their own small arms lacked stopping power. 'They just poured down the hillside, wherever you looked, they were everywhere, bodies coming at you,' said Langton. The SBS corporal was armed with a .30 calibre carbine, a weapon popular for its light weight, its light ammunition and its automatic option, but its low-velocity round was not doing the job against the adrenalised enemy bound up in multiple layers of gear and clothing. Langton fired at one man – certain he'd hit him, he switched his sights onto another enemy – the Chinese were streaming past – in his peripheral vision, he glimpsed his original target continuing towards him – the corporal pivoted and rapid-fired. 'Eventually he fell,' said Langton. 'I formed the impression that this carbine did not pack enough punch.'

Lieutenant Peter Thomas, had procured a more satisfactory weapon: A Thompson submachine gun, the 'Chicago Typewriter' of the gangster era. Its heavy .45 bullet was a man-stopper, but without tracers, Thomas could not see his fall of fire in the darkness. He was snap-shooting at movement when he heard a crack and felt something whipping at his trousers: A round had passed between his legs. Thomas retaliated with a burst of fire and a blast of swearing that shocked his men; he had previously criticised instructors who used bad language. Thomas impressed one of his troops. 'We were walking alongside the trucks by this waist-high bank at what we called "the marine crouch" – you keep your head down! – and we came to a 20 or 30-yard break in the bank,' Payne said. 'Thomas stood in the centre, enemy were 100 yards away, bullets were coming in thick and fast, and he was standing in full view, encouraging us. I thought that was brilliant.'

A classic leadership lesson taught to British officers is, 'If your men are wet – you should be wetter!' A junior officer's job is to communicate, manage and inspire, but most critically, these tasks need to be done in the thick of things, leading by example. This – and the fact that by concentrating on leading, they are less aware of incoming fire – makes officers high-visibility targets who customarily suffer the highest casualty rates. Such would be the fate of a number of commando officers this night.

When a truck brewed up, it was critical to shove it off the road or it became a de facto roadblock. O'Brien's truck was passing a section of the road where it fell away on the left, when Chinese swarmed down the hillside on the right. He and fellow commandos leapt overboard and fired across the road. 'Chinese were heaving grenades,' he said. 'I saw chaps being blown apart, you'd see his head just go.' A passing driver was hit; as it came to a halt, blocking the road, O'Brien's Troop Commander, Captain Parkinson-Cumine jumped onto the running board and grabbed the steering wheel. 'He shouted "All push, lads!"' said O'Brien. 'We pushed if off the road and it started to trundle left, down the hillside, and I heard him shout, "Back to the road!" – he was a very forceful man.' The commandos scrambled up and resumed shooting. One man was missing: Parkinson-Cumine. As Walter's truck drove by, he caught a split-second glimpse of a prone man attempting to rise – then he was past. If it was Parkinson-Cumine, it was the last time he was seen. 'He saved so many lives,' said O'Brien. 'This is where awards should have been made, but weren't.'

41's medical officer, Surgeon Lieutenant Knock was furiously busy, dashing from casualty to casualty. 'He was a very brave man,' said Richards. 'I saw him jump out of a truck, treat wounded, get hit himself in the leg, but get back in the truck; twice I saw him wounded.' Then Doug Knock himself was killed. Another KIA was Corporal Joe Belsey, the marine who had begged to join 41 despite Drysdale's prohibition on married men: he fell with a bullet in his head.

Todd and his section were having ammunition problems. Their bullets were packed into five-round clips for the old US Springfield rifles, rather than in eight-round clips for the Garands. Lying beside a truck Todd fumbled frantically with numb fingers, transferring rounds from one type of loader into the other, when someone kicked

SCORCHED EARTH, BLACK SNOW

him in the sole of his boot. It was the RSM. Upright in full view of the enemy, ignoring all incoming, Baines was carrying correctly packed ammunition. 'How much do you need?' Baines asked. 'Two bandoleers, please,' Todd answered, adding, 'Don't you think you should be taking cover?' 'When I want your opinion, I'll ask for it!' Baines snarled, and moved on. 'We were under heavy fire and he just ignored it,' Todd said. 'It saved the day.'[55]

But even in the commandos, there were weak links, and combat of the intensity now underway ruthlessly exposed anyone found wanting. 'One corporal panicked and we had to deal with him,' said Moyse. 'Somebody thumped him.'

The column was experiencing in the most literal sense, that phrase beloved of military historians: 'cut up'. 'We were getting chopped up like a snake getting chopped up into little pieces,' said O'Brien. By fragmenting the convoy, the Chinese could cut off and overrun isolated sections. This tactic granted different segments of the column short breathing spaces between one firefight and the next. 'A group 100 yards ahead could be in pitched battle, and your group could be looking around, sizing up the situation, not taking any fire at all,' Todd recalled.

Edmonds was unable to see what was happening to his front, and was annoyed that his section was split between two trucks. His own truck had already lost three drivers, when the Chinese opened fire from the doorways of cottages lining the road 15 yards away. But with the cottages on fire – their thatch ignited by tracer or phosphorous – the enemy were silhouetted. Edmonds spotted a target. 'I could see him in the glow,' the SBS man said. 'I fired and hit him.' Another Chinese ran to assist the casualty. Edmonds killed him. He felt no emotion. For the youthful O'Brien, the action – Chinese and commandos blazing away across the width of the road – was a fearsome ordeal. 'It's not like an atom bomb dropping, this is hand-to-hand fighting, you're fighting for your life, you're killing a chap right opposite you,' he said.

Yet even amid this high-velocity melee were dashes of humour.

Marine Fred Hayhurst was shot in the leg. His truck juddered to a halt; Hayhurst toppled into the monsoon ditch along the road. A commando medic, SBA Bill Stanley, thudded down beside him. The two were close friends. On hearing that his mate was wounded, Stanley told him, 'No favouritism! Sick parade, eight o'clock in the morning!'[56] When firing temporarily eased, Hayhurst was shoved into the back of a truck piled with wounded.

In a lull, Major Dennis Aldridge, the 2I/C, spotted a glove lying on the ground. 'We came under fire, and we were in the ditches and Aldridge, a rum character, picked up this glove and amid all this chaos he was just walking up and down, asking, "Alright, who's lost a glove?"' remembered Edmonds. The show of nonchalance injected a priceless – if temporary – morale boost. And the glove was important, for in the hyper-excitement of combat, few men noticed the cold, but once out of action, its insidious effect would be impossible to ignore and by then, frostbite might already have set in: Thermometers at Hagaru were registering minus 24 degrees that night.[57]

Aldridge proved a tower of strength directing the fighting. 'American fieldcraft was not as good as ours,' said Moyse. 'They'd just stand up and fire.' Moyse watched the commando officer dash over to a US marine standing by the roadside blazing away, and render him prone with a boot to the backside.

Chinese mortars were deadly accurate. One scored a direct hit on 41's ammunition truck. It went up like a shower of fireworks, then blazed furiously, rounds cooking off in every direction. Lance Corporal Gersham Maindonald, the Guernseyman who had been the best recruit, was in a truck immediately behind. He yelled at Baines – who, being responsible for ammunition supply, was nearby – asking permission to try and squeeze past the blaze. It was a risky proposition: The truck could catch fire, or be blown apart by a secondary explosion. Baines assented. The Chinese opened up all around. The American driver inched past, while Maindonald and his mate, Jimmy Pepper, fired ahead with a BAR.[58]

By now, many men had realised that vehicles drew fire. Abandoning trucks they fought through on foot.

Among them was Todd: He and his mates had created a 'foxhole' in the back of their truck by piling stores around themselves and firing from within. Then an enemy machine gun found the range and a burst 'cut straight through'. Two men were killed outright. Todd was shot through the arm. Survivors baled out. Todd noticed groups of men who appeared aimless; a US marine pointed out that they were American soldiers who had no *esprit de corps*. Then Todd was flung down; he'd been hit again, in the chest. Still, he kept on, reaching tents pitched off the road where the spearhead had been shot up earlier. Expecting them to be occupied by Americans he shouted out. Chinese within responded with a fusillade. Todd stumbled back to the road, when a truck jerked up alongside. 'Like a lift, corporal?' a voice asked. It was Maindonald. Momentarily taken aback at the polite enquiry, Todd assented, and was dragged inboard by Pepper. The truck continued to a point where the valley was extremely hilly, with acutely angled cliff faces. Up a re-entrant, Maindonald could see, in the firelight, Chinese massing to attack. He let rip with his BAR, scattering the assault force. Then, just ahead, he heard voices shouting, 'Hi, Limey!' They were inside the perimeter.[59]

Still crashing through the firefights was the Heavy Weapons Troop truck, driven by Saunchegrow. The American Bath and Fumigation corporal had expected only to ferry commandos up to Koto before returning south, but in the hellish gauntlet, he rose to the occasion. His weapons carrier, 'Old Faithful' was riddled. The tarpaulin was shredded, the wooden deck slats in the back shattered from grenades and box mines. Wounded crammed in the back clung to the framework over sleeping bags and packs acting as a temporary floor. On the road ahead, a line of seven trucks was blazing furiously in the night. There was no way past. Saunchegrow swung his steering wheel, juddered off the road, and continued cross-country, rattling and banging over frozen ground.[60]

The truck was a mobile fortress: A machine gun was mounted on the bonnet, while an escort of unwounded commandos led by Thomas jogged along in front of and to the flanks of the vehicle. Ahead, they could see long, yellow-white flashes jetting from the barrels of Hagaru's artillery, but the muzzle flashes could not explain the surreal sight that Hayhurst, lying in the pile of wounded in the back, made out ahead. 'As we approached Hagaru it was like approaching the Blackpool Illuminations; the array of lights seemed to be silhouetting us to enemy fire.'[61] The mysterious lights, so utterly out of place on a night-time battlefield, were like a beacon in a storm, luring the splintered taskforce onward.

Suddenly the truck's flank escort – Thomas' running arrowhead – was challenged; they had run into a marine sentry post. Thomas went forward, grabbed an officer by the hand and blurted, 'I've never been so glad to see an American!' They had made it. The arrivals were informed that they had just driven over a minefield but had been saved by the permafrost, which had hardened the earth to such an extent that there was no give in the ground to trigger the pressure detonators.[62]

Inside the perimeter – there was no trench system, just strong points – it became clear what the lights were. Engineers with bulldozers were using massive arc lights for illumination as they worked round the clock and under the gaze of enemy on the high ground to complete the emergency airstrip. 'It was like being in the middle of Times Square,' said O'Brien. 'Lights noises, people working – it was unbelievable, these Americans with cigars in their mouths were carrying on as if nothing was wrong.'

Saunchegrow's pepper-potted vehicle would be the last into the base. Other groups were arriving on foot. RSM Baines formed one party into a Waterloo-style square, with wounded in the centre, unwounded on the outside to fend off attackers. Among them was Langton, scouting ahead. 'Everywhere was turmoil: flares, gunfire, tracers even Chinese going past us, they appeared to be running toward trucks or running away, or to get their share of booty – I am not sure what was happening,' he said. 'If they came within close range, we fired and moved on.' Baines' group made it in.

Inside the perimeter, Drysdale* had found his way to General Smith's CP. In the operations tent at midnight, by the dim light of the Coleman lamp, the tall officer – green beret on head, iced blood

---

* For his 'courageous action' and 'outstanding leadership' of the Taskforce, Drysdale was awarded the US Silver Star.

dripping from two shrapnel wounds in his arm — saluted and reported to leadership: '41 Commando present for duty!'[63]

In fact, Drysdale's Commando was very much attrited. Trapped behind the leading troops were elements of the Heavy Weapons Troop, Assault Engineers Troop, and the Commando HQ. Mixed up with them were the soldiers of B Company, and a variety of US marine echelon elements. The vehicles still in the valley had now lost all momentum: they were sitting targets.

* * *

Modern warfare is, in many ways, a matter of mathematics. The range, rate and angle of fire of weapons; the quantities of ammunition supplied; the numbers in a certain zone; the killing range and radius; the siting, observation and communications of units; and so on. However, such calculations cannot account for certain factors. One is luck. The other, for which no mathematical formula yet exists, and for which predictive indicators are little help, is the human factor. In desperate circumstances, many persons bow to the inevitable. In identical circumstances, others – notably, trained and motivated men – defy the inevitable; rise to the occasion and battle odds that are, on paper, insurmountable.

Trailing Saunchegrow's vehicle had been Payne. He was shooting down from the back of his truck at countless muzzle flashes winking alongside the road: He could see enemy falling, but was unsure if it was due to his own shooting or someone else's; everyone in the truck was shooting with every available weapon. Things seemed to move in a blur: Payne felt a sense of self-preservation, but no real fear. Programming had taken over; he was returning fire as he had been trained to do. They were halted by something in the road. Then there was 'a terrific bang' – probably a mine or mortar – and the sagging truck shuddered to a halt. Rounds whined into mortar ammunition crates. Fire raked the rear of the 6-6 truck; Payne's friend Joe McCourt was hit by a full burst of fire and killed immediately; a ricochet ripped across Payne's forehead, knocking him temporarily unconscious. He came to seconds later, to find another corporal, Chris Hill, lying dead. (In fact, Hill was badly wounded but would die in captivity). Like many men that night, Payne felt nothing from his wound, the combined cold and adrenalin killed the pain. The truck was finished. Ahead, the track was completely blocked by the burning vehicles Saunchegrow had avoided. Payne leaped to the frozen ground and with five other commandos, fled into the countryside. After a couple of hundred yards, they paused to look over their shoulders. Enemy had come down onto the road to loot the stationary trucks, blazing like funeral pyres. Darting in and out of the darkness, quilted Chinese looked like goblins dancing in the flames.

Payne's small group scrunched through the snow in silence but in the hills, could hear the echoes of movement and the clink of metal on metal of men digging in, or adjusting weapons. The commandos held a whispered conference. Perhaps it was other members of the taskforce who, having abandoned their vehicles, were preparing a defensive position? Warily, they advanced up the hill. As they broke the skyline, a challenge rang out. Chinese. Just two or three yards ahead of them stood a black silhouette, its weapon levelled. Thinking fast, Corporal Joe Cruise responded with a line of gibberish that was obviously not English. With a 'huh?' the enemy soldier hesitated for an instant.

Engaging the man's brain was a brilliant gambit by Cruise, a fatal mistake by the Chinese, for it gave Cruise the instant needed to raise his own weapon and shoot. He could not miss. The enemy soldier tumbled, dead. The commandos dropped prone, anticipating an immediate counterattack. 'The Alamo!' thought Payne, bringing his carbine into his shoulder and laying a Colt .45 on the snow in front of him for last-ditch use. Seconds passed. To his amazement, nothing happened. The commandos scrambled backwards down the hill. Ahead was the frozen river. There was no choice but to cross. Its banks were lined with frozen clusters of reeds, and as the commandos stepped on them, they cracked like gunshots. Then they were on the ice. Payne looked back. Just 100 yards behind, pursuers had appeared. 'Christ Almighty!' Payne thought: They were sitting targets. Yet the Chinese did not shoot; perhaps the commandos were indistinguishable from the dark river. They kept moving as silently as possible, but the ice proved thin. It cracked. One step, two steps, then the water rose over their boot tops and seeped down into their socks. The frigid shock took Payne's breath away, but there was nothing for it but to wade on, climb out of the river and head north. The battle was well behind them, but there were innumerable footprints in the snow. Friend? Enemy? They continued. Payne's water bottle was frozen solid and now the same thing was happening to his feet: he could feel them solidifying into boots of ice. Suddenly a challenge stabbed out of the darkness. The commandos dived instinctively for cover, before realising that the voice –'Who goes there?' – was American. They had reached Hagaru. They yelled back, but the marine guards were not convinced of their identity. The freezing commandos began singing, 'God save the King' as proof of nationality. They were ushered inside the perimeter. They would be the last group of Taskforce Drysdale to make it.

Back on the road, battle raged. Brady had been with three members of his Assault Engineer section when the truck ahead of him exploded; there was an eerie silence, then the sound of whistles signalling a Chinese assault. He and fellow commandos rolled over the side of their truck and into the monsoon ditch just as a volley raked the vehicle. Around him American soldiers were blazing away in response, but Brady could make out no targets in the darkness. Like all commandos, he had been trained in night fighting and knew that wild shooting gives the enemy a muzzle flash to register on. He held his fire, waiting. Shadows ahead. Brady squeezed off a double tap. The response was an intense burst of automatic fire that forced Brady to scrabble even lower. Then Chinese soldiers in quilted uniforms were charging all around him, past him. Overrun! Brady became 'a berserk inhabitant of an abattoir'. He shot down several of the enemy, then whipped out his bayonet and tried to slit it onto his muzzle. To his horror, it would not hold. It took him microseconds to remember that the blade he was fumbling was made for a carbine he had ditched earlier in favour of a rifle. Illuminated by flashes of grenades and tracer, another squad of Chinese charged out of the darkness. One ran straight into Brady. He lashed out with the bayonet he was holding – the blade caught in the enemy's face – the man screamed – then the hilt was wrenched out of Brady's hand as his victim tumbled to the ground.

The attack was past. Sudden silence, then an American voice calling, 'God help me . . . medic! Medic!' Brady was torn between assistance and self-preservation. More fire overhead. Self-preservation won. Rifle cradled in his forearms, Brady crawled frantically forward, though a scatter of bodies. Behind him, someone screamed, 'Surrender! Every man for himself!' Yet another line of Chinese was advancing directly ahead of him. Brady lay as still as he could among the bodies; enemy padded by on both sides of him, intent on the convoy. He continued crawling through the snow. Shooting on the road died down. Looking back, he could see Americans, identifiable by their helmets, jumping down from trucks, hands in the air. He looked for the berets of fellow commandos, but could see none.

He continued toward the silent hills then ahead of him, a dark figure rose from the snow. Brady caught a split-second glimpse of an Asian face, illuminated by the fires from the road, and the motion of throwing. A grenade! Brady was so terrified that he 'would have definitely defecated' had there been time. He tried to bury himself in the snow and counted . . . one, two, three, four . . . nothing. Like many Chinese grenades it was a dud. Brady could not believe his luck. He twisted into a firing position, hardly daring to breathe. 'Where are you, you bastard?' he wondered. About 10 yards away, the enemy broke cover. Brady made out empty hands flailing for balance as the man fled clumsily through the snow: Suddenly, he tumbled. To his astonishment, Brady registered smoke whisping from his own muzzle: He had fired on pure instinct. Slogging through the snow he continued upward; he knew he had to find a lying-up point in the hills before daybreak. He felt desperately lonely.[64]

Geoff King, the Pounds Force veteran, had been firing from the running board of a moving vehicle, when everything went blank. He came round on the road – he was not sure if he had been out for minutes or seconds – temporarily deafened. He heard nothing, just saw enemy faces hurtling forward out of the darkness: 'They were all around us, through us,' he said. Everywhere men were struggling, fighting. Suddenly, he was winded, doubled over by an impact to the stomach. A Chinese had run right into him, spitting him with a bayonet in the abdomen – he was so close King could feel the breath on his face – the Chinese pulled up with his weapon, a disemboweling stroke – King straightened up reflexively, bringing his BAR up into firing position. 'I let him have it!' King said. The Chinese was thrown violently backward by a full magazine. 'I was a Christian, but you have got to destroy what is in front of you,' said King. Then the pain hit: 'It was like someone pushing a stick into my stomach.' The melee passed; his hearing returned. Someone was talking about surrender. Remembering the atrocity he had witnessed in Pounds Force, King was having none of it. He hurled a phosphorous grenade and staggered off, alone, for the hills, praying under his breath. His wound had frozen. Ahead, he heard American voices, but was not sure if they were POWs. He crawled carefully past. They were all armed. He returned to one and tapped him on the shoulder, to be told that he had just come through Hagaru's minefield. He was directed to a dressing station.

In the valley behind, the column had ground to a terminal halt. Some 500 Americans, Britons and South Koreans were trapped among the line of stalled and wrecked vehicles that stood on approximately a mile of road, midway between Koto and Hagaru. These scratch groups formed several pockets of resistance.[65] Compressed into narrow perimeters on, in and under vehicles and in roadside ditches; illuminated by burning vehicles; the desperate survivors of Taskforce Drysdale faced an enemy who surrounded them, outnumbered them and dominated them.

At the rear of the Commando were HQ Troop and the engineers of Captain Pat Ovens. The commandos were mixed up with American soldiers, who were preparing to surrender.[66] Ovens, however, was determined to try to escape. He asked nearby commandos – about twelve men, in the monsoon ditch – if they would join him on his risky venture. Among them was the Scottish commando Andrew Condron, the man who had felt himself fully trained to get out of tight situations. That training would now be tested. 'I didn't have much hesitation,' said Condron in response to

Ovens' enquiry. Condron knew there was no assistance imminent: as a signaller, he had tried several radios, reaching nobody. Ovens led the commandos in a fast crawl along the ditch to a point where there seemed to be no enemy. Ahead, lay snow-covered open ground to the east of the road, but the combination of burning trucks, mortar detonations, sizzling flares and shining moon, lit the area, Condron thought, as brightly as day. The order came to dash across the open ground, one-by-one, at 10-second intervals. The first half a dozen men made it – then they were spotted.

Mortars plunged down, tracers whipped overhead: 'It was a bee's nest!' Condron said. He and the last few commandos ran, dived, crawled, ran again. Making the cover of a dark hill, Condron and two others found that Ovens and his group had disappeared. Ahead, trickled a stream. An NCO, who Condron did not know, led them into the freezing water, but as he rounded a tree growing out of the bank, he jerked back as a shot rang out, tearing through his neck and exiting through his head. Condron and the other commando froze. In the silence following the gunshot, they heard American voices. 'You've shot my mate!' Condron roared, then cursed. The Americans, who had also escaped the road, were apologetic. They had made out a figure, and, not recognising an American helmet had fired. Condron ripped off the man's ID tags and retrieved his pay book. A captain told Condron that he and his group were going to stay where they were until it got light, when hopefully a rescue force would arrive. Condron decided to remain with them. He removed his shoepacs and soaked socks, which he hung from the tree. They immediately froze solid. He rubbed circulation into his feet, wrapped his beret round one foot, his scarf round the other, and replaced his shoepacs. In a few hours it would be dawn.

Trapped on the road with a mixed group was Richards. Earlier, he had piled into a canvas-sided truck, full of Christmas mail. When the convoy had stalled for the last time, someone leapt over the tailgate. Two or three followed him, but the next man to go was shot in midair; a sniper had sighted in. To stay on the truck was suicide. Those left inside whipped out bayonets, slashed through the canvas and tumbled into the ditch like laundry. There, a commando corporal was trying to care for wounded South Koreans and Americans, injecting them with morphine, bandaging. Richards could see the burning trucks blocking the road ahead. Firing at any noise or flashes we could see, he was awed at the noise of incoming fire from many different calibres: 'Czzrrrrr! Crash! Snap!' A night fighter skimmed over the column, dropping a string of flares in its wake. All they did was illuminate marines and commandos for the enemy.

In the same ragged perimeter was Underwood, the commando who had been wary of entering heavy ground combat. Now he was under a crossfire: Tracers were streaking along the length of the road from a promontory ahead, as well as from the flanks. Enemy bugles added an eerie quality to the battle. Mortars thunked from the hills, blasting trucks to scrap. 'It was dreadful, and it was so cold that those wounded under trucks were screaming, they were freezing and dying, but there were no orderlies,' said Underwood. 'There were bodies around, it was pretty hairy. Up till then I had not been scared, but I was terrified then.'

Commandos and marines returned fire with whatever was at hand. Underwood's carbine froze. He grabbed a Garand from a wounded man, and resumed shooting. There were few clear targets: 'We were firing into the unknown.' He was deeply impressed by a group of marines operating a 75mm recoilless rifle. That weapon is essentially a giant bazooka, but while it packed a heavy punch, it also had a terrific back blast which illuminated the crew. Using the flash as their aiming point, the Chinese responded with a fusillade each time the gun fired, hitting a man here, another there. But the Americans continued to step up and serve the weapon, fighting back. 'You go through procedures,' said Underwood. 'We were using what we had.' Leadership was absent: no commando officer in this segment of the convoy had survived. A corporal ordered Underwood, 'Stay here, I'll find out what's happening!' He disappeared, never to return.

But one officer was moving from man to man, group to group, re-positioning, supplying a few extra rounds, urging men to fight on. US Marine Major John McLaughlin had been liaison officer with X Corps assigned to Hagaru; here, he knew that if his group could hold out until daylight, when the marine air would come on-station, they had a chance. But the position was past desperate. His enclave was surrounded, wounded were dying from the cold, and the only means of self-defence – ammunition – was dwindling. By now it was approximately 04:00; there were another two hours to daybreak. Firing was becoming desultory as defenders clicked on empty chambers. An American prisoner, taken down the road, appeared out of the darkness with a message from the Chinese. McLaughlin opted to bluff, telling the man to tell the Chinese that if they surrendered, he would treat them according to the Geneva Convention – and feed them hot food. It was a brave attempt, but a Chinese officer responded that if the pocket did not surrender in 10 minutes, it would be liquidated. McLaughlin tried to stall again, saying he had to sort out his wounded. The Chinese downgraded his offer: five minutes.[67]

McLaughlin moved among survivors, spelling out options. 'He was a good man,' said Underwood. 'He explained the predicament to everybody, he said, "I'll try and get a surrender if we can get medical supplies." He asked me, "What do you want to do: Fight to the last, our position being hopeless, or surrender?"' Realistically, there could be only one answer. 'We threw away the working parts of our weapons,' said Underwood. 'We'd take our chances.'

Firing dwindled. Wary squads of Chinese emerged from the pre-dawn murk. 'We thought they'd be gun-happy,' Richards said, but when he raised his hands, a Chinese soldier pushed them down, saying, 'No, OK, OK!' Some had already been looting trucks; Richards spotted an enemy wearing his own Denison smock – it had his name written on the back. A Commando SBA, seriously wounded, appeared. He wanted a drink, but there was no way he could have one. His jaw had been shot away, leaving him without a mouth. The Chinese placed him in a roadside hut, where he would soon die. In broken English, unwounded prisoners were told that they would be looked after. Then they were herded into groups and marched into the hills. The sky was lightening.

As day broke, the white-clad Chinese battalions south of Hagaru faded into the landscape to avoid early combat air patrols. Seventy-five vehicles – some blackened and smouldering, others in near-perfect working order – jammed the road in a hopeless tangle. In them, beside them, on them and under them, corpses sat and lay among the detritus, frozen like toppled statues.

The valley between Koto and Hagaru bore no name on issue maps, but after the night of 29–30 November 1950, it gained one; a name coined by the leader of 41 Commando himself. It is this name which has gone down in marine legend, denoting the funnel up which 'Taskforce Drysdale' drove, fought and died: 'Hellfire Valley'.

Chapter Eleven

Black Snow

You may come to the moment when you will have to
fight with all the odds against you and only a
precarious chance of survival.

Sir Winston Churchill

Dawn, 30 November. South of Hagaru-ri.

A lone figure in bulky khaki trudged through a white wilderness: Corporal Dave Brady. The commando who had escaped 'Hellfire Valley' was lost among the hills, but as the temperature inched up with sunrise, appetite asserted itself. He sat, dug into a pocket, fished out a tin of rations and cracked it open: frozen fruit. He shovelled it down. Then, in shock from the previous night, exhausted from his exertions and knowing that the hills around were infested with enemy, Brady subsided into a depression in the snow. Common sense and commando training told him this was suicidal in the savage cold, but he was past caring. He curled into a foetal position.

Brady dreamed. In his dream, he was soaring high above the snowscape: a ground attack pilot. Looking down, he saw a figure below: himself. Realisation: He was indistinguishable from a Chinese. Terror of napalm jerked him awake. His subconscious had saved him. He struggled to his feet – then dropped back into the snow.

Figures had appeared on a ridge ahead. 'This is it!' he thought. Then he caught a glimpse of colour: green headgear. Brady's heart jumped. He staggered forward. The big joker – one of the most visible characters in 41 Commando – was recognised instantly, and welcomed by a half a dozen commandos, led by Captain Pat Ovens, his troop commander. But this was no time for a joyous reunion. The group set off through the hills, plodding south, parallel to the road.

Among them was a US marine, shot through the leg; the commandos took it in turns to assist him. Despite his wound, the American remained cheerful, lifting Brady's spirits. The landscape was motionless; only the commandos moved through the silent hills and valleys. A clatter above: A helicopter! The aircraft circled, then began to descend. A hidden machine gun spat a burst of fire – invisible enemy were still wide awake – the helicopter, vulnerable to ground fire, lifted away. Ovens' group walked on. Looking around their faces, Brady was reminded of post-battle photos he had seen: Each man wore a harrowed expression, but Ovens' bloodshot eyes retained a spark of determination.

For hours, they walked. Once again, light began to die. Mindful that darkness would summon the enemy, Brady – no churchgoer – found himself praying. 'Let me survive,' he pleaded under his breath. The religious conversion was interrupted by a metallic click ahead: a weapon. There followed a whispered conversation between Ovens and someone – someone with an American accent. In the gloom, Brady made out holes occupied by marines. It was the Koto perimeter. 'Thank you, God!' Brady exulted. Ovens had led them to safety.[1]

Other members of the Assault Engineer Troop had greeted sunup in different circumstances. Marine Andrew Condron, the Scottish commando separated from Ovens in the chaos, remained huddled among the Americans who had escaped the road. Some had lit fires. By dawn's light, Condron recognised a wounded US marine driver. The man had been shot in the hip, so Condron dragged him over to a fire, cut away his trousers, shook disinfectant powder into the bullet hole, and dressed the wound. Kneeling in the snow, tending the marine, he heard a grunt behind him. Looking round he saw a South Korean in a snow cape. 'This chap was standing there pointing a Thompson at me, so I ignored him,' he said. Another grunt. Condron guessed the man was shell shocked, but was getting fed up; he unslung his own rifle and was about to 'have a go at him' when an American said, 'Hey buddy, you better throw down that rifle – we've surrendered!' The 'South Korean' was a Chinese. Enemy appeared all around. He and the Americans stood glumly around the fires as Chinese relieved them of weapons. Then they were marched off into the hills.

In another desolate group was George Richards, the corporal who had expected to meet only 'stray guerillas' in North Korea. He gazed wistfully skyward. To the north, aircraft were circling, objects dropping from their rears. Parachutes flared as supplies in swaying lines drifted down to the airhead that had been the taskforce's target.

* * *

Those commandos who had battled through to Hagaru – many still coming down from the adrenalin peaks scaled while running the gauntlet – gazed around as dawn illuminated their surroundings. The village-base was as bleak as Koto, but more open to the elements. There was the settlement itself: Several hundred wooden cottages and huts; a handful of brick buildings; a sawmill cutting timber to strengthen defensive positions. Around the buildings were hundreds of grey-green US marine tents, canvas roofs sagging under snow. Equipment – ration boxes, ammunition crates, fuel drums – was heaped everywhere. Radio aerials jutted skyward; elevated artillery barrels pointed at the hills. Splashes of yellow, orange, red, blue and green enlivened the bleakness: parachute silks draped over the terrain. Engineers' bulldozers were still grinding though the snow, dredging the emergency airstrip from the deep-frozen terrain. Dotted all around, on the ridges and the low ground, was a ragged necklace of foxholes, with, among them, stationary, snow-coated tanks, cannons outboard. Looking across the frozen Changjin River, with its stone bridge, was the great bulk of East Hill, dominating Hagaru like an ogre's castle, its crest scoured by the ferocious winds the marines called 'the Siberian Express'.

The outlook remained grim. The break-in through Hellfire Valley had entangled them further in the Chinese net, 11 miles deeper in enemy territory. Hagaru was no sanctuary: it was surrounded, besieged. Germans on the Eastern Front in the Second World War would have dubbed Hagaru a *kessel* – a cauldron. Taskforce Drysdale's survivors had exchanged the frying pan for the fire.

Among those checking the lay of the land was Lieutenant John Walter, the officer whose first driving experience had been the night before. After crashing through into the base, Walter had crashed out in a peasant hut. Beside the hut was a large, marquee-style tent; stacked outside were weapons of every calibre. Walter – armed with the derided carbine that so many men found lacked stopping power in the cold – 'went rummaging', acquiring a Colt .45 and a .45 calibre sub-machine gun. 'A .45 does the job marvellously well,' he said. But it was no armoury that Walter had stumbled upon. Those inside the tent had no further use for their weapons. This was a field hospital.

None of the twenty-five wounded members of 41 Commando at Hagaru would ever forget the medical conditions inside the cauldron. Gordon Payne, who had waded across the river then crunched for hours through the snow on frozen feet, had been taken directly to the dressing station with the rest of his party. 'I could not feel my feet at all,' he said. 'They were absolutely dead.' Stumbling through the frosted canvas flaps and into the tent's dim interior, Payne was taken aback: This was not the well-equipped MASH that UNC troops had come to expect.

Petrol lamps illuminated a Crimean scene. Stretchers were strewn everywhere, piled with young men reclining in various states. In one corner was a jumble of used dressings, crusted with blood and pus. Behind a screen at the end of the tent was the operating theatre. The fuggy heat triggered re-function of iced-up nasal passages, accessing a sickly, rotten stench: gas gangrene. Above all hummed a strange sound: The low keening of scores of agonised men moaning quietly.

Orderlies arrived. Payne's boots were cut away, then socks; the wool had frozen to the flesh of his feet. The rest of his party was undergoing the same treatment. 'We all had frostbite to some degree,' Payne said: his own toes had turned dark blue. But he was not the worst: 'One had all black toes, and the front parts of his feet [were] also black,' Payne recalled. 'He lost all his toes and parts of his feet.' Payne was placed near the stove. In the heat, circulation gradually returned. And with sensation, agony – for in one of nature's cruel ironies, frost burns like fire. 'It was terrible, absolutely painful,' he recalled. 'There was no anaesthetic, they had nothing to give us for pain, just coffee laced with medical alcohol to thin the blood and get circulation going.' Payne's time at the stove did not last. Urgent wounded were carried in from the perimeter. Payne was moved outside, where, on straw among mounds of wounded, he drifted to sleep under an ice-stiff tarpaulin.

Another man outside was Marine Geoff King. Waking up in the dressing station, his memory was a blank, but he had a pad and brace on his stomach; sharp, cramping pain brought back the memory of the Chinese bayonet. Seeing amputations underway, he asked to be taken outside. Bullets cracked in from infiltrators; King, lying wounded, got hold of an M1.

Corporal Raymond Todd, with a round through his right arm and another in his left chest, was helped to a different medical station, in the village schoolhouse. The medics were swamped. For the first time, Todd saw triage in action. 'One man was assessing the wounded,' he said. 'Dead or dying were left outside and eventually moved to a small tent.' Scanning bodies, recognition hit Todd, 'like a kick in the stomach.' One of his best friends, Petty Officer Tate, lay among them. Todd was motioned inside, but only after reluctantly giving up his hand grenades and pistol: 'I thought they were crazy, Chinese were 400 yards away,' he said. He was lifted onto a trestle where, 'they patched me up, enough to keep me alive'. Then he was handed a mug of steaming coffee.

Looking around, Todd winced at the condition of some ROK troops, horribly frostbitten: Their hands were bloated lumps of great black blisters. Nursing his coffee, Todd felt 'quite restful', despite the occasional bullet hitting the outside walls. Friends were at hand. A commando officer shot through both lungs was propped against one wall: he seemed 'quite cheerful'. Later, a Commando SBA arrived and offered to remove the bullet in Todd's chest; the round was visible under a black bruise near a rib. 'I managed to dissuade him,' Todd said. 'I don't think he had the right equipment even though he was keen to have a go.'

One commando ended up on the wrong end of triage. Fred Hayhurst, shot through the leg, had been deposited in a hut by marines, who then departed. Inside was dark and silent. There were no lanterns, no stove. As his eyes accustomed to the gloom, Hayhurst could make out other wounded stacked around him. He started asking questions. Nobody replied. Nobody seemed to be moving. Nor did any orderly arrive. Some time later, the door opened and a head poked in. Hayhurst begged for a drink. The head disappeared as the man took off running. Hayhurst was mystified, until the runner returned, reinforced with two more marines. A torch was thrust into the commando's face. 'You're not supposed to be in here,' a voice drawled. 'This is the morgue!' Every man stacked around him, Hayhurst realised, was dead.

He was taken to a dressing station in a village cottage; mercifully, it was equipped with a cosy Korean underfloor heating system. By now, his leg had completely seized up. A field dressing was clagged on and he was given a tetanus shot but no other treatment was available. 'I just had to sit there and listen to this firing, mortar fire, and everything else going on,' he said.

*   *   *

Other commandos were discovering what close shaves they had had. Jack Edmonds, the SBS man, had slept in a hut with his pack still on. When he awoke, someone drew his attention to it: It had been shredded by a burst of fire but the rations stashed inside had saved him: The frozen tins were embedded with bullets. In the combat chaos, Edmonds had not even felt the impact.

41's morale reasserted itself. 'We felt that whenever things were going well, the Americans were probably better than we were, they had tremendous dash,' said Marine Teddy Allen, the sharpshooter who had made his first kill the previous morning. 'But when things were not going very well, we were better than they were. We didn't lose morale the way they did.'

How many men had cleared Hellfire Valley? This was not yet known. Corporal Ron Moyse found his commanding officer and the RSM sitting on 44-gallon drums in the peasant hut serving as Commando HQ. 'Drysdale asked me, "Where have you come from?" I told him. He said, "How many men were with you?"' Just 125 members of the Commando who had started out from Koto-ri the previous morning – a lifetime away for so many members of the unit – had made it to Hagaru; the unit had suffered sixty-one killed, wounded or missing.[2] Moyse told Drysdale of the losses. For a moment, it looked as if the iron commander's resolution would crack. 'He was nearly in tears,' Moyse said. 'But being the kind of guy he was he pulled himself up; he had to come to terms with it. He was a very strong man.'

Taskforce Drysdale had lost 321 men and 75 vehicles, but its mission had been accomplished: It had reinforced the lynchpin of 1st MARDIV's survival. 'By its partial success, the taskforce made a significant contribution to the holding of Hagaru,' Major General OP Smith would later state. 'To the slender garrison . . . were added a tank company and some 300 seasoned infantry.'[3] The tanks, and the US marines of George Company – the first elements to punch into the base – had been inserted into the perimeter immediately upon arrival.

The decimated commando, reformed into two amalgamated fighting troops, was tasked as garrison mobile reserve, to be used to plug any gaps in the perimeter if the Chinese broke through, as well as for offensive jobs. In a siege, reserve is the critical role. 'A situation like Hagaru required that you had your best in reserve,' said the base's infantry commander, Lieutenant Colonel Thomas Ridge of the 3rd Battalion, First Marines.[4] 'OP Smith knew the strength of Drysdale,' added Lieutenant 'John' Lee Jong-yun, the Korean student assigned to the marines in the summer and now division liaison with local civilians. 'He wanted them in the pivotal section.'

Lee was astounded by the strange new arrivals. 'Usually any unit – regardless of whether they were marines or soldiers – after they engage in severe fighting, they are full of concern, but these were joking with each other,' he said. 'They were real professionals. I thought they'd be half-dead, but they were upright, full of fighting spirit: green berets!'

The commandos' numbers were paltry, yet US marines seemed delighted to see another UNC contingent joining the battle. 'We were welcomed out of all proportion to the benefit they were getting,' said

Walter. 'It was just the feeling of someone on their side.' And one American was formally welcomed to 41 Commando. When Drysdale noticed that US Corporal Don Saunchegrow, who had driven so brilliantly the previous night, was short of kit, he ordered him to outfit himself from the pack of one of the commandos who had not made it; the CO then made him a gift of his own beret.[5]

41 Commando's first day at Hagaru passed. Daylight faded; early winter darkness descended. With it came the murderous cold. Base thermometers dropped to minus 25 degrees. And out of the darkness, came the enemy.

The first indication of impending assault was an unnerving sound beyond the perimeter: clashing cymbals. Then, at 20:15 a bugle blared, and a green flare burst in the sky. Action commenced on the low ground. Rounds from marine tanks ignited a pair of huts; their blaze illuminated charging crowds of attackers. Massed machine gun fire tore across their ranks, leaving lines of dead and wounded on the snow. On the high ground, on an outcrop of East Hill, was positioned Captain Carl Sitter's George Company, the commandos' comrades from Hellfire Valley. The attacking force, visible due to flares sputtering above and seventy drums of blazing aviation fuel ignited by a mortar bomb below, appeared like a 'great shadow' moving over the snow. Marine mortars and artillery blew terrible holes in their ranks.[6] 'There were machine guns and everything firing that night, a mass of light,' said the young Marine Michael O'Brien. 'You don't see a perimeter, you just see pockets of people firing out.' This was now a general attack; Hagaru was being assaulted by elements of two enemy divisions.[7]

In his CP – a peasant cottage with a portrait of Stalin adorning the wall – a pipe-smoking figure stood in the doorway, silently watching the fighting. General OP Smith had moved his base from the lowlands and set up here on 28 November, at the centre of the beleaguered division. The quiet general did not interfere with battle management at the tactical level; Smith let his subordinate commanders carry out their tasks. As the dark hours ticked by, the danger on the East Hill foothold mounted; Sitter's men were being overrun. The garrison reserve was called upon for its first task. 41

Commando's Baker Troop was ordered to counterattack on George's flank and secure Sitter's marines.

* * *

B Troop was considered 41's best sub-unit, an elite within an elite.[8] Lieutenant Gerald Roberts briefed his commandos. 'We were told the Chinese had broken through, they had overrun the position on the hill that overlooked the village,' said Edmonds. 'We were sent up.' Given his numbers – B Troop numbered only thirty-seven men[9] – Roberts opted not to assault in the American style: 'We'll do it the Royal Marines way!' he told his men.[10] Roberts would generate battlefield shock by stealth and surprise; this operation would be stiletto rather than sledgehammer.

The troop spread out into assault lines and advanced silently across the open ground between the village and the objective. It loomed, a great black mass, topped by violent flashes of light where George Company was battling. Approaching, Allen watched green and red tracers crisscrossing overhead in the blackness. 'One was not conscious of being under fire, but you could see it incoming,' he said. 'It was rather beautiful.' As the range closed, Allen's concern mounted: 'I was sort of ridiculously trying to walk closely behind the chap in front, lining him up so he'd be hit first!'

On the hill, Sitter remained in charge, but wounded and anxious: he had no reserves left and the enemy was poised to overrun the remnants of his men. It was now approximately 04:00, 1 December.[11]

Roberts led his men up the steepest spur of the hill, using rock gullies as his avenues of advance. Iced up, these were tricky to climb and the angle of the rock was so abrupt that the commandos approaching the crest were crawling. Tanks below shot cover over the commandos' heads, their fire was so close that the crawling line halted, hugging frosted rock. 'There were tanks firing, we did not know if they were theirs or ours,' said Allen. 'One was just lying there, one froze up completely.' By now the commandos were just below the skyline. O'Brien could hear wounded marines screaming for corpsmen. Leopard-crawling past casualties, he whispered, 'You'll be alright in a minute.'[12] The tank fire lifted. For the commandos on the rock face, the tension wound up to its maximum – then was released. Roberts ordered the assault.

The silent attack went noisy. Sliding and struggling to their feet, the commandos stormed forward, hurling hand grenades and firing on the run. Edmonds watched a fellow commando, Jim Stanley get shot. Stanley spun down with a bullet through the arm – his shooter turned to run – he was gunned down. Few other enemy reacted so effectively. The majority were completely shocked by these attackers who had materialised out of nowhere that they scattered, fleeing before the assault wave.

After the long, dicey approach, the attack had taken mere minutes to clear the position. Roberts' surprise tactic was vindicated: B Troop suffered just three men wounded. Stanley, the gunshot commando – his arm almost torn off by an explosive bullet – was laid on a groundsheet and slid down one of the hillside gullies, 'like a sledge,' recalled Edmonds. The commandos dug in to secure the height. 'All you were doing was scraping in,' said Allen. 'There were trees in front of us, and I am sure I saw someone climbing up, but in the morning it looked completely different, it did not look anything like it had hours earlier.'

With daylight, the commandos and marines saw the gruesome cost of the attacks that had swarmed over George's position throughout the hours of darkness: More than 500 enemy lay dead. 'We pushed them out of foxholes, we just heaved them out,' said O'Brien. 'Within minutes of being killed, they froze solid, so if you had to move a dead Chink, you tipped him over like a piece of wood.'[13] Edmonds found the man who had shot Stanley: 'We'd shot him in the back of the skull, and his brain spilled out of his head,' he said. 'I searched him and found a picture of his wife and kids in front of his house . . .'

But the callousness of combat was taking affect. Edmonds rolled a dead Chinese out of a mountain sleeping bag the man had obviously taken from a dead American. The SBS man had no superstitious compunction that his new possession had been occupied by at least two deceased combatants in the previous night: 'We did not have sleeping bags,' he said simply. 'So we took them.' The enemy fallen were so numerous that the commandos began stacking them into a pile 7 feet high. US marines later erected a lean-to in its lee, huddling in shelter with the frosted faces of dead Chinese peering over their shoulders. So prominent was the stack that it was visible from below; the grisly new feature became a landmark.[14]

The counterattack had been successful, but commandos later learned that disaster had been narrowly averted: No message had been sent signalling the gaining of the objective, so a daylight assault on the hilltop was in the works; airstrikes were just called off when word got down.[15] With the position secure, the base reserve were relieved; the commandos headed back down to the village.

On the way, O'Brien was amazed at the ability of the Americans to dish up what was, by British standards, quality fare while under siege. He was walking past a field kitchen 'like a hot dog stand in a lay-by', when one of the Americans manning it called out, 'Hey Brit!' – the commandos berets made them recognisable – 'You want something to eat?' O'Brien had not eaten a proper meal since Hamhung three days ago, so wandered over. 'What can I have?' he asked. 'We got flapjacks!' the American replied. O'Brien had never heard of them; he was delighted when the cook dished fourteen pancakes onto his makeshift platter of ration pack cardboard, drizzled treacle over the top and shoved a hot coffee into his hand. 'In the middle of everything, they were so organised: A mortar could have blown them asunder, but they were there, talking casually as if they were in Central Park,' O'Brien said. 'The marines were fantastic fighters, there were youngsters there the same age as me; we just smiled, talked and moved on.'

However precarious things seemed for the defenders, Hagaru was proving a furnace for the attackers. In the fight to overcome massed marine firepower on the previous night, the Chinese 58th Division had been burned out.

*   *   *

It is an odd facet of human behaviour that even those facing the most extreme circumstances acclimatise themselves to their lot. So it was at Hagaru. Commandos slipped into the routine of a besieged base.

The Chinese did not attack during daylight hours, but snipers were active. 'It was potluck whether you got hit or not,' said SBS Corporal Harry Langton. Extreme danger bred a disregard for risk and death. O'Brien, queuing in the open with American marines at a field kitchen, noticed that a nearby latrine, a rickety, wooden shack, was riddled with bullets – a sniper had it zeroed – yet marines were still using it. O'Brien was ruminating on this when a shot rang out. A marine in the queue crumpled, the sniper's latest victim. But a stationary tank had spotted the shooter. Its engine roared and the tank jerked into motion, clanked over to a pile of rubble and began rolling back and forth over it, pivoting on its axis. Facing being crushed, the sniper's nerve broke. He broke cover and fled awkwardly through the snow. The metal beast pursued, accelerated and caught him; churning the man under its tracks. 'There was an imprint of him in the snow, like the jokey thing of a steamroller going over him,' said O'Brien, who, with others in the chow line, had watched the fatal drama with mild interest. 'You just carried on eating, "Oh, that's got rid of one."'

The 4-mile perimeter was a line of unconnected holes in the snow. 'When your mate was on sentry, you dropped off to sleep and your feet froze and when you wakened you had to spend 15 minutes getting your feet moving,' said Edmonds. It was critical to regularly get into warming tents or cottages inside the perimeter, but the contrast between external frigidity and interior warmth held its own risks. 'In the huts, there [were] these barrels which were keeping the huts warm, on bricks, glowing red hot,' said Lance Corporal Gersham Maindonald. 'One American came in and said, "Goddamn, it's cold out there!" took his shoepacs and socks off and lay down with his feet toward the barrel. Within a few minutes one smelt burning; the soles of his feet were burning and he did not know it, his feet were so numb.'

There were some tremendous characters among the US marines. Lieutenant Peter Thomas' Heavy Weapons Troop had been taken in by a transport unit commanded by Lieutenant Colonel Olin Beall. 'He was an old fashioned marine with a Springfield rifle,' said Thomas. 'He used to go out, come back and cut another notch in his butt and say, "I got me another Gook today!"' Moyse's section was sent to reinforce a dugout, a large hole with overhead cover – though so widely spaced, a mortar bomb could easily have landed inside; offense-focused US marines were not great builders of defences. The resident was a grizzled marine sergeant. 'He had been there for several days, he had a fire in a tin can, and I thought it was amazing that instead of wearing boots, he had several pairs of thick, white socks on,' Moyse said. The two got talking; the marine was a Guadalcanal veteran. 'He was so calm and collected, we asked about his feet and he said, "I ain't goin' nowhere!"' In front of the dugout, a pair of frozen enemy dead dangled on a thicket of barbed wire, 'almost within reaching distance'. The men settled in for the night. A runner arrived and warned them to prepare to repel cavalry. 'We all said, "What!?"' recalled Moyse. The cavalry – probably supply mules – never appeared but the sergeant was momentarily enthused, telling the commandos he would capture one and ride it out. It was a weak joke but like many men in combat, they found it funnier than it was.

Not all attacks were assaults. 'At one stage an enemy officer – rather smartly dressed in a dark uniform – just walked through,' said Allen. 'He was as bold as brass! Only afterwards did people think he might have been a North Korean.' Probes – some men surmised the Chinese were raiding for supplies – could bypass strong points. 'They'd come in from behind, or from another part of the perimeter; whether they were trying to get out or heading for us, I did not dwell on this,' said Langton, recalling replacing one of his men on sentry. 'One of the lads said to me, "A machine gun followed you all the way here." Tracers had been hitting behind me – I hadn't realised.'

Lee, in charge of Korean porters, shared a tent with General Smith's bodyguard detachment – yet even this, in the centre of the base, was perforated by bullets. 'We were the last unit to guard the HQ, so our personnel were good fighters,' Lee said. 'A couple of Chinese made it to our tent then surrendered: They'd penetrated our perimeter, but knew that they would be killed instantly if they carried on.' Smith kept a pistol belted on at all times. It was no affectation. In a siege in which the perimeter was threatened nightly, even the division commander might have to defend himself.

* * *

The catastrophe overwhelming both Walker's 8th Army and Almond's 10th Corps was by now staring even MacArthur in the face. High Command in Tokyo had conferenced late into the night on 28 November; Almond was ordered to pull back and consolidate, albeit still with a view to somehow assisting Walkers' embattled men in the west.[16] On 29 November, Almond placed all forces in the reservoir area of operations – including 31st RCT – under Smith's command. On 30 November, he ordered the 5th and 7th Marine Regiments at Yudam, and the soldiers of 31st RCT east of the reservoir, to fall back on Hagaru.[17] Once concentrated, the marines and soldiers would fight their way to Koto, down Funchilin Pass into the lowlands, thence to the sea.

News of the disaster in Korea was reaching all branches of the US Armed Forces. The commander of the US Naval Forces in the Far East, Admiral Charles Turner Joy, ordered naval units from across the Pacific to steam for the peninsula with all possible speed.[18] Ploughing through the grey swells of the northern Pacific, a vast American armada converged to support 1st MARDIV's upcoming break for freedom.

Off northeast Korea, prowled Taskforce 77, a swarm of mine-sweepers, destroyers and cruisers, screening the fast US aircraft carriers *Philippine Sea* and *Leyte* and the light carrier *Badoeng Strait;* the fast carrier *Princeton* would arrive on 5 December; the light carrier *Sicily* on 7 December. Even though MIG 15s were now duelling the US Air Force high above the Manchurian–Korean frontier, some 350 aircraft were committed to the Chosin area. The land- and carrier-based squadrons tasked to assist the marines totalled fifteen on 1 December; by 10 December, these had increased to twenty.[19]

With besieged troops demanding ammunition and medical supplies, a massive air bridge was under construction. Every USAF C-119 'Flying Boxcar' in theatre was assigned to operations at Chosin on 1 December. In the skies above the reservoir, the planes orbited. Inside the vibrating cargo bays sat lines of plywood pallets, with parachutes attached, on skaterollers. Given that the perimeters were so restricted, the aircraft's rear, clamshell doors had been removed, granting the USAF quartermasters – 'kickers' – in the back of each plane an awesome view of snow-covered, embattled mountains unfolding below them. Once each aircraft neared the Drop Zone it slowed to 110 knots; when the pilot, in radio communication with ACTs on the ground, sounded the alarm, the kickers sliced through a sling restraining the pallets, and the bundle tumbled out of the aircraft belly in six seconds, parachutes billowing. Between 1 and 6 December, 238 C-119 sorties dropped 970.6 tons of cargo.[20]

The eyes of the world were now focused on the bleak little mountain settlement, but previously Hagaru had been an overlooked backwater in the communist republic. This isolation had made it a sanctuary for a certain group. 'Some Christians had escaped to Changjin from the Japanese,' said Lee; the community had practised their forbidden religion despite Hirohito's, and later Kim Il-sung's, strictures against it. After the marines arrived, they had begun openly holding services. Their salvation was being cut short. With the marines preparing to depart, the population of Hagaru decided to abandon their homes, taking their chances on the perilous retreat to the sea. Lee was dismayed at the suffering this would entail. 'God is too harsh,' he said.

* * *

The first stage of the withdrawal – the pullback of the 5th and 7th Marines and the 31st Regimental Combat Team to Hagaru – got underway on 1 December.

By this time, the US Army unit east of the reservoir, was crumbling. With its CO, Lieutenant Colonel Allen MacLean lost, Lieutenant Colonel Don Faith assumed command. Leaving aside training and motivation, the RCT was already weaker than its marine equivalents. Approximately one third of its men were half-trained Koreans who spoke little or no English. When Faith gave the order to break out, artillery and vehicles were blown up; the RCT would keep only twenty-two runners to transport their 600 wounded. The column hit resistance as soon as they moved beyond their perimeter, and the covering aircraft drenched the front of their column with napalm. Faith personally led a charge on a roadblock; he was wounded, and soon died. He had hurled away a Silver Star in his fury at High Command's indifference to his unit's predicament; for his leadership, he was awarded a posthumous Medal of Honour. The column struggled on to the hamlet of Hudong-ri, half way to Hagaru, to find it occupied by enemy in strength. In despair, vehicles tried to crash through, but were raked and halted. The RCT disintegrated. It had occupied the attention, for three nights, of two Chinese divisions that could otherwise have joined the assault on Hagaru. The cost had been horrific. Originally 2,500-men strong, just over 1,000 men made it to Hagaru; of those, only 385 were found combat effective; they were formed into a provisional battalion.[21] 31st RCT had been virtually wiped out.*

The 5th and 7th Marine Regiments were a tougher proposition. Surrounded by three divisions, they had been fighting ferociously at Yudam since the night of 27 November. On 1 December, they began their 14-mile breakout toward Hagaru, down what Colonel Raymond Murray, the 5th Marines' CO, called 'a nightmare alley'.[22] This would not replicate 2nd Infantry Division's motorised race into disaster at Kunu-ri; this was a tactical move. The column was led by a lone tank, flanked by marine companies fighting along the ridgelines and shepherded overhead by US Marine Corsair squadrons and the Royal Australian Air Force's Mustangs. Painstakingly, marines cleared high ground, jury-rigged blown bridges and smashed aside roadblocks. In a brilliant feat of soldiering, Lieutenant Colonel Ray Davis, led his 1st Battalion, 7th Marines, cross-country through knee-deep snow to relieve a lone company holding the key Toktong pass that overlooked the road. In an epic private battle, the 237 men of Fox Company, 2nd Battalion, 7th Marines, surrounded on a hilltop, had been under siege since the first night of battle; when

---

* The ill-fated 31st RCT has become known to posterity as 'Taskforce Faith'. The latter designation, however, was not in use at the time.

Davies' men arrived on 2 December, Fox was reduced to eighty-six effectives.[23] Their position was encircled by enemy dead. One survivor could not avoid walking over a 50-yard wide carpet of Chinese corpses as he abandoned the hill.[24]

The 5th and 7th Marines were expected to make Hagaru on 3 December; their 14-mile breakout had taken nearly 48 hours. At 16:30, the garrison reserve was ordered to advance to Hagaru's northern roadblock to link up with the column and cover it in.

The commandos and tanks took up defensive positions. Darkness fell. Nobody arrived. Then, emerging out of the gloom, the convoy's point element appeared. 'I had never seen anything so dreadful,' said Walter. Jeeps and trucks, crammed with wounded and dead – the two regiments had 1,500 casualties – dripped bloody icicles. For want of space on vehicles, frozen dead were lashed across bonnets and dangled from artillery barrels. The living were wide-eyed, slack-jawed, gaunt, unshaven. 'Talk about the retreat from Moscow!' said Allen. 'Some had straw round their feet, they looked totally defeated.' Wounded were hanging 'like grim death' to trundling vehicles.

But their spirit was unbroken: The 5th and 7th Marines' entrance to Hagaru would become a Korean War legend. 'They'd been through it, they'd been hammered, but they came out carrying their wounded and their weapons,' Moyse said. 'Pretty good.' Approaching the perimeter, some marched in singing *The Marine Hymn*. Thomas, deeply moved, wondered whether 41 Commando should transition from covering force to honour guard. 'We should have presented arms,' he said. 'They were magnificent!'

The Americans were surprised at the identity of their greeters. 'Thank God we're not the only guys fighting this goddamned war!' one told Thomas. 'Their spirits were lifted when they saw us,' said Moyse. 'They thought we were mad to wear berets!' Commandos were detailed to assist the wounded, a group of whom had been secured with cord. A commando cut loose one man and gave him a cigarette. 'Harry, give me a hand, they got this fucking Yank tied up for Christmas!' he remarked to a mate. 'It sure felt good to know these people were on our side,' was the wounded marine's comment.[25] Inside the base, the unwounded new arrivals settled into positions alongside the commandos. 'They bow to no man in the bloody business of the foxhole,' one US marine wrote of the commandos.[26]

Field kitchens fed the arrivals a hot meal; Hagaru marines who knew men in the 5th and 7th regiments approached them to ask about the fate of buddies. Many would receive bad news. The most relieved man to see his haggard regiments, though, was their divisional commander. Watching them arrive, Smith wrote, was 'quite an emotional experience'.[27] Some members of the 5th and 7th had been stunned to see what looked like thousands of dead Chinese heaped outside Hagaru's perimeter.[28] Having escaped Yudam, they had hoped Hagaru would be a haven. In fact, they had just escaped the first link in the trap.

On 4 December, 41 Commando went out again, accompanied by marine engineers. The commandos clambered onto snow-covered tanks – their armour was frozen but their engines pleasantly warm – which clattered past the northern roadblock, out of the perimeter. Mounted on one steel beast was Langton. The treads of the tank in front were churning up shards of ice from the road, which lashed him in the face, but he could not raise a hand; he was too busy hanging on. Chinese were visible in the distance, but did not attack. The commando rode into the wasteland to where, up the track, 5th and 7th Marines had abandoned eight 155mm howitzers when their prime movers ran out of fuel. Arriving at the guns, commandos spread out: 'It was merely a question of being a protection party,' Moyse recalled. The artillery, engineers discovered, was unrecoverable. The party remounted on the tanks as Chinese began appearing over ridges. As the little convoy churned back to Hagaru, an air strike roared in to destroy the guns.

* * *

At Hagaru, the engineers' work was paying off. A trickle of wounded had been escaping the siege, flying down to the lowlands, in light observation planes. Among them were Payne and Todd. Payne was told, 'You are getting out!' He was taken to the landing strip where a one-seater scout plane crouched. The canopy swung open and Payne – armed with a carbine and a .45 pistol under his parka – was crammed into the space behind the pilot's seat. The plane shook and bucked as it picked up speed, then lurched into the air and away over the hills. 'I was fully expecting to stay there recovering then join what was left of the commando,' Payne said. 'The reaction was relief but also shock – of the suddenness in which it happened.'

Todd had a similar experience. While B Troop had been fighting up East Hill, the Chinese skirmished close to the aid post. The following morning the commando was asked if he wanted to be evacuated: Single-seaters could get in. Todd agreed, so was stretchered out to the airstrip, where a small plane was waiting. 'The chap flying was a dentist from Tokyo, a major or a colonel and he told me he had a private pilot's licence and they had brought in all these kinds of people, anyone who could fly, for this evacuation,' he said. 'He was quite a cheery chap.' Todd crouched behind the pilot's seat: 'We had to wait as Chinese had infiltrated the airstrip.' Marines counterattacked, then the plane climbed up, giving Todd a last chance to see 41. 'Whilst he was banking he said, "Have a look at your boys down there".' 'We could see lines of marines clearing the hills.'

King was awaiting air-evac' with a friend when he felt 'as if someone had hit me with a bat'. A mortar had burst, sending a piece of shrapnel into his un-helmeted scalp. Both he and his friend were covered in blood – head wounds bleed heavily – but the man helped him up onto the evacuation plane. When he came round, he was in a hospital in Japan, being offered an American purple heart.

But the massive numbers of wounded required bigger transports. With Hagaru lying 4,000 feet above sea level, manuals demanded a minimum runway of 7,600 feet to accommodate C-47s.[29] On 30 November, it still measured only 2,500 by 50 feet; moreover, it had a hump at one end and a 25-foot dyke at the other.[30] Yet – though the strip was unfinished; though its 'control tower' was a jeep with a radio – Smith decided, on 30 November, to chance large aircraft.[31] Among those scheduled for one of the first flights was the leg-shot Hayhurst.

He was driven by vehicle to the airstrip, then lined up to board the next aircraft, a C47, the famous 'Dakota' transport. 'When we started moving toward the aircraft, a group of us were stopped, and they said, "No, there are people on stretchers and they were going on," and they were put on,' he said. 'We were not too happy.' The stretcher cases were loaded, the aircraft's rear door slammed. Its props hummed, then it turned, gathered speed down the icy runway, wobbled into the air – and flew directly into the hillside ahead.

Hayhurst was stunned. Marine squads raced to rescue survivors. But there was no time to lose. The next aircraft taxied up. Hayhurst and the wounded around him were loaded – with trepidation – into the C47's belly. It raced down the strip, lifted, and cleared the wall of mountains. The besieged base receded. Relief. Twenty minutes later, Hayhurst landed at Hamhung.[32]

The air bridge was in place. From 1 December, a full-scale lift got underway: It would carry 4,312 wounded and frostbitten men, including 25 commandos [33] to safety.[34] Remarkably, only two C-47s were lost. At Smith's insistence, 138 marine dead were also flown out. X Corps ordered him to cease the funeral arrangements; Smith 'didn't pay them any attention'.[35]

The chance to end the ordeal was too much for some: It became necessary to screen evacuees when some men were caught feigning wounds in order to escape.[36] There was no doubt of the state of many wounded, though; when the four-day evacuation was complete, the ground between the main aid post and the landing strip was a sheen of frozen blood.[37]

And traffic was not one-way: 537 marine volunteers from echelons in the lowlands and Japan were flown in to reinforce the decimated ranks of the combat units 'up at the reservoir'.[38] Necessary supplies were also flown in, including, for some reason known only to a quartermaster far in the rear, a shipment of condoms.[39]

With the Hagaru strip operational, the USAF proposed flying out the entire garrison. Smith declined, but it was not pride on the part of the marine general.[40] Once the garrison's manpower was reduced to a certain size, a tipping point would inevitably be reached, and the rearguard would be overrun. Smith was determined to get his entire command – heavy weapons and equipment intact – out.

The addition of the 5th and 7th Regiments, and the incoming reinforcements, boosted Smith's decimated companies, but did not alter 1st MARDIV's overall strategic position. Nobody needed a situation map – maps that were by now crisscrossed with red arrows – to understand that; the position was clear to anyone who gazed beyond the perimeter of the fortified airhead. 'We were completely entrapped, an island in a sea of Chinese,' said Lee. 'In the mountains we could see people on top, and we could see the smoke from their cooking fires.'

On 5 December, Almond flew into Hagaru as Smith's staff presented plans for the breakout from the mountain arena. The movement – 56 miles from Hagaru to Hungnam – would commence on 6 December. The Hagaru garrison would fight south in a moving pocket. Infantry would lead the way; other companies would clear the heights. Soft-skinned vehicles would drive loaded with gear, wounded and dead. Hellfire Valley's lesson had been learned: tanks would be spread through the column for fire support, while bulldozers on point would smash aside roadblocks. Overhead, twenty-four fighter bombers would orbit.[41] But air support could not trump ground fighting. When Almond told Smith that he had arranged for bombers to 'clear a path for you all the way to the sea', Smith responded: 'I think there will be plenty of fighting for all of us.'[42]

The 7th Marines would spearhead on 6 December; the 5th Marines would rearguard on the 7 December. 41 Commando was assigned to the 5th Marines. Smith himself would fly his CP to join Puller, and control operations from Koto. Once the 5th, 7th and 41 Commando joined Puller's 1st Marines, the concentrated division would strike south.

The obstacles facing the breakout were daunting. The 5th and 7th Marines had had to fight, mile by mile, from Yudam, and 41 Commando had to run the Chinese gauntlet in Hellfire Valley – the same 11-mile route that led from Hagaru to Koto. Then, to exit the highlands, the escape hatch led through Funchilin Pass. The winding, narrow, 10-mile track carved into the cliffs was custom-made for ambush.

* * *

If the troops' outlook was grim, the prospects for anti-communist civilians were equally frightening. Though official information sources were silent, word of the defeat of the UNC and the communist descent through the mountains was reaching the lowlands.

'We knew, through the grapevine, that something terrible had happened,' said Lim Geum-sook, the 19-year-old girl who had hidden in a bunker dug in a cemetery prior to the arrival of UNC troops. 'Every day, people were passing through and they talked: news spread fast.' The teenager was astonished that the UNC – 'the most modern troops' – were retreating. 'We knew the Chinese were approaching,' she said. 'The fear, the impact, was so great.'

Most of Lim's staunchly anti-communist family had departed for the south in previous weeks after her older brother had volunteered for the ROK Army. The only members remaining in Hamhung were Lim's parents and her 13-year-old brother. The family decided to escape. Precious goods – fabrics and jewellery – and provisions – rice, red pepper paste and power – were boxed. The family bundled on all their winter clothes and left a home they would never see again. At Hamhung Station they hoped to catch a train for the coast, but chaos reigned, and soldiers prevented civilians from boarding. 'They were saying, "Get away! Hamhung is safe!"' Lim said. She did not believe them. Trains were reserved for military personnel, and, she guessed, for those with connections. The station doors were slammed.

Korean civilians were not the only ones growing aware of the situation around the reservoir; the high drama was not lost on editors around the world. On 4 December, Peking Radio announced: 'The annihilation of the United States 1st Marine Division is only a matter of time.'[43] British and American newspapers did not demur. A Philadelphia columnist wrote that the marines were being 'sliced to ribbons'.[44] Marines were unimpressed by press statements from High Command, which evidenced little faith in their survival.[45]

On 5 December, that would change, for the airlift brought journalists to Smith's CP, and it was one of those who provided Smith with the phrase that would not only re-animate the battered spirits of his own men, but would brand the breakout for posterity.

Smith was asked by a British correspondent if his division was retreating. The general explained patiently that this could not be a retreat: 'Heck, all we're doing is attacking in a different direction,' he said. The quote somehow morphed into, 'Retreat – hell!' It was seized upon as bold defiance of overwhelming odds. Marines were electrified, and the phrase blazed across US headlines.[46] Eleven miles south, Puller also rose to the occasion. When doubts were raised by his staff, he leapt onto a table. 'I don't give a good goddam how many Chinese laundrymen there are between us and Hungnam!' he roared. 'There aren't enough in the world to stop a marine regiment going where it wants to go!'[47]

Fighting words may read like hyperbole, but in desperate situations, theatrics like Puller's are motivational. And Smith was no drama queen; his statement was factual. 'There was no word of withdrawal,' said Smith of his breakout orders. 'That was an attack order because we were attacking, and we gave them objectives to capture enroute.'[48]

1st MARDIV would have to hack its way through everything the enemy could throw in its path. Two Chinese regiments, spearheading a fresh corps from Manchuria, were arriving to reinforce General Song at the reservoir.[49] Song himself was manoeuvring: He ordered the 76th and 77th Divisions to block the route between Hagaru and Koto, while his 60th and 89th Divisions massed around Koto and took up positions overlooking Funchilin.[50]

It was amid the soaring cliffs of the pass that Song pulled off his masterpiece – a spectacle worthy of a Hollywood cliffhanger: Chinese infiltrators blew the bridge in front of the power station. Even if they fought through 11 miles of enemy-held hills from Hagaru to Koto, 1st MARDIV's escape route to the lowlands led not to safety, but to an abyss 2,900 feet deep, over rock, ice and snow. The division's rat run was now a rat trap.

The situation, 1st MARDIV's operations officer thought, was 'not promising'.[51] yet intelligence about the blown bridge did not delay the breakout. On 5 December, flames flickered through snow flurries as Hagaru-ri was put to the torch. Among the stores being hurled onto bonfires were piles of marine dress uniforms; why they were at

Hagaru was anyone's guess.[52] Vehicles were loaded. Remarkably, Corporal Don Saunchegrow's truck – its bodywork shot to pieces – was still a runner. The vehicle, christened 'Old Faithful' would comprise, along with Drysdale's jeep, 41 Commando's sole load-carrying vehicles; the US marine corporal, posted as missing by his own unit, elected to remain with 'the crazy Brits'.[53] On 6 December, the breakout began as 7th Marines attacked toward Koto. That afternoon, the radio relay station at Hagaru – the base's link with the outside world – was closed. The air bridge shut down. Smith helicoptered for Koto.[54]

* * *

Dusk, 6 December. General Song had smashed 31st RCT, but the 5th and 7th Marines had slipped through his grasp at Yudam. Now, the situation was being repeated at Hagaru. With the 7th Marines having jumped off south, the force at Hagaru was halved. A key military principal is: 'Fix the enemy in position. Then destroy him.' Song was determined to exterminate the marines before they could escape his clutches again.

Some time after 16:00, 41 Commando had joined the column and started toward Koto. Reports were negative: The 7th Marines vanguard was engaged in heavy combat. Soon after 19:00 sounds of fighting to their rear reached them; the commandos had barely advanced 400 yards. The situation was deteriorating. 'About 21:00 hrs . . . a heavy attack on Hagaru developed,' 41 Commando's war diary noted. 'By midnight . . . the position at Hagaru was looking a bit sticky . . . soon after this, 41 Commando were recalled and were committed to the perimeter.' The commandos were deployed near the stone bridge under East Hill to help repel the last and greatest Chinese attack on the base. The events of the night of 6–7 December would be described by the US Marine history as 'spectacular'.

For the marines and commandos manning the Hagaru perimeter, straining to see in the darkness, the first indication was bugles sounding as the invisible enemy manoeuvred. Bursts of firing crackled here or there on the perimeter: probes. Then – illuminated by flares and burning buildings – the ghostly, white-clad masses emerged from the darkness, rolling forward: a wall of men. 'You could see hordes of them on the skyline – literally hordes! – like a Western when you see Indians suddenly appear on the hilltops,' said Maindonald. 'You just waited for the bugle as you knew then they were forcing their attack home.'

If the Chinese assault was cinematic, the American response was operatic. As the perimeter lacked obstacles – mines were invalidated by the permafrost; barbed wire was minimal; field fortifications poorly constructed – defence depended upon firepower. Positions lit up with laser-like streaks of machine gun tracers, their chatter a relentless popping crackle; mortars and artillery dropped DF tasks with flashing crumps; tanks rocked back on their suspensions as they fired out. Invisible in the darkness overhead, American night fighters droned, guided onto enemy concentrations by parachute flares fired by the artillery, or by solid lines of red tracer from heavy machine guns – their crossfire marking bomb aiming points – then adjusted by radio from ACTs. 'They had a very slick system of fire control,' said Thomas, awed by the god-like firestorm the Americans were summoning from the skies. 'Imagine a hill with these figures all over it coming down with a background of white snow, lit up by flares, by tracers going up in the air,' recalled Langton. 'Fireworks night!'

Still – incredibly – the crowds surged in.

Those enemy who made it through the beaten zone of marine heavy weapons had a better chance, as the cold affected the propellants – and so the muzzle velocity and knockdown power – of small arms. Weapons work was intense: shooting, reloading, clearing stoppages, giving or responding to fire commands. 'You got engulfed with Chinese attacks, literally masses in the dark,' O'Brien said. 'You are firing into hordes of them, they are falling down and another lot come on.'

The main attack hit the marines on East Hill, but the commandos caught the flank of the attack. Edmonds watched Chinese hit three or four times, yet – as if in a nightmare – continue advancing. This was not all-arms warfare, or even fire and manoeuvre: the Chinese approach was simply mass. Echeloned units charging over the bodies of their comrades to swamp the defenders. The enemy numbers necessitated the shelving of the commandos' precision shooting, in favour of more profligate American drills. 'It is not like on a rifle range where you took careful aim,' said Langton. 'The only thing that would beat the enemy was firepower, so you would not aim with one round, you would let two, three or four go at one target before you switched to the next: bang-bang-bang!' Men armed with semiautomatic weapons found themselves suffering an unusual ache: trigger finger fatigue.[55]

In winter darkness, it was impossible to see the foresights of weapons, so commandos loaded every third or fourth round with tracer to mark their fire. With the frozen Changjin in front of his position, Langton squeezed off bursts onto the surface of the river with his BAR: the ice was so hard, the bullets ricocheted up into the enemies' lower bodies.[56] Moyse's section was forced into cover behind a wall of what turned out to be frozen excrement. His night vision was useless; he could see no individual targets to pinpoint. All that was visible was a violent, flashing kaleidoscope.

The marines and commandos were fuelled by a potent blend of adrenalin and caffeine from black coffee, but the astonishing courage of their attackers – and their apparent ability to absorb several rounds before collapsing – led many defenders to conclude that they were doped. 'It was said that a lot were fighting under influence of drugs,' said Maindonald. 'They certainly must have had something to spur them on.' Benzedrine – a stimulant – and opium – probably a pain-killer – were, indeed, recovered from some corpses. But there was another motivation driving this incredible assault: the cruel cold and feeble Chinese logistics. The enemy knew the Americans had food, heating equipment and warm clothing and boots. If they could take Hagaru before the dumps were fired, that loot would be theirs.

They were generally poor shots, but were taking an inevitable toll. In lulls, commandos and marines whispered in low voices. 'We were fighting to survive, you were laid shoulder to shoulder on the ground, a New Yorker speaking to a Cockney,' recalled O'Brien.'The conversation was not about the war, it was about anything but. In a quiet moment, you'd say, "Where you from?" and he'd say

"Nebraska" and next thing he's lying dead, his head blown off.'

As dawn broke over East Hill's crags on 7 December, the attack dwindled away. Charging into the teeth of the defences, the attackers had been slaughtered. 'It was amazing and frightening to find Chinese dead within 3, 4 or 5 yards. You'd seen a silhouette and fired,' said Maindonald. 'If we had not stopped them, they would have been right in amongst us.' Langton's ricochet fire had proven effective. '[The Chinese] had died in all sorts of positions – the severe cold must have frozen them as they dropped,' he said. The 5th Marines' CO, Colonel Raymond Murray, walked along the lines that morning. Though he had fought the Japanese on Guam and Saipan, he had never seen so many enemy dead.[57]

It was time to move out. Once again, Drysdale paraded his men, checking weapons, appearance, clothing. Once again, watching American marines were astounded. Orders were delivered. The only persons to be allowed on vehicles were the wounded, the dead and the drivers. Everyone else – including those wounded in the arms – had to walk.[58] The parade broke up. For the first – and almost certainly the last – time in the village's history, Hagaru was serenaded with, 'We're a Shower o' Bastards.' Then the commandos separated into their sections for the breakout.

Nothing was being left for the Chinese, neither equipment, nor shelter. Yudam had been obliterated by artillery as soon as the 5th and 7th had withdrawn.[59] Even the wreckage of 31st RCT's truck column – complete with dead aboard – had been incinerated by napalm on Almond's orders.[60] Now, as the rearguard headed for Koto, Hagaru and its supply dumps blew up: the firework-like explosions reminded some marines of 4 July.[61] As well as the supply dumps, wrecked aircraft were destroyed, the timber village torched. Through billows of snow, the shadowy figures of marines were silhouetted against yellow flames dancing across the dark wood of buildings. Hagaru-ri was scorched off the map.

The commandos were among the last of the 5th Marines to leave. Chinese had infiltrated a small hill inside the perimeter, and at daybreak they tried to escape. Corporal Jerry Maill, Heavy Weapons Troop's ace machine gunner, opened up with long bursts, tumbling them down in the snow, Thomas recalled. By the time Maill was finished, he had burned out the barrel of his weapon, firing cover while vehicles pulled out.[62]

By now, some commandos, samurai-like, had accepted the inevitability of death. 'I think I became resigned that I'd had it: I'd be killed,' Langton, the SBS corporal, said. 'I can't say I welcomed it, but I was not frightened, you just felt: "We are not going to get out of here." I was not ready to surrender. The end to me would be the end.'

* * *

On either side of the grey ribbon of road, loomed the snow-covered hills, stubbled here and there with scraggy forest. Beyond, rose the glittering bulk of the mountains. Having cleared the blazing pyre of Hagaru, the column began passing a long tangle of wrecked trucks and jeeps, shoved off the road by the 7th Marines the previous day. Among this blackened monument to Taskforce Drysdale were wrecked men, too. The marines and commandos were now entering a nightmare wonderland, for battle in Siberian temperatures had transformed Hellfire Valley into a surreal gallery of cartoonish monstrosities, of hideous grotesqueries.

In normal circumstances – even allowing for the rigidity of rigor mortis – tensile integrity deserts corpses, gives them their rag-doll appearance as they lie sprawled or flat. Not so at Chosin Reservoir. Here, the bodies – like victims of an icy Pompeii – had frozen into rigid postures, limbs sticking out at peculiar angles: 'stiffs' in every sense of the word. Even though the corpses had been lying in the valley for six days and nights, they looked freshly killed, Moyse thought. Some tableaux were reminiscent of an abattoir: spilled blood had not coagulated to its usual brownish scab, but frozen into streams and puddles of crimson. The feelings and emotions that the men had been undergoing at their moment of death – shock, terror, agony – remained frozen in their faces. O'Brien recognised some. They were 'terrible to see', lying, trouserless, with their feet up in the air where the Chinese had stripped them to clothe themselves; their legs had frozen in the extended position. Edmonds spotted a commando he had once served with on HMS *Sheffield*; his corpse was frozen 'absolutely solid'. There were greater indignities. The Korean interpreter, Lieutenant Lee, could not help noticing how many corpses displayed signs of having soiled themselves. And Allen passed a marine who had been sniped while defecating. Dead, trousers round his ankles, he squatted at the side of the track, a frozen sentinel.

Scattered among the wreckage and the dead were letters and brightly wrapped Christmas gifts from the blown-up mail truck; Thomas found the sight pathetic. The necessity to break south as fast as possible meant there was no time to properly police up the slaughter. Dead marines were heaved onto trucks for later burial. Bodies were impossible to stack in any order. 'There were people twisted and in agonised positions, it was grotesque,' said Moyse. 'Some had bullet holes in their bodies and faces, but others, you would not know they had been shot.' With crooked arms and legs jutting over their tailgates, the trundling hearses appeared to be conveying a cargo of butchered waxworks. Still, at least the marines took pains to carry their own out. In an unusually callous example of inter-service rivalry, a number of army corpses were left *in situ* by the marines.[63]

Chinese dead fared worse of all. Enemy bodies, rolled over again and again by tanks and trucks, were flattened; straw stuffed into their uniforms for insulation made them look like dead scarecrows. Oddly, on these one-dimensional corpses, Walter noted that individual facial features on 'foot-and-a-half wide heads' were recognisable. Enemy carrion not steamrollered flat into the surface of the track was booted into the parallel ditches, though some offered an opportunity for marine humour. Moyse passed a roasted Chinese corpse that, like many victims of extreme heat, had contorted, due to the shortening of the tendons, into a 'pugilist pose', body bowed, hands pulled up, fingers clawed inward.[64] In this posture, the blackened and shrivelled body appeared to be kneeling beside the track hands extended. A passing comedian had carefully dropped a boiled sweet onto the outstretched palm. Other enemy dead had had cigarettes placed in their mouths; passing marines amused themselves by shooting the cigarettes out as they passed.[65] Yet along this charnel house of a road, the terrible cold proved an effective mortician. By refrigerating the fallen, the weather obviated the rotten stench that permeates battlefields in more gentle climes.

There were other incongruities. The columns were continually stopping, starting and concertinaing, making it near impossible to light fires to thaw out frozen cans. Trail rations were called for, and at Chosin, it had been discovered that not only did candy not freeze solid, but Hagaru held a massive supply of the stuff, for before the Chinese struck, the basis of a PX – the American NAAFI – had been established.[66] General Smith had ordered the sweets be doled out to the troops, with the result that the dull-eyed fighting men forged south chewing on caramel Tootsie Rolls and sucking on Lifesavers sweets – rations more suitable for a kindergarten picnic than a fighting withdrawal through a screaming wasteland.[67]

While the cold preserved the dead, it gnawed at the living. Trifling injuries were the white patches of frozen skin that appeared on the face, the strips of flesh that peeled off around the fingernails, the cracks that cut through lips. Ears and earlobes, fingers and the tip of the nose were equally at risk, but as these areas were visible, men warned each other when danger signs appeared. More seriously, a design fault of the shoepacs was becoming painfully apparent. The impermeable rubber boots did not 'breathe' so sweat could not evaporate; moisture froze into a film of ice around the feet. Frostbite comes in stages, and for those marines and commandos who did not have the chance to remove their boots – often for days at a time – they could not know how serious their condition would be. In the first stage, the feet feel icy cold; the flesh turns white. This is treatable. In the second stage, blisters develop, accompanied by a burn-like pain. At this stage, toenails may come off with socks. In the third and most severe stage, blisters and affected flesh turn greenish-black as gangrene sets in. This is when toes and chunks of feet fall off, an effect that may require amputation. Of frostbite casualties, ninety-five per cent would be to the feet.[68]

Water bottles were carried inside clothing, to prevent freezing. Commandos constantly kept one pair of socks slung under their armpits, drying out from body heat. A sergeant ordered O'Brien to kick empty ration cans along the road. O'Brien concurred with the order – it took him a while to realise that the move was designed to keep circulation in his feet. 'My insteps were numb, but I did not get frostbite,' he said. With so many men losing toes, he was grateful for the advice.

At the rear of the column came the exodus from Hagaru. Some civilians piled their belongings in ox carts, but many just walked with what they had carried on A-frames on their backs or in bound bags on their heads. Edmonds was to experience one of those odd coincidences that would be a feature of the campaign: He halted near a group of Korean refugees, carrying both their own belongings and gear salvaged from the battlefield. On one A-frame Edmonds spotted his kitbag, lost in Hellfire Valley, recognisable by the stencil. He did not have the heart to reclaim it.

Amid the horrors, one angelic-looking refugee stood out. 'I remember this girl – she was beautiful, skin like alabaster, she must have been sixteen or seventeen, and everyone remarked on her, even in that situation,' said Moyse. 'It was so sad to see people displaced like that.' The spectacle of their suffering tore at witnesses. Lee's Christian faith was wracked. 'I don't see that kind of suffering as God's grace,' he said.

But the exiles were kept at a distance. 'The refugees tried to follow us,' said Thomas. 'The US marines got jittery about infiltration and fired on them.'*

Firefights continued to break out all along the column, for the Chinese lay in ambush in the hills; bullets hitting the iron-hard road sounded like stones hitting a tin roof. One of these brief combats spelt tragedy for the approximately 300 Chinese prisoners taken at Hagaru. 'The Chinese on the hills thought we were Chinese and flashed a signal with a mirror or something, then shouted to the POWs from the hills,' said Lee. 'About half the POWs ran off, then immediately

* Thomas told the author how haunted he was by the sight of the refugees; he wondered if any made it out. In fact – remarkably – many did. Over twenty years later, John Lee, by then retired from the military and a successful lawyer, met a group of Hagaru exiles in Seoul. They were keen to tell him how successful they were in South Korea; Lee was moved to tears.

afterwards, the Chinese opened fire and we returned fire.' Taking cover in the ditch, bullets bounced off Lee's helmet; for the first time in the battle, he prayed, 'really sincerely'. The prisoners were mown down in the crossfire.

41 Commando's C Troop was tasked to clear a hill. A US tank halted to fire support. The cover offered, however, was not as accurate as the commandos liked; one dashed back and told the astonished tank commander, 'Excuse me, this is our show!'[69]

More formidable support circled overhead, where the ground attack squadrons circled like birds of prey. Outnumbered in infantry terms, the marines had dubbed the Corsairs 'The Equalizers'. Captain Lyle Bradley of the 'Black Sheep' squadron – who had been so stunned to see the footprints in the mountains – was among them.

Bradley's squadron was staging from Yonpo Airfield near Hamhung where the subzero temperatures, though milder than in the highlands, made aircraft maintenance – a precise mechanical job – agonizing for ground crews. The aircrews shared some discomforts of the infantry, sleeping in sleeping bags in a windowless concrete building with North Korean artwork on the walls. Bradley was prepared to survive on the ground if he went down. He dressed in fatigues instead of a flight suit, stuffed his pockets with emergency rations, and packed a .38 revolver and a knife. He also carried a suicide kit: 'I was determined not to be captured,' he said. 'Aviators were very unpopular.' For good reason: If their quilted uniforms were splashed by napalm, Chinese soldiers flared up like human torches.

Perils started at takeoff: Wintering geese were common over Yonpo's runway, and were disastrous if sucked into the 13-feet props of the Corsairs, heavily laden with explosive and fuel. The combat zone was only a twenty-minute 'hop' away, granting pilots two hours overflight above the column. On days when the cloud ceiling was just 300 feet, the pilots reached the marines by flying over the road snaking up into the mountain plateau. The heavy overcast – 'soup' in pilot parlance – and frequent snow flurries made low flying high risk. 'We lost several pilots who ploughed into the sides of valleys,' Bradley said. 'You are not going to hurt a mountain, but you tear hell out of an airplane!'

Once over the column, pilots contacted the ACTs on the ground, whose radios were manned by marine pilots with the infantry. 'We never did any type of action unless we were under positive control with the air controller,' Bradley said. One of the best ACTs Bradley dealt with had an appropriate call sign: Dunkirk 14. Attack precision was critical, for Corsairs bristled with a fearsome array of killing instruments: 500lb bombs or rocket clusters dangled under the wings; a napalm tank hung in the centre of the fuselage; and there were the four 20mm cannon in the wings. The control stick of the Corsair held the trigger for the cannons and the rockets; the bombs and napalm tanks were released by switches.

Once a pilot had visual ID, it was easy to tell the combatants apart, even when skimming over the battle at 350 knots: 'The Chinese were dressed in white uniforms but not quite white – I don't know if they realised it, but the snow was much whiter – and some of their uniforms were dirty,' Bradley said. 'The marines were all in dark uniforms.'

Prior to an attack run, Bradley – despite the screaming, subzero wind chill – wrenched open his cockpit canopy. 'When bombing low, you don't know exactly what the blast will do – it could cut the engine or send up a piece of rock,' he said; his open canopy enabled a split-second bale-out. Bomb drops necessitated a steep Stuka-style plunge on top of the enemy, releasing the 500lb bomb at the same angle as the diving plane and pulling up and out of the blast zone before the explosion overtook the Corsair. Hurtling down like a rollercoaster – hitting the bomb release – jerking violently up – Bradley could feel the shockwave through his airframe.

Rockets were fired as much as a mile ahead of the aircraft, though their explosive force was not as great as the bombs. Napalm runs – used to mark the drop zone for bombs as well as to incinerate troops – were made with shallow dives as low as 20 feet. On a napalm run, Bradley made one near-fatal error: 'When I got low to drop napalm, I accidentally hit the rocket trigger,' he said. Flying into the explosions, his aircraft shook as objects clattered against it; rock fragments had blown nineteen holes in his airframe.

After expending their explosives, the Corsairs had their 20mm wing cannon – effectively giant machine guns. These had no tracer ammunition, but tracer proved unnecessary: Loaded alternatively with incendiary and explosive rounds, the cannons' fall of shot was marked by the churning lines of fountains in the snow. 'You could see the Chinese diving for cover, running,' Bradley said. 'Some hugged tree trunks for cover.' Some fighting was incredibly close, safety margins razor thin: Flying up the road as marines and Chinese shot into each other across the width of it, Bradley was only able to fire the cannon in one wing. Keeping his Corsair flying straight was a struggle as recoil almost threw him into a corkscrew.

When the aircraft swooped on enemy roadblocks on the track or fireblocks in the hills, marines and commandos halted to watch the effect. Sweeping down, the dark blue, crooked-wing hellions were awesome apparitions, their menace compounded by the roar of their engines, and the siren-like shriek a diving Corsair emitted as wind whistled through its wing-mounted air intakes – an effect that had caused World War II Japanese to dub the aircraft 'Whistling Death'.

'People on the hills tried it on but nothing very seriously because the air control kept it to a minimum,' said Moyse. Allen was reminded of nature films of flocks of birds wheeling across the sky in formation as a unit of Chinese zigzagged through a snowfield, taking desperate evasive action to shake a strafing Corsair.

Still, after exploding, the napalm offered the enemy one advantage. 'We could see Chinese coming out and warming themselves over where the napalm had been dropped,' Allen said. Thomas was fascinated to see the effect of Chinese camouflage reversed, for the jellied petroleum transformed long streaks of snow into black sludge. 'The Chinese were wearing white quilted jackets,' he recalled. 'You could see them when they ran across the blackened bits quite prominently.'

After an air strike, the column had about fifteen minutes before the Chinese recovered and resumed shooting. The convoy inched down the road at less than one mile per hour, constantly halting to dismantle or shove over the timber-and-earth road blocks the Chinese had thrown across the track, load wounded or dead onto vehicles, take cover and return fire, or watch more air strikes pounding the flanks. By 17:00, all members of 41 Commando were inside the Koto perimeter; by midnight, the last of the 5th Marines had made it to the village.

For the first time in the Chosin Reservoir campaign, 1st MARDIV was concentrated.

* * *

Inside Koto, the commandos reunited with twenty-five men, including Ovens' party, who had escaped Hellfire Valley after that first night; 41 Commando was now 150 strong.[70] The meeting was not entirely joyful: The many silences as names were called forced men to confront the losses suffered: 'Lots of familiar faces were missing,' Brady realised [71]

One commando, Corporal Williams, had a remarkable tale. In the confused fighting he had been wounded and captured, but had managed to convince Chinese that he was a British war correspondent, not a combatant. The enemy had put him on a shot-up, tyreless, jeep with a pair of US soldiers, and helped them charge the battery. The jeep trundled south, stopping on the night of 30 November under a bridge. When Williams awoke the following morning, the jeep, and the two US soldiers, had gone. Williams was furious. The Chinese took him into a roadside hut with another American prisoner. For days, the pair slowly froze until, on 6 December, they heard tanks clanking past. It was the 7th Marines. The two yelled out, were spotted, stretchered onto a truck and carried to Koto.[72]

Bivouacs had been prepared inside the perimeter, but Allen first went looking for his kit and had an almost supernatural experience. On the march from Hagaru, he had got fed up with the weight of his pack, and slung it into a passing jeep. At Koto there was an enormous park of 1,400 vehicles – trucks, weapons carriers, jeeps. 'I emptied my mind and headed off, I allowed myself to be guided to my pack,' he said. 'I went to the right corner of the park and there was the vehicle on which I had put my pack – I just found it. Very strange!'

There were other odd events underway – events that would later

convince some exhausted survivors of divine intervention. Snow had
fallen through much of 7 December and on the evening of 8
December, storm clouds were settling heavily over the plateau. Yet
intermittently, through breaks in the air cover shrouding the
mountains, sentries made out a lone, white star glittering over the
combat base. Word spread. Cheers rang up from warming tents and
perimeter positions, then songs. As a symbol of hope, 'The White Star
of Koto-ri' would enter marine legend.*[73] But when daylight came on
8 December, it brought with it a mix of fog and snow flurries; the
skies were unflyable. 'The familiar drone of planes was strangely
absent, and a glacial, primeval silence settled over the hundreds of
tents,' wrote the war's most famous correspondent, Margueritte
Higgins, who had arrived at Koto's tiny airstrip.[74] On 9 December,
the skies cleared.

The dead were consigned to the frozen ground they had fought
over. Three mass graves were blown in the rock-hard earth and on 8
December, 113 men were laid to rest. Among the waxy corpses of US
marines and soldiers, the commandos were identifiable by their green
berets. 'The Lord is My Shepherd' was recited by an American
chaplain but the shrieking wind carried away his words. A graves
registration officer paced the spot and sketched a map – just in case
UN forces should return.[75] 'It was "ashes to ashes, dust to dust," then
the bulldozer covered them,' said Thomas.†

One attendee at the funeral would not join the fight through
Funchilin. Puller had been indignant at her presence and Smith,
suffering 'an attack of chivalry' insisted Higgins be flown out.[76] No
proponents of womens' lib, the commandos had been among those
unimpressed with her presence. 'Ridiculous!' sniffed Thomas. Koto's
short runway could not accommodate larger aircraft, so torpedo
bombers were being used to fly wounded out. Higgins flew out in

* The 'Star of Koto-ri' became the official logo of the veterans' group 'The Chosin Few'.
Today, it shines on in the stained glass of the US Marine chapel in Kaneoe, Hawaii.
† As part of the 1953 Korean War truce terms, the 113 men buried at Koto were exhumed
and turned over to the UNC. 'I've got to hand it to the North Koreans,' said General Smith.
'They did an excellent job of digging up those bodies and put them in bags and sent them
to Panmunjom,' he said. (See his interview with Roe at www.chosinreservoir.com)

one – under fire from ridges above. Her co-passenger was General Lemuel Shephard, commander of all marines across the Pacific: He had flown into Koto to join his men on the battleground; Smith persuaded him to depart.[77]

For the descent through Funchilin Pass, the 7th Marines would break trail, followed by the 5th Marines and 41 Commando. Puller's 1st Marines, together with tanks and the divisional reconnaissance platoon, would be rearguard. There was one advantage at this stage of the operation, a fellow commando told Brady: 'At least it's all downhill, mate!'[78] But there a critical obstacle remained: the felled bridge.

The Chinese had blown a 30-foot gap; below it, yawned a chasm 2,900 feet deep.[79] While infantry could scramble around the slope behind the power station, there was no space to build a by-pass; 1st MARDIV's 1,400 vehicles, many loaded with wounded, were lost unless the gap could be bridged. Four sections of treadway bridge would be needed for MARDIV to cross – but it had no treadway.

In a brilliant feat of improvisation, salvation fell from the sky. The USAF loaded bridge sections – each weighing 2 tons – and attached parachutes to their ends, an operation never previously undertaken anywhere. Mindful that the equipment might not survive the fall, marine engineers ordered eight sections. The drop took place on 7 December from C-119s. One piece fell into Chinese hands and one was damaged, but the rest landed inside the Koto perimeter. The next challenge was moving them down through the pass to the chasm. By a fortunate coincidence, Almond had, in the heady days of the advance to the Yalu ordered a section of treadway-carrying trucks to Hagaru. These trucks had survived the journey from Hagaru and were deployed to move the bridge sections.[80]

At minus 30 degrees, 8 December was the coldest day of the campaign: On that day, the final stage of 1st MARDIV's epic breakout – the withdrawal through the eleven winding miles of the towering pass – began. As the 7th Marines and the engineers with the bridge rolled out of Koto, 41 Commando was ordered to hold high ground covering one of the hairpin 'switchbacks' on the road.

The commandos laboured up the face of the hill, buffeted by the frigid blast of the 30-knot wind. Upon reaching a trench cut in the ridge, Edmonds was shocked to find it piled with scores – perhaps hundreds – of frozen Chinese. Below, visible through breaks in the blizzard, the divisional column passed. As light faded, the commandos settled in for the coldest night of their lives. The attack they had been sent up to repel never came, but even Drysdale thought, 'daylight would never come'.[81] The next morning, 41 was ordered back to Koto.

Upon arrival at the chasm on 9 December with the bridge loaded, the engineers discovered that their sections were too short – by seven feet. However, there was a ledge, about 8 feet below the level of the road, at the southern end, and railway timber had been left by the roadside. The timber could be used to create a lattice to bridge that final gap, but it needed filler, and this would require another – much grimmer – feat of improvisation than parachuting bridge sections. Though the ground was too hard to dig for soil, there was one construction material which was plentiful.

The relentless cold that was corroding the commandos and marines was killing their enemy. The marines' scorched earth tactics meant that the Chinese were unable to secure either shelter or food. Having outrun their own supply lines, many were now subsisting on 'a handful of parched flour and a handful of snow'.[82] While their cotton quilted uniforms were reasonably effective, most had no gloves, and their canvas boots, designed for an invasion of the subtropical island of Taiwan, proved gruesomely inadequate for the subzero rigours of Chosin Reservoir.[83] The weather was proving as murderous as bullets and napalm, and nowhere was this more true than in front of the valve station. A Chinese battalion had been ordered to establish an ambush there on the freezing night of 8 December. They had jogged there, but once they arrived and set up positions in the snow, most froze to death in the ice of their own sweat; a few dozen pathetic survivors surrendered to the marines.[84]

As the wooden lattice was constructed, frozen corpses were slung onto the ledge by Chinese POWs.[85] Engineers were the first to cross, then one by one, divisional traffic began rolling. 1st MARDIV was exiting the high country via a bridge built over the bodies of their enemies: human cement.

The only 1st MARDIV battalion not thus far engaged was joining the fight. 1st Battalion, 1st Marines had held Chinhung-ni, the town that was the entrance to and exit from, the highlands. On 8 December, they had been ordered to fight up through enemy roadblocks below Funchilin, seize a key ridge – Hill 1801 – and link up with the marines fighting south. They had impressive fire support: An army armoured artillery battalion and an antiaircraft battalion, armed with double 40mm cannon and the fearsome quad .50 calibre machine guns, mounted on eighteen half tracks. Behind the 1st Marines, an army unit from the 3rd Infantry Division in the lowlands – Taskforce Dog – occupied Chinhung to cover the marines' exit.

Following a second sleepless night holding a section of Koto's perimeter, 41 Commando started moving down the pass at 09:00 on 9 December with the 5th Marines. A blizzard whipped stinging snow into the faces of the marching men. Drysdale had earlier ordered that nobody would ride in vehicles; despite his wounded arm, 41's CO marched among his commandos.

Fighting continued. While the wheeling Corsairs obviated much ground combat, Maindonald's troop, Charlie, was tasked to eliminate a machine gun sweeping the road from the head of a gully. One commando, Jimmy Pepper was hit in the shoulder. Maindonald's section deployed into line for a frontal assault – the machine gun opened fire – commandos dived for cover. Maindonald could see bullets churning the 18-inch deep snow with a 'fluttering' effect. He hid behind a tree, but it was only a sapling, the trunk just inches wide; he crawled into a fold in the ground. An officer yelled orders for a flanking manoeuvre, but when they moved right, the valley dropped away, sheer. The machine gun was well emplaced; there was no avenue of attack, but by now, the column had passed. The commandos were recalled, abandoning their attempt on the gun. 41 tramped over the jury-rigged bridge. 'It was a great job, marvellous,' Moyse said. 'There are two things I really admired about the Americans: engineers and fliers.'

To one side of the road, where it dropped away sheer for

thousands of feet, were dramatic vistas of snow and mist filled valley bottoms. On the other side. towered granite cliffs. Commanding hilltops – notably Hill 1801, taken by the fresh 1st Marines after a torrid assault – were black with napalm. From positions up-slope, squads of refrigerated Chinese dead sightlessly watched their enemies escaping.

Thomas' gaze was drawn to an eviscerated Chinese: The man's frozen intestines were spread across the entire width of the track. More enemy lay crushed, flattened into the ice-glazed road surface. 'We were walking on human beings,' thought Brady the desire to survive overcoming revulsion. While he habitually marched head down, he could no longer bear to look at the road surface. His thoughts turned to other legendary retreats; Brady wondered if conditions had been as bad for Napoleon in Russia. Mulling this amid the almost ghostly spectacle of lines of marines and commandos marching through the mist along the twisting mountain road Brady sensed, for the first time, history in the making.[86]

Brady's reverie was interrupted when someone started to hesitatingly sing: 'She's a big fat bastard, twice the size of me . . .' Above the wind, Brady bellowed back, 'With hairs on her belly like the branches of a tree!'[87] The song was taken up, echoing off the cliffs.

In the late afternoon, a barrage of heavy artillery thundered down into the surrounding hills. 'We thought we were home and dry when the Puerto Ricans brought down fire on us,' said Thomas. The Puerto Rican 65th Infantry was establishing blocking positions in the lowlands; fortunately, nobody was hit. 'I suspect the fire was friendly, but it was nonetheless unpleasant,' Drysdale commented.[88]

Daylight died. In the darkness, Chinese began firing light mortars. Each time they fired, they flashed. The commandos, who had lost their own mortars in Hellfire Valley, put small arms fire down on the flashes. It was unclear if they were hitting anything, but the flashes were moving all the time, meaning the Chinese were being forced to move and redeploy their weapons.[89] But there was now a feeling that the enemy's back had been broken: their frozen dead were visible all around, they were not attacking with their previous élan. 'From that point on, you felt safe,' said O'Brien. 'You still had odd attacks causing a bit of disruption, but not mass attacks: They'd come up on a hillside and fire down.'

The last unit casualty would come in darkness, as Saunchegrow conned his shot-up truck down through the pass at walking pace. A commando was striding ahead, guiding him by verbal commands, but at a turn, the track crumbled. The truck tipped over and disappeared down the slope, scattering commandos and equipment. Drysdale and Aldridge dashed over to supervise the rescue, but none was needed; remarkably, the vehicle had come to rest on a ledge 20 feet down; equally remarkably, nobody was wounded. Saunchegrow, hanging upside down at the steering wheel, crawled out. The US marine corporal was 'mighty sad' at the demise of 'Old Faithful'.[90] The vehicle had been carrying the last of the unit's kit: Now, all the commandos had left was on their backs or hanging from their belts.

The slow, cold miles passed. When the column halted yet again, the commandos belted out, 'Why are we waiting?' Morton Silver, a US Navy corpsman accompanying 41, was as astonished by the singing as much as by the fact that the commandos were 'disdaining any and all forms of motorised transport'.[91]

Rumours spread: There were trucks waiting around the next bend. Yet around each bend, the promised vehicles proved illusory. By now, abandoned personal equipment – packs, shovels, bed rolls – littered the track, dropped by exhausted men ahead. Still 41 Commando trudged on. Brady, almost hallucinating with exhaustion, registered something: the road he was on no longer sloped, it was flat. Then there came a ragged cheer: A long line of empty trucks was waiting on the road ahead.[92]

Thomas was near the front of the column with Drysdale, ordering that every commando would march out, but when he looked back it was too late: his men were swarming over the vehicles. The commandos had marched 23 miles; none had slept for 72 hours.[93] Thomas happened to glance across at Drysdale as he gazed back up the grim pass they had fought out of. A look of utter desolation passed momentarily across his face as, Thomas guessed, Drysdale remembered the men left behind.

1st MARDIV's spearhead had reached Chinhung at 02:30 on 10 December. 41 Commando were in at 21:30 hours.[94] Behind 41, the 1st Marines pulled back. The last elements were a column of tanks, a reconnaissance platoon, and a group of engineers. The bridge was blown; the treadway sections tumbled 2,900 feet into the abyss. Refugees were left stranded on the northern side, though many scrambled around the slope behind the valve station and down to the lowlands. Six heavy tanks of the rearguard, trapped by a tank that stalled on the road ahead, were abandoned. They were blasted by air strike. By 11 December, the last marines had cleared the highlands.

* * *

Sprawled over one another in the backs of the trucks, shattered commandos dozed. 'The vibration of the truck as it moved off was the psychological equivalent of manna from heaven,' thought Brady. 'I have never since felt the release of tension so vehemently.'[95]

The survivors disembarked at a tented camp in Hungnam. While cold, the camp was not nearly as frigid as the highlands: the mud was liquid, not frozen, the snow merely patchy. A field kitchen was dishing up hot stew and coffee. Men wolfed it down. No member of the commando had removed his clothing since 27 November. 'It will be an interesting moment when the time comes!' Drysdale reckoned.[96]

41 Commando was a shadow of its former self. RSM Baines called the roll. The murderous combat in Hellfire Valley, the subsequent fighting at Hagaru and during the breakout the insidious frost had bled the unit white. Of 217 men who had entered the mountains twelve days earlier, ninety-eight were casualties: thirteen killed; twenty-seven missing or captured; thirty-nine wounded; and nineteen suffering from frostbite, exposure or pneumonia.[97] Having been 'pretty badly cut about', the Commando was reduced to, in its CO's words, 'virtually three independent platoons'.[98]

The US marines suffered terrible losses. Between 11 October and 11 December 1950, 1st MARDIV lost 704 killed; 187 missing, 3,489 wounded and 6,000 non-battle casualties, largely frostbite cases. Overall, X Corps suffered 11,500 casualties.[99]

On 12 December, 41 Commando, together with the 5th Marines,

loaded onto LSTs at Hungnam's Green Beach and chugged out to the troopship USS *General Randall*. The next day, she set sail. Silver, the US Navy medical officer, was approached by an SBA with a request to examine the commandos. 'The Britishers removed their shoes and hosiery to reveal frozen, gangrenous, blackened toes and feet,' Silver wrote. 'They had marched, crippled and in pain, fought, singing and swearing, down the road from Chosin to the sea. The US Marines were proud to have the Royal Marines fight alongside us in that hellish place.'[100]

Bound for Pusan, *General Randall* was carrying 5,000 men aboard a ship designed for 2,000.[101] Administration was impressive. 'They gave us a ticket: Four people to share every bunk,' said Edmonds. 'The pipe would come: "Red tickets! Crash now!"' Galley queues jammed companionways. 'As soon as you got to the end of the queue, it was time for the next meal!' Edmonds recalled. 'The showers were knee-deep in underwear where people had thrown stuff off,' said Moyse – yet new, clean underwear was on hand for every man. In the showers, Maindonald noted how odd some looked: 'The combination of C-ration diet and temperatures which had dissuaded men from defecating for days on end, had left many bloated.'[102]

The gangways, mess halls and bunkroom were animated by a delirious atmosphere of explosive emotional decompression. Crowds of marines were squatting in any spare space, gambling away hundreds of dollars. 'Money was nothing to them,' said O'Brien. 'They had come out of hell, and being typical Americans, the dice was going. Every one of them was laughing.'[103]

Drysdale was not sharing the joy. Determined that Whitehall grasped the ordeal his men had endured, he wrote to the Admiralty on 12 December. 'I should like Commandant General Royal Marines to know that the chaps have been absolutely magnificent under quite the bloodiest conditions that I have ever experienced,' he wrote. 'I'm not ashamed to admit that I'm proud of them.' His letter – a single page, but containing several typos – reveals that the carnage in the mountains had affected the commando leader. 'What I am desperately in need of is future guidance, 41 Commando is no longer an operation (sic) unit,' Drysdale continued. It would need to be 'either very considerably reinforced . . . or be disbanded'. For the CO even to suggest that the unit of which he was so proud might lack a future indicates his desolation. 'I'm sorry this is so short, but conditions are not ideal,' Drysdale concluded, 'and I'm a spot weary.'[104]

He was not the only one. Looking at himself in a washroom mirror, O'Brien noticed grey hairs. He was nineteen.

* * *

On 11 December – the day the marines exited the highlands – X Corps issued orders for a total withdrawal from northeast Korea. The battleworn 1st MARDIV was just the first unit to depart. In all 105,000 military personnel and 17,500 tanks and vehicles would be carried away into the northern Pacific.[105]

To cover this exodus, four fast aircraft carriers, one light carrier and two escort carriers were on station. To this was added, the naval gunfire of two heavy cruisers, six destroyers and three rocket ships. Off the coast, some 200 ships were undertaking the biggest seaborne evacuation since Dunkirk.[106]

While the Chinese were gunning for 1st MARDIV, X Corps' other units – 7th Infantry Division and ROK 1st Corps – had withdrawn, largely without interference from the enemy.* Corps rearguard was the US 3rd Infantry Division. After their savaging at the hands of the marines, the Chinese did not pursue closely. 3ID withdrew through a series of concentric phase lines, methodically blowing everything behind them. The Puerto Rican troops of the division commandeered ox carts to carry kit as explosions rigged by demolition engineers brought factory chimneys crashing down behind them.[107]

Hungnam's rail yards provided another canvas for the engineers' art. On 15 December, fifteen locomotives and 275 cars were set on a viaduct, a span of which was blown. The engines and carriages were then rolled, one by one, into the chasm. The last pieces of rolling stock were a locomotive and several tankers of petrol, sitting on a wooden

---

* While some in the US Army contend that 31st RCT's sacrifice saved the marines, it is worth noting that by holding down the Chinese mass of manoeuvre, it was 1st MARDIV that permitted ROK and US Army units further north to escape to the coast unscathed.

section of the viaduct. The wood was ignited. The flames climbed. The engine's whistle blew forlornly; it turned pink, then scarlet, before the wooden supports collapsed and it plunged to destruction.[108]

For tens of thousands of Koreans, the sky was falling. With the thunder in the mountains descending to destroy them, the UNC defeat triggered a desperate race for survival.

Four of them, turned away at Hamhung train station, knew their lives rested on reaching the coast. After nightfall the Lims crept into the station, and hid inside a single cargo car. 'There was no engine, we just hid there,' Lim said. Her hands nearly froze in the night. The next day, there came clangs from outside; they were being connected to a locomotive. The car started rolling. 'We did not know our destination,' she said. 'We just hoped and hoped.' The train stopped at the end of the line: Hungnam.

Bundled up in thick layers of clothing, their few possessions bound up, carted or carried on heads or backs, refugees swarmed over the frost-glazed quays of the port and the freezing black mud of the evacuation beaches, hoping to be ferried out into the Pacific.

The Lims had reached the port, but not safety; they hid in the house of a cousin. 'Hungnam was a port and industrial city, so was full of communists,' Lim said. 'Every day, we waited to hear if we could get on a boat.' They did not dare go out; instead, every day, their cousin left to see if there was space. Every day she returned with the same litany: 'Not today.' 'We were terrified, we could not sleep,' said Lim. 'If we could not escape, it meant death.' Then her cousin roused them: 'There's a ship!' she said. Fearful of marauding troops, her mother bundled the teenaged Geum-sook up in a muffler to hide her gender. 'We were afraid of soldiers,' she said. 'Russian, communist or UN – soldiers are soldiers.' The family hurried down to the port and joined one of several long queues thronging the icy docks.

The atmosphere was one of fearful anticipation. Lights were winking out to sea and the air over the refugees' heads was rent with express train shrieks as the US Navy bombardment group rained destruction far inland. 'I knew my hometown was being destroyed,' Lim said. 'How can I explain my feelings? My heart felt like it was being squeezed, I could barely breathe with terror.'

The ship Lim's cousin had spoken of was a freighter, the SS *Meredith Victory;* the last civilian ship to leave Hungnam. Her master, Captain Leonard La Rue, had not been ordered inshore, but scanning the scene through binoculars and seeing thousands of refugees still hoping, somehow, to get away, he volunteered. On 22 December, he docked. 'There were families with eight and ten children,' La Rue, remembered. 'There was a man with a violin, a woman with a sewing machine, a young girl with triplets. There were seventeen wounded, some stretcher cases, many aged, hundreds of babies.'[109] While the ship was only designed to carry twelve passengers, Koreans were herded aboard throughout the night. Among those piling up the gangways were the Lims. The family was ushered into the hold, well below the waterline. It was heaving with people. 'There was no room even to sit, but it was a horrible situation, life or death,' she said. 'I did not think of discomfort.' For the first time in weeks, the 19-year-old was safe.

Enemy forces were reportedly only 4,000 yards away. 'My main memory was the anxiety of getting all those people aboard as communist forces closed in,' said Robert Lunney, a US naval ensign. 'We had men on shore with axes ready to cut our lines, our boilers were up and running.' Cables were cast off on 23 December and the ship's bows turned seaward, but risk had not receded: In the northern Pacific chill, some refugees lit fires near barrels of fuel. Yet not only did everyone aboard the ship survive, the *Meredith Victory** docked on Boxing Day near Pusan with five more passengers than she had departed with: babies born in transit.[110] Of 91,000 Koreans civilians evacuated from Hungnam; 14,000 sailed aboard the 'Ship of Miracles'.[111] 'That Christmastide, in the bleak and bitter waters off the shores of Korea,' La Rue, who later entered the church, stated, 'God's own hand was at the helm of my ship.'[112]

The background overture to the tragedy now reached its crescendo. The great battleship USS *Missouri* – the vessel on whose

---

* The *Meredith Victory*, the 'Ship of Miracles', earned a mention in the *Guinness Book of Records* for carrying out the world's largest ever seaborne rescue, as well as a special citation from President Dwight Eisenhower. In 1993, she was sold for scrap – without apparent irony – to China.

deck the Japanese surrender ending the Second World War had been signed – had been summoned. On 23 December, the three 16-inch turrets of the floating fortress joined the cruisers and rocket ships as they fired a rolling barrage a mile and a half inland.[113] The 16-inch shells each cost the price of a Cadillac; when fired, they caused a displacement of water; when they detonated, they blew a crater 30 feet across in the frozen soil. The avalanche of explosives was part tactical necessity, part impotent fury. Viewed from an observation aircraft, even the greatest of America's fighting ships appeared like a toy against Hamgyong's snow-capped mountains.

On 24 December, the last unit ashore, demolition experts of the US Navy's Underwater Demolition Team (UDT) Detachment Bravo, were working feverishly. Their orders from Admiral James Doyle, the commander of the evacuation, were simple: Hungnam's port was to be turned into 'a wasteland'. The UDT men found it strange to be preparing demolitions with a naval barrage howling over their heads; they had to 'work fast and be damn cautious', recalled a team member, Royal Vanatta, who was praying silently. Hundreds of yards of explosive hose were connected; charges were lowered off quays into the water. The UDT rigged the docks with tons of explosives, as well as wiring a nearby train loaded with aerial bombs. Enemy closed. A flare was fired to summon the scattered detachment to the end of the breakwater, their extraction point. Setting a last charge in the lighthouse, the frogmen boarded the APD USS *Begor,* which swiftly departed out to sea.[114]

Christmas Eve, 1950 was one of those crystalline winter days – an appropriate backdrop for the most spectacular, most terrible manifestation of the UNC's scorched earth policy. Admiral Doyle and General Almond watched through binoculars from the USS *Mount McKinley*; closer inshore, the UDT men on the *Begor* had a grandstand view of their handiwork. First, an ammunition dump blew, crackling like a firework display. Then, a long line of synchronised explosions detonated, rippling along the shoreline. Thunder boomed across the water. The eruptions tore apart the docks, blasting their facilities – quays, cranes, warehouses, lighthouse – into obliteration. Seconds later, tons of debris began splashing down into the Pacific. Colossal clouds of white, grey and black smoke and dust billowed up into a merciless blue sky.

The UNC's foray into North Korea was over. It was an apocalyptic finale.*

*   *   *

For overseeing the successful evacuation of northeast Korea with minimal losses of men or materiel, General Almond, X Corps' commander, received his third general's star.[115] Such platitudes did nothing to sweeten the overall outlook. For the UNC, that believed it stood on the brink of victory at the end of November, the situation at the end of December was catastrophic.

In the west, the 8th Army had been routed. In the east, X Corps had retreated. North Korea was lost to the UN. UNC troops regrouped in the South. In the winter winds, the red banner fluttered once more over Kim Il-sung's land, now a blasted wilderness.

Within that wilderness, a strange new feature had appeared. In the high country around Chosin Reservoir – in and around the ashen ruins of Chinhung-ni; up through the winding Funchilin Pass to Koto, Hagaru and Yudam; along the roads linking them; and in the mountains overlooking them – countless oval hummocks lay in irregular patterns across the terrain.

The Chinese had planned to annihilate the marines. Instead – against an enemy who could not be panicked, and who deployed grit, tactical skill and firepower – the Chinese, themselves, had been decimated. On 8 December, in a cable to Mao, Peng estimated that 9th Army needed 60,000 replacements.[116]

Hamgyong Province had become the Army Group's graveyard: Each hummock marked one of General Song's fallen soldiers.[117] The countless frost-blackened corpses would not be revealed until their snow shrouds melted in the spring thaw.

---

* A popular South Korean song of the post war years, 'Be Strong, Keumsun' tells of a couple separated at Hungnam: *Amid a raging blizzard at Hungnam Port, I shouted your name and searched desperately/ Where are you Keumsun?/ Keep alive behind the iron curtain/ The day will come when we will reunite/ The day will come when we will dance hand in hand.* Sixty years later, that day has yet to arrive.

Chapter Twelve

Dark Christmas

*I see the world gradually being turned into a
wilderness, I hear the ever approaching
thunder, which will destroy us too. . .*

Anne Frank

Under heavy grey skies, the snowfields lay in winter silence.

The last elements of 8th Army had retreated from North Korea
by 15 December. There was no pursuit. In the hills, 27th Brigade's
soldiers dug positions, and when not on duty, stripped the twisted,
blackened ruins of Uijongbu to build shelters. Against a backdrop of
craggy hills, constructions of corrugated iron, planking, rice straw
matting and tent canvas sprouted in the snow. Bonfires and lanterns
flickered in the shanty town.

Inside their shacks, men filled shell cases with earth soaked in
petrol and lit them. As improvised heaters the devices worked, but
many men would wake up black. Baths were rigged: 44-gallon drums
cut lengthways, filled with water, and fires lit in trenches underneath.
'It was a question of getting in, soaping, up, getting out into the snow
and getting dressed as soon as possible,' recalled Diehard Corporal
John Pluck, who, like others, found his chest and stomach infested
with body lice.

Brigadier Basil Coad, recovered after his breakdown, returned
from Japan on 18 December. Known to the 3 RAR as 'the grey-haired
old bastard', his return was greeted in uproarious fashion. 'All the
Diggers were shouting, "Hi Bas, get any geishas did you?"' recalled
sniper Ian Robertson. 'He loved it, but the brigade major came out
and said, "You can't speak to the brigadier like that!" And one

Digger said, "Go on Bas, give him a couple of lashes with the cane" – and he did! He said to the brigade major, "I am speaking to my mates" – and gave him a couple of ceremonial whacks! He knew how to win the troops over.' Lieutenant Peter Baldwin was surprised at how touched Coad was by the Australians' welcome: He seemed to have tears in his eyes.

Another player exited the stage. 8th Army Commander General Walton Walker, who had orchestrated the defence of the Pusan Perimeter then overseen the rout at the hands of the Chinese, was on his way to present 27th Brigade with a South Korean Presidential Unit Citation for its Naktong actions, when a ROK truck pulled out in front of his jeep. Walker was flung out, sustaining serious head injuries. He died hours later.

News of the UNC catastrophe in North Korea had by now reached Seoul. Late at night, the young artist, Kim Song-hwan, sketched trams trundling from the railway station, through dark, battered streets. Their destinations were city hospitals, their cargoes heaps of soldiers wounded from up north. With the fighting burning south once again, the ancient Korean folk fear of a Chinese invasion was reignited.

Middlesex majors John Willoughby and Roly Gwynne went into the battered capital for a day. The two men were invited into the British Embassy for tea and sandwiches, served – remarkably, given the circumstances – on fine China. They had hoped to view the National Museum's pottery collection, but it was closed. Hearing Western music down an alleyway they investigated. The music emanated from a building, outside which were stacked firearms of every model: 'I suppose when you left, you just took your pick,' Willoughby thought. Inside, were jammed soldiers from every contingent of the UNC, most lolling drunkenly against the walls. Through a fug of tobacco smoke, the two majors made out a woman dancing in the centre of the room. 'It was such a debased sight that two minutes were enough,' Willoughby wrote. 'Thankfully we made our way out.' In the streets, apart from new ROK recruits being hastily drilled, the civilian population appeared listless, but at the Han River, the two majors were confronted by the sight of thousands of refugees, belongings piled upon ox carts, crowding around the entrances to the bridges south.[1]

Even the gentlest hollows of Korea's landscape contained death. On a road recce of the brigade's LOC, Willoughby came across a pretty village buried in the hills, overlooked by, 'a most attractive little pleasure garden' – probably a Buddhist temple. He hiked up. 'Looking down . . . over a precipice directly below was a slab of rock. In the middle was a body, a skeleton in fact, the flesh had gone and most of the clothes. It must have been there for months and was now part of the view.'[2]

* * *

Though the enemy was out of contact, the killing continued. Australian journalist Harry Gordon joined a B26 Intruder raid into North Korea. The bomber's crew was obliging: Gordon was belted into the co-pilot's seat, then the bomber droned up into the night sky. Over enemy territory, the mission became a rushing, flashing nightmare of explosions in the blackness. 'It was frightening: At times, we would screech down to track level, then roar up again.' Anything moving, even ox carts, were targets. The dark, frozen landscape was soon dotted with blazes. 'They did not want to return with any weapons on board,' said Gordon. 'They were attacking anything that moved, blasting any light; I thought it was needless slaughter.'

Many victims of the strafing were refugees escaping the devastated north. Foot patrols were detailed to search those stumbling in. 'One of our jobs was to carry out roadblocks to search and strip civvies – they would carry arms strapped to their waist, or to their legs,' said Diehard Ted Haywood. 'It was not a very nice thing to search them in the intense cold, every morning you would see women, children, old people frozen to death on the sides of road: They walked till they dropped, then that was it.' The brutality of the times was not ameliorating. A South Korean attached to 3 RAR who raped a woman was handed to a South Korean officer. 'This captain spoke English, he said, "Thank you very much," pulled out a pistol and shot him,' said Sergeant Jack Gallaway. 'This was common.'

Defences were emplaced against guerillas, and the luck of Second Lieutenant Owen Light continued to hold. He had placed booby-traps – live grenades, pin removed and levers depressed, in tins strung from wire; if the wire was kicked, the bomb would tumble out of the tin, releasing the lever, and it would detonate – around his position. The next morning, a heavy snowfall had obscured the traps – until Light kicked one. 'It was under my feet, it was smoking,' he said. He leapt sideways and to the ground as it erupted. 'Grenades blow up and out, if you are close to it, you get away with it; I was unharmed. Relief!'

With ROK units dug in to the north, 27th Brigade was made IX Corps reserve. Patrols tailed off as units prepared for Christmas.

*   *   *

In the distant southeast, 41 Commando – the final toll on the 235-man unit was ninety-three casualties, almost half of those who had fought at Chosin Reservoir – was attached to 1st MARDIV in a huge tented camp at Masan.[3] 'We were reorganising, licking our wounds,' said Marine Michael O'Brien. A Christmas tree was set up, decorated with pieces of brass from ammunition boxes and inflated condoms for balloons. While the US Women's Temperance League blocked a dispatch by the Milwaukee Brewers' Association of one million cases of beer for troops in Korea, 41 was well supplied by the British Embassy in Tokyo, enabling a cocktail party in the officers' mess tent.[4] But with so many men still getting to mental grips with their experience in the Chosin crucible, it was a quiet Christmas.

27th Brigade's Christmas preparations demanded some initiative. The Middlesex officers' mess was established in marquee; officers were best advised not to ask its source. 'I got the tent from the Yankee rear echelon!' said Sergeant Paddy Redmond, a popular man among the Americans for his Irish songs. 'We went down and dismantled it and a staff sergeant said, "What are doing?" and we said, "We've been told to move it." It was the Yanks' toilet tent!' One of Alan Lauder's Jocks obtained sheets of white linen for the Argyll lunch tables in a Quonset hut. The subaltern was taken aback when he heard the material's origin: undertakers' shrouds. 'We developed a strange sense of humour as a kind of defence mechanism,' he said.

Christmas Day was a blizzard. For lunch, American turkeys, roasted in 44-gallon drums, were served. Men were warned to avoid local moonshine, such as 'Hwarang Brandy', its label denoting a sword-wielding warrior, and 'Old Hawk Whisky', reputedly coloured with horse urine. Instead, bottles of Japanese Asahi beer passed around as officers served men: 'Colonel Man was in the thick of it, just like at home,' said Private Ken Mankelow. The Middlesex received gifts of knitwear from the people of Middlesex – 'there were some bloody funny colours!' recalled Private Edgar Green – and letters: Man insisted his men write thank-you notes. Most men's priorities were simple. 'I got drunk,' recalled Middlesex Corporal Bob Yerby. 'We met up with an Aussie who had some black navy rum it was just, "Cheers, thank God we've survived, and it's Christmas!"'

The Argylls – who received Christmas puddings from their colonel-in-chief, Princess Elizabeth – found themselves oversupplied with food. Quartermaster Andrew Brown had heard of an orphanage nearby, so invited the children over. The orphans had an orchestra, which played 'God Save the King', then they were fed. 'There were these hard-bitten Jocks saying, "Come on, eat up!"' said Brown. 'But the kids probably had a bad night, they had not eaten that much in ages.'

3 RAR's A Company cooks had adopted a pair of boys in their field kitchen when a ROK recruiting squad arrived, demanding the lads be handed over. The Digger cooks cocked their rifles and told the ROKs that the two were performing their war service with the Australian Army. The squad backed off – to the relief of Captain Ben O'Dowd, who had serious doubts about the cooks' martial abilities.[5]

Individual soldiers did what they could for children. Frank Screeche-Powell, the Irish corporal so disturbed by the murder of the old Korean by a Middlesex mortar man, took care of a tiny brother and sister, giving them rations and a gift of a mouth organ. Their father, a refugee, wrote him a letter:

Dear sir
I thank you very mutch your kindly and many present to my
childrens Siho and Whaja. they are very like you. I think present
some thing to you but I can not it because I all losted in this war and
from came Seoul. please you understand to me
Lee

New Year's Eve. Above Uijongbu's ruins, the winter sky faded into translucene, the mountains turned purple and darkness fell on the last day of 1950. A three-quarter moon rose, glittering on the snow.

'We went down to the Argylls' Sergeants Mess for the Hogmanay Party in a big tent and there was the RSM, a big fella, and a little bloke was playing the bagpipes, you couldn't hear yourself speak,' said 3 RAR Sergeant Jack Gallaway. 'The RSM handed you a tumbler of whisky and said, "Drink! If ye dinnae drink, ye dinnae get in!"' The whisky flowed, to the point where the Digger RAP sergeant lost his false teeth when the truck taking the Australian NCOs back to their shelters overturned. 'We all got a bit charged,' admitted Gallaway, who was expecting the war to wind down. 'There was not a Chinese within miles and miles of the place and we could not believe that MacArthur was going to carry on after getting his nose busted in North Korea, we thought he'd try and come to some kind of agreement.'

There would be no agreement. On 15 December, the UN had proposed a ceasefire. On 16 December, President Harry Truman declared a US state of emergency. On 22 December, Peking rejected the ceasefire offer. While Gallaway and other sergeants caroused, those soldiers of 27th Brigade still sober and alert as the final hours of the Year of the Tiger ticked away, heard an ominous rumbling a dozen miles to their north.

Marshal Peng Te-huai had not been idle. Of the CPVA who had been fighting in Korea since late October, perhaps twenty-five per cent were dead or disabled. But a regrouped and refitted NKPA – a fresh force, 75,000 strong – had now united with the Chinese. Mao had demanded a new offensive, designed to seize Seoul and lay the groundwork for a spring attack that would drive the UNC into the sea.[6]

The rumble heard at twilight on New Year's Eve, 1950, was a barrage fired by six Chinese artillery regiments. On New Year's Day, 1951, 267,000 communist bayonets surged across the 38th parallel.

Appendix

Where are They Now?

Armies march by tower and spire
Of cities blazing, in the fire; –
Till as I gaze with staring eyes,
The armies fade, the lustre dies.
Robert Louis Stevenson

1st Argylls: One of its Korea officers, Colin Mitchell, led a successful campaign to resist amalgamation in the 1960s, but in the midst of British Army reorganisation, the regiment became the 5th Battalion, Royal Regiment of Scotland, in 2006.

1st Middlesex: The Diehards were merged into the Queens Regiment in 1966, and the Princess of Wales Royal Regiment in 1992. In 2004 in Al Amara, Iraq, PWRR soldiers launched a bayonet charge against insurgents to free soldiers pinned down by insurgents. The freed men were the Argylls – the PWRR's former comrades in Korea.

3 RAR: Nicknamed 'Old Faithful' for its utter reliability in Korea – it was the key unit at the desperate battle of Kapyong in April 1951 – the battalion remains a regular unit of the Australian Army with a parachute role.

41 Commando: After further raiding operations in Korea in 1951, the commando was disbanded in 1952. For its heroism at Chosin, US 1st MARDIV was awarded a US Presidential Unit Citation. Following lobbying by US marines, 41 Commando was also awarded the PUC. However, due to issues over foreign awards, Whitehall only grudgingly accepted the award. In 1957, the PUC was attached to the colour of the disbanded commando, though individual men were not permitted to wear the flash However, some, in defiance of orders, did so.

Teddy Allen: The crack-shot commando was commissioned after Korea, and served in the Suez invasion and the Borneo confrontation with 40 Commando. He retired as a major, and lives in the same village as John Walter.

Alf Argent: 3 RAR's intelligence officer later served in military aviation in Vietnam and retired from the Army as a colonel.

Peter Baldwin: The signals officer served in Borneo, retired as a major general, and was one of the pioneers of commercial radio in the UK. To this day, underfloor heating reminds him of the Korean cottages of 1950.

Reg Bandy: After Korea, the 3 RAR sergeant and three mates entered a Returned and Service League (RSL) bar in Perth for a drink. 'Six old blokes were at the bar and they said, "Korea wasn't a war: Piss off!"' That bitter experience was shared by many Diggers. Bandy later served two tours in Vietnam, which he found more amenable than Korea: 'Vietnam was alright, we had a firm base.' As for PTSD, he offers a simple solution: 'A few blokes went "milko" but we used to go on the piss and talk it out of them.' Today, he lectures at schools on his war experiences.

Don Barrett: The Middlesex corporal became, after the war, the unofficial historian of the Diehards and 27th Brigade in Korea: His detailed writings are kept in the National Army Museum.

Sir Phillip Bennett: The Australian mortars officer commanded a battalion in Vietnam, and later the Australian Defence Force, from 1984–87. He was subsequently Governor of Tasmania. He still carries souvenirs of that grenade attack in the North. 'There are bits of things floating around in my body!' he said. 'Doctors are bit surprised at annual medicals that I still carry it sixty years later.'

James Beverly: The Bermondsey lad who watched the hillside turn colour as Chinese surged down its slopes returned to Korea in 2009. 'Back then it was a shit-hole, now it's marvellous,' he said. Handing out a scholarship to a Korean schoolgirl at Gloster Hill*, he was

---

*Every April, visiting British Korean War veterans, after a memorial service at the site of the Gloster Battalion's last stand in 1951, hand out scholarships provided by Korea-based UK companies to local schoolchildren.

embraced. 'When she thanked me, I choked up. The feeling I got, money could not have bought.' He never unfolded his good luck charm – the sackcloth flag he was handed at Pusan in 1950 – until interviewed by the author at his London home in 2010.

Sir Alexander 'Sandy' Boswell: The Argyll Intelligence Officer served in Borneo and Belfast, commanded the Argylls, was commander-in-chief in Guernsey, and retired as a general. Of his Korea experience, Boswell is succinct: 'I think I grew up a hell of a lot!'

Stanley Boydell: The Middlesex MO's wife told him he went to Korea a boy and came back completely different; he found the experience bonded him with his father-in-law, a First World War veteran. 'The worst was the cold,' he said. 'I think perhaps I have never been warm since.'

Lyle Bradley: The USMC pilot considered Chosin the worst flying conditions he had ever encountered. Twenty-five years after the war, he was at a meeting in Wyoming, when he noticed another participant wearing a marine tiepin. They began talking and Bradley realised he was 'Dunkirk 14' the ground callsign he had liaised with. 'He jumped up and threw his arms around me,' said Bradley. 'It was quite a shock to everybody to see two marines hugging!'

Dave Brady: 41 Commando's joker left the marines and joined the Metropolitan Police where the self-described 'coward' went on to win two awards for gallantry, for taking on armed robbers unarmed; on the second occasion he was shot through the arm. He retired in Norfolk near his old CO, who was running a sheep farm, and taught police driving tactics. One day he drove to Drysdale's farm in a police car where he informed the colonel, 'I am investigating allegations of bestiality on this farm.' Drysdale, belatedly recognising the policeman, 'jumped in the air and roared, "Brady! You bastard!"' Brady's lively *One of the Chosin Few,* a source for this work, was published in 2003.

Andrew Brown: The Argyll quartermaster retired as a Lieutenant Colonel and retains a twinkle in his eye: In his nineties, he turned up at a 'senior aerobics' class in Aberdeen to find the next oldest person was in her fifties. He is active in Argyll veterans groups.

David Butler: The commander of the spearhead in the 'Apple Orchard' did another tour in Korea, finishing the conflict on 'The Bloody Hook', and commanded a battalion in Vietnam. As for Korea being 'The Forgotten War', he said: 'It does not affect me. I have been a regular soldier and gone to wars that are all forgotten – nobody is interested in Vietnam, either. I am rather pleased wars are forgotten and glad the whole of society did not get exposed.'

Basil Coad: 27th Brigade's commander retired as a major general. His secret report about Korea to the British government – a source for this work – was never made public, perhaps due to Coad's heavy criticism of the US military. It is now viewable at the National Archive. Many of his men praise his prudent leadership, which they believe prevented 27th Brigade from suffering the disasters that befell 29th Brigade at Koyang and Imjin River in 1951. He died in 1980.

Andrew Condron: The captured Scottish commando took part in Chinese propaganda broadcasts in the POW camps, and was the only British prisoner to refuse repatriation at the war's end. In China, he taught English and married, returning quietly to the UK in 1962. Though fellow commandos say everything Condron did in the camps assisted fellow prisoners, he remained controversial, and was assaulted at one 41 Commando reunion. He died in 1996.

Edward 'Ted' Cunningham: Despite losing a leg to mortar fire, he is not bitter. 'I was damned lucky not to be more severely injured,' he said. After Korea, he studied at Cambridge and Harvard Business School, and worked at the World Bank and the Scottish Development Agency. Today, he is active in venture capital in Edinburgh.

Max Desfor: After the winter retreat, the photojournalist was on leave in a Japanese inn when the phone rang. It was his bureau chief: His photograph of the Taedong bridge had won the Pulitzer Prize. It is now arguably the most famed photograph of the war. Desfor covered other wars, and retired as photo editor of *US News and World Report*. In Korea in 2002, he lectured to journalism students, and was delighted to be stuck in a traffic jam: 'It was amazing, the vehicles – what a difference!' Today his photography is limited to family snapshots: 'Nice pictures!' For his 95th birthday, his wife bought him a Nikon digital.

Douglas Drysdale: After leaving Korea in 1951, Drysdale spent two years teaching at the US marine officer schools at Quantico. He retired from the corps in 1962, but remained uncompromising. In the 1980s, he was dining with Ron Moyse at a 41 reunion when he heard about a fracas that had taken place the previous evening. Drysdale roared, 'I will have no indiscipline in this unit!' Moyse was taken aback: 'This was thirty years later!' Drysdale died in 1990.

Jack Edmonds: The SBS commando remained in the corps and took part in a range of clandestine operations, 'but nothing on the scale of Korea'. He lives close to Ron Moyse.

Jack Gallaway: 3 RAR's signals sergeant suffered occasional nightmares of a GI crushed by a tank – 'his body seemed to end in a splash of strawberry jam' – but settled into civilian life as a journalist. After hearing in RSLs that Korea was, after the Second World War, 'just a bloody sideshow', he decided to set the record straight. His lively *The Last Call of the Bugle* is the finest book on 3 RAR in Korea.

Harry Gordon: The Australian journalist subsequently covered the Algerian War, became chief editor of the *Herald Weekly Times* and official historian of the Australian Olympic Committee. He remains surprised at the Korean War's lack of recognition. 'For all its huge dimensions, its characters, its grand theatre, it seems easy to forget if you were not there,' he said. '*MASH*, for all its fierce satire, hardly did justice to the harshness of the conflict.'

Edgar Green: When he arrived home in 1951, his father held up the letter Green had written during the voyage to Korea and warned him, 'Don't ever write a letter like that again – if your mother'd seen it, she wouldn't be here now!' Having returned on several veteran revisits to South Korea, Green is a huge fan of the nation. In 2010, he flew the Korean flag during the World Cup; when neighbours laughed he said, 'Wait and see!' Indeed, Korea proved far more entertaining than a dire England.

Eric Gurr: The Argyll overrun at Pakchon still carries a Chinese bullet in his chest. Though he has no regrets, the war returns to him: 'I think of the guys I was close to who never came back. I had a good life, good marriage, a couple of great kids – they never had that chance.' During a revisit in 2005 – where he posed with a Chinese burp gun – he was delighted by South Korea. 'I thought it was amazing,' he said. 'It puts this country to shame a wee bit, ye know!'

Doug Haldane: 'Jock the Doc' left the Army in 1952, but plays golf with the Highland Brigade and curls with fellow Argylls Andrew Brown and Alan Lauder.

Kim Song-hwan: The student watercolourist served as a war artist with the ROK Army, and after the war, started a political cartoon *Gobau* – the pen name he adopted while hiding from the NKPA. By the 1970s, he was Korea's most famous cartoonist. Now retired, he paints back alleys, country villages and thatched cottages – the Korea that has been submerged by modernity. His war paintings reside at the National Museum of Contemporary Art, and a full gallery is displayed on the author's website.

Geoff King: The commando bayoneted in 'Hellfire Valley' served three more years in the marines, but suffered mental trauma: 'I used to dream I'd murdered people and buried them,' he said. 'If you're Christian and you kill, it preys on your mind.' In 2010, he returned to Korea, where, with US marines, he led a street parade for Inchon veterans. 'To see that the results have been so good, my book is closed,' he said.

Alan Lauder: After Korea, the Argyll subaltern took over the family photo business – 'As my wife says, I've given a lot of women a lot of pleasure!' – and in 1986, revisited Korea, where his son was working. And the war? 'Not a day goes by when I don't think about it,' he said.

Lee (John) Jong-yun: The student served with US marines throughout the war; post-war, marine officers sponsored him to study law in Virginia, and he became a successful lawyer. He later met refugees from Hagaru: He wept to recall their sufferings during the breakout, but they were keen to tell him how successful they were in the South. In 2010, he published a book on the Chosin campaign. Like many Koreans separated by the war, he never discovered the fate of his parents.

Owen Light: The deadliest Argyll platoon commander was the only one in the battalion to survive the full tour unscathed. He later served in the RAF and the Foreign Service, and became director of the PTSD charity, Combat Stress. In his late 70s, he still runs half marathons: 'It's an opportunity to see young women wearing almost nothing!'

Lim Geum-sook: 'The *Meredith Victory* was the greatest Christmas gift I could have had,' the teenager who escaped on the last civilian ship from Hungnam, said. But like many who fled North Korea, she feels survivors' guilt, certain that many who did not get out were punished or killed by vengeful communists.

Adam MacKenzie: The mortar man did thirty-four years in the Argylls, retiring as a colour sergeant. 'I never wore any other cap badge,' he said. 'It was family.' But the combat he recalls best is not a Korea War action, but the Battle of Fanling – a legendary 1951 punch-up between the Argylls and the Ulster Rifles in Hong Kong. 'We don't let anyone walk over us!' he said.

Andrew Man: The feisty little colonel retired in 1959, but his men's affection was evident when they asked him to head their veterans' association, 'The Korea Club'. Many ex-Diehards continued to seek his advice until his death in 2000.

Ken 'Ted' Mankelow: After returning to London, Mankelow heard that the Australian Army was recruiting. He volunteered, and was made an instructor. After retirement, he settled in Melbourne. A respected member of ex-serviceman's clubs in Victoria, the expatriate Briton died in 2010.

Colin Mitchell: The aggressive captain commanded his regiment in Aden, where, as 'Mad Mitch' he won a legendary reputation for unleashing 'Argyll Justice' in Crater, a campaign that some, today, consider a benchmark for counter-insurgency. After the Army, he served a brief stint as an MP, then headed a charity removing mines from former war zones. He died in 1996.

Ron Moyse: The big commando remained in the marines, and was RSM of 42 Commando in Borneo and Aden. In the 1980s, he was in a pub in Inverness when a visiting US marine colonel heard he had been in 41 Commando, stood up, and announced: 'This man saved my goddamned life, he got through to us at Hagaru!' In 1997, Moyse organised a reunion with US marines that included American wives taking part in an amphibious raid. His two sons were also commandos, but the line halted with his grandchildren – all female.

Tom Muggleton: The Digger sergeant spent thirty-five years in the Army, including a tour in Vietnam and postings to Sandhurst and

Duntroon. Of his three wars – the Second World War, Korea and Vietnam – he considered Korea the most intense. When a general once opined that 3 RAR's early battles in Korea were 'skirmishes', Muggleton, remembering the Broken Bridge and the prowling tanks, responded, 'If you were staring down the barrel of a T34, you might have a different view!'

Jake Mutch: The mortar man wounded at Naktong Crossing served in Borneo and Aden, then became a recruiter at Stirling Castle. He later visited his son, a commodities executive, working under a Korean boss in New York. Upon hearing that Mutch Sr had served in the Korean War, the Korean ordered everyone to cease working, and stood the floor of traders a drink to toast Mutch. He retains a fondness for Korea: 'It's a nice little country, some things are the same as our own,' he mused. 'Mountains, little farms, people going about their business – though we don't have topless apple pickers!'

Leslie Neilson: The Argylls' CO handed over command after leaving Korea in April 1951 to command the Highland Brigade. He retired a full colonel and died in 1980.

Ben O'Dowd: The tough Australian company commander was the unsung hero of the epic battle of Kapyong in 1951, where he commanded the forward company, then led 3 RAR's masterly retreat through hills infested with enemy. After Korea he fought in Malaya as liaison with the British Army. He retired as a colonel and wrote a book *In Valiant Company* – not bad going for an uneducated lad who had left the Outback to join the Army. Asked if he suffered PTSD, his reply was laconic: 'No, it was all in a day's work. I don't brood.'

Len Opie: After Korea, the frighteningly effective Digger's interest in military history led him to buy a bookshop, but he soon volunteered for Vietnam: 'There's nothing like combat.' There, he worked with the CIA, leading local irregulars against Viet Cong infrastructure in the notorious Phoenix Program (criticised by some as an assassination strategy). Among the Second World War, Korea and Vietnam, Korea was his career highlight: 'Korea was the best war, the first seven months,' he said. 'Every time we went into a fight, we won it.' At his funeral in 2008, Opie was eulogised as 'a warrior among warriors'.

Gordon Payne: The commando evacuated from Hagaru with frostbite considers the night in Hellfire Valley, 'the most significant part of my life, something you'd never dream of'. But Korea is so unknown, on the rare occasions when people ask him about his experiences, he has a suspicion that they will not believe what he tells them, so remains quiet

Paddy Redmond: The Irish sergeant is today a full-time carer for his severely handicapped daughter, Bernadette. Once certified as dead, Bernadette opened her eyes when nuns visited, making her one of the most famous Catholics in the UK, and the first confirmed by Pope John Paul II: 'Another first for the Middlesex!' Redmond said.

Ian 'Robbie' Robertson: 'The Hitman' was wounded in 1951, but recovered to serve in Vietnam. 'In Korea it was hand-to-hand, but in Vietnam, I didn't come across a lot of fighting and the weather was better,' he said. Though his sniping exploits led the *Sydney Morning Herald* to dub him 'The Deadliest Man in Australia' in 2004, he is an animal lover, who, in recent years, has ridden a horse in Anzac Day parades.

Ray Rogers: After leaving the army, Rogers emigrated to Australia where he keeps in touch with other Down Under Diehards. 'I can't say it was not worth it,' he said of Korea. 'I don't regret it, given the blokes I met, but I wouldn't advise my sons to do it.'

Frank Screeche-Powell: The Irishman never forgot the old Korean murdered by the Middlesex mortar man, nor the tiny Korean brother and sister he cared for over Christmas. Having emigrated to Australia, he wrote to the Korean Embassy to see if there was any chance of tracking the children down. He never received a reply, but treasures the rough note the children's father gave him.

Mick Servos: Having recovered from the machine gun burst through his thigh at Pakchon, Servos, returned to fight at Kapyong. He retired from the army as RSM of the Royal Queensland Regiment in 1976 and is active in veterans groups. Having enjoyed the combat, he finds the war remains with him: 'I dream of it quite often,' he said. 'The attacks... forming up... going in...'

John Shipster: Back in Hong Kong, the major's wife asked him about the golf and tennis gear he had abandoned at Taegu, so he filed an insurance claim. To his surprise, his insurers paid out double, 'in view of the hardships' he had suffered. Of Korea, he said: 'We had all the elation of chasing a beaten army and all the misery of being part of a beaten army ourselves.' A compiler of *The Diehards in Korea*, he penned his own memoirs, *Mist over the Rice Fields*. Having retired from the Army as a colonel, he died in 2001.

Viscount John Slim: After Korea, 'Big John' joined the fledgling SAS, fighting with it in Borneo, Yemen 'and in other places I don't talk about'. He advised the Australian Army on their establishment of an SAS regiment, and commanded the British unit. Today, as Viscount Slim of Burma, he is active in the Lords, in charity work in Burma and Pakistan, and as head of the SAS Regimental Association. During a veterans' revisit to Korea in 2010, he lunched with President Lee Myung-bak and invited him to the House of Lords. He is one of the last living Englishmen to use the term 'old boy' without irony.

Harry Spicer: After Korea, Spicer served in the crack Parachute Regiment, then emigrated to Australia, where he is active in charities and veterans' groups and holds a 5th dan black belt in taekwondo. In a 1989 letter to John Willoughby, Sergeant Paddy Bermingham wrote of Spicer: 'Disgustingly respectable and successful for one who appeared to be a potential rogue at the time!' But Spicer still has anger issues stemming from his wartime experiences, and remains haunted by the memory of the charred North Korean tank commander: 'Not a day goes by without thinking about Korea,' he said.

Sir James Stirling: The subaltern wounded alongside Kenny Muir recovered, served in the Territorial Argylls, and became Lord Lieutenant of Stirlingshire, where he lives amid stunning scenery. His son Archie also joined the Argylls, serving in Northern Ireland.

Peter Thomas: The commando heavy weapons officer remained in the corps, retiring as a colonel. He remains disturbed by the memory of the refugees from Hagaru who followed the marine column to Koto. His granddaughter, on a visit to Korea, laid a wreath for 41 Commando's dead at the UN Cemetery in Pusan in 2009.

Reginald Thompson: The brilliant reporter died in 1977, but his vivid 1951 work, *Cry Korea* – a key source for this book – was republished in 2009. Unflinching in its portrayal of UNC 'collateral damage' it is arguably the most powerful journalistic work on the war.

Julian Tunstall: The sensitive Diehard's *I Fought in Korea* was controversial among some. But in its afterword, Tunstall wrote: 'There is a great future for Korea . . . before very long . . . the Korean people will push themselves to the front and claim their rightful place among the great nations of the earth.' Given that the book was written in 1951, Tunstall's prescience was extraordinary.

John Underwood: The commando captured in Hellfire Valley survived captivity, and worked his way back to health. He has three times visited the USA to meet Chosin marines. 'Korea was not a brushfire war, not a police action, it was a war, when you think how many died – millions,' he said. 'Now, people don't mention the Korean War, they mention the Falklands and others, but they were very small compared to Korea. It annoys me intensely.'

John Walter: The subaltern who had not earned his green beret before deploying retired as a major. Today a keen ecologist, tree surgeon and furniture maker, he lives close to Teddy Allen.

Frank Whitehouse: 'After Korea, I was not frightened of anyone or anything,' Whitehouse said; he found himself drinking and fighting, but settled down after marriage. He is sad that the war is forgotten: 'Nobody knows anything about it,' he said. 'Nobody was interested, it was happening miles away.'

Sir John Willoughby: After Korea, Willoughby led 1st Middlesex in Austria and Cyprus during the EOKA Emergency. Promoted to major-general, he was knighted, retired in 1972 and died in 1991. His notebooks, in the Imperial War Museum, are the finest unpublished first-hand accounts of the Korean War the author has encountered.

David Wilson: The popular company commander never commanded the Argylls, but was military assistant to Field Marshal Bernard Montgomery and made brigadier. He also served as military attaché to Seoul in 1968, where he was moved to watch Korean school-children tending the 'field of graves', the UN Cemetery in Pusan, amid bitter October weather. His autobiography *The Sum of Things* was published in 2000. He died in 2001; John Slim spoke at his funeral.

Don Woods: The Digger machine gunner left the Army and married; today he has four children, nine grandchildren and four great-grandchildren. Of the war he says: 'I would not wish that experience on anyone, but I learned what mateship means and I learned what trust means. I am probably a better person for it.'

Bob Yerby: During a 2009 presentation on 29th Brigade's stand on the Imjin River, the Diehard asked the author not to overlook the 'forgotten' 27th Brigade. That conversation planted the seeds of this book.

Harry Young: The tough Argyll served in Borneo and Aden before retiring as a warrant officer. 'You never clear your mind of Korea, you dream of it, you are going into a gunfight, you see all your pals,' he said. 'It keeps me younger than I am!' He married his NAAFI sweetheart; their two sons both served in the Argylls.

Acknowledgements and Sources

The author expresses his gratitude to all interviewees (listed below), and to the staffs of: The Argyll and Sutherland Highlanders Regimental Museum and Regimental HQ; The Australian National War Memorial; The Imperial War Museum; The National Archive; The National Army Museum; and The Royal Marines Museum. I must also especially thank a number of persons for supplying me with information and/or images, permitting me to quote from their books, arranging contacts/interviews or otherwise rendering assistance. They are: John Ambler Alf Argent, Joe Bermudez, Sunny Choi, Graham Coster, David Brady, Vince Courtney, Bob Elliot, Frank Ellison, Frank Fallows, Chelsey Fox, Jack Gallaway, Edgar Green, Olwyn Green, Jack Harris, Kim Song-hwan, Andrei Lankov, Jean Main, Maria and Nicholas Man, Ben O'Dowd, Maurie Pears, Barry Reed, Tony Rooney, Shim Jae-hoon, Viscount John Slim and David Thomson. Finally, I must apologise to my wife and daughter for endless late nights and the paper-strewn chaos they lived amongst.

Oral Sources

1st Battalion, Argyll and Sutherland Highlanders:
Author Interviews: Sir Alexander 'Sandy' Boswell, Andrew Brown, Edward 'Ted' Cunningham, Eric Gurr, Dr Douglas Haldane, Alan Lauder, Owen Light, Adam MacKenzie, Jake Mutch, Viscount John Slim, Sir James Stirling, Harry Young

Imperial War Museum (IWM) Interviews: Henry 'Chick' Cochrane (18453), Joseph Fairhurst (18347), Ralph Horsfield (17968), Richard Peet (18344), Robert Searle (18470), Roy Vincent (17987), David Wilson (18699), Ronald Yetman (18003)

1st Battalion, Middlesex Regiment:
Author Interviews: Don Barrett, James Beverly, Tony Bradley, Edgar Green, Ken Mankelow, Edward 'Paddy' Redmond, Barry Reed, Ray Rogers, Frank Screeche-Powell, Harry Spicer, Frank Whitehouse, Bob Yerby
IWM Interviews: Albert Avis (18746), Stanley Boydell (18625), Edwin 'Ted' Haywood (20268), Arthur 'Nick' Hutley (18205), Reverend William Jones (18733), Ralph Main (30400), Andrew Man (9537), John Pluck (17430), Dennis Rendell (19055), John Shipster (18443)

3rd Battalion, Royal Australian Regiment:
Author Interviews: Alf Argent, Reg Bandy, Sir Phillip Bennett, David Butler, Stan Connelly, Jack Gallaway, Stan Gallop, Tom Muggleton, Ben O'Dowd, John 'Lofty' Portener, Ian 'Robbie' Robertson, William 'Dusty' Ryan, Mick Servos, Don Woods
Australian War Memorial Interviews: Leonard Opie

27th Brigade Headquarters:
Author Interview: Peter Baldwin. *IWM Interview*: Reggie Jeffes (17155)

41 Commando, Royal Marines:
Author Interviews: Teddy Allen, David Brady, Jack Edmonds, Geoff King, Ron Moyse, Gordon Payne, Peter Thomas, John Underwood, John Walter
IWM Interviews:
Andrew Condron (9693), Leslie Coote (14964), Fred Hayhurst (15576), Henry Langton (16761), Gersham Maindonald (16627), Michael O'Brien (13522), George Richards (9859), Edward Stock (16790), Raymond Todd (16656)

Others:

Author Interviews: Lyle Bradley, 1st US MARDIV Air Wing; Max Desfor, AP Photojournalist; Harry Gordon, *Melbourne Sun* reporter; Olywn Green, widow of Charles Green; Hahm Sock-young, ROK Army attacked 1st MARDIV; Kim Song-hwan, artist; John Lee, ROK Army attached 1st MARDIV; Lim Geum-sook, refugee; Robert Lunney, US Navy, SS *Meredith Victory;* Father Richard Rubie, 1st US MARDIV

Books

Anderson, RCB, *History of the Argyll and Sutherland Highlanders, 1st Battalion, 1939–1954*, Edinburgh, 1956

Anon, *Kim Il-sung, Condensed Biography,* Pyongyang, 2001

Appleman, Roy, *Disaster in Korea: The Chinese Confront MacArthur,* Texas, 1989

Appleman, Roy, *Escaping the Trap: The US Army X Corps in Northeast Korea, 1950,* Texas, 1990

Appleman, Roy, *South to the Naktong, North to the Yalu*, Washington DC, 1992 edition

Brady, Dave, *One of the Chosin Few: A Royal Marine Commando's Fight for Survival Behind Enemy Lines in Korea*, Essex, 2003

Brown, Andrew, *A Memoir: From Music to Wars,* Aberdeen, 2001

Cameron, James, *Point of Departure*, London, 1967

Carew, Tim, *How the Regiments Got their Nicknames,* London, 1974

Carew, Tim, *The Korean War: The Story of the Fighting Commonwealth Regiments,* London, 1967

Cunningham-Boothe, Ashley and Farrar, Peter (ed) *British Forces in the Korean War,* London, 1998

Department of the Army, *Handbook on the Chinese Communist Army*, Washington DC, 1952

Drury, Bob, and Clavin, Tom, *The Last Stand of Fox Company,* New York, 2009

Evans, Ben, *Out in the Cold: Australia's Involvement in the Korean War – 1950–53*, Canberra, 2001

Farrar-Hockley, Anthony, *The British Part in the Korean War, Volume 1: A Distant Obligation,* London, 1990

Foley, James, *Korea's Divided Families: Fifty Years of Separation*, London, 2003

Gallaway, Jack, *The Last Call of the Bugle: The Long Road to Kapyong*, Queensland, 1994

George, Alexander L, *The Chinese Communist Army in Action: The Korean War and its Aftermath*, New York, 1967

Goncharov, Sergei Nikolaevich, Lewis, John Wilson, Xue Yitai, *Uncertain Partners: Stalin, Mao and the Korean War*, Stanford, 1993

Green, Olwyn, *The Name's Still Charlie*, Queensland, 1993

Halberstam, David, *The Coldest Winter*, New York, 2007

Hammel, Eric, *Chosin: Heroic Ordeal of the Korean War*, New York, 1981

Harris, Alfred 'Jack,' *Only One River to Cross: An Australian Soldier Behind Enemy Lines in Korea*, Canberra, 2004

Hayhurst, Fred, *Green Berets in Korea*, Cambridge, 2001

Hickey, Michael, *The Korean War: The West Confronts Communism*, New York, 2000

Higgins, Margueritte, *War in Korea: The Report of a Woman Combat Correspondent*, New York, 1951

Leary, William, H., *Anything, Anywhere, Anytime: Combat Cargo in the Korean War,* Washington DC, 2000

Li Xiao-bing, Alan Millet, Bin Yu, *Mao's Generals Remember Korea,* Kansas, 2001

Mahoney, Kevin, *Formidable Enemies: The North Korean and Chinese Soldier in the Korean War,* New York, 2001

Malcolm, GI, *The Argylls in Korea*, Edinburgh, 1952

Millett, Allan, *They Came from the North: The Korean War 1950–1951,* Kansas, 2010

Mossman, Billy, *The United States Army in the Korean War: Ebb and Flow*, Washington DC, 1990

Neillands, Robin, *By Sea and Land: The Story of the Royal Marine Commandos*, London, 1987

O'Neill, Robert, *Australia in the Korean War 1950–53 Volume II: Combat Operations,* Canberra, 1985

Roe, Patrick, C., *The Dragon Strikes: China and the Korean War, June–December, 1950,* New York, 2000

Russ, Martin, *Breakout: The Chosin Reservoir Campaign, Korea, 1950,* New York, 1999

Salisbury, Harrison, *The Long March: The Untold Story,* New York, 1985

Shipster, John (ed), *The Diehards in Korea* (revised edition), Privately published, 1983

Shipster, John, *Mist on the Rice Fields,* Yorkshire, 2000

Spurr, Russell, *Enter the Dragon: China's Undeclared War Against the US in Korea, 1950–51,* New York, 1988

Thomas, Peter, *41 Independent Commando R.M., Korea 1950–1952,* Portsmouth, 1990

Thompson, Reginald, *Cry Korea: The Korean War: A Reporters' Notebook,* London, 1951

Tucker, Spencer, C., (ed), *Encyclopedia of the Korean War,* New York, 2002

Tunstall, Julian, *I Fought in Korea,* London, 1953

Wilson, David, *The Sum of Things,* Kent, 2001

Wilson, Jim, *Retreat, Hell!* New York, *1988*

Zhang Shu-guang, *Mao's Military Romanticism: China and the Korean War, 1950–1953,* Kansas, 1995

Articles

Anon, 'Argylls Ordeal in Bombing,' *Glasgow Herald,* 25 September 1950

Anon, 'B Coy, Sariwon and Pakchon,' *The Thin Red Line,* January 1951

Anon, 'Fighting Withdrawal in N.E. Korea: 41 Commando in Action with American Marines,' *Globe and Laurel,* 1951.

Anon, *Hansard,* 23 January 1951

Anon, 'Hill 282' in *The Thin Red Line,* January 1951

Anon, 'American Commentary,' in *The Thin Red Line,* September 1951

Camp, Dick, '41 Independent Commando, Royal Marines,' *Leatherneck* magazine, January, 2001

Charlesworth, NR, 'Pakchon – 4 Platoon Commander,' in *Duty First: The Royal Australian Regiment Association,* Spring 1997

Clark, LG, 'Through OC A Coy's Eyes,' in *Duty First,* Spring 1997

Connor, Steve, 'War, what is it Good for? It Made us less Selfish,' *The Independent,* 5 June 2009

Dicker, MC, 'Paddo to Pakchon,' *Duty First: The Royal Australian Regiment Association,* Volume 2, Number 5, Spring 1997

Dowling, Chuck, 'Task Force Drysdale: The Story of 41 Commando and their 'Cousins' the US Marines,' http://www.chuckdowling.com

Driberg, Tom, 'Commando Raid on North Korea,' *Reynolds News Service/Japan Times,* 18 October 1950

Dwyer, John, B, 'Any Purpose Designated,' *Naval History,* May/June 1996

Edmonds, Jack, 'SBS Operations in Korea, 1950–1951' *Croaker* (magazine of the SBS), 2009

Goldstein, Richard, 'Leonard La Rue, Rescuer in the Korean War, Dies at 87,' *New York Times,* 22 October 2001

Gurr, Eric; Charlesworth, Chick; Meighan, John; *A Hill in Korea,* www.britains-smallwars.com

Hegarty, John, *HMS Jamaica, Korean War Service,* www.britains-smallwars.com

Jones, Peter C, le P, *Argylls in Korea,* www.britains-smallwars.com

Koone, Howard, W., 'Fox Seven' in *Changjin Journal,* 15 June 2000

Macleod, Angus, 'Death on Hill 282,' *Sunday Mail,* January 21 1993

Man, Andrew, *The Naktong River and Middlesex Hill: September 1950,* in Cunningham-Boothe and Farrar, *op cit.* 1998

Mansourov, Alexandre, 'Stalin, Mao, Kim and China's Decision to Enter the Korean War, September 16–October 15, 1950: New Evidence from the Russian National Archive,' *The Cold War International History Project Bulletin 6/7*

Robson, Seth, 'Korean War Battle of Kunu-ri Remembered,' *Stars and Stripes,* 5 December 2004

Roe, P, 'Interview with General OP Smith' at www.chosin reservoir.com

Walden, Corporal JT, USMC, 'British Royal Marines' in *Leatherneck* magazine, reprinted in *Globe and Laurel,* 1952, p. 129.

Warner, Denis, 'A Warm Quayside Welcome,' the *Daily Telegraph,*

20 August 1950

Zabecki, David, *Stand or Die; 1950 Defense of Korea's Pusan Perimeter*, www.armchairgeneral.com

Unpublished Letters

Douglas Drysdale to General WI Nonweiler, The Admiralty, 2 November 1950. Held in RM Museum Archive

Douglas Drysdale to General WI Nonweiler, The Admiralty, 24 November 1950. Held in RM Museum Archive

Douglas Drysdale to General WI Nonweiler, The Admiralty, 12 December 1950. Held in RM Museum Archive

Morton Silver (US Navy, attached 1st USMC) to author Robin Neillands, 28 October 1995. Held in Royal Marines Museum Archive

John Smallbridge to BH Gandevia, 12 June 1992. Passed to the author by Dr. Douglas Haldane

Unpublished Documents

Anon, *USS Perch, Report of 1st War Patrol,* 7 Oct. 1950. Held in Royal Marines Museum

Anon, *War Diary, 1st Battalion, Argyll and Sutherland Highlanders.* (Annotated by Don Barrett). Held in National Army Museum

Anon, *War Diary, 3rd Battalion, Royal Australian Regiment.* Held at Australian War Memorial, Canberra

Anon, *War Diary, 27th British (later Commonwealth) Infantry Brigade.* Held in Public Record Office, Kew, London

Barrett, Don, *1st Battalion The Middlesex Regiment, Duke of Cambridge's Own, The Korean War, August 1950–May 1951,* 2005. Copy held in National Army Museum (Note: This work was collated by Barrett from the battalion War Diary and Signals Log)

Bermingham, Sergeant Edward, Package of papers covering his memories of 1st Middlesex in Korea, 1992. Presentation copy to Don Barrett. Held in National Army Museum

Bentinck, Major VN, *41 Independent Commando RM and the US Presidential Citation,* Held in Royal Marines Museum

Coad, Major General, Basil, *Report on Operations of 27th Brigade 29*

August–31 March 1951. Held in Public Record Office, Kew, London

Green, Olwyn, *Max Eberle Interview*, 2002. Held at Australian War Memorial

Green Olwyn, *Tim Holt Interview,* Undated. Held at Australian War Memorial

Hanson, Major Thomas, *America's First Cold War Army: Combat Readiness in the Eighth US Army, 1949–1950*, 2006. PhD Thesis, Ohio State University

Pounds, Captain EGD, *All in a Night's Work: An Account of a Raid in Korea, September (sic) 1950*, 1960. Held in Royal Marines Museum

Willoughby, Major General John, *Notebooks, 1950*. Held in Imperial War Museum

Audio Visual Materials

Korea: The Unknown War, Thames Television, 1988

Combat Bulletin Nos 102, 105, 106 of the Armed Forces, US Department of Defense, 1950

War in Korea: Looking Back, Part 1 Holding on the Naktong, British Defense Film Library, 1979

Websites

www.armchairgeneral.com

www.arrse.com

www.awm.gov.au

www.britains-smallwars.com

www.chosinreservoir.com

http://www.chuckdowling.com

www.frozenchosin.com

www.globalsecurity.org

www.moore-mccormack.com

www.navyfrogmen.com

www.wikipedia.com

www.youtube.com

Notes

Introduction

1 For casualty figures: see *Tributes to Soldier Killed in Helmand*, AFP, 2 Jan 2011; UK *Military Deaths in Afghanistan and Iraq*; BBC 12 February 2009; and *Falklands Islands History Roll of Honour* at www.raf.mod.uk/falklands/rollofhonour.html

Part One: Triumph

Prologue: Strangers in the Night

1 27th Brigade War Diary.
2 Anon., Jan 1951, p. 27.
3 Thompson, 1951, p. 187.
4 Yetman, IWM interview.
5 Malcolm, 1952, p. 39.
6 Mitchell, 1969, p. 75.
7 Carew, 1967, pp. 115–116.
8 Malcolm, 1952, p. 40.
9 Edward Searle, IWM Interview.
10 Anderson, 1956, p. 209.
11 Malcolm, 1952, p. 40.
12 Mitchell, 1969, p. 77.
13 Author interview, Adam MacKenzie.
14 Malcolm, 1952, p. 40.
15 Cochrane, IWM Recording.

Chapter One: Thunder in the East

1 Rendell, IWM.
2 Richard Peet, IWM.
3 Brown, 2001, p. 117.
4 Author interview, Edgar Green.
5 Author interview, Stan Tomenson, Royal Northumberland Fusiliers.
6 Farrar-Hockley, 1990, p. 125.

7 author interview, Rah Jong-yil.

8 Boose, Donald W, *The United Nations Command*, in Tucker, 2002, pp. 679–680.

9 from *Korean War Timeline*, in Tucker, 2002, p. 776.

10 Hanson, 2006, p. 34.

11 Zabecki, David, *Stand or Die; 1950 Defense of Korea's Pusan Perimeter*, www.armchairgeneral.com

12 Hayhurst, 2001, pp. 28–29.

13 Peter C le P Jones,*The Argylls in Korea*, and Hegarty, John, *HMS Jamaica, Korean War Service,* both at www.britains-smallwars.com. For casualty figures on 8 July, see Farrar-Hockley, 1990, p. 67.

14 Farrar-Hockley, 1990, pp. 117–119.

15 Farrar-Hockley, 1990, pp. 115–121.

16 Farrar-Hockley, 1990, p. 126.

17 Author interview, Owen Light.

18 O'Neill, 1985, p. 16.

19 Author interview, Major-General David Thomson, who later became colonel-in-chief of the regiment.

20 Malcolm, 1952, Chapter 1.

21 James Stirling, author interview.

22 Author interview, Harry Young.

23 Carew, 1974, p. 90.

24 Andrew Man obituary, 'The Diehards, 2000'.

25 Farrar-Hockley, 1990, p. 127.

26 Andrew Man, *The Naktong River and 'Middlesex Hill',* in Cunningham-Booth and Farrer, ed. 1998, p. 15.

27 Farrar-Hockley, 1999, p. 128.

28 Willoughby, 23 August.

29 Carew, 1967, p. 65.

30 Carew, 1967, p. 66.

31 Robert Searle, IWM interview.

32 Willoughby, 28 August.

33 Willoughby, 25 August.

34 Willoughby, 28 August.

35 Reggie Jeffes, IWM sound archive.

Chapter Two: Under Korean Skies

1 Harry Young, author interview.

2 Willoughby, 28 August.

3 Don Barrett, author interview.

4 Denis Warner, 'Warm Quayside Welcome', the *Daily Telegraph*, 20 August 1950.

5 Ralph Main, IWM interview.

6 This pen portrait of the refugee chaos of 1950 is sourced from contemporary photographs, film, and the life-size, walk-through display in the Korean National War Memorial in Yongsan, Seoul.

7 Willoughby, 31 August.

8 Willoughby, 2 September.

9 Willoughby, 31 August.

10 Willoughby, Diary, 3 September.

11 27th Brigade War Diary.

12 Willoughby Notebook, 1 September.

13 Willoughby Notebook, 1 September.

14 Willoughby Notebook, 2 September.

15 Willoughby, 3 September.

16 Coad, Report.

17 Reggie Jeffes, IWM interview.

18 Willoughby, 4 September.

19 Willoughby Diary, 4–6 September.

20 Shipster, 1975, p. 10.

21 Reggie Jeffes, IWM Interview.

22 Coad Report.

23 Willoughby Notebook, 13 September.

24 Willoughby, 6 September.

25 Willoughby, 19 September.

26 Willoughby Diary, 6 September.

27 Willoughby Notebook, 31 August.

28 Author interview, Rah Jong-yil.

29 Jones, Peter C le P, Argylls in Korea, at www.britains-smallwars.com

30 Willoughby, 8 September.

31 Willoughby Notebook, 12 September.

32 Tunstall, 1953, p. 16.

33 Willoughby Notebook, 5 September.

34 1st Argylls War Diary, 5 September.

35 Author interview, Edgar Green and Bob Yerby.

36 1st Argyll Highlanders War Diary, 8 September, 1950.

37 Coad Report.

38 This account of the patrol blends two accounts: an author interview with Harry Young, and the Argyll's official history by Malcolm, 1952. Where the accounts are at mild variance I have gone with Young.

39 1st Argylls War Diary, 7 September.

40 Coad Report.

41 Shipster, 1975, p. 11.

42 Tunstall, 1953, pp. 22–23.

43 A Company after-action report in 1st Argylls War Diary.

44 The account of the firefight and its aftermath comes from the A Company After-Action Report in 1 Argylls War Diary and an author interview with Owen Light.

45 Coad Report.

46 Willoughby, 8 September.

47 Barrett, 2005, p. 12.

48 Willoughby Notebook, 19 September.

49 Bermingham,1992, p. 4.

50 Bermingham, 1992, pp. 4–5.

51 Willoughby Diary, 19 September.

52 Willoughby Notebook, 25 September.

53 Zabecki, David, 'The Pusan Perimeter', Tucker, ed. 2002, pp. 544–545.

54 Millett, 2010, p. 269.

55 Coad Report.

56 Willoughby Notebook, 25 September.

57 Wilson, 2001, p.164.

Chapter Three: Into the Inferno

1 Barrett, 2005, p. 13.

2 Carew, 1967, p. 90.

3 Barrett, 2005, p. 13.

4 Willoughby Notebook, 25 September.

5 Willoughby, 25 September.

6 Man, in Cunningham and Farrar-Hockley, p. 17.

7 Shipster, 1975, p.10.

8 Barrett, 2005, p. 13

9 Willoughby, 25 September.

10 Farrar-Hockley, 1990, p. 167.

11 27th Brigade War Diary, 21 September.

12 Farrar-Hockley, 1990, p. 167.

13 Willoughby, 25 September.

14 Barrett, 2005, p. 14.

15 Willoughby, 25 September.

16 Barrett, 2005, p. 14.

17 Barrett, 2005, p. 14.

18 Willoughby, 25 September.

19 Man, in Cunningham and Farrar-Hockley, eds, *op cit.*, p. 20.

20 British Defence Film Library, 1979.

21 Willoughby Notebook, 25 September.

22 Bermingham, 1992, p. 7.

23 Willoughby, 25 September.

24 Bermingham, 1992, p. 7.

25 Willoughby, 25 September.

26 Willoughby, 25 September.

27 Willoughby, 25 September.

28 Willoughby Notebook, 25 September.

29 Willougbhy Notebook, 25 September.

30 Willoughby Notebook, 25 September.

31 Willoughby, 25 September.

32 Willoughby, 25 September.

33 Bermingham, 1992, p. 8.

34 Farrar-Hockley, 1990, p. 170. Some Middlesex accounts state that the last attack was a dawn attack, but Beverly and Yerby both recall fighting in darkness.

35 Farrar-Hockley, 1900, p. 170.
36 Bermingham, 1992, p. 7.
37 Barrett, 2005, p. 15.
38 Farrar-Hockley, 1990, p. 166.
39 Wilson, 2001, p. 164.
40 Timing from 1st Argylls War Diary.
41 Farrar–Hockley, 1990, p. 171.
42 1st Argylls War Diary.
43 Malcolm, 1952, p.18.
44 1st Argylls War Diary.
45 1st Argylls War Diary.
46 Anderson, 1956, pp. 195–196.
47 C Company after-action report, in 1st Argylls War Diary.
48 1st Argylls War Diary.
49 Malcolm, 1952, p. 19.
50 Coad Report.
51 C Company after-action report, 1st Argylls War Diary.
52 1st Argylls War Diary.
53 C Company after-action report, 1st Argylls' War Diary.
54 Napalm entry on www.globalsecurity.org
55 Napalm entry at www.globalsecurity.org
56 Don Barrett, author interview.
57 Author interview, Owen Light.
58 Angus Macleod, 'Death on Hill 282', *Sunday Mail,* 21 January, 1993.
59 Sir Alexander Boswell, Viscount John Slim, Sir James Stirling, author interviews.
60 An Argyll officer interviewed by the author who requested anonymity.
61 Wilson, 2001, p. 165.
62 Anon, *Hill 282*, in 'The Thin Red Line', January 1951, p. 25.
63 B Company after-action report, 1st Argylls War Diary.
64 According to the Argylls War Diary, all men had withdrawn off the hill and regrouped at the bottom by 15:30. As it took approximately an hour to get down, 14:00 seems about right for the final act on the summit.
65 B Company after-action report, in 1st Argylls War Diary.
66 B Company after-action report, 1st Argylls War Diary.
67 Connor, Steve, 'War What is it Good For? It Made Us Less Selfish', the *Independent,* 5 June, 2009.
68 B Company after-action report, in 1st Argylls War Diary.
69 This anecdote was passed to the author by an employee of Westlands Helicopter during a function at the British Embassy, Seoul.
70 Don Barrett, author interview.
71 Anon, 'Argylls Ordeal in Bombing', *Glasgow Herald,* 25 September.
72 27th Brigade War Diary, 23 September.
73 Anderson, 1956, p. 198.
74 Millett, 2010, p. 270.
75 Coad Report, p. 2.

76 Coad Report, p. 2.
77 Farrar-Hockley, 1990, p. 177.
78 Millett, 2010, p. 271.
79 Anon, 'Argylls Ordeal in Bombing', *Glasgow Herald*, 25 September.
80 Jan 1951 edition of *Thin Red Line*, p. 5.
81 Farrar-Hockley, 1990, p. 177.
82 Willoughby, 26 September.
83 Albert Avis, IWM interview.
84 Willoughby Notebook, 26 September.
85 Willoughby Notebook, 30 September.
86 Tunstall, 1953, p. 23.
87 Barrett 2005, p. 17.
88 Willoughby, 29 September.
89 Willoughby, 30 September.
90 Willoughby, 28 September.
91 Willoughby Notebook, 28 September.
92 Willoughby Notebook, 30 September.
93 1st Middlesex War Diary, 29 September.
94 Willoughby Notebook, 28 September.

Chapter Four: Turned Tide and New Allies
1 Farrar-Hockley, 1990, p. 149.
2 Farrar-Hockley, 1990, p. 149.
3 Millet, pp. 249–250.
4 Millet, 2010, p. 244.
5 Ent, Uzel W, 'Korea Democratic People's Republic Army', Tucker, 2002, p. 339.
6 Zabecki, David, 'Pusan Perimeter and Breakout', Tucker, 2002, p. 545.
7 Esposito, Matthew, 'Australia' in Tucker 2002, pp. 61–62.
8 O'Neill, 1985, pp. 1–6.
9 Gallaway, 1994, p. 26.
10 O'Neill, 1985, pp. 6–10.
11 Tim Holt interview, Green, undated.
12 Author interview, David Butler.
13 Gallaway, 1993, pp. 23–24.
14 Green, 1993, pp. 214–22.
15 Author interview, Harry Gordon.
16 O'Dowd, 2000, p. 7.
17 O'Neill, 1985, p. 19.
18 Gallaway, 1993, p. 46.
19 27th Brigade War Diary.
20 Gallaway, 1994, p. 54.
21 Reggie Jeffes, IWM interview.
22 Willoughby Notebook, 8 October.
23 Author interview, Harry Gordon.
24 Gallaway, 1994, p. 56.

25 Willoughby Notebook, 7 October.

Chapter Five: Behind Enemy Lines
1 Thomas, 1990, p. 8.
2 Farrar-Hockley, 1990, p. 121.
3 Thomas, 1990, p. 6.
4 Farrar-Hockley, 1990, p. 326.
5 Neillands, 2004, p. 38.
6 Author interviews, Gordon Payne and Ron Moyse.
7 Hayhurst, 2001, p. 21.
8 Brady, 2003, p. 8.
9 Brady, 2003, p. 9.
10 Author interview, John Walter.
11 Brady, 2003, p. 10.
12 Farrar-Hockley, 1990, p. 326.
13 Brady, 2003, pp. 16–19.
14 O'Brien, IWM interview.
15 Hayhurst, 2001, p. 62.
16 Author interview, Peter Thomas.
17 Driberg, Tom, 'Commando Raid on North Korea', *Reynolds News Service/Japan Times,* 18 October 1950.
18 Author interview, Gordon Payne.
19 Hayhurst, 2001, p. 63.
20 Hayhurst, 2001, p. 69.
21 Hayhurst, 2001, p. 72.
22 Pounds, *All in a Night's Work,* 1960.
23 Pounds, 1960.
24 Driberg, Tom, 'Commando Raid on North Korea', *Reynolds News Service/Japan Times,* 18 October 1950.
25 Hayhurst, 2001, p. 49.
26 Thomas, 1990, p. 8.
27 Brady, 2003, p. 38.
28 Brady, 2003, pp. 43–44.
29 Brady, 2003, pp. 49–50.
30 Brady, 2003, p. 56.
31 Hayhurst, 2001, p. 57.
32 Hayhurst, 2001, p. 57.
33 Brady, 2003, p. 57.
34 Driberg, Tom, 'Commando Raid on North Korea', *Reynolds News Service/Japan Times,* 18 October 1950.
35 USS Perch, Report of 1st War Patrol, 7 October 1950.
36 Driberg, Tom, 'Commando Raid on North Korea', *Reynolds News Service/Japan Times,* 18 October 1950.
37 Hayhurst, 2001, p. 83.
38 Drysdale letter, November 2 1950.

Chapter Six: Dust Clouds and Burning Towns

1 Millett, 2010, p. 278.
2 Millett, 2010, p. 275.
3 Coad Report.
4 Millett, p. 275.
5 Farrar-Hockley, 1990, p. 237.
6 27th Brigade War Diary.
7 Zabecki, David, T, *Walker, Walton Harris*, in Tucker, ed, 2002, p. 731.
8 Farrar-Hockley, p. 237.
9 27th Brigade War Diary.
10 Coad Report, p. 8.
11 Farrar-Hockley, 1990, p. 239.
12 Coad Report, p. 8.
13 Wilson, 2001, p.167. See also Wilson IWM interview.
14 1st Argylls War Diary.
15 Wilson, 2001, p. 168.
16 Thompson, 1951, p. 191.
17 1st Argylls War Diary.
18 27th Brigade War Diary, 17 October.
19 A Company After-action Report, in 1st Argylls War Diary.
20 Appleman, 1992, p. 644.
21 A Company After-action Report, in 1st Argylls War Diary.
22 Wilson, 2001, p. 171.
23 From *Newsweek*, 30 October 1950. Un-bylined fragment in *The Thin Red Line*, September, 1951, Volume 5, Number 3.
24 Wilson, 2001, p. 170.
25 Wilson, 2001, p. 170.
26 Coad Report, p. 8.
27 Harris, 2004, p. 4.
28 Harris, 2004, p. 4.
29 Harris, 2004, p. 5.
30 Farrar-Hockley, p. 244.
31 Willoughby, 18 October.
32 Willoughby, 18 October.
33 Shipster, 1983, p. 19.
34 Farrar-Hockley, 1990, pp. 244–245.
35 Gay letter to Coad, in 27th Brigade War Diary.
36 Bermingham, 1992, p. 10.
37 Coad Report, p. 9.
38 Len Opie, AWM interview; 3 RAR War Diary, 19 October.
39 Thompson, 1951, p. 200.
40 Willoughby Notebook, 20 October.
41 Mick Servos, author interview.
42 Willoughby Notebook, 20 October.
43 Thompson 1951, p. 208.

44 Thompson pp. 214–215.
45 Anon, 2001.
46 Appleman 1989, p. 11.
47 Willoughby Notebook, 20 October.
48 Millett, 2010, p. 283.
49 Coad Report, p. 9.

Chapter Seven: At the Tip of the Spear
 1 Combat Bulletin No 103, 1950.
 2 Millett, 2010, p. 274.
 3 Coad Report, p. 11.
 4 27th Brigade War Diary, 21 October.
 5 Coad Report, p. 11.
 6 Willoughby, 21 October.
 7 Coad Report, p. 10.
 8 Farrar-Hockley, 1990, p. 250.
 9 27th Brigade War Diary.
10 Wilson, 2001. p. 172.
11 Coad Report.
12 Coad Report.
13 Barrett, 2005, p. 8.
14 Author interview, Owen Light.
15 Jones, www.britains-smallwars.com
16 Coad Report, p. 10.
17 Jones, www.britains-smallwars.com
18 Author interview, David Butler.
19 Harris, 2004, pp. 15–16.
20 Harris, 2004, p. 16.
21 Appleman, 1992, p. 660.
22 Carew, 1967, pp. 124–125.
23 Appleman, 1992, p. 660.
24 Coad Report.
25 Quoted in O'Dowd, 2000, p. 12.
26 Casualty figures in Gallaway, p. 77.
27 Millett, 2010, p. 289.
28 Harris, 2004, p. 19.
29 27th Brigade War Diary.
30 Coad Report.
31 Willoughby Notebook, 23 October.
32 Coad Report.
33 Barrett, 2005, p. 24.
34 Willoughby Notebooks, 23 October.
35 Coad Report.
36 Willoughby Notebook, 24 October.
37 27th Brigade War Diary, 24 October.

38 Farrar-Hockley, 1990, p. 254.
39 27 Brigade War Diary, 24 October.
40 Coad Report.
41 Farrar-Hockley, 1990, p. 253.
42 Barrett, 2005, p. 25.
43 27th Brigade War Diary, 25 October.
44 O'Neill, 1985, pp. 41–43.
45 O'Neill, 1985, p. 43.
46 Harris, 2004, p. 21.
47 Reg Bandy, author interview.
48 Evans, 2001, p. 28.
49 O'Neill, 1985, p. 45.
50 Gallaway, 1989, p. 88.
51 Gallaway, 1989 p. 86.
52 O'Neill, 1985, p. 46.
53 Harris, 2004, p. 23.
54 Barrett, 2005, p. 25.
55 Arthur Hutley, IWM interview.
56 Willoughby, 27 October.
57 Barrett, 2005, p. 36.
58 Farrar-Hockley, pp. 256–257.
59 Don Barrett, author interview.
60 Shipster ed. 1975, p. 25.
61 Willoughby, 27 October.
62 Willoughby Notebook, 27 October.
63 Coad Report.
64 27th Brigade War Diary, 27 October.
65 Farrar-Hockley, 1990, p. 257.
66 27th Brigade War Diary, 28 October.
67 Farrar-Hockley, 1990, p. 258.
68 Gallaway, 1989, p. 92.
69 From 3 RAR War Diary, as quoted in Green, 1993, p. 281.
70 Gallaway, 1989, p. 93.
71 Millett, 2010, p. 289.
72 Coad Report.
73 O'Neill, 1985, p. 49.
74 Coad Report.
75 O'Neill, 1985, p. 49.
76 Willoughby Notebook, 30 October.
77 Brigade War Diary, 30 October.
78 Fragment of Australian newspaper *The Age,* in 27th Brigade War Diary appendix.
79 Harris, 2004, pp. 26–27.
80 Green, 1993, p. 270, p. 284.
81 O'Dowd, 2000, p. 16.
82 Green, 1993, p. 283.

83 Gallaway, 1994, p. 97.

84 Green, 1993, p. 283.

85 Author interview, Olwyn Green.

86 *Silver Star;* Extract from 'Stars and Stripes', 4 November, 1950, in 28th Brigade War Diary.

87 Shipster, 2000, p. 125.

88 Appleman 1992, pp. 669; Millett, 2010, p. 288.

89 Appleman, 1992, pp. 670.

90 27th Brigade War Diary, 31 October.

91 Farrar-Hockley, 1990, p. 290.

92 Willoughby Notebook, 31 October.

93 O'Neill, 1985, p. 45.

94 Millett, 2010, p. 290.

95 Farrar-Hockley, 1990, p. 261.

Part Two: Catastrophe

Chapter Eight: North Wind

1 Wilson, 2001, pp. 174–175; also A Company After-Action Report in 1st Argylls War Diary.

2 Salisbury, 1985, pp. 191–193.

3 Goncharov et al., 1993, p. 181.

4 Goncharov et al., 1993, p. 182.

5 Roberts, Priscilla, 'Pannikar, Sardar', Tucker, 2002, p. 510.

6 Goncharov et al., 1993, p. 181.

7 Li et al., 2001, p. 31.

8 Goncharov et al., 1993, p. 182.

9 Goncharov at al., 1993, p. 185.

10 Goncharov et al., 1993, p. 195.

11 George, New York, 1967, p. 193.

12 George, 1967, p. 130.

13 Appleman, 1998, p. 14.

14 George, 1967, p. 164.

15 Author interview, Rah Jong-yil .

16 Millett, 2010, p. 275..

17 Li et al., 2001, p. 43 and p. 254.

18 Spurr, 1988, p. 129.

19 Millett, 2010, p. 295.

20 Appleman, 1989, p. 14.

21 George, 1967, p. 170.

22 Goncharov et al., p. 165.

23 Coad Report.

24 Appleman, 1989, pp. 19–20.

25 Willoughby Notebook, 2 November.

26 Coad Report.

27 27th Brigade War Diary, 3 November.

28 1st Argylls War Diary, 3 November.
29 Coad Report.
30 Coad Report.
31 Bermingham, 1992, p. 13.
32 Bermingham, 1992.
33 Willoughby Notebook, 7 November; also Don Barrett's notes to Shipster ed. 1975.
34 Coad Report.
35 Coad Report.
36 Coad Report.
37 Appleman, 1992, p. 711.
38 Barrett, 2005, p. 31.
39 Coad Report.
40 Coad Report.
41 Author interview, Peter Baldwin.
42 Tunstall, p. 37.
43 A Company After-Action Report, in 1st Argylls War Diary; also Wilson, 2001, p.175.
44 A Company After-Action Report, 1st Argylls War Diary.
45 1st Argyll War Diary.
46 Mitchell, 1969, p. 80.
47 IWM Interview, Robert Searle.
48 Gurr, Eric; Charlesworth, Chick; Meighan, John; *A Hill in Korea*, www.britains–smallwars.com
49 A Company After-Action Report, in 1st Argylls War Diary.
50 Charlesworth, N.R., 'Packchon – 3 Platoon Commander', in *Duty First*, 1997.
51 Author interview, Ben O'Dowd.
52 Gurr, Eric; Charlesworth, Chick; Meighan, John; *A Hill in Korea* at www.britains–smallwars.com
53 3 RAR War Diary.
54 Mitchell, 1969, p. 81.
55 Barrett, 2005, p. 31.
56 Willoughby, 7 November.
57 Willoughby Notebook, 7 November.
58 Willoughby Notebook, 7 November.
59 Coad Report.
60 27th Brigade War Diary, 5 November.
61 O'Dowd, 2000, pp. 21–22.
62 Clark, 'Through OC A Coy's Eyes', *Duty First,* 1997.
63 Charlesworth, 1997.
64 Clark, 1997.
65 O'Neill, 1985, p. 63.
66 Willoughby Notebook, 7 November.
67 3 RAR War Diary, 6 November.
68 1st Argylls War Diary, 7 November.
69 Thompson, 1951, p. 266.

70 Author interview, Andrew Brown.

71 Thompson, 1951, p. 267.

72 Millett, 2010, p. 310.

73 Farrar-Hockley, 1990, pp. 290–291.

74 Willoughby Notebook, 10 November.

75 Malcolm, 1952, p. 56.

76 Thompson, 1951, p. 269.

77 Shipster, 2000, p. 134.

78 Shipster ed., 1983.

79 27th Brigade War Diary, 13–17 November.

80 Thompson, 1951, p. 267.

81 O'Neill, 1985, p. 66.

82 Willoughby, 13 Nov.

83 27th Brigade War Diary.

84 Thompson, 1951, p. 266.

85 O'Neill, 1985, p. 68.

86 Author interview, Don Barrett.

87 Barrett, 2005, p. 25.

88 Harris, 2004, p. 17.

89 Green, Max Eberle Interview, 2002.

90 Tunstall, 1953, p. 10.

91 Tunstall, 1953, pp. 24–25.

92 Thompson, 1951, p. 55.

93 Beirne, Daniel, 'Chinese Military Disengagement', Tucker ed., 2002, p. 132–133.

94 Appleman 1989, pp. 24–26.

95 Thompson, 1951, p. 272.

96 Thompson, 1951, p. 275.

97 Millett, 2010, pp. 312–313.

98 Millett, 2010, p. 317, 335.

99 Appleman, 1989, p. 47.

100 Millet, 2010, p. 335.

Chapter Nine: Scorched Earth

1 Willoughby Notebook, 26 November.

2 27th Brigade War Diary, 25 November.

3 Willoughby Notebook, 24 November.

4 Willoughby, 24 November.

5 Coad Report.

6 Schafer, Elizabeth, Coulter, John Breitling, Tucker ed. 2002. p. 174.

7 Thompson, 1951, pp. 282–283.

8 Coad Report.

9 Shipster, 1975, p. 33.

10 27th Brigade War Diary, 27 November.

11 Willoughby Notebook, 8 December.

12 Coad Report.

13 27th Brigade War Diary, 27 November.

14 Daniel Bierne; Chonchong River, Battle of, in Tucker ed. 2002, pp. 146–7.

15 Coad Report.

16 Reggie Jeffes, IWM Interview; see also O'Dowd, 2000, p. 48.

17 Coad Report.

18 Farrar-Hockley, 1990, p. 333, and Coad Report.

19 Quoted in Shipster, 1983, p.105.

20 Appleman, 1989, p. 201.

21 Farrar-Hockley, 1990, p. 333.

22 Bermingham, 1992, p. 15.

23 Shipster, 1983, p. 105.

24 Malcolm, 1952, p. 59.

25 Willoughby Notebook, 8 December.

26 Wilson, 2001, p. 180.

27 Bermingham, 1992, pp. 15–16.

28 27th Brigade War Diary, 18–19 November.

29 Millet, pp. 340–341.

30 Millet 2010, p. 341.

31 Coad Report.

32 27th Brigade War Diary, 29 November.

33 Willoughby Notebook, 8 December.

34 Willoughby Notebook, 8 December.

35 Shipster, 2000, p. 136.

36 Barrett, 2005, p. 38.

37 Willoughby Notebook, 8 December.

38 Barrett, 2005, pp. 38–39.

39 Willoughby, 8 December.

40 Coad Report.

41 Bermingham, 1992, p. 18.

42 Bermingham, 1992, pp. 18–19.

43 Barrett, 2005, p. 39.

44 Willoughby, 8 December.

45 Coad Report, *Yongwon;* 27th Brigade War Diary, 30 November.

46 Author interview, Ray Rogers and Harry Spicer of Middlesex; also Peter Baldwin of Brigade Headquarters.

47 Willoughby Notebook, 8 December.

48 Bermingham, 1992 p. 20.

49 Willoughby Notebook, 8 December.

50 Shipster, 2000, p. 138.

51 Willoughby Notebook, 8 December.

52 Appleman, 1989, p. 242.

53 Appleman, 1989, p. 254.

54 Appleman, 1989, p. 257.

55 Willoughby Notebook, 8 December.

56 Wilson, 2001, p. 180.

57 Author interview, Don Barrett.

58 Barrett, 2005, p. 40.

59 Willoughby Notebook, 8 December.

60 Arthur Hutley, IWM Interview.

61 John Pluck, IWM Interview.

62 Willoughby Notebook, 8 December.

63 Thompson, 1951, p. 299.

64 Appleman, 1989, p. 289.

65 Appleman, 1989, p. 284.

66 Thompson, pp. 294–295.

67 Appleman, 1989, p. 299.

68 Appleman, 1989, p. 296.

69 Barrett, 2005, p. 41.

70 Appleman, 1989, p. 303.

71 27th Brigade War Diary, 1–2 December.

72 O'Dowd, 2000, p. 56.

73 Wilson, 2001, pp. 181–182.

74 Coad Report.

75 Willoughby Notebook, 8 December.

76 Coad Report.

77 Willoughby Notebook, 8 November.

78 Roy Vincent, IWM Interview.

79 Gallaway, 1994, p. 150.

80 Ted Haywood, IWM Interview.

81 Appleman, 1989, pp. 309, 317–8, 321, 334.

82 Foley, 2003, Chapter 2.

83 Willoughby, 8 December.

84 Thompson, 1951, p. 284.

85 Appleman, 1989, p. 297.

86 Appleman, 1989, p. 313.

87 Appleman, 1989, p. 321.

88 Appleman, 1989.

89 Appleman, p. 321.

90 Hickey, 2000, p. 143; Letter from Australian historian John Smallbridge to Dr B. Gandevia, 12 June 1992.

91 Coad Report.

92 Appleman, 1989, p. 331.

93 Appleman, p. 340.

94 Appleman, 1989, p. 328.

95 O'Dowd, 2000, p. 59.

96 Willoughby Notebook, 8 December.

97 27th Brigade War Diary.

98 Tunstall, 1953, p. 50.

99 Millett, 2010, p. 318.

NOTES | 449

Chapter Ten: White Hell

1 For vehicle numbers, see Thomas, 1990, p. 14.
2 Drysdale, Letter, 24 November.
3 George Richards, IWM interview.
4 The author is thankful to Chosin Reservoir veteran Lee Jong-yoon for historical background.
5 Drysdale, letter 24 November.
6 Brady, 2004, p. 72.
7 Raymond Todd, IWM 16656.
8 Timing from Anon, 'Fighting Withdrawal in N.E. Korea: 41 Commando in Action with American Marines', *Globe and Laurel*, 1951, p. 58.
9 Brady, 2004, p. 78.
10 Brady, 2004, p. 75.
11 See Tucker, *Puller, Lewis Burwell* in Tucker, ed., 2002, pp. 538–539.
12 Quote: See Puller's Wikipedia entry.
13 Author interview, Father Richard Rubie.
14 Brady, 2004, p. 75.
15 Wilson, 1988, p. 226.
16 Halberstam, 2007, p. 163.
17 Russ, 1999, p. 17.
18 Tucker, ed. 2002, pp. 59–600.
19 Halberstam, 2007, p. 431.
20 For Chinese army and division numbers in the reservoir areas, see Zhang, 1995, pp. 116–117; also Mahoney, 2001, pp. 128 and 130.
21 For UNC troop numbers around the reservoir, see Russ, 1999, p. 114.
22 Quoted in Hayhurst, 2001, pp. 152–153.
23 Remembered by Teddy Allen, author interview.
24 Hayhurst, 2001, p. 110.
25 Quoted in Halberstam, 2007, p. 439.
26 Mossman, 1990, p. 101.
27 Column numbers from Thomas, 1990, p. 14.
28 Camp, Dick, 2001, p. 16.
29 Hayhurst, 2001, p. 109.
30 Neillands, Robin, 1987, pp. 286–287.
31 Hayhurst, 2001, p. 112.
32 Hayhurst, 2001, pp. 94–95.
33 Brady, 2000, p. 80.
34 Brady, 2000, p. 71.
35 Hayhurst, 2001, p. 113.
36 Hammel, 1981, p. 145.
37 Hammel, 1981, p. 152.
38 Wilson, 1988, p. 226; see also 41 Commando War Diary. *58th and 60th Divisions;* Mossman, 1990, p. 102.
39 Brady, 1990, pp. 81–82.
40 Brady, 1990, pp. 81–82.

41 Brady, 2000, pp. 83–85.
42 Wilson, 1988, p. 229.
43 41 Commando War Diary.
44 41 Commando War Diary.
45 41 Commando War Diary.
46 Quoted in Russ, 1999, p. 224.
47 O'Brien, IWM 13522.
48 Kirk 1988, p. 230.
49 www.chosinreservoir.com
50 Russ, p. 235.
51 Neillands, 1987, p. 287.
52 Timing from 41 Commando War Diary.
53 Hammel, 1981, p. 180.
54 Wilson, 1989, p. 239.
55 Raymond Todd, 16656.
56 Hayhurst, 2001, p. 130.
57 Dowling, Chuck, *Task Force Drysdale* http://www.chuckdowling.com
58 Gersham Maindonald, IWM 16627.
59 Gersham Maindonald, IWM 16627.
60 Kirk 1998, pp. 239–243.
61 Fred Hayhurst, IWM 15576.
62 Hayhurst, 2002, p. 132.
63 Russ, 1999, p. 237.
64 Brady 2004, pp. 93–98.
65 Hammel, 1981, p. 201. Hammel puts the pockets at five; Russ, 1999, at four. Given the chaos of that night, it is impossible to accurately establish what happened with certainty.
66 Neillands, 1987, p. 290.
67 Russ, 1989, pp. 241–242.

Chapter Eleven: Black Snow

1 Brady, 2003, pp. 99–106.
2 Thomas, 1990, p. 16.
3 Wilson, 1988, p. 252.
4 Wilson, 1988, p. 253.
5 Wilson, 1988, p. 254.
6 Russ, 1999, pp. 263–267.
7 Thomas, 1990, p. 17.
8 Teddy Allen and John Walter.
9 Farrar-Hockley, 1990, p. 340.
10 O'Brien, IWM 13522.
11 Farrar-Hockley, 1990, p. 338.
12 O'Brien, IWM 13522.
13 O'Brien, IWM 13522.
14 Russ, 1999, p. 266.
15 Hayhurst, 2001, p. 156.

16 Mossman, 1990, p. 105.
17 Mossman, 1990, pp. 129–130.
18 Mossman, 1990, p. 129.
19 Naval and air strengths from James A Field, *History of US Naval Operations: Korea*, Washington DC, Chapter 9.
20 Leary, 2000, pp. 19–20.
21 Tucker, Spencer, C, 'Changjin, Chosin Reservoir Campaign', in Tucker, ed. 2002, p. 111.
22 Higgins, 1951, p. 186.
23 Russ, 1999, p. 317.
24 Drury and Clavin, 2009, p. 277.
25 Koone, 2000.
26 Walden, Corporal JT, USMC, 'British Royal Marines' in *Leatherneck* Magazine, reprinted in *Globe and Laurel* 1952, p. 129.
27 Russ, 1999, p. 322.
28 Russ, 1999, p. 328.
29 Leary, 2000, p. 17.
30 Leary, 2000, p. 20.
31 Russ, 1999, p. 338.
32 Hayhurst, IWM 15576.
33 Thomas, 1990, p. 21.
34 Hammel, 1981, p. 300.
35 CP Roe interview with General OP Smith at www.chosinreservoir.com
36 Russ, 1999, p. 337.
37 Wilson, 1988, p. 267.
38 Hammel, 1981, p. 300.
39 Hayhurst, 2001, p. 168.
40 Hammel, 1981, p. 301.
41 Mossman, 1990, p. 139.
42 Hammel, 1981, p. 304.
43 Higgins, 1951, p. 181.
44 Russ, 1999, p. 328.
45 Russ, 1999, p. 341.
46 Russ, 1999, p. 355.
47 Hastings, 1987, p. 160.
48 Pat Roe interview with General OP Smith, www.chosinreservoir.com
49 Russ, 1999, p. 373.
50 Mossman, 1990, p. 141.
51 Russ, 1999, p. 361.
52 Hahm Sock-young, author interview.
53 Hayhurst, 1999, p. 175.
54 Russ, 1999, p. 376.
55 Roe, Patrick C, 2000, p. 435.
56 Langton, IWM 16761.
57 Russ, 1990, p. 388.
58 O'Brien, IWM 13522.

59 Russ, 1999, p. 324.

60 Russ, 1999, p. 239.

61 Wilson, 1988, p. 288.

62 Wilson, 1988, p. 289.

63 A veteran of the march, speaking on condition of anonymity; author interview.

64 The author is grateful to British and American veterans on the Army Rumour Service website for this insight into the effect of napalm on corpses.

65 O'Brien, IWM 13522.

66 Drury and Clavin, 2009, p. 20.

67 Hayhurst, 1999, p. 168.

68 Anon in *Changjin Journal*, 03.31.00.

69 Peter Thomas, author interview.

70 Thomas, 1990, p. 22.

71 Brady, 2003, p. 114.

72 Peter Thomas, author interview; Hayhurst, 1999, pp. 179–180.

73 Russ, 1999, p. 398.

74 Higgins, 1951, p. 105.

75 Higgins, 1951, p. 106.

76 Higgins, 1951, p. 107.

77 Russ, 1999, p. 398.

78 Brady, 2003, p. 116.

79 Russ, 1999, p. 412.

80 CP Roe interview with General OP Smith, www.chosinreservoir.com

81 Hayhurst, 2001, p. 190.

82 Li, Millet, Yu, 2001, p. 154.

83 Spurr, Russell, *Enter the Dragon*, New York, 1988, p. 270.

84 Hammel, 1981, p. 379.

85 Hammel, 1981, p. 391.

86 Brady, 2003, p. 116.

87 Brady, 2003, p. 118.

88 41 Commando War Diary.

89 Leslie Coote, IWM 14964.

90 Wilson, 1988, p. 317.

91 Letter from Morton Silver, to author Robin Neillands, 28 October, 1995.

92 Brady, 2003, p. 120.

93 Farrar-Hockley, 1990, p. 341.

94 41 Commando War Diary.

95 Brady, 2003, p. 122.

96 Drysdale, letter, 12 December 1950.

97 Casualty figures from 41 Commando War Diary.

98 Drysdale, letter, 12 December 1950.

99 Casualty figures from Tucker, Spencer, C, Changjin 'Chosin Reservoir Campaign', in Tucker, ed. 2002, p. 112.

100 Silver, Morton, Letter, 1995.

101 Farrar-Hockley, 1990, p. 341.

102 Maindonald, IWM 16627.
103 O'Brien, IWM 13522.
104 Drysdale, letter, 12 December 1950.
105 For statistics on the evacuation, see Marolda, Edward J, *Hungnam Evacuation* in Tucker, ed. 2002, pp. 267–269.
106 For statistics on the evacuation, see Marolda, Edward J, *Hungnam Evacuation* in Tucker, ed. 2002, pp. 267–269.
107 The scene was captured in a vivid photograph.
108 Hickey, Michael, *The Korean War: The West Confronts Communism*; New York, 2000, p. 141.
109 Goldstein, Richard, 'Leonard La Rue, Rescuer in the Korean War, Dies at 87', *New York Times;* 22 October 2001.
110 Author interview, Robert Lunney.
111 Marolda in Tucker, ed., 2002, p. 269. 14,000. Lunney, author interview.
112 Goldstein, 2001.
113 Mossman 1990, p. 174.
114 Information on the UDT comes from accounts by veterans Royal Vanatta and Mack Boyton at: http://www.navyfrogmen.com/
115 Schafer, Elizabeth, *X Corps*, in Tucker, ed. 2002, p. 642.
116 Zhang, 1995, p. 123.
117 Spour, 1988, p. 265.

Chapter Twelve: Dark Christmas

1 Willoughby Notebook, 20 December.
2 Willoughby Notebook, 16 December.
3 Thomas, 1990, p. 26.
4 Thomas, 1990, p. 26.
5 O'Dowd, 2000, pp. 62–63.
6 Millett, 2010, p. 381.

Index